## Additional Comments on *Pakistan's Drift to Extremism*

"Hassan Abbas has written a book that will be required reading for anyone hoping to understand the dense thicket of Pakistan's jihadist organizations and the social and political milieu in which they have flourished. Abbas draws on his wide experience as a senior Pakistani police officer and government official, allied to his experience as an academic, to write a book that is nuanced, authoritative, and well written. Any student of Pakistan will find Abbas's work richly rewarding."

—PETER BERGEN, Terrorism Analyst, CNN, and Author of
*THE HOLY WAR INC.:INSIDE THE SECRET WORLD OF OSAMA BIN LADEN*

"After a long but mixed history as a sometime-ally of the United States, Pakistan itself might evolve into Washington's worst foreign policy nightmare: a nuclear-armed state, rife with Islamic terrorists, and in direct conflict with its neighbors. No one is better prepared to explain how Pakistan arrived at this point than Hassan Abbas, who knows the country and especially its Islamic radicals from the inside. This book not only traces Pakistan's trajectory over the last forty years, but it provides valuable insights into the workings of its establishment and should be required reading for anyone interested in a deep understanding of this troubled state."

—STEPHEN PHILIP COHEN, Brookings Institution

"Hassan Abbas is a brilliant geopolitical psychoanalyst who has put schizophrenic Pakistan on his couch and discovered the roots of the country's permanent state of denial as it slipped into the clutches of religious extremists and condescending spooks. The remedy lies in a new America that finally learns how to conjugate soft and hard power."

—ARNAUD DE BORCHGRAVE, Editor-at-Large of
*THE WASHINGTON TIMES* and UNITED PRESS INTERNATIONAL

"Abbas warns of a frightening future—one in which extremists gain more military support and more military might, and tensions between India and Pakistan continue to rise, partly as a result of domestic pressures on both sides. But he also offers us hope by suggesting a way out of this frightening morass, detailing a role for the United States and the international community. It is to be fervently hoped that his message will be heard worldwide, especially in Washington."

—from the Foreword by JESSICA STERN, Harvard University

# Pakistan's Drift into Extremism

## Allah, the Army, and America's War on Terror

Foreword by Jessica Stern

## Hassan Abbas

An East Gate Book

### M.E.Sharpe

Armonk, New York
London, England

**An East Gate Book**

Map on pg. ix is from Owen Bennett Jones, *Pakistan: Eye of the Storm*
(New Haven, CT: Yale University Press, 2002), p. 20.
Copyright 2002 by Yale University Press. Used with permission.

Photographs, where noted, are courtesy of Online International News
Network, Islamabad, Pakistan.

**Library of Congress Cataloging-in-Publication Data**

Abbas, Hassan.
    Pakistan's drift into extremism : Allah, the army, and America's war on terror / Hassan
Abbas.
        p. cm.
    "East gate book."
    Includes bibliographical references and index.
    ISBN 0-7656-1496-0 (hardcover : alk. paper); ISBN 0-7656-1497-9 (pbk.: alk. paper)
    1. Pakistan–Politics and government. 2. Islamic fundamentalism—Pakistan. 3. Islam and
politics—Pakistan. 4. Pakistan—Armed Forces—Political activity. 5. Radicalism—Pakistan.
I. Title.

DS384.A27 2004
320.95491'09'045—dc22                                                     2004007993

Printed in the United States of America

The paper used in this publication meets the minimum requirements of
American National Standard for Information Sciences
Permanence of Paper for Printed Library Materials,
ANSI Z 39.48-1984.

| BM (c) | 10 | 9 | 8 | 7 | 6 | 5 | 4 | 3 | 2 |
| BM (p) | 10 | 9 | 8 | 7 | 6 | 5 | 4 | 3 | |

Dedicated to the innocent victims
of terrorism all around the world.

# Contents

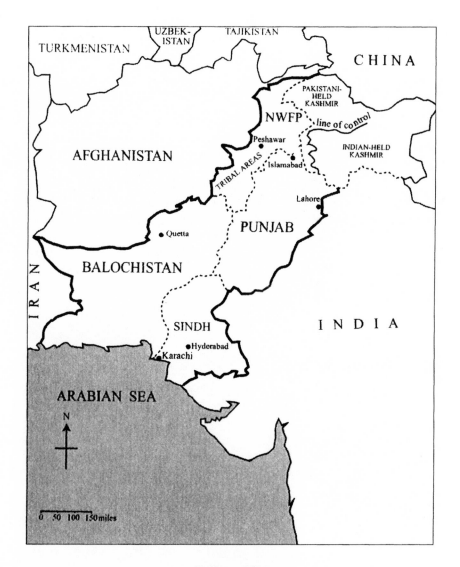

**Pakistan 2004**

# Foreword

Hassan Abbas contributes this important volume at a critically important juncture in Pakistan's history. Will it continue on the path of Islamic extremism and sectarian strife? Or will the Pakistani people learn to value tolerance and peace more than fundamentalist certainties and divisive ethno-religious identities? Will tensions with India continue to rise, or will both parties' nuclear weapons make war increasingly unthinkable?

Hassan Abbas's unusually broad background enables him to address these questions at many levels. He explains the forces pushing Pakistan toward "Talibanization" and sectarian violence as only a police investigator can—with knowledge from the field. His experience working at high levels in the Musharraf government enables him to explain how the general's early idealism served the country well when Musharraf first came to power; but that idealism eventually gave way to more traditional power politics, including the military's courting of the mullah for political gain. But Abbas does not rely on his own practical experience to describe these developments. He spent years studying Islamic law and South Asian politics as a fellow at Harvard Law School and as a graduate student at Tufts, and we, his readers, are the beneficiaries of his scholarship.

In *Pakistan's Drift into Extremism: Allah, the Army, and America's War on Terror*, Hassan Abbas explains many mysteries. Why does Pakistan consistently lurch back and forth between democratic regimes and military dictatorships? And why do Pakistan and the United States have such a complicated relationship? Abbas explains that it has long been clear to Pakistan that despite its stated goal of promoting democracies around the world, the United States cares far more about Pakistan's compliance to its wishes than the nature of its leadership. The United States is often prepared to overlook military coups, corruption, and, most recently, extraordinary nuclear crimes perpetrated by a Pakistani citizen, as long as Pakistan provides the United States what it needs.

On the one hand, Pakistan has played a crucial role in the war on terrorism, turning over hundreds of Al-Qaeda suspects to U.S. law-enforcement authorities. Without Pakistan's assistance, few of the most important successes in the "war on terrorism" could have occurred. On the other hand, why do terrorists choose Pakistan as their refuge? And why was Dr. A.Q. Khan, the father of Pakistan's nuclear weapon and a self-described Islamic fundamentalist, allowed to go free after confessing to unprecedented nuclear crimes?

Twin devils plague Pakistan, Abbas explains: fundamentalist extremism and corruption.

Abbas attributes much of Pakistan's woes to the Pakistani military's historical practice of courting the "mullah," a figure he describes as a barely educated religious leader largely ignorant of true Islamic principles, likely to be corrupt, and likely to have a great deal of pull with various political factions. Abbas also describes the history of this practice and traces its development through the alternating civilian and military regimes that have ruled Pakistan since its birth as a nation in 1947.

To look different from previous military rulers, Abbas explains, Musharraf suspended only parts of the constitution and did not impose martial law. He also made fighting the corruption that has dragged down Pakistan's economy the centerpiece of his early tenure. His decision to establish the National Accountability Bureau (NAB), and to appoint as its leader a general widely admired for his integrity, generated excitement among all those interested in seeing Pakistan thrive. But who in Pakistan could be relied on to force the people with political power—mullahs, industrialists, politicians, and military personnel—to comply with laws they had long grown used to ignoring? The Inter Services Intelligence (ISI) was known to have monitored civilian government, known for its corruption, and the NAB assumed that the ISI had acquired sufficient data to prosecute. But, much to the dismay of the new anticorruption officers (of which Mr. Abbas was one), the data were sketchy. In the end, Musharraf chose to compromise with those willing to play along with his regime. He sidelined the liberals, and cozied up to the religious parties, facilitating their unprecedented victory in the October 2002 parliamentary elections. Abbas explains Musharraf's difficulty: the masses wanted Musharraf to stamp out corruption and political patronage, while the political and military elite wanted the status quo to continue. Musharraf began swinging in between.

This swinging applies not only to the anticorruption campaign, but also to Musharraf's relationship with the jihadis. Pakistan's intelligence agency, the ISI, has long supported numerous jihadi groups, which it used as "volunteer fighters" in the conflict with India over Kashmir. Pakistan looked the other way as the groups began to harbor ambitions that reached beyond their original mission. They established close links with Al-Qaeda, the Taliban, and other international jihadi organizations that emerged from the earlier Afghan war against the Soviets. After 9/11, Musharraf officially banned a number of these jihadi groups, renounced the Taliban, and arrested hundreds of Al-Qaeda suspects, turning them over to the U.S. government. But even as Pakistani officials were arresting some terrorists, factions within the Pakistani military continued to support those same terrorist groups. Pakistani jihadi groups fought beside Al-Qaeda and the Taliban against the United States and its allies. They are leading suspects in a number of terrorist strikes since September 11. Sunni sectarian terrorists, also assisted by the military since their inception, have grown increasingly brazen, gunning down large numbers of Shia civilians in broad daylight. Shia terrorists have responded in kind. But the jihadi groups seem to have crossed a line when they attempted—apparently with assistance from members of the military—to assassinate Musharraf himself in December 2003. Musharraf's swinging in regard to the jihadis may have ended for good, but it may eventually spell the end of his regime. It is not clear that Musharraf can completely control the military he ostensibly commands. The power of the army to control the mullahs is increasingly a façade, Abbas argues. Mr. Abbas is uniquely qualified to teach us about these issues. A former senior police officer, Mr. Abbas has earned several master's degrees, and recently completed a fellowship at Harvard Law School, where he studied Islamic law pertaining to jihad. He also served in the administrations of Prime Minister Benazir Bhutto and President Musharraf.

The fate of Pakistan will affect the entire world. Will Pakistan's military continue to use the mullahs to achieve its short-term political and military goals? Will the sectarian killers—created by the ISI—get involved in sectarian crimes in other countries, for example in Iraq, further destabilizing that country? Will terrorists continue to see Pakistan as a hospitable place of refuge? If Pakistan is to be saved from a Taliban-like future, and the rest of the world saved from future Dr. Khans, it will have to make accommodations with India over Kashmir, and stop flirting with the mullahs. It will have to spend less of its national income on defense, and more on educating its youth. It will require that a true democracy take hold. But none of this will happen, Abbas warns, without assistance from the United States. After all, the U.S. government helped to design and fund the strategy of employing violent Islamist cadres to serve as "volunteer" fighters in a war that seemed critically important at the time, but left those cadres to their own devices once they were no longer important for achieving U.S. strategic goals. The idea of international jihad—which was promoted by the United States and Pakistan when it was expedient, took hold and spread, ultimately resulting in deadly terrorist crimes throughout Asia as well as the September 11 strikes.

U.S. assistance to Pakistan helped to create the problem we now face; and U.S. assistance will be required to undo it. But that assistance cannot be exclusively military. The enemy is not just a military target, but a bad idea.

Fighting that idea will require providing alternatives to the youth who are currently educated at extremist schools, who find solace in hate. Targeted development assistance, especially in regard to education, is the most important aspect of the war on terrorism, as Mr. Abbas makes clear.

Mr. Abbas warns of a frightening future—one in which extremists gain more military support and more military might; and tensions between India and Pakistan continue to rise, partly as a result of domestic pressures on both sides. But he also offers us hope by suggesting a way out of this frightening morass, detailing a role for the United States and the international community. It is to be fervently hoped that his message will be heard worldwide, especially in Washington.

Jessica Stern
Harvard University
April 2004

# Preface

This is a story of Pakistan. The three main characters of this story are the Pakistan Army, the jihadi actors, and the United States of America. It is an inside account of how these players have shaped the development of Pakistan in its fifty-six years of history—for better or for worse. It is my candid and straightforward analysis of what went wrong with Pakistan. But it is more than just that. It is also my jihad against the injustices inflicted upon the people of Pakistan. It is my hope that this book helps explain how Pakistan came to be what it is today because it is only through understanding its journey that we can hope to help the nation overcome its troubles and build a brighter future.

The information I collected for this book is from various sources, including the major works published on the related issues in Pakistan and the West in different languages, declassified American documents, and interviews with dozens of Pakistani politicians, military officials, journalists, and many American political analysts and diplomats. The last few chapters that cover General Pervez Musharraf, the Kargil episode, and the profiles of jihadi groups and their linkages with Al-Qaeda and the Inter-Services Intelligence (ISI) are largely based on interviews with militants of the jihadi groups and officials of the ISI. Due to sensitivities involved with these issues, all the sources are not identified by name in this book. But I have confirmed the information with many credible sources for accuracy. My access to these avenues was possible due to my being a former government official in Pakistan, having served in Prime Minister Benazir Bhutto's administration in 1994–96 as a staff officer and in General Pervez Musharraf's Chief Executive Secretariat (National Accountability Bureau) during 1999–2000 as a deputy director. My service as an assistant superintendent of police in the North-West Frontier Province in 1996–98 also provided me an opportunity to witness the ground realities vis-à-vis the *Madrasa* network in the region and the Pakistan-Taliban–al-Qaeda linkages.

All together, the writing of this book is a work of six years of investigation and research. The effort to translate and analyze this information in a book form, however, started a couple of years ago and was made possible through a research fellowship at the Islamic Legal Studies Program at the Harvard

Law School (2002–3). I am indebted to Professor Frank Vogel and Peri Bearman for this support. Professor Emeritus Roger Fisher at the Harvard Law School, managing the Harvard Negotiation Project, was also very kind to provide me access to the Harvard library and research facilities during the final phase of my work as a research fellow. Studying at the Fletcher School of Law and Diplomacy, Tufts University (2001–2) was another valuable experience in this context. I greatly benefited from the classes that I took with Professors Andrew Hess, Alan Henrikson, and Richard Shultz at the Fletcher School and Dr. Jessica Stern at the Kennedy School of Government, Harvard University. From these professors I learned how to scrutinize and evaluate events and data from a political analyst's perspective. Jessica Stern especially had been a source of guidance for me while working on this book project.

Many friends and colleagues read various chapters of the book and provided immense help in improving the text with their valuable comments and encouragement. I am very thankful to Ahmed Rashid, Marvin Weinbaum, Khalid Hasan, Peter Bergen, Samiullah Ibrahim, Sohail Iqbal, Mahnaz Ispahani, Professor Robert Wirsing, Professor Saeed Shafqat, Professor Christopher Candland, Arnaud de Borchgrave, and Barry Bearak in this regard. I am deeply grateful to Silbi Stainton, my dear friend who read almost the entire manuscript and gave excellent suggestions. Many thanks are due to my Pakistani-American friends Shahid Ahmed Khan and Javed Sultan, who supported my research endeavors. My gratitude is also due to Salman Haider and Jaspal Singh, who helped me comprehend issues from an Indian perspective. I gained considerably from my discussions with Usman Rahim Khan, Yasin Malik, Farooq Khatwari, Moeed Pirzada, and Ghulam Nabi Fai about the plight, dreams, and opinions of Kashmiris. I also greatly benefited from my interaction with Stephen Cohen, Ambassadors Teresita Shaffer and Steven Monblatt, and most of all Professor Ayesha Jalal, whose seminal work on Jinnah many years ago had motivated me to turn to academia besides giving the realization that the history textbook I was taught in Pakistan had many distortions embedded in it.

Barry Hoffman, Pakistan's honorary consul general in Boston, was always patient listening to my conspiracy theories about the American role in Pakistan over the years. He facilitated my understanding of the issues from an American perspective, though in the process I found a Pakistani patriot in him. He also kindly provided most of the pictures of Pakistani and American heads of state printed in the book, from his private collections. I am thankful to my editor at M.E. Sharpe, Patricia Loo, for her encouragement and support. Managing editor Angela Piliouras and editorial assistant Amy Albert earned my gratitude for their cooperation and help in the publication process. Finally, for loving support and patience, I wish to give my warmest thanks of all to my wife Benish.

The book could not have been written without the support of a mentor, who despite my insistence wants to remain anonymous. Besides providing useful information, he was of enormous help in making the book readable. In this sense the book is a collaboration—his as much as mine.

Any errors of fact, interpretation, or judgment expressed in this book are of course entirely my own and should not be attributed to the institutions I remained associated with or the individuals mentioned above.

# Pakistan's Drift into Extremism

# ——Chapter 1——

# Introduction

In A.D. 712, Mohammad bin Qasim, an Arab general at the age of seventeen, conquered a part of the Sindh region of India, and thus Islam touched the Indian subcontinent. Here the predominant religion was Hinduism, which had evolved in India after the Aryans came from the north many thousands of years earlier.

India then, as now, had much diversity. The great traditions of Hinduism were nurtured by a "conglomeration of sects,"[1] each sect having different religious texts and believing in various gods and goddesses. The religion itself possessed little in the way of a formal central structure. But Brahmans, the clergy, undermined this religion by instituting a stratification of Hindu society into four watertight castes.[2] At the bottom of the scale, the *shudra* (the untouchable) has eked out his subhuman existence more or less unchanged for many generations.

The caste system thus was largely intolerant of social mobility within Indian society. By the same token it was expected to be equally intolerant of the outsider. And the Islam that met Hinduism then, being sternly monotheistic, was prejudiced against all pluralistic worship. Thus, when these two faiths met, it was to be expected that the resultant collision could lead to a catastrophe. But this is not quite what happened. The reason for this was that the Islam that came to India had yet to be subverted by its own brand of "Brahmanism," that is, the power of the clergy. Mohammad bin Qasim won the hearts of his new subjects, but his stay was so short that soon he and the religion he professed were a distant memory.[3]

The next to come to India were the Muslim conquerors from the north who consisted of Central Asians, Afghans, and Persians. Many of them were more prone to plunder and pillage for achieving military glory[4] rather than pursuing any Islamic ideals. But in their train came the Sufis (mystic saints) and with them Islam came to stay. They presented the softest and most tolerant face of Islam, and it was this Sufi tolerance that cushioned the meeting of Islam and Hinduism. They gained thousands of Hindu disciples, many of whom converted to Islam. Also, many who did not convert remained disciples because association with the saints was not made conditional on one's religious identity. Their core message was love for humanity and its creator. Thus, such was the Allah to which India was first introduced. Even in today's India the annual feasts in honor of these saints are celebrated and massively attended.[5] And even, at times, surpassing the Muslim disciples in number and enthusiasm are those of Hindu and Sikh faith—the great-grandchildren of the original disciples.[6]

Historically, most Sufis were rebels against the degeneration of the despotic rulers in the Arab and other predominantly Muslim regions. When the Sufi threat to despotism increased, it was thought expedient to discourage Sufism. Consequently the mullah class (clergy) that originally had no place in Islam was built up. Mullah, distinct from an *alim* (learned religious scholar), stands for a narrow-minded and semiliterate person who is the product of the decadent *Madrasa* system and oftentimes leads prayers in mosques and poses as a religious authority claiming the discretion to interpret religious texts for all Muslims. The term mullah is also used throughout the book to portray the general mentality of the majority of Pakistani religious parties' leadership. And as the mullah influence increased, with the passage of time the population of the Indian subcontinent began to see the not-very-alluring face of Islam. Today's Pakistan is seeing the flowering of this phenomenon that started so far back.

Starting with Mahmud of Ghazni in the eleventh century, many Muslim conquerors ruled the Indian subcontinent for a better part of the millennium. Each one established a kingdom, settled down, and became effete, only to be supplanted by a new and more vigorous successor. By the time the British trader had sufficiently organized himself to unveil the bayonet, the sun of Islamic power in India had set. By the early nineteenth century, the Mughal king in Delhi reigned but did not rule. Nevertheless, when British ambitions in India started to take tangible shape in the form of conquered territories, Muslim princes were still ruling a large part of the subcontinent. To remedy this situation the British pursued a policy of divide-and-defeat the country. The British had a natural ally in the Hindu population of the Indian subcontinent for two reasons. The first was the nascent sense of Hindu patriotism that regarded the Muslim ruler as a usurper. It can be argued that this perception encouraged the Hindu to align with any power holding the promise of sending the usurper packing. Second, the education of the average British officer was just barely adequate to have kept the memory of the Crusades alive, which cast the Muslim in an adversarial role.

Thus, slowly but surely, a handful of British officers, administrators, and traders got India where they wanted it—as a colony divided between the fiction of self-ruling Indian states and the fact of the rest of the country being ruled from London through its governor-generals and later the viceroys.

Because the Hindu was the ally of the British in this new dispensation, his lot stood to improve at the cost of the Muslim subjects of the Crown. At a time like this, the Muslims needed a voice of sanity and vision. What they got instead was the mullah, who was enlightened enough to block the only avenue of advancement open to them. He promptly proscribed British schools and the learning of the English language. Against the prospective violators of these prohibitions he pronounced many oaths, invoked many curses, and listed many areas of a fall from grace. Among the latter was a promise that, in the eyes of Allah, the marriage vows of the transgressors shall stand annulled. And the subject of marriage being a matter of grave concern among the believers, many a good Muslim decided to save his wedlock at the cost of a modern education! And when Sir Syed Ahmed Khan (1817–98) decided to reclaim his coreligionists from the morass of ignorance unrelieved by any hint of the bliss that is supposed to go with it, he was promptly dubbed "infidel" by the outraged majesty of the mullah. This situation has improved sufficiently in the Pakistan of today so that each school of thought has managed to put the other well outside the pale of Islam.

Conversely, the Hindus, not being overly concerned with the fragility of their vows of matrimony, enrolled happily in the network of schools opened by the British. Unfortunately, however, education sowed the seeds of a different type of problem in the Hindu psyche. As he came to study his history book, he found that among other things, this was a history of an unbroken series of conquerors issuing from the north, debouching onto the plains of India, defeating the Indian forces, and settling down to rule without let or hindrance. But the historical singularity that was most galling to Indian pride was that very few of these adventurers had ever been defeated and turned back. And it did not augur well for the future of Hindu-Muslim amity to be reminded that for the previous eight hundred years or so almost all the conquerors were Muslims.

These calculated moves infected the Hindu mind with a collective inferiority complex, a condition normally associated with individuals. The Muslims of India did not by any chance escape this complex, but instead executed a neat little sidestep. They have conveniently chosen to forget that they are the children of Hindu converts and have equally conveniently chosen instead to range themselves with the Muslim conquerors of India—the position least likely to enamor them with the Hindus. Many roads and places of note in Pakistan are named after Arabs, Moors, and Turks with whom they share little history.

As the deck eventually came to be stacked, Pakistan would always have an army anyway, and the army would probably have the toe of its haloed boot in uncomfortable proximity to the anterior of the politician. But if there was a chance to the contrary, brothers Kaiser and Adolf scotched it. The world wars that they unleashed created the requirement of gun fodder from India. And the Muslims of India, having been left behind in terms of education due to the assiduous efforts of their clergy, now wanted nevertheless to advance. And because the semi- or the uneducated had few better routes to advancement than service in the army during those times, they enlisted in disproportionate numbers, compared with their representation in other fields. Hence, Pakistan was destined to inherit a well-trained army.

In terms of political development, Muslims were far behind Hindus for the aforementioned reasons. In 1885 the Indian National Congress, primarily a Hindu-dominated party, was formed. Originating as a platform of the British loyalists comprising the cosmopolitan rich, the leisurely, and the powerful imbued with a zeal for social service and political recognition, it acquired by the early twentieth century a fervent nationalist character, and with Mohandas Karamchand Gandhi's entry in 1915, it transformed into a bulwark against British imperialism. They decided that India had had enough of "civilized" governance from Britain. It took the Muslims of India two more decades to wake up to all this, though some Muslims were part of the Hindu-dominated Congress Party. They eventually formed their party, the Muslim League, in 1906 with almost similar motives as that of the early days' Congress, and later joined the chorus for independence but were not too clear about what they really wanted. The Muslim League was organized as an immediate reaction to political developments in Bengal Province—British authorities had divided this large province into two, resulting in the creation of a Muslim-dominant province in 1905. The Hindu Mahasabha, a militant group, violently opposed the Bengal partition through a campaign of terror that enflamed communal passions. Muslim League leadership at this juncture got convinced that they must speak for the rights and interests of Muslims as Congress had done very little to thwart or condemn the role of Hindu militants in this episode. They needed therefore a leader who could define the primary needs of the Muslims of India and voice it effectively. They found such a leader in Mohammad Ali Jinnah, who joined the Muslim League in 1913, though without abandoning his membership in the Congress.

A lawyer who had spent his formative years in Britain, Jinnah was a Muslim primarily by birth and loyalty, and in all other ways was more British than the British. He was not overly keen on independence, but he was only too aware that the Muslims of India were far too backward compared with the Hindu majority, and thus the withdrawal of the British authority would lay the Muslims open to the possibility of exploitation by this majority. His first priority therefore was to obtain guarantees to obviate this eventuality, or at least make such exploitation less probable. The demand for Pakistan as a separate homeland for the Muslims of India was seriously considered by Jinnah much later, and then too as a bargaining chip for obtaining these self-same guarantees. Up to the second decade of the twentieth century he was a member of both the Congress Party and the Muslim League and was called the greatest ambassador of Hindu-Muslim unity. And so he would have remained had the march of events not decided differently.

In 1916, in what came to be known as the Lucknow Pact between Congress and the Muslim League, Jinnah sought and received from Congress such constitutional guarantees, which in his estimate were an adequate constitutional insurance for the minority Muslims against the might of the Hindu majority.[7] But the deal was wrecked by the Nehru Report[8] in 1928. Jinnah tried his best to save the spirit of the Lucknow Pact, but without success. This was a severe rebuke to Jinnah's faith in Indian nationalism.[9] Soon, he left the Congress Party.

In such a political atmosphere, Dr. Mohammad Iqbal, a respected Muslim philosopher and poet, came up with the idea of an independent Muslim state in the subcontinent. He presented this proposal at the 1930 annual meeting of the Muslim League and questioned Jinnah's insistence on the unity of India. Jinnah, though increasingly disillusioned with Congress, saw the issue of a separate Muslim homeland as a nonstarter.

Earlier, after Gandhi had joined the Khilafat Movement,[10] Jinnah refused to be associated with it by saying that "it was a crime to mix up politics and religion the way he had done."[11] At that time he had little doubt left that the soul of the Congress was in fact communal, but the sabotage of the Lucknow Pact was the one act that more than any other issue led to the "parting of the ways"[12] between Muslims and Hindus and to the eventual partition of British India. It stunned Jinnah, broke his faith in the word of the Hindu leadership, and he henceforth regarded all assurances and commitments issuing from that quarter as mere expedients. He thereafter believed that the secularist slogan of the Congress was a mere hoax meant to calm the fears of the Muslims and gain credit with the secular democracies of the West.

As Jinnah progressively came to represent the Muslim opinion in India, a number of the better organized Muslim religious parties, most of these anti-Pakistan, lost little time in branding him an infidel—a time-honored label for all such who did not conform. The battle lines between the moderate, westernized Muslims and the potentially militant groups were beginning to be drawn way back then. The Muslim religious groups had devoted their energies and time to the cause of freeing the Muslims from colonial rule and had concluded that the British were the chief enemy of Islam. For them British control of India was the reason behind the decline of Islamic civilization in the region. And they saw Jinnah as a lackey of the British.

Because of the general backwardness of the Muslims, the organizational structure of the Muslim League was much weaker than that of the Congress. And when the Congress started agitational politics against British rule during the Second World War and most of its top leadership was clapped into prison, the very challenge posed by this situation further honed and strengthened the second-tier leadership of this party. But Jinnah supported the British effort in the war. He was only too keenly aware of the weakness of the Muslims and was in dire need of a strong ally, which he saw in the British. And he could not hope to obtain their support by withholding his support from them at an hour so crucial for the Western democracies. Thus the already weak leadership of the league was further denied the opportunity to learn in the hard school of agitational politics. With the exception of Jinnah, Pakistan was destined to inherit a generally lightweight political leadership, a hash of comparatively well-organized religious parties, and a much stronger and better-organized army. This power equation was to play a very important role in the emerging Pakistan.

As India lumbered and lurched its way toward independence, Jinnah nevertheless hoped for a compromise that would keep India's unity intact while at the same time he was trying to obtain the minimal security guarantees on behalf of his Muslim followers. As such, he played the consummate lawyer. He built up the case for Pakistan but steadfastly refrained from defining it to any degree of exactitude,[13] using it as a card to achieve his main aim and keeping the gratitude of the British (earned through active cooperation in their war effort) as a resource of last resort should the formation of an independent Pakistan become necessary. Unfortunately for him, except for Maulana Abul Kalam Azad, none in the top leadership of the Congress was ready to make the sort of compromise Jinnah was hoping for, and he had a visceral dislike for Azad. Worse than this, the Congress Party gave enough cause to confirm Jinnah in his opinion of the basic hypocrisy of that party.[14] The elections of 1937 were one such event that did little to rehabilitate his faith in the honesty of his chief adversary. Having a firm understanding with the Muslim League to form coalition governments in all provinces irrespective of the election results, the Congress, after returning with large majorities in nearly all the provinces, promptly reneged on its commitment. It not only dumped the Muslim League, but soon stood accused of serious instances of abuse of power by the Muslims in a number of provinces. This further destroyed Muslim trust in the Congress and was considered the second major demonstration of bad faith by it.

As time ran out for the British in India, they resorted to their last major effort to leave India a united country in which the Muslims could hope for advancement in an atmosphere of security. In 1946, through the Cabinet Mission Plan, a proposal was made to group the Muslim majority provinces in both the east and the west of British India. These two groups were to have considerable autonomy under a weak center handling a few subjects. Ten years later there was to be a referendum in these two groups to stay within the union or to opt out. Both Jinnah and Jawaharlal Nehru agreed to the plan. When Gandhi was apprised of the details of the agreement, he immediately advised Nehru to make his acceptance conditional and thus torpedo the last effort of keeping India united. This brought down the curtain on Jinnah's hopes, compelled him to solicit the support of as many of the religious parties as possible, and led to the bloodshed and tragedy that accompanied the emergence of a moth-eaten Pakistan in 1947. The dream of a united India was dashed by the Congress in search of a strong center, though it artfully blamed the partition on the intransigence of Jinnah.

And if there was any chance left for the economic uplift for either peoples, Nehru decided to annex Kashmir, a state contiguous with Pakistan with an overwhelming Muslim majority. This effectively robbed the peoples of both countries of the promise of their days in the sun. From then on these two poor countries were to spend their scarce resources feeding their mutual animus and building up their armed forces. Because of its large economy, the effect of such sterile expenditure, though vexatious, was at least bearable for India. For Pakistan it was a disaster. Over the years it meant enhancing the power of the army at the expense of all the other institutions of the country. For the people of Pakistan it meant progressive and gathering poverty, with any expectation of reclamation through mass education going out the window.

As soon as India was partitioned, the region saw another divide in the foreign policy orientation of the two newborn countries. The Cold War had set in, and the socialist leaning of the Indian leadership helped it gravitate toward the USSR and become firmly aligned with it while the anticommunist bias of Pakistani leadership coupled with the country's security needs ensured its alignment with the United States. And for all of America's commitment to the noble cause of democracy, its first commitment was to anticommunism. Thus it looked for strong anticommunist allies. In many such countries of the Third World the governments came in the form of dictators, civil or military, which was all very well with their sponsors. The army's influence in Pakistan was increasing as politicians were failing and the limited revenues of the country were insufficient to support a huge army, which Pakistan needed to defend itself from India. The Kashmir crisis was also a potent factor behind the army's demand for more funds. This made the army even stronger in Pakistan and a competitive contender for U.S. funds. Thus the army became the major recipient of U.S. financial aid. The rabidly anticommunist religious parties also got their share of support from the United States, which kept them financially alive at a crucial phase of their lives.

In its long association with Pakistan, America lost the forest for the trees. It saw only its army, but behind it, it lost sight of Pakistan itself. The continued advancement of the army meant the concomitant impoverishment of the country and the emasculation of the nascent political process. Each dollar spent on the steel helmet meant a dollar taken away from education, health, and industrial infrastructure. As the army grew in strength, it frequently took over the task of governance, diluted its own fiber, and weakened all the other institutions, including the judiciary and the political parties. In all of this, the growth of religious parties' influence seemed arrested. Their poor showing at the ballot was held up as proof of this and was celebrated by the many who wanted to see in this a settled fact that they had no political future in Pakistan. But religious elements, due to politicians' failure, were making enough progress to take on the government from time to time with increasing vigor, irrespective of the result of the previous engagement. And there was just the right amount of education among the ruling elite not to be able to take the long-term view of history. And, most important, few seemed conscious of the fact that as poverty and insecurity increase, humans are driven to seek the embrace of religion. And it was the mullah whose influence would grow in such circumstances.

As Pakistan progressed in its regression, as the army became stronger and stronger, and particularly as the army subdued and outlasted the few genuine political leaders of the old guard around whom a political process and governing consensus could be built, a political vacuum was created within the first decade of Pakistan's birth. In this vacuum the army became an acceptable alternative. From then on the army never gave up the privilege of imposing martial law whenever it wished or whenever the incompetent Pakistani politicians provided them even the slightest opportunity.

In 1971 the Indian subcontinent witnessed yet another partition when Pakistan broke into two and Bangladesh emerged—a direct result of Ayub Khan's policies, West Pakistani chauvinism, and insensitivity to its Bengali brethren. With this, the country was given the taste of its first popular civilian leader in the shape of Mr. Zulfikar Ali Bhutto, who rode to victory on his socialist slogan. He started on the road to break feudal power and to emancipate the oppressed of the land, but could not deliver what he promised. He gave the country a legitimate democratic constitution and successfully initiated the work on acquiring nuclear technology, but on the other hand he handed over to the mullah his first significant victory when, under pressure from the religious parties of Pakistan, he amended the constitution of the country to declare the Ahmedis[15] as non-Muslim. This was the community whose active help was solicited and received by Pakistan's founding father Jinnah at the creation of the country.[16] In 1936, Jinnah had successfully resisted an effort by a religious group, Ahrars, to make it incumbent upon Muslim League candidates for legislatures to take an oath vowing to expel the Ahmedis from the Muslim community.[17] In the words of leading scholar of South Asian studies Ayesha Jalal, Jinnah had done so because he "saw no reason to strip the Ahmedis of their Muslim identity simply on account of a doctrinal dispute."[18] Thus, declaring them non-Muslim after the creation of Pakistan was considered a breach of contract by the Ahmedis.

The next ruler the people of Pakistan had to bear was a general—Zia ul-Haq. He was basically a politician in uniform and a very scheming one at that. His ready smile covered a vast range of malice. Under him, lip service to Islam became the official creed, and hypocrisy became the lubricant of easy passage to positions of pelf and power. And the officialdom of Pakistan, already hovering around the outer limits of politeness, did not find it too difficult to make a transition into the brave new world of obsequiousness. And just when bets began to be taken as to when Zia was likely to bow out, the Soviets marched into Afghanistan, Zia became indispensable to the West, and Pakistan became the most allied ally of America.

No one could have guessed it then, but the onset of the Afghan war was the most fateful dagger driven into the heart of Pakistan. America could never forget its Vietnam experience. It would do anything to reverse a Vietnam on the Soviet Union. When Brezhnev walked into Kabul, the United States had the USSR right where it wanted. A long-forgotten Pakistan was the only country that could help America avenge itself. A U.S. ally since its inception and in very poor economic health, it decided to play the role of an ally to the hilt.

The Afghan war indeed reversed Vietnam on the USSR and in such a manner that it not only withdrew its forces from Afghanistan but broke up into pieces. As soon as the Soviets left Afghanistan, the Americans left Pakistan. Pakistan had helped America sow the wind in Afghanistan, but when the time came to reap the whirlwind, it had to do it alone. The abandonment of Pakistan by America left it more than 3 million Afghan refugees to care for; thousands of *Madrasas* (religious seminaries) funded by Saudi money to militarize the youth and convert them to the intolerant brand of Wahhabi Islam; a Kalashnikov culture such that one could rent an automatic gun in Karachi at less than two dollars an hour; and last but not least—the drug trade.

The people who actually did the fighting and gave their lives were not just Afghans themselves but Muslims drawn from all over the world, including thousands of Pakistanis, most of whom were the students of *Madrasas*. They were motivated to fight a jihad (religious war) against an infidel communist aggressor and take martyrdom in the process. Their religious fervor was not only due to the motivation provided by the *Madrasa* or the mullah; it was also fully backed by the Pakistani Inter Services Intelligence (ISI) and financed by the U.S. Central Intelligence Agency (CIA). Not just the Pakistanis but the United States well knew of, and welcomed, Saudi funding of the *Madrasas* that produced the holy warrior who was now fighting a war not only for the freedom of Afghanistan, but also a vicarious one for the United States. As far as this was being achieved, the United States quite welcomed this Muslim holy warrior brought alive from the Middle Ages.

General Zia ul-Haq and his shortsighted generals, who did not have a clue about Afghan history, were pursuing their own agenda. They had it as their aim to impose upon the new postwar Afghanistan a regime of their own choice in order to have strategic depth against India. Toward this end the ISI devoted a disproportionate amount of U.S. aid to Gulbadin Hikmatyar for the good reason that he was expected to play their game. Furthermore, some Pakistani generals started charity from home in strict compliance with the moral precept of such distribution, and enriched themselves. Thus the most tangible result of this policy was their own fat fortunes, which continue to smile on their children and shall continue to do so on their grandchildren as well. However, they could not seat their chosen king on the throne in Kabul because Hikmatyar, who had few followers, lost out. And the real warriors like Ahmad Shah Masud, who had the following but little aid, turned against Pakistan. So the end result was unity among the many warring groups of Afghanistan, that is, in their contempt for Pakistan, the country that had risked the most in standing up against the USSR for the cause of Afghan freedom!

After the Soviets withdrew from Afghanistan, and particularly after it settled down into an ordered anarchy imposed by the Taliban, Pakistan was awash with unemployed mujahideen (holy warriors) who were no longer needed there. These heroes of yore, the likes of the bin Ladens and Mullah Omars, whom it was possible to switch on, could not as easily be switched off. These battle-hardened fundamentalists trained, supported, and motivated both by Pakistan and the United States were now without a cause to fight for.

By this time, Zia ul-Haq had died in a mysterious plane crash in 1988, and Benazir Bhutto and Nawaz Sharif were taking turns at the helm of Pakistan. The problem of the mushrooming militants did not occupy the politicians, as it meant direct confrontation with the ISI, which had opened up enough avenues for the jihadis to remain busy. Sectarian violence also reached its peak during the 1990s, but the political leadership failed to gather the courage to counter the growing strength of the jihadis. By the time General Pervez Musharraf, a moderate and progressive Muslim, came to the scene, the very scale of religious extremism had reached its climax. When he halfheartedly tried to halt this trend before the tragedy on 9/11, the army found that it was faced with a potential adversary that it was not willing or able to bring to heel. Many of these groups had developed independent channels of financing, giving them increased maneuverability. This was the beginning of a shift in the power equation away from the army and toward the jihadi groups, the latter being supported by the mullah parties acting as their political wings.

No one realized this shift. In part this had to do with the sloth and inertia inherent in any bureaucracy, civil or military, which is generally disposed not to disturb the prevailing status quo. Also, the ISI, the organ responsible for drawing up analyses and presenting them to the government, failed to awaken the government to the emerging exigency. They were not aware perhaps that their tools were fast becoming Frankenstein monsters. Apart from the religious parties, it was the ISI that had grown most in size, in influence, and in resources during the Afghan war. In the aftermath of the Afghan war, Pakistan not only inherited thousands of mujahideen, but also their handlers in the shape of a vastly expanded and powerful ISI.

The ISI, having its natural sympathies with the mujahideen, which it had helped motivate and train, could not obviously see in them a potential menace. And those few who did were too few in number to swim against the tide of inertia and settled opinion. And last, the very scale of the problem gave it immunity from redress. It was therefore a predicament more conveniently ignored than faced. It was in this atmosphere of self-imposed ignorance and enforced bliss that the problem continued to expand and found three directions in which to focus its attention and unleash its pent-up energies, that is, within Pakistan itself in terms of sectarian violence; against the West (primarily U.S. interests); and against the oppression of the Indian forces in Jammu and Kashmir.

At first the diversion of the mujahideen effort to Kashmir was spontaneous. Kashmir was contiguous with Pakistan, and the cause of the Kashmiri fight for freedom had much in common with that of the Afghans, and the Indian atrocities in Kashmir were such that very little was required in the way of motivation for the veterans of the Afghan war to change direction toward Kashmir. With the passage of time, ISI increasingly got involved with directing and diverting the effort of the erstwhile mujahideen into Kashmir. This suited the ISI both because it was the logical extension of Pakistan's policy on Kashmir and, equally important, it suited the ISI to divert elsewhere a problem that Pakistan was in no position to address. India, on the other hand, took advantage of this situation. It refused to accept its own complicity and responsibility in the creation of the Kashmir imbroglio and brazenly went a step further by denying totally that there was in fact any problem in Kashmir, except at the instigation of Pakistan. It has cynically used Pakistani involvement in Kashmir to cover up the atrocities of its own forces of occupation in that unhappy land. These forces have thus far sent many thousands of Kashmiris to their deaths, maimed and crippled thousands more, raped countless women, and put to the torch entire villages.

The largest democracy in the world, in having pledged and then having consistently broken this pledge of providing the right of self-determination to a small part of its population, is directly responsible for lighting the fires of a freedom struggle in Kashmir. And though Pakistan has contributed both through a policy of commission and acts of omission, it is India that initiated the Kashmir conflict. This dispute is primarily responsible for providing to the militant factories of Pakistan an endless stream of willing recruits. Unless a just solution of the Kashmir issue is achieved and *Madrasas* are reformed, the prospect of a Pakistan going down the extremism path must not be discounted.

A peace process is taking shape lately, but more needs to be done. It is time India heeds the voice of sanity and, in a leadership role that is natural to its size and position, leads the region out of the impending catastrophe. Only then can the Pakistan Army be "convinced" to take up the challenge of tackling religious militancy with full force. The Pakistan Army, because of its institutional and corporate interests, will never allow Musharraf or for that matter any other general to completely clamp down on militants before achieving something on the Kashmir front. It is not inferred that Kashmir has to come into Pakistan's lap—it is the promise of self-determination for Kashmiris that must be fulfilled. An increasing number of Kashmiris, after helplessly witnessing the sectarian and politically motivated killings orchestrated by Pakistani-sponsored militant groups in Indian-held Jammu and Kashmir, have lost their dream of joining Pakistan. The Pakistan Army and the jihadi forces must understand that the Kashmiris alone have the right to decide about their future. A jointly controlled Kashmir Valley with an autonomous political setup in this scenario may turn out to be the only viable option. But India is not likely to focus on the reality and significance of this issue unless the West, especially the United States, recognizes its seriousness.

In the post–September 11 scenario, the U.S. military campaign in Afghanistan and the ostensible destruction of the Taliban and Al-Qaeda forces was hailed as the first victory of this war. But as the dust begins to settle, so has the euphoria of many who had hastened to call this a victory. In its aftermath there have been elections in Pakistan, and the mullahs have been returned to the national and provincial houses of the legislature in unprecedented numbers. This has been a vote against both the United States and Musharraf for his pro-American policies. It has also been a vote that has announced a paradigm shift in the traditional equation of power in Pakistan. For the first time, a large number of Pakistanis have considered the mullahs fit to rule over them. Potentially, this betokens the handing over of the baton by the army to the religious forces, as one of the most powerful forces in the politics of Pakistan. The U.S. military campaign in Iraq and its aftermath have made this power shift complete. And close behind the mullahs are the forces of militant extremism. Thus, where the United States has cut off one head of the hydra in Afghanistan, many more heads are now growing in Pakistan. Arguably, the way Musharraf has mishandled the domestic political situation and the way the U.S. campaign in Afghanistan and Iraq is progressing, the barely surviving Muslim moderate in Pakistan will soon be heading toward extinction, further reinforcing the already abundant reserves of extremists in the Muslim world.

Despite these negative tendencies and indicators, the silent majority in Pakistan wants the country to be a moderate and progressive state. But the problem is that this segment of society is silent. Civil society at large has failed to stand up to the extremist forces. A credible democratic system would have provided an avenue to moderate forces to voice their opinions but General Musharraf opted to manipulate the elections (October 2002) and introduced autocratic amendments to the constitution to ensure that he remains in power. And, to this end, he co-opted a group of politicians who are known to be turncoats and corrupt, and consequently in this process he is losing his credibility among Pakistanis. The U.S. administration, however, does not appear to be concerned about this trend. But both the United States and General Musharraf must realize that Pakistan's crucial support of the U.S.-led war on terror can be sustained only through strengthening democracy in the country.

# ——Chapter 2——

# The Early Years

## A Dream Deferred

On the fourteenth of August 1947, the Union Jack was lowered for the last time and its place was taken by the green-crescent-and-star standard of Pakistan, in acknowledgment of the birth of a new state. The new nation was awkwardly cut out from British India in two separate pieces, an East and a West Pakistan that happened to be eight hundred miles apart, with India situated in between. The partition was accompanied by a merciless communal slaughter of Muslims by Hindus and Sikhs and vice versa—17 million people were shunted across the frontiers of the two states created by partition to reach their designated homelands—millions vanished.[1] For the Muslim migrants, the road to Pakistan was covered in blood and ashes.

Pakistan's straits were dire, and its immediate financial position was not much improved when Viceroy Mountbatten, forever on the lookout to reinforce his immortality, let it be known that after their independence, he would like to be the head of state (governor-general) of both India and Pakistan. In pursuit of this historic first, his vanity blinded him to the obvious anomaly of his ambition, that is, trying to be the joint head of two mutually hostile states, and in this position taking instructions from two mutually antagonistic cabinets. Thus, when Jinnah refused to accede to his desire and chose to become the governor-general of Pakistan himself, he not only wounded Mountbatten's rather large ego but also allowed Pakistan to become a victim of his malevolence. Mountbatten has left a record of his feelings on this issue: "I asked him [Jinnah], 'Do you realize what this will cost you?' He said sadly, 'It may cost me several crores of rupees in assets,' to which I replied somewhat acidly, 'It may well cost you the whole of your assets and the future of Pakistan.' I then got up and left the room."[2] Thus, to all the other ills inherited by a weak and fledgling Pakistan was added the injured majesty of Mountbatten, who seemed determined not to easily forget this injury, nor forgive it.[3] As a direct result of the rebuff, Pakistan greatly suffered in the division of assets.[4]

At partition, Pakistan's single most valuable asset was Jinnah. But he was a dying man ravaged by years of a losing war against tuberculosis—a secret strictly kept by his personal physician. Few could pick up the courage to openly defy him, and thus upset a very unsettled applecart, while he was still alive. He was essentially the glue that kept everything together.

Those who believed that Pakistan would not be able to sustain itself were right. It had neither industry nor money.[5] Vast numbers of professionals who ran the essential services were Hindus and Sikhs who emigrated from Pakistan to India. There were no resources of essential items to fall back on. More so, there were millions of homeless refugees from India to house, clothe, and feed. It was in these circumstances that India dispatched a contingent of Indian forces to pressure the hesitant Hindu maharaja of Kashmir, an overwhelmingly Muslim state contiguous to Pakistan, to opt for India. Pakistani tribesmen with discreet and limited official support were also crossing over into Kashmir.[6] It is ironic that the whole debate revolving around the Kashmir issue was deflected to blatant technicalities like, when did the maharaja of Kashmir sign the instrument of succession to opt for joining India; whether he signed the document willingly or under duress; did the Indian forces enter Kashmir first or did they do this in response to raids by Pakistani tribesmen in Kashmir; and so forth. This was deliberately done to obfuscate the heart of the matter that could admit of no debate, that is, that the princely states of India were under a legal as well as moral obligation to choose between India and Pakistan, keeping in view the geographic location of the territory concerned as well as the wishes of the people of the state.

Having thus successfully diverted the thrust of the debate away from the core issue, India has continued to deny freedom to the people of Kashmir on the basis of one technicality or the other, and might has held brutal sway over the just aspirations of a groaning people. Within a year of independence, this crisis led to the first India-Pakistan war, which was brought to an end by a United Nations–(U.N.) sponsored cease-fire. Afterward, a series of U.N. Security Council Resolutions called for a plebiscite to allow the people of Kashmir to opt either for India or Pakistan. Two-thirds of Kashmir by then was under Indian control and the rest was with Pakistan. Both countries signified their acceptance of the proposal for a plebiscite on a January 5, 1949, resolution providing: "The question of the accession of the State of Jammu and Kashmir to India or Pakistan will be decided through the democratic method of a free and impartial plebiscite."[7] India never allowed that to happen. Thus from day one, this conflict landed Pakistan in a security dilemma, and the military budget became a priority, indirectly increasing the strength and power of the military and furthering the poverty of the country. And though the people of India and Pakistan have celebrated their respective independence many times since, few seem to have realized that this independence has remained enslaved by the Kashmir dispute. And if there is this realization at all, few on either side have let out the secret.

But for Jinnah, the matter of urgency was to initiate the process of consti-tution-making. He had the stature and the competence to impose this (and in the light of what happened later, many now wish he had done so), but he was a committed constitutionalist and abhorred the subversion of the constitu-tional path. As such, he convened the Constituent Assembly on August 11, 1947, and helped them on their way with the following words: "You are free; you are free to go to your temples, you are free to go to your mosques or to any other place of worship in this state of Pakistan. You may belong to any religion or caste or creed—that has nothing to do with the business of the state. . . . We are starting with this fundamental principle that we are all citizens and equal citizens of one state."[8]

The extent to which Pakistan diverged from the spirit of these words of its great leader is the real measure of the tragedy that Pakistan's subsequent leadership collectively inflicted on their country and the people they misled and misruled. The available political elite was a strange mix of people—only a few were committed and capable. The rest were a bunch of feudal lords who had joined the movement in the last days to reap the benefits and save their lands. Chaudhry Mohammad Ali, a close associate of Jinnah who later became the prime minister of Pakistan (1956–57), substantiates this by say-ing: "As public support for the idea of Pakistan gathered strength, Muslim politicians who were in training under the British in the art of contesting elections and in capturing such crumbs of power as the British allowed to fall turned more and more toward the Muslim League. They were shrewd and hardheaded men capable of being infected temporarily by mass enthusiasm but never forgetful of their own advantage."[9]

The composition of the sixty-nine-member Constituent Assembly of Pa-kistan (CAP) provides insights into the stature of the political leaders. Given the nation's scarce resources, it was almost impossible to have organized elections at that stage, so the CAP was constituted from members of the provincial assemblies who were elected in 1946 under the British. Interest-ingly, the provincial members largely chose themselves to go to the CAP while keeping membership in the provincial legislatures as well. Moreover, many members remained members of the CAP even after their appointments as ministers in provincial cabinets, governors, and ambassadors. In many cases, provincial chief ministers were also found in this august house. It is quite easy to judge whether it was out of love for the country or a reflection of a lust for power.

While Pakistan's honeymoon time was running out, Jinnah passed away on October 11, 1948. It is perhaps justly said that no man is indispensable, but it may also be as just to say that if ever a leader was indispensable to his people, that man was Jinnah. Just as was the case with his life, here was a man whose death so soon after the creation of his country also changed the course of history. The bereavement felt by the people of Pakistan was as near a collective sense of being orphaned as it was possible to feel. Obituaries poured in eulogizing the singular achievements of a man whose integrity, incorruptibility, and sheer power of will had forged a new nation. The least complimentary of these was by Lord Archibald Wavell (a former viceroy of India): "I never liked Jinnah, but had a reluctant admiration for him and his uncompromising attitude. He certainly had much justification for his mistrust of Congress and its leaders."[10] And years later came a historical appraisal of Jinnah from Professor Stanley Wolpert: "Few individuals alter the course of history. Fewer still modify the map of the world. Hardly anyone can be credited with the creation of a nation-state: Jinnah did all three."[11]

With Jinnah out of the way, the political leaders left to carry his mantle did not waste much time coming out in their true colors, each gravitating to the side of the many-sided toast as he felt was buttered for him. And in this mad rush after self-interest, few felt burdened by any sense of shame or modesty. The many private agendas were guaranteed to make the prevailing confusion worse. Their prime purpose was no longer to draft a constitution, but to delay it as much as possible. After eighteen long months, all that the Constituent Assembly had to show for its efforts was a page and a half of a "vaguely worded Objectives Resolution, which was contradictory in itself."[12] The ulema (religious scholars), many of whom had opposed the Pakistan movement tooth and nail (and some who had supported it), were nevertheless united in trying to give the constitution an Islamic character. It was convenient for them to forget that the entire struggle that eventually saw the birth of Pakistan had revolved around Jinnah's efforts to find a formula that would ensure the security of the Muslims of India, preferably within a united India, and as a last resort, without. His whole thrust was on the word "Muslim," which is not always easily translatable into "Islamic." He made this clear at every opportunity. In his radio address to the American people in February 1948, he maintained that he was certain that the ultimate shape of Pakistan's constitution would be of a democratic type, embodying the essential principles of Islam. He then went a part of the way to give an interpretation of these principles. He said: "In any case Pakistan is not going to be a theocratic state to be ruled by priests with a divine mission. We have many non-Muslims, Hindus, Christians, and Parsi—but they are all Pakistanis. They will enjoy the same rights and privileges as any other citizens and will play their rightful part in the affairs of Pakistan."[13] This speech along with the one delivered on August 11, 1947, gives a fair idea of the Pakistan envisioned by the father of the nation. The spirit of these two speeches should have formed the heart of the Objectives Resolution.

But that was not to be. The divergent views of ulema and other members of the CAP about the definition of an Islamic state created much confusion in this regard. Prolonged and futile discussions on nonissues such as *shoora-* (consultation) based *Khilafat,* transterritorial pan-Islamic remedies, and democracy versus Islam all blurred the real issue of framing a constitution for establishing an efficient and accountable government.[14] But after prolonged wrangling, the ulema managed to get in the opening sentence of the Objectives Resolution, that is, "Sovereignty over the whole universe belongs to God Almighty alone, and the authority which He has delegated to the State of Pakistan through its people for being exercised within the limits prescribed by Him is a sacred trust." This was an innocuous enough insertion. The lieutenants of Jinnah either could not or would not see any further significance in this sentence beyond what it strictly stated, but the minorities could see well beyond it and they were alarmed. They saw here a foot of the clergy in the door and feared that as time passed this simple statement would be progressively enlarged and interpreted anew until it reached its logical conclusion, that is, that Pakistan was an Islamic state to be ruled under the law of the *Sharia,* which would be interpreted by the mullahs. And the moment this happened, in its wake would follow its natural corollary, that is, that non-Muslims in Pakistan will be declared second-class citizens.

For the moment the anxieties of the minorities were mollified by the assurances of the moderates in the CAP to the effect that the Objectives Resolution was exactly what it was, and would not take the place of the constitution, nor would it be allowed to be interpreted so as to reduce the status of any citizen of Pakistan. Prime Minister Liaquat Ali Khan clarified that Pakistan would not be a theocracy.[15] But half a century down the line, the clergy has used its foot to open the door ever wider. They have as yet not all got through this door to entirely fill and take over the hall where it leads, but they have succeeded nevertheless in disenfranchising hundreds of thousands of Pakistanis; reducing thousands more to second-class citizens; and rendering the country divided along its myriad sectarian fault lines, often to the accompaniment of random bloodshed. Jinnah's stark warning to Gandhi to desist from intermingling religion with politics was both apt and portentous. Jinnah had told Gandhi: "Your methods have already caused split and division in almost every institution that you have approached hitherto . . . not amongst Hindus and Muslims but between Hindus and Hindus and Muslims and Muslims. . . . All this means complete disorganization and chaos. What the consequence of this may be, I shudder to contemplate."[16] Both India and Pakistan have proceeded well beyond the prophetic shudder of Jinnah. Had the Congress leadership realized this, the Indian subcontinent could have been spared a lot of misery inflicted upon it by the religious fanatics of both sides.

But that still lay in the future. For the moment, Pakistan's clergy was well under control, for the good reason that the process of constitution-making itself was headed nowhere. The framers of the constitution seemed quite happy with a spruced-up version of the Government of India Act of 1935 to masquerade as the genuine constitution. After meeting at the average of no more than sixteen days a year over a period of seven years,[17] this is all they could produce apart from the Objectives Resolution. Time seems to have stopped still in the East yet once again!

But this madness was not entirely without a method. It is true that a fair amount of time was spent losing a bit of the ground to the mullahs in the framing of the constitution, and there was the question of reconciling different agendas as well, but most of the time was lost in devising ways to constitutionally deny the due representation to East Pakistan (Bengalis) in the central legislature. There is also a stronger than faint suspicion that many members of the CAP, who were immigrants from India, had left their constituencies behind and were not overly keen to complete the task. Such completion would have led to the dissolution of this body, and fresh elections would have had to follow, and many of the latter could not have looked forward to this with much enthusiasm. And here lay an irony, because it was the Muslims, of what had now become India, who were a threatened minority. It is they that had the greatest role in the creation of Pakistan, and who had made the greatest sacrifices in the process.

The first serious internal upheaval that Pakistan had to encounter was the language controversy in East Pakistan. Urdu, which came to be the national language, was not used as the first language in any of the provinces of Pakistan. Urdu was an amalgam of Sanskrit, Persian, Arabic, and Turkish. It had evolved as a language of the caravan and by the seventeenth century it was sufficiently developed to supplant Persian as the court language at Delhi. Primarily it was the language of the Muslim elite of India, and it had a respectable enough array of literature to stake such a claim. It is thus that Urdu came to be chosen as the national language of Pakistan, though all the five provinces of Pakistan had different and well-developed languages of their own.[18] Bengalis, the largest ethnic group in Pakistan, whose population was a little more than 50 percent of the country's whole populace, demanded that Bengali should also be declared a national language along with Urdu, but this legitimate demand fell on deaf ears. It became a controversial issue, and political and economic frustrations led the Bengalis to become more assertive in this regard. In 1948 the problem became sufficiently alarming for the government to ask an ailing Jinnah to travel all the way to Dhaka, the capital of East Pakistan, and douse this fire by the strength of his personal prestige.

Jinnah was booed while addressing a huge gathering when he declared that only Urdu could be the national language. There was a repeat of the problem in 1952, resulting in the deaths of four of the protesting students, and the army had to be called out to restore order.

Both the language riots and the army's role in quelling these were highly significant, setting the tone for the future struggle for power in Pakistan. Coming on the heels of West Pakistani efforts in the CAP aimed at denying the East Pakistanis their due share of representation in the future legislature, the language issue was one further cause for disillusionment in East Pakistan. These grievances, given adequate cause, would build up to the point where they would explode in a crescendo of violence to sunder Pakistan in an orgy of blood. The underdog mullah with just a "foot in the door" would in time also exact a terrible price for his long wait as the outsider. But it would be the army that would take the first heat hands down. The incompetent politician made a mess of things and then asked the army to clean it up by coming out "in aid of civil power." Each time the army moved out to restore order at the insistence of the politician, it not only returned with an exaggerated opinion of itself, but also with a proportionately disparaging opinion of the politician. And what is more, the army liked the little crumbs of power it was allowed to taste from time to time, which kept its appetite well whetted.

The politicians made the most serious recourse to the army in 1953 in what came to be euphemistically called the Punjab Disturbances. These were engineered by the mullahs as their first serious bid to take power in a country that they had first opposed the creation of. The troubles of 1953 did not start out of the blue. As observed earlier, the clergy had done all it could to hijack the constitution-making process and give it a theocratic character, but they did not have much success until then; but as soon as Jinnah passed away, it was the signal for the clergy to emerge from the shadows. Leading the pack was Jinnah's inveterate foe, Maulana Maududi (1903–79) of the Jamaat-i-Islami (Party of Islam), who had considered this country "na-Pakistan"[19] (an impure land). He immediately found himself dictating to the country's ruling elite. Lawrence Ziring rightly wonders why the political leadership after Jinnah "allowed those heretofore opposed to the Pakistan idea, namely the Muslim clerics, to intrude themselves into the nation's constitution-making activities."[20] But Maududi had to wait till 1953 to do some real damage, and thus far he had achieved little more than cause a great fright to Mr. A.K. Brohi, one of the country's leading jurists, who thought that the problem of constitution-making had become unnecessarily complicated due to "a wrong insistence on a slogan viz. that the constitution of Pakistan would be based on Islamic law."[21] For this effort at stating the obvious, he received such a telling broadside from Maududi and his cohorts that he hastened to make an undignified retraction,[22] and was so chastened by the experience that he seldom took any principled stand thereafter.

At partition, the government of Punjab Province was rent by all manner of petty squabbles and sordid intrigues. The ambitious and unscrupulous minister of finance (Mumtaz Daultana) was not entirely satisfied with the ministerial office held by a man as brilliant as himself. He eyed the scalp of his chief minister (Iftikhar Mamdot) with special relish. In 1949, Daultana did manage to create conditions that warranted the dismissal of the Punjab legislature.

By the time the political process was restored in Punjab Province, there were severe food shortages in the province, against which the *Ahrar* (another hard-line anti-Pakistan religious organization) and some other religious forces had started an effective agitation. With the help of these elements, Daultana had swept to power and soon they diverted the course of the agitation from an economic issue to a religious one. Maududi and his party joined in as well. As a foil to the hardship that the people of Pakistan were undergoing, they threw up the supposed prosperity of the Ahmedis, holding them responsible for the economic misery of the people. From there they diverted the agitation to the person of the foreign minister Zafarullah Khan, an internationally well-respected diplomat who was an Ahmedi. They now started demanding that Zafarullah Khan be dismissed from office and that Ahmedis be declared non-Muslim. With some difficulty, a similar crisis situation in Karachi was restored, but Daultana, who wanted to embarrass the prime minister, did not move a muscle to defuse the problem despite appeals by his chief of police, Mr. Qurban Ali Khan.[23]

Finally, as the incidence of arson, looting of Ahmedi properties, and murder increased to shake the rulers out of their torpor, the authorities began to take notice of the plight of the Ahmedis. Iskander Mirza, the defense secretary, was moved to write to the prime minister, Khawaja Nazimuddin, a top-secret letter on February 26, 1953, saying that:

> [T]he problems created by your personal enemies including the Mullahs, if not dealt with firmly and *now*, will destroy the administration and the country. . . . In Cairo, Sir Zafarullah Khan is being received with the utmost honor and respect. He is also meeting the heads of all the Arab countries, where he has a very high reputation. Whereas in Karachi he is being abused in public meetings . . . and his photographs are being spat upon. . . . For God's sake, become a courageous leader and take decisive action. Once you do this, the whole country, with the exception of rascals, will rally around you, and the prestige of Pakistan will go up. The country will be saved.[24]

To a great extent it was Jinnah's early demise that plunged Pakistan into such an abyss of intolerance. After Jinnah, the only man who commanded sufficient obedience in the ranks of the ruling elite was Prime Minister Liaquat Ali Khan. But he had already fallen to an assassin's[25] bullet in 1951. At Jinnah's death, Bengali politician Khawaja Nazimuddin had became governor-general. He was as weak as he was amenable, and when Liaquat was gone, he moved over to fill the prime minister's slot, making way for Ghulam Mohammad, a former bureaucrat, to become governor-general. This move was the first overt assertion of power by a bureaucrat at the expense of the politicians.

Shortly after Iskander Mirza's letter to Nazimuddin, the situation in Daultana's burning fortress of Lahore, which he had willfully abandoned to the religious extremists, had to be redressed by the imposition of local martial law in March 1953. Daultana, who had acquiesced in a criminal agitation of the religious fanatics, was dismissed, and Maududi and many of the leaders who had spread the turmoil were arrested. Maududi and a few other leaders were given death sentences for the part they played in the upheaval, later to be reprieved by the Supreme Court. And thus was peace brought to Punjab. But the clergy had already made its first concerted bid for power.

Demonstrating the tactics it would follow in the future, the clergy had succeeded in holding the government hostage for a fair while. This performance could only bolster its confidence in its own strength, of which it was largely unaware before 1953. And though it still remained largely an outsider among power players of the first rank, it had served adequate notice that such would not be the case for long. It was the army alone that could stop them, and eventually did. And through martial law, limited though it was, the army got its first real taste of power.

After the ugly episode, the government also held an inquiry report on the subject. The two learned members of the commission, Justice Mohammad Munir and Justice Rustam Kayani, having asked a number of ulema (religious scholars) to define the word Muslim, concluded:

> Keeping in view the several definitions given by the Ulema, need we make any comment except that no two learned divines are agreed on this fundamental. If we attempt our own definition as each learned divine has done, and that definition differs from that given by all others, we unanimously go out of Islam. And if we adopt the definition given, say by any one of the Ulema, we remain Muslims according to the view of that *alim* but Kafirs [infidels] according to the definition of everyone else.[26]

Though unknown to most Pakistanis, it is in these early years that the United States started to play its increasingly significant role in the internal politics of Pakistan, which can be clearly mapped out from the declassified

American documents despite the blacking out of large sections of the same. It has been the view of many that Pakistan veered westward in its orientation in 1951 when Prime Minister Liaquat Ali Khan turned down the Soviet invitation and went to Washington instead. That is not quite true. From its very inception Pakistan saw itself as a state that could not abide by communism. As early as September 9, 1947, Jinnah stated in a cabinet meeting: "Our interests lie with the two great democratic countries, namely [the] UK and USA, rather than with Russia."[27] Jinnah knew that the United States was supporting a united India and in fact had cautioned the Muslim League in 1945–46 that its hard-line stance of sticking to the partition idea would cost it America's sympathy.[28] But Jinnah was clear about what he wanted for Pakistan—he and his lieutenants took the initiative of approaching the U.S. diplomats in India to ask for establishing diplomatic relations between the two countries and besides expressing his great admiration for the United States, he conveyed to them that "he was hopeful the U.S. would aid Pakistan in its many problems."[29] However, it took the United States a few years to develop sufficient interest in the region to consider such prospects.

The U.S. National Security Council "top secret" report prepared in early 1951 maintained that, "in Pakistan, the communists have acquired considerable influence in press circles, among intellectuals and in certain labor unions" and argued that domination of "Pakistan by unfriendly powers, either directly or through subservient indigenous regimes, would constitute a serious threat to the national security of the U.S."[30] The said report, while considering U.S. strategic interests, mentions that possible air bases at three major Pakistani cities (Karachi, Rawalpindi, and Lahore) "would be nearer a larger portion of Soviet territory, . . . than bases in any other available location in Asia or the Near East," thus implying that a strategic military relationship with Pakistan had become crucial for the United States.

Interestingly, according to Ian Talbot, a British historian specializing in South Asia, the alleged motive of the killers of Prime Minister Liaquat was his consideration of a shift away from a pro-western foreign policy orientation in the Middle East.[31] However, a senior Pakistani bureaucrat who had read the Liaquat assassination inquiry report, still under lock and key in Islamabad, says that though the conclusions of the inquiry commission were vague, there was enough indication that Liaquat's political successors tried to close the investigations.[32] Ayub Khan also writes in his autobiography that he observed that Liaquat's murder did not entirely displease Mr. Ghulam Mohammad, the then–governor-general.[33]

So the first stirrings of a friendship between the leader of the First World and one bringing up the rear of the Third was now beginning to be felt. But one not too friendly with the United States was Khawaja Nazimuddin, the pious but naïve prime minister of Pakistan, whose affinity with delicious fare outranked his knowledge of the reality of a poor man's plight. He was ambivalent about Pakistan's pro-U.S. policies and was inclined to look for allies elsewhere.[34] Soon he was dismissed by Governor-General Ghulam Mohammad (April 1953) for his general incompetence, the last nail in his coffin being driven by Daultana and the Punjab Disturbances. Failure to devise a constitution for the country was given as the prime reason for his departure, though the step was controversial, being in violation of constitutional norms. But the genial old man was so naïve as to try and appeal to the queen of England to bail him out—perhaps he thought that the United States was behind his removal from office!

This brought in Mohammad Ali Bogra as the next prime minister, a third-tier Bengali politician who had been Pakistan's ambassador to the United States and living outside Pakistan for the previous six years. Being a close American friend, a lightweight politician, and largely ignorant of the real political situation at home, he was thought to be the ideal choice for the job. The U.S. embassy in Islamabad reported back to the State Department that Bogra's appointment was a "welcome gain as far as U.S. interests are concerned."[35]

Bogra stood in as prime minister for only eighteen months. During his brief tenure the Mutual Aid Assistance Agreement was signed with the United States in May 1954. In September 1954, Pakistan joined the Southeast Asia Treaty Organization (SEATO), and in February 1955 it entered the Baghdad Pact (later called CENTO). The Pakistan army was desperate to get military hardware and weapons from the United States, as the perceived threat from India was rising with every passing year. In pursuance of this goal, Ayub Khan, while talking to Assistant Secretary of State Henry Byroade in 1953, even went to the extent of saying that: "Our army can be your army if you want us."[36] The foundation of a solid Pakistan Army–Pentagon relationship had been laid.

But in Pakistan, another alliance was in the making—that between the army and a bedridden governor-general, who had been alerted to the fact that his newly chosen prime minister (Bogra) was conspiring to pull the rug out from under him. The old man, though he could not get up, was determined nevertheless not to take this lying down. Each power player around this time started looking to gain the army's support, overtly or otherwise, to bring down its rival.

The Pakistan Army by now had become a very powerful institution, playing a significant role in the decision-making processes. In this context, a watershed incident occurred in 1949 that had a huge impact on the military and political history of Pakistan, but is often ignored by historians. Major General Iftikhar Khan, who was designated as the next commander in chief (C-in-C) but had not taken over yet, died in a plane crash at Jungshahi along with a few other officers. According to his contemporary, Major General Sher Ali, the history of Pakistan would have been different if General Iftikhar Khan had become C-in-C of the Pakistan Army, because he would never have allowed the army to be used for political purposes and would never have used his position as a doorway to political power.[37] Ayub Khan, who had risen from the rank of lieutenant colonel to four-star general in only four years, was appointed C-in-C in 1951. There is many a conspiracy theory as to how General Iftikhar's plane crashed, but no evidence has ever come to light.

Certainly, all was not well within the army circles. In March 1951 a group of military officers and some prominent civilians with a leftist/communist orientation led by Major General Akbar Khan were planning a coup, with the aim of overthrowing the government, appointing a military council to hold elections to the Parliament, and resolving the Kashmir dispute through use of military force.[38] Luckily the plan, later known as the Rawalpindi conspiracy case, was unearthed well in time.[39]

Due to weak political management of the state, the army as an institution was increasingly becoming independent. For instance, the instructions given to Brigadier Ghulam Gillani, Pakistan's first military attaché to Washington, by General Ayub Khan in 1952 are noteworthy. He was told that his main task was to procure military equipment from the Pentagon, and he need not take either the ambassador or foreign office into confidence because in his view, "these civilians cannot be trusted with such sensitive matters of national security."[40] According to Mushahid Hussain and Akmal Hussain, it was in fact "the American connection, which made the Army the most important institutional vehicle for U.S. political influence in Pakistan."[41]

Bogra by now had seen and handled a bit of power as prime minister, and what he had seen he had liked. But the summary manner in which his predecessor (Nazimuddin) was bundled out of office could not have done much for his confidence. So he thought it would not be a bad idea to enhance his power at the cost of the governor-general's. Ordinarily Bogra would have been too scared of entertaining such an idea, but Ghulam Mohammad had suffered a stroke and his speech was severely impaired, and he needed an interpreter to be understood. His florid speech, which used to issue forth in torrents of the choicest curses, could now be understood only by his nurse. And though she was usually good enough to render a faithful enough interpretation of his volleys of enraged abuse, this could not match the original for sheer effect.

This must have brought about a corresponding reduction of the dread that

Bogra had of the governor-general as he gathered enough courage to reduce his powers to that of a mere constitutional head of state in October 1954. Having due regard for the old man's reputation for immediate counterattack, he timed the measure so that, immediately as it was through, he would be airborne on his way to the United States on an official trip. He was in Washington when the froth hit the fan. Ghulam Mohammad ordered Bogra to report to him forthwith. Ayub Khan was also in the United States, and he too was told to return. The flight back was one of a thoroughly frightened prime minister churning out one scenario after another about the fate that probably awaited him upon landing, with his general Ayub Khan discounting his worst fears and consoling him.

In any event, it was Ayub Khan and Iskander Mirza who decided to face Ghulam Mohammad in full spate. They mollified him sufficiently for a highly nervous Bogra to be ushered in to bear the lion's portion of the invective via the kindly nurse. It was during this "meeting," with the ailing governor-general sprawled on a white bedsheet on the floor and hurling abuse at all and sundry, that Ayub Khan received from him the offer to take over the reins of government. He refused.[42] Not being one for legal niceties, the governor-general lost little time in bundling out the Constituent Assembly that had dared to pare down his powers. The main reason he cited for the dissolution was the monumental incompetence of this body, with which few could disagree. And even if some could, he was not to care.

Ayub was not offered this crown for any reasons of altruism. Ghulam Mohammad knew that he was very sick and that he had barely avoided dethronement by the skin of his teeth. He knew it was time to go, but if power were to be handed over, it was best handed over to the one who was most likely to step in and take it anyhow. But once Ayub refused, the old man did not give the slightest indication that he was in any hurry to leave. Crippled or not, he was confident that he was more of a match for the rest of them. He had Bogra reconstitute the cabinet, in which Ayub was taken on as defense minister. This was the first time that military influence was openly induced to bolster the power of one of the power players.

These events were ominous for the politicians of Pakistan. They saw in these their diminishing role in the power game—a firm shift in favor of the bureaucracy and the army. To redress this imbalance in their favor, a recourse was made to the higher courts, challenging the dissolution of the late Constituent Assembly by the governor-general, but the superior court upheld the dissolution, thereby discrediting itself. A new assembly was cobbled together in 1955 through indirect elections and was charged with the task of framing the long overdue constitution. Meanwhile, the governor-general, that doughty old survivor who had absolute faith in his own indestructibility, was being fast overtaken by senility and in August 1955, Iskander Mirza, another former bureaucrat, stepped in as acting governor-general.

The composition of the new legislature obliged Bogra to resign as prime minister. He went back as an ambassador to Washington and Chaudhry Mohammad Ali succeeded him, and the task of constitution-making fell on him. Like Ghulam Mohammad, he too was a civil servant, but he neither had the former's backbone nor his rapier of a tongue. U.S. interest in the internal political affairs of Pakistan was obvious from what the U.S. ambassador to Pakistan, Horace Hildreth, wrote in a dispatch to the Department of State, dated August 26, 1955:

> Chaudhry Mohammad Ali has become Prime Minister. Mohammad Ali will shortly become Ambassador to Washington. . . . General Ayub, though relinquishing his Cabinet post, continues as Commander in Chief of the Army, and final arbiter of the destiny of Cabinets. These men have been among the most powerful friends of the United States in Pakistan. I believe that their continuance in positions of power and their continued friendliness toward the United States are important to our policy objectives here.[43]

Chaudhry Mohammad Ali, a gentleman, cast in the mold of an ideal number two man, produced a constitution in a matter of seven months. The constitution also had the "blessings" of Governor-General Iskander Mirza, who believed in "controlled democracy" because the masses, he believed, were "bound to act foolishly sometimes."[44] Politicians were hardly involved in the constitution-making process and, as aptly narrated by Ayesha Jalal, "intimidation, outright coercion and extension of patronage had been critical in the central leadership's success in forcing the constitutional bill through the Constituent Assembly."[45] Iskander Mirza signed the constitution bill only after getting the assurance that he would be nominated as the provisional president. The opposition parties severely criticized the new constitution, calling it a sellout to Americans and a black day for Bengalis.[46]

The 1956 constitution was a bundle of contradictions. Not adhering to the established norm of parliamentary democracy, which the constitution claimed to be ushering in, the office of president was unduly equipped with the authority to not only dissolve the National Assembly before expiration of its term of five years (Article 50), but also to appoint a prime minister at its discretion.

By the time the 1956 constitution came into being, the religious forces of the country had consolidated their position quite considerably. Among other things, the communist-inspired military coup attempt in 1951 had inclined the government of the day to view religious parties with a certain detached, if not benign, neutrality. But it was Maududi's religious learning and intellectual powers along with the dedication and organizational strength of the Jamaat-i-Islami that had done the most to strengthen the disparate forces of the religious right. He had assessed early that there was little chance for parties like his to become the main players in the power game. But knowing the fickle balance of political power in the country, he saw that becoming a power broker was an attainable possibility.

Here the consequences of the peculiar circumstances of the birth of the country were to come and rescue the religious parties from their comparative obscurity. When Pakistan came into being, it did so as a state but not as a nation. The historic experiences of the Muslims of India were not such as would forge the spirit of nationhood among a disparate peoples, who were developing separately along different lines in different locales. The underlying unity that is central to being a nation was therefore lacking, and whatever little unity there was, was reactive. It manifested itself only in the insecurity engendered by a fear of Hindu domination. As soon as this fear fell into the background, so did the unity that it had thrown up as reflex. And without this, a drift into chaos and anarchy was a more natural phenomenon than was order, especially because of the huge upheaval and carnage that had accompanied the partition. This had destroyed the fine political, economic, and social balance that had passed for harmony in an undivided India. Unity was therefore essential to contain the forces unleashed by the shattering of a delicate equilibrium. Top quality leadership could have done much to arrest the destabilizing effects of such forces, but the leadership after Jinnah, such as it was, mostly added to chaos in order to exploit it.

In these circumstances the only commonly shared notion of nationhood was Islam. Thus the political leadership of the day was frequently forced to fall back on the slogan of Islam to bring order out of chaos. And here lay the central dilemma of the Pakistan Muslim League and other like-minded parties, a majority of whose leadership in these early years was either secular, or at the very least moderate enough to abhor the prospect of religion being formally inducted into politics. They wanted to appeal to the slogan of Islam to forge national unity and discipline, but they did not want it to go any further than that. But the moment this slogan was out of the bag, it was up for grabs, and none but the religious parties was better qualified to pick it up and take it to its natural conclusion, that is, the call for an Islamic state with an Islamic constitution.

Maududi led the charge against the "secular" parties and mercilessly exposed the contradiction inherent in their position—that of their use of the slogan of Islam, but for rejecting its ideology when it came to the framing of the constitution. In the event, what the clergy got in the constitution of 1956 did not seem to be much, but it was a fair advance on what they had managed to get earlier. Pakistan was henceforth to be called "the Islamic Republic of Pakistan." Also inserted into the new constitution was the veto of "the repugnancy clause," that is, that no laws could henceforth be passed that were repugnant to the teachings of the Quran and the Hadith, and all previous laws were also to be vetted to ensure that they so conformed.

The mullahs were not near being half satisfied with these concessions, but Jamaat-i-Islami knew that a fair advance had been made over what they had previously achieved and that the door had been opened a little wider. Besides, Maududi was aware of a parallel attempt being made by Ismail Ibrahim Chundrigar (the law minister) to frame a constitution with the assistance of Britain's parliamentary counsel, Mr. John Rowlatt.[47] It is not known whether he was also aware that a CIA-sponsored "constitutional adviser" Charles Burton Marshall,[48] was also in the country. He, however, knew that Chundrigar's document was bound to be entirely secular and would be more acceptable to the bureaucrats and the leadership of the army, who were already the real power in the country. It was therefore entirely possible that if a deadlock prevented ratification of the constitution, it could be thrown out the window, and Chundrigar's document would then likely be imposed. Thus, rather than lose the few concessions prized out with great difficulty, he was all for securing these gains, and for having the constitution ratified. He therefore declared the constitution "Islamic" and gave his support for its ratification.

Whatever the perceived merits and demerits of the new constitution, the central fact was that political leaders were not much affected by those, as they had the unique commitment to not play by any set of laws except those of unrestrained greed, self-interest, and quest for power. Laws alone can achieve little in the face of such fierce dedication. Their performance over the next two years was poor even by their already very abysmal standards. Four prime ministers tasted power under the enlightened presidential tenure of Iskander Mirza during this period. Elections to be held under the new constitution were delayed for no reason, depriving the citizens of voicing their views about the policies of the ruling elite. This period has been called the era of political musical chairs. Beyond the hissing derision that greeted their malfunction, there was no music. But there were chairs. In the Provincial Assembly in Dhaka, the right of parliamentary dissent was radically redefined when, on September 26, 1958, using chairs as weapons, members of the opposition attacked and killed the deputy speaker.

Pakistan's desultory love affair with parliamentary democracy was just about to come to an end. A well-pleased General Ayub Khan put on his best look of national concern and began polishing his gun. Iskander Mirza had much the same thoughts, but he did not have a gun. Mirza had little doubt, though, that his friend Ayub would lend him one—but for how long he did not know.

————Chapter 3————

# Ayub Era

## Kashmir and the 1965 War with India

At partition, the Pakistan Army was in a lamentable state. It was short of everything in the way of men, defense stores, weapons, ammunition, and officers. It had one major general, two brigadiers, and fifty-three colonels. Of the six hundred officers required in the army corps of engineers, it had to do with just a hundred, most of whom were unqualified.[1] Besides, not a single complete regiment could come to Pakistan. Though there were pure Sikh regiments and various all-Hindu regiments in the Indian Army, there was no such thing as an all-Muslim unit. After the War of Independence of 1857 (the mutiny, to the British), the British decided that, though they needed Muslim soldiery, they could not trust it enough to form independent all-Muslim units. Muslim elements had therefore to be scattered and mixed with others to dilute their strength.

Further, most of the military assets were located on the Indian side, and because of the ill-concealed hostility between the two emergent states, it was a forlorn hope for Pakistan to expect a fair distribution of the same. Pakistan's hopes of fair play lay only with Field Marshal Auchinleck, the supreme commander. In his capacity as head of the Armed Forces Reconstruction Committee, he was in part responsible for the fair distribution of defense stores and materials. His attempts at being fair were looked upon as bias in favor of Pakistan by the senior Indian officers and political leaders. As a campaign of vilification built up against him, he proposed that the supreme commander's headquarters be closed down in November 1947 rather than on the date of its scheduled closure in April 1948. Pakistan protested against this proposal but the Indians supported the move, and Mountbatten had little difficulty in going along with the Indian demand.[2] With this evaporated Pakistan's slender hope of getting its fair share of military assets.

In these circumstances, the Pakistan Army could not do without the experienced lot of senior British officers, two of whom became its first two commanders in chief (C-in-C). In the building up and reorganization of the Pakistan Army, the role of Generals Frank Messervy and Douglas Gracey has to be lauded without reservation. That so soon it could be called an army at all had much to do with their efforts.

Toward the end of 1949, as General Gracey's term of office neared its end, he tapped Major General Akbar Khan (the seniormost Pakistani officer) to take over. But Akbar refused the offer on the grounds that the job was beyond his competence—an admission never made by any Pakistani Army officer again, though many were eminently qualified to make it. But for the army, a better professional beginning could hardly have been made. The next in line was Major General Iftikhar Khan, Akbar's younger brother. Iftikhar was a highly respected senior officer of the day, known for his professional ability, integrity, and incapacity to suffer fools with joy. Before he could assume the responsibility as C-in-C, he was killed in an air crash. This was a tragic loss for the fledgling institution, but it was also a watershed event of grave significance for the army. Instead of landing in the sure hands of incontrovertibly its finest officer, it fell into hands not quite as sure. General Ayub Khan was appointed as C-in-C in 1951.

Ayub Khan was a graduate of the Royal Military College, Sandhurst, U.K., and though not an arrogant man, he was sufficiently free of the restraint of humility to recount in his autobiography all the reasons why he thought Iftikhar would not have made a good army chief.[3] But arrogant or not, he was about the handsomest senior officer, apart from which there was little in his previous career to make it especially distinguished. Indeed, in the early years of Pakistan he was known more for a rumored dereliction of duty when posted in the Punjab Boundary Force (PBF), from the consequences of which he was believed to have been rescued by Iskander Mirza, who was defense secretary at the time.[4] It was also suggested that Mirza helped his promotion to the rank of major general by ensuring that Jinnah did not see his entire service record, and that this was where Ayub's friendship with Mirza took root. Whether these rumors had a basis in fact is difficult to tell, but they are difficult to entirely discount either, because Ayub has made reference to the criticism he drew on account of his service on the PBF in his autobiography and has tried hard to prove that he "was placed in a hopeless situation."[5] Irrespective of this, there is no denying that Ayub Khan greatly contributed in stabilizing, organizing, and building the Pakistan Army.

Very soon after taking over as C-in-C, Ayub was jolted by an abortive coup from within the military. This attempt was led by the brilliant but temperamental Major General Akbar Khan, who had a strong socialist bias plus an equally healthy prejudice for his wife, with whom he shared all the secrets. Surprisingly, it was Akbar's wife who spilled the beans. The main reason for the disgruntlement of the officers involved was what they believed to be an inept handling of Pakistan's war effort in Kashmir. As a result of the consequent court-martial, the army lost a number of very good senior officers—a loss it could ill afford. But within the army the court-martial produced a scare, which could only have helped Ayub consolidate and secure his position against any possible challenge. What further helped him in this was a four-year extension of his term as C-in-C in 1954, and then another two-year extension in June 1958 given by President Iskander Mirza. By 1958, Ayub had been the head of the army for a better part of eight years. His position was beyond challenge, but not as yet above criticism, because there was a sufficient number of senior officers not junior enough to be awestruck by him. But that would soon be put right. He was already seriously thinking about a coup and had started to show disloyalty to his benefactor Iskander Mirza, and before the year was out he had probably received the required clearance from the director of the Central Intelligence Agency of the United States. An extremely revealing top secret telegram of April 19, 1958, from the U.S. ambassador James Langley in Pakistan to the secretary of state in Washington, D.C., reads in part:

> This is the story of the dreams of Empire of two of the stronger men in Pakistan, President Mirza and General Ayub Khan. . . . It is a story developed in search of an answer to why Ayub, who is being sent by his government to the U.S. to plead the case of Pakistan for a gift of bombers, should seek an appointment with Allen Dulles (Director of the CIA) without the knowledge of Mirza. . . . Ayub said Pakistan was nearly ripe for a dictatorship. He said a dictatorship must have popular support, and that it must come into being as a result of some violence. He thought elections were going to be held, and that they would provide the bloodshed which could make a dictatorship inevitable . . . got the definitive impression that Ayub wanted very much to enlist Allen Dulles' support for the dictatorship which Ayub felt was inevitable.[6]

Iskander Mirza, who belonged to the Nawab family of Bengal, was the first Indian officer to receive the king's commission from Sandhurst's Royal Military College. He was commissioned as a second lieutenant in a cavalry regiment (Poona Horse), and by the rank of colonel had transferred to the political service of India. He was an administrator who drew favorable notice and whose meteoric rise was much helped by the partition. As defense secretary, Mirza had seen and participated in the palace intrigues that defined Pakistan's early years. By 1958, however, both Mirza and Ayub were after the same prize, that is, absolute power in Pakistan. And both were looking toward American support to achieve this end, but Mirza probably did not know that Ayub had stolen a march on him by approaching the Americans a good few months before he made his own approach. On October 4, 1958, Ambassador Langley reported to the State Department that Mirza would take over the government of Pakistan within a week and would simultaneously proclaim martial law.[7]

On October 7, 1958, President Iskander Mirza proclaimed martial law in Pakistan. According to his son, he planned to lift martial law after a month or so,[8] but if at all he wanted to do this, he was forestalled by Ayub's palace coup on October 27, arrested, and sent to London a few days later. The treatment meted out to Mirza was humiliating. He could have been relieved with a little more grace. That this was not the case must redound to Ayub's discredit.

Ayub's takeover was duly christened a "revolution," and the day of the takeover entered the national calendar as a holiday. There was relief among the people of Pakistan, though there was no overt celebration. They thanked Allah that the day had dawned for them to see the backs of the accursed politicians. Many petty crooks, plying their trades in the bazaars of towns and cities, went into hiding. Senior crooks, not as petty, underwent a change of faith, went into recess, and started to praise the savior in public while privately they waited for things to "settle down," as they knew they eventually would. The mullahs shut their mouths, waiting for the opportune moment to open them again. Trains, by miraculous coincidence, started to run on time. Optimism and hope, for once, were on the ascendance. The entire country seemed to have turned a new page, and emerged in its Sunday best.

But then Ayub had promoted himself to the rank of field marshal. It was said at the time that this was done at the unwavering insistence of the generals, who would just not take "no" for an answer. The truth seems to be that the suggestion came from young politician Zulfikar Ali Bhutto[9] and Ayub slipped on the unction, and by the time he recovered himself, he was already field marshal. With this elevation, the first eyebrow was raised and the first little bit of hope was shattered. He next raised Musa Khan to the rank of a four-star general and appointed him as the C-in-C of the army. Unlike Ayub, the Sandhurst-commissioned officer, Musa had risen from the ranks. He belonged to Quetta and was from the Hazara tribe—those brave and sturdy descendants of Genghis Khan (1162–1227) one finds in small pockets all over Asia. Musa was a big, bluff man who played excellent field hockey as a defender. In the old Indian Army, Dhian Chand of the Punjab Regiment was the legendary forward. And it was said that if anyone could stop him, it was Musa Khan of the Frontier Force. But his new assignment was not hockey and was far removed from his turf. Few could match Musa as a gentleman, but as C-in-C he was not all there. It was quite clear to the discerning that this revolution was to be a long-drawn-out affair and that Musa had been promoted primarily for his inability to pull off a coup. Resenting this elevation as unjust, six senior generals resigned. Ayub could only have rejoiced in these resignations because all those who could have looked him in the eye in dissent had bowed out voluntarily. Those who were left were far too junior to him, and among them he could play the demigod with considerable ease.

Ayub had charm and an impressive physical presence, and he came across as a sincere man and he meant well for Pakistan. He was realistic enough to sign an agreement on the sharing of the waters of the Indus Basin with India. He further strengthened ties with the United States and, because of the enhanced credibility of Pakistan, secured substantial aid from it, though primarily for the military sector. He also tried to come to a negotiated settlement with Nehru over Kashmir, but there he ran into a brick wall.[10] Among his achievements, developing a close friendship with China also deserves mention, for which much of the credit is due to Z.A. Bhutto, who soon became foreign minister.

To seek legitimacy for his power, Ayub held a restricted[11] referendum in 1960, which he won without a hitch. And then he decided to have a new constitution that would suit the needs of Pakistan, which "incidentally" coincided with his own as well. By 1962 this was duly produced. It envisioned a presidential system, with a president being elected by an indirect method and various safeguards to ensure that, unless he was an absolute dolt, there was nothing to remove him from power. In the words of Ayub's right-hand man, Altaf Gauhar, democracy "was a concept alien to Ayub's mind."[12]

Ayub was not very religious, but he was not irreligious either. He believed that if politics and religion were mixed, such a mixture would be to the mutual detriment of both, for neither would remain pure. His constitution amply reflected this.[13] He also renamed the country simply as the Republic of Pakistan, by removing the word "Islamic." He wanted to remove any ambiguity that could give discretionary latitude of interpretation to the clergy.

As a sop to the clergy, however, the new constitution provided establishment of an Advisory Council of Islamic Ideology. This council was to make recommendations to the government on issues relating to Islam, but the body's advice was not to be binding. To this body Ayub appointed liberal Islamic scholars so as to avoid a narrow interpretation of issues examined by it. He was very conscious of the danger that, unless averted, conservatives among Muslims with the passage of time would fall back on the dogmatic interpretation of Islam, with all its attendant prejudices. He even expressed this view in public while addressing the Dar-ul-Uloom Islamia, a leading seminary, in March 1959.[14] In furtherance of presenting a progressive view of Islam, he also established the Institute of Islamic Research to "interpret Islam in a liberal manner and in the context of the modern world." Toward this end he introduced the Family Law Ordinance in 1961, which emancipated the lot of women in Pakistan and was contrary to the established conservative wisdom on the subject.

The mullahs did not like any of this and did not take long to start agitating to protest these measures. Denying a concession is one thing, but withdrawing it once having given is quite another. This protest was again led by the Jamaat-i-Islami, and Ayub reacted by banning the party, freezing its funds, closing its offices and publications, and throwing its leaders in jail. He also realized that much of the increasing militancy of the mullahs had to do with the *Madrasas,* where they were getting their education. There was a time when the *Madrasas* were producing the intellectual elite of the Muslims, but that time was long past, and now what they were breeding was "uncompromising cynicism."[15] A commission was thus appointed to examine what could be done to integrate the curriculum of these institutions into modern secular education—a good idea that died of neglect.

After the crackdown on religious hard-liners, Ayub surprisingly and unaccountably started to backslide on the very issues that had given rise to the agitation. His great leap forward all of a sudden halted. One after the other, he took back nearly all such measures, which he had taken to hold the dogmatic version of Islam at bay. This was enough indication that, though the president had his head screwed on right, the heart needed shoring up. What had started as containment of the forces of the right and a recovery of the ground lost to them ended up as a surrender to these forces. To make a military dictator back down was the most significant battle won by the religious forces thus far. From the disorganized and discordant groups of 1947 that largely neutralized themselves by their mutual squabbles, they had come a long way indeed. Perhaps they could unite only under the impulse provided by a common threat, but the very fact that they could get together at all would prove significant for the future. Another seed sown about this time, and quite as significant in its own way, was the falsification of the meaning of one word of the lexicon, that is, "secular." It increasingly came to be equated with being antireligion, and by extension with being anti-Allah.

Ayub next committed the blunder of taking two of his sons out of the army and putting them into the corporate world. Soon Captain Gohar Ayub Khan, the elder of the two, earned the despicable reputation of being an arrogant upstart moderated only by high-handedness—a man on the make in the business world who played the political gangster in his off hours. Slowly Ayub's name came to be linked to corruption from which even his most able courtiers were unable to detach it. The effectiveness of Ayub's splendid isolation can be gauged from the fact that while people were increasingly being disillusioned by him, others were suggesting that he become a hereditary monarch, to which idea he did not seem entirely averse.[16] The first real jolt to shake him out of the aura of infallibility that had been built around him came with the 1964 elections, which he won against Miss Fatima Jinnah, the sister of Mohammad Ali Jinnah, with considerable difficulty. Many attributed his victory to rigging. That this charge was widely believed was the first sign that perhaps the colossus was not so infallible after all.

Concurrently with all this, Pakistan went one strategic step closer to the United States. During the brief stint of H.S. Suhrawardy as prime minister (1957–58), Pakistan had agreed in principle for the establishment of an American base in Peshawar, but this decision was finalized after detailed discussions in 1959, when Ayub was president. This was to be a secret intelligence facility, which would allow the United States to operate U-2 spy planes from this base. This was considered an excellent place from which to monitor signals from Soviet missile test sites and to intercept other sensitive communications. Photo intelligence gathered by the U-2 had vital strategic importance in the years before the United States developed space satellites.[17] It was the view of the U.S. that until the establishment and the operation of this base, it was Pakistan that was hogging the best from the U.S.-Pakistan alliance, and that it was only after this that "the Americans received in return something that they judged to be of great importance for U.S. national security."[18]

Before this base could be established, however, the United States got a first-class scare. Pakistan was expecting U.S. B-57 bombers, delivery of which was being delayed, and meanwhile India was getting the latest military equipment from the United States. An impulsive Feroz Khan Noon, then briefly Pakistan's prime minister (1958), went off the handle to declare in the National Assembly that, "We will break all pacts in the world and shake hands with all those whom we have made our enemies for the sake of others" if Pakistan's independence was considered to be in jeopardy.[19] But things were soon put on an even keel, and the U.S. secretary of state, John Foster Dulles, assured Pakistan that U.S. feelings for Pakistan were, in a sense, totally different from those for India. He said, "The basic relationship with India was intellectual in contrast to its relationship with Pakistan, which came from the heart."[20]

However, these feelings from the heart were soon to land Pakistan in thick soup with the Soviets. In May 1960 a U-2 plane flown by Francis Gary Powers took off from Peshawar and was shot down over USSR territory. Nikita Khrushchev, the Soviet leader, was not amused. He first conned the Americans into denying the loss of the U-2 and then, to its embarrassment, gave out the details, including the fact that Mr. Powers was with them and that he was cooperating. It must have really rankled President Eisenhower to have to come clean about the affair, and extremely difficult to do so with a face straighter than the one used in the denial. For Pakistan, Mr. Khrushchev reserved a severe warning: "We warn those countries that make their territory available for launching planes with anti-Soviet intentions. Do not play with fire, gentlemen."[21] Later he sternly informed the Pakistani ambassador to the USSR that Peshawar had been marked in red on their maps. And though he did not take off his fabled shoe and bang it on a table to emphasize the gravity of the issue, for Pakistan it was enough to get a bad attack of nerves.

Though very few top-ranking Pakistanis could have known about the operation of the U-2s from Peshawar, the Soviets certainly did. According to a report in the Pakistani intelligence records, the KGB had managed to infiltrate an agent into the U.S. base fairly early on. The agent was an Afghan who was able to get a job at the air base as a cook. And as per this report, it was this agent who managed to sufficiently tamper with the gadgetry of the ill-fated plane so that when Gary Powers thought that he was flying well outside the Soviet missile range, the delusion was laid to rest with a missile hit.[22] And the resultant fall was too long for the rest of beans not to have spilled.

Ironically, it was not Khrushchev's warning that disturbed the composure of the Pakistanis half so much as the words of the next American president. When President John F. Kennedy took over in Washington in 1962, he packed his team with many who had a pronounced pro-India leaning. When in his first State of the Union address he praised the "soaring idealism"[23] of Jawaharlal Nehru, who was better known to the Pakistanis for his soaring duplicity, the U.S.-Pakistan honeymoon suffered a jolt. This was not helped when some members of the U.S. administration suggested that military aid to Pakistan was a blunder and that it be reduced. As if this were not enough, President Kennedy started advocating increased economic aid to India. Pakistan could not see the U.S. rationale behind this cozying up to India and insisted that if such aid was to be given at all, the resulting leverage that this would give to the Americans ought to be used by them to lean on India to solve the Kashmir issue. The U.S. administration did not believe that it had such leverage and also consistently discounted Pakistani fears that U.S. economic aid to India would free funds for the Indian military, which could result in an increased threat for Pakistan. The only assurance the United States was ready to give to Pakistan was that in any eventuality, such as an impending war against China, if the United States were to give military aid to India, it would consult with Pakistan first.[24]

This U.S. assurance was dogged by bad timing as much as it was prescient, because in October 1962, China attacked India, reacting to India's imprudent "forward policy," that is, establishing military posts behind Chinese positions in the mountains. The United States immediately promised military aid to India without consulting Pakistan, despite their recent assurances to do so. Pakistan was miffed. Further, Ayub was not amused when he was asked by the United States to "make a positive gesture of sympathy and restraint" toward India.[25] Nevertheless, despite considerable pressure to take advantage of India's difficulties, Ayub assured the Americans that he would not hamper the Indian effort, that is, that he would abstain from launching a military strike in Kashmir. To the abiding regret of many Pakistanis, Ayub kept his word. Thus Pakistan lost its best chance to settle Kashmir through force of arms, and most ironically, whether Pakistan gained anything substantial from its friendship with the United States or not, it was India that became the greatest beneficiary of this relationship.

Pakistan soon started to think in terms of lessening its almost total dependence on the United States. The U-2 incident made this all the more urgent. Toward this end, Ayub authorized Z.A. Bhutto, the then minister of natural resources, to sign an agreement with the former USSR, allowing it to explore for oil and gas in Pakistan. And in 1961, Bhutto prevailed over Ayub to give Pakistan's support to communist China to be seated at the U.N., in place of Taiwan, and this could only have made Kennedy livid. Then Pakistan announced that it had reached a border agreement with China, and though the Chinese premier offered Pakistan a limited package of economic aid as well as a nonaggression pact, this was refused to keep the United States in a relatively good humor. Not too long thereafter, Pakistan went ahead and signed an aviation accord with China, coming further into its orbit, and to that extent out of that of the United States. This could not have pleased the latter. The policies of the United States and Pakistan were such that they could no longer be reconciled. For Pakistan, the mortal threat to its security lay in India, which the United States saw as a country to be salvaged and indemnified against the Chinese threat, while Pakistan saw in China an insurance against India. This was a vicious circle that was to be accentuated further with the passage of time.

That time was not too far off. In April 1965 the Pakistan Army clashed with Indian forces in the Rann of Kutch area. The Indian Army had moved into a disputed territory, which elicited an immediate response from the Pakistani armed forces. In the desultory fighting that followed, Pakistani forces came out better. The lessons that Pakistan drew from this engagement were to have fateful results. Not too far back, when the Indian Army had received a bloody nose at the hands of the Chinese, and Pakistan had refrained from taking advantage of Indian discomfiture, it was hoping that as a quid pro quo, India would be amenable to a peaceful resolution of the Kashmir problem. That did not happen. Pakistan came to the conclusion that in Kashmir it will have to help itself. It believed that the Himalayan war had destroyed the morale of the Indian Army. The Rann of Kutch experience went further to confirm the Pakistan Army in this opinion. This confirmation indicated to them that the time to take on the Indians had come.

Soon after the Rann of Kutch run-in, India and Pakistan went to war over Kashmir. Whatever little economic consolidation these two very poor countries had achieved since their independence was frittered away in the space of a mere seventeen days. It is pertinent here to briefly refer to the developments vis-à-vis the Kashmir dispute between the two countries after 1947 in order to analyze and understand the causes and effects of the 1965 war.

India's position on Kashmir had changed many times. After the controversial accession of the 77-percent-Muslim-majority Jammu and Kashmir state to India by a Hindu ruler who had already lost control over the state machinery,[26] the matter was deliberated upon many times at the U.N. Security Council. The conclusion was that the matter could be resolved only through a plebiscite seeking the wishes of the people of Kashmir. The accession in 1948 was accepted by Mounbatten conditionally, specifying that the "question of the State's accession should be settled by a reference to the people." Jawaharlal Nehru, the first prime minister of India, had fully supported such a plebiscite in many of his public pronouncements.[27] But progressively, India started to cite the local elections in Jammu and Kashmir (1954) as being a substitute for a plebiscite. Yet, off and on, Nehru came back to uphold his old pledge of holding a plebiscite. On May 10, 1954, Nehru, while addressing the Indian Council of States, had said: "India, honestly and sincerely, does not want to tarnish its image in the world, and it is high time that the tyranny and brutalisation in the valley must cease. Kashmir is neither an inseparable nor an integral part of India . . . [India] must accept the facts and start making arrangements for allowing the people of the disputed territory to exercise their inalienable right of self-determination."[28] It was astonishing, however, that Nehru tried to wriggle out of the promised plebiscite in 1961 by saying, "There is no question of any plebiscite in Kashmir, now or later. I am sick of the talk about plebiscite, which does not interest anybody."[29] That was not all. In August 1963 he changed his stance yet again, when he met Pakistan's foreign minister in New Delhi, and the resulting communiqué of their talks clearly stated that the Kashmir "dispute would be settled in accordance with the wishes of the people of Kashmir . . . by a fair and impartial plebiscite."[30] Nothing came of this as well.

In October 1963, when Pakistan approached the U.N. Security Council to plead for the implementation of its resolutions on Kashmir, the Soviet veto put an end to this effort. By this time India had completely "nonaligned" itself with the former Soviet Union. However, in December 1963 an event took place in Srinagar that unified the Muslim population of Kashmir to rock India out of its smugness. A rumor spread through Srinagar (capital of Jammu and Kashmir) that the holiest relic of the Prophet of Islam had been stolen from the shrine at Hazratbal. As this rumor received confirmation, the entire Muslim population of Kashmir rose up in a raging torrent of protest, which was as antigovernment of Kashmir as it was anti-India in content. These protests spread rapidly to both the wings of Pakistan and also to the Muslim population in India.

But for the moment, passions in Kashmir were doused by the miraculous recovery of the relic, followed by a declaration of a body of Muslim divines that this was indeed the genuine article. The spontaneity of the protests and unity of the Muslim masses during this episode sent a very clear message to India that, notwithstanding the myths about Kashmir, spun and sold by it, the Kashmiri people were on their way to taking an adverse position vis-à-vis India. This—coupled with the fact that after releasing Sheikh Abdullah, a pro-India Muslim leader in Kashmir, the Indian government had to lock him up again on charges of conspiring with Pakistan to suborn the loyalty of the state— could have done little to allay either the alarm or the embarrassment occasioned by the recent happenings. It was therefore considered essential that India restructure the core of its argument on Kashmir. Thus it finally repudiated its pledge of plebiscite in Kashmir and replaced it with a new myth, that is, that Kashmir had become an inseparable and integral part of India and it was therefore not prepared to discuss the issue at all. In consonance with this new stance, it moved to nullify the special constitutional status of Jammu and Kashmir and, in December 1964, a presidential order was passed whereby the president of India could impose direct presidential rule over Kashmir. Then in January 1965 it was announced that the National Conference Party of Sheikh Abdullah was to be disbanded. It was this party's support on which the central Indian pretense of enjoying the backing of the majority of the people of Kashmir was based. Now that Sheikh Abdullah refused to toe India's line, the pretense could no longer be supported.

India had taken a very long and tortuous route to shift from a position of hypocrisy to one of truth. But the explanation of why and how this shift came to be made still had to be supported on pillars of mendacity—a fate it cannot be rescued from by all the wiles of casuistry that it must employ to justify itself. Countless attempts at a solution of the Kashmir problem had foundered on the rock of Indian intransigence even while officially it held to the pledge of plebiscite. With the repudiation of this pledge, hopelessness in Kashmir and frustration in Pakistan could only rise.

New developments in Pakistan's relationship with the United States also had consequences. As mentioned above, when President Kennedy entered the White House, he did so with a decided bent toward India, which was deeply annoying for Pakistan. The U.S. military aid to India had brought about the first discernable bit of anti-American feeling in various Pakistani circles. But when President Johnson took over the presidency in Washington, logically things ought to have favored Pakistan because the new president had a good rapport with Ayub Khan, ever since he had first visited Pakistan as vice president a few years earlier. Johnson once reacted to the pro-India bias of his administration with the words: "Why is it that Jack Kennedy and you India lovers in the State Department are so God dammed ornery to my friend Ayub?"[31] Unfortunately for Pakistan, Johnson's friend Ayub was so irked by the United States that instead of going to President Kennedy's funeral himself and renewing his friendship with Johnson, he chose to send Z.A. Bhutto, who, being the architect of Pakistan's pro-China policy, was least likely to get a favorable reception in Washington.

As relations with the United States continued to sour, Ayub visited China in February 1965 to the warmest and the most elaborate reception ever given to any foreign leader in Beijing. This was followed a month later by a visit to Moscow, the first such trip by a Pakistani leader. The reception here of course was not as warm as the one in China. As a matter of fact, there was a considerable chill about it. But as talks progressed and both sides got over airing their reservations about the other, the atmosphere thawed considerably. By the time the visit ended, it did so with the promise of better things to come in the future. The next destination on Ayub's itinerary was Washington, and just when he was packed and ready to go, he was stunned to be told that the visit had been put off. Johnson thought that in view of Pakistan's pro-China tilt and the American position on Vietnam, the timing of the visit was not appropriate. Ayub was stricken over this cancellation, but because Pakistan was still an ally, Johnson thought he needed to balance things up a bit. So he also canceled the Indian prime minister's visit, which was to follow. This revived Ayub's spirits considerably.

And when the Pakistan Army inflicted a short, sharp reverse on the Indians in the Rann of Kutch in mid-1965, his spirits got a further boost. More important, the international arbitration that followed the Kutch dispute (resulting in favor of Pakistan) put Pakistan under the assumption that if the Kashmir problem was to be solved, the Rann of Kutch route would have to be replicated—a limited clash in Kashmir leading to a threat of all-out war, and then an intervention and arbitration by the great powers.[32] Hence at this point there was considerable confidence among the Pakistanis about the strength of their own arms, which was bolstered by their newfound friendship with China. Utter frustration over Indian intransigence on Kashmir coupled with sympathy for the gathering hopelessness of the Kashmiris and concern over the rapid rearmament of the Indian armed forces on account of Western military aid were factors that played a crucial role in Pakistan's drift toward considering a military solution of the Kashmir issue. Bhutto, in his letter to Ayub of May 12, 1965, drew his attention to increasing Western military aid to India and how fast the balance of power in the region was shifting in India's favor as a result. He expanded on this theme and recommended that "a bold and courageous stand" would "open up greater possibility for a negotiated settlement."[33]

Ayub Khan was won over by the force of this logic, and he tasked the Kashmir Cell under the foreign secretary, Aziz Ahmed, to draw up plans to stir up some trouble in Indian-held Jammu and Kashmir, which could then be exploited in Pakistan's favor by limited military involvement. The Kashmir Cell was a nondescript body working without direction and producing no results. It laid the broad concept of Operation Gibraltar, but did not get very far beyond this in terms of coming up with anything concrete. When Ayub saw that the Kashmir Cell was making painfully little headway in translating his directions into a plan of action, he personally handed responsibility for the operation over to Major General Akhtar Hussain Malik, commander of the 12th Division of the Pakistan Army. This division was responsible for the defense of the entire length of the cease-fire line (CFL) in the Kashmir region.

General Akhtar Malik was a man of towering presence and was known for his acuteness of mind and boldness of spirit. He was loved and admired by his subordinates, but was far too outspoken to be of any comfort to most of his superiors. His professional excellence, however, was acknowledged both in military and civilian circles.

The plan of this operation (Gibraltar) as finalized by General Malik and approved by Ayub Khan was to infiltrate a sizable armed force across the CFL into Indian Kashmir to carry out acts of sabotage in order to destabilize the government of the state and encourage the local population to rise up against Indian occupation.[34] In order to be able to retrieve the situation in case this operation got into trouble, to give it a new lease on life, or to fully exploit the advantage gained in the event of its success, Operation Grand Slam was planned. This was to be a quick strike by armored and infantry forces from the southern tip of the CFL to Akhnur, a town astride the Jammu-Srinagar Road. This would cut the main Indian artery into the Kashmir valley, bottle up the Indian forces there, and so open up a number of options that could then be exploited as the situation demanded. According to some Pakistani Army officers, it was foreseen then that the value of Operation Gibraltar would be fully enchased after Grand Slam succeeded in wresting control of Akhnur.

There was not enough time to fully prepare and train the men who were to infiltrate, and the three-month deadline given was considered to be not nearly enough for this, but the 12th Division was told that, because of certain considerations, no further time could be given. Most of the men to be trained belonged to the Azad Kashmir Regular Forces, which meant that they would have to be withdrawn from the defensive positions along the CFL. The denuded front lines therefore had to be beefed up by other elements. Having no reserves for this purpose, General Malik decided that the only option for him was to simultaneously train a force of Azad Kashmiri irregulars (mujahids) for this purpose. But when he called the C-in-C General Musa to ask for weapons to equip this force, the latter refused. General Malik then made a call to Ayub, apprised him of the difficulty he was having with the C-in-C, and concluded that if the Kashmiris were not to be trusted, they were not worth fighting for. Ayub then called Musa, told him why the new Mujahid Companies needed to be armed and equipped, and ended with the same note, that is, people who cannot be trusted were not worth fighting for. Soon General Malik got a call from Musa: "Malik, people who cannot be trusted are not worth fighting for—go ahead, arm them."[35]

Operation Gibraltar was launched in the first week of August 1965, and all the infiltrators made it across the CFL without a single case of detection by the Indians. This was possible only because of the high standards of Pakistan's security measures, as acknowledged by a senior Indian Army general.[36] The pro-Pakistan elements in Kashmir had not been taken into confidence prior to this operation, and there was no help forthcoming for the infiltrators in most areas. Overall, despite lack of support from the local population, the operation managed to cause anxiety to the Indians, at times verging on panic. On August 8 the Kashmir government recommended that martial law be imposed in Kashmir. It seemed that the right time to launch operation Grand Slam was when such anxiety was at its height. But it was General Malik's opinion that this be delayed till the Indians had committed their reserves to seal off the infiltration routes, which he felt was certain to happen eventually.

On August 24, India concentrated its forces to launch its operations in order to seal off Haji Pir Pass, through which lay the main infiltration routes. That same day General Malik asked General Headquarters (GHQ) permission to launch Operation Grand Slam. The director of military operations, Brigadier Gul Hassan, passed on the request to General Musa, and when he failed to respond, reminded him again the following day. But Musa could not manage to gather the confidence to give the decision himself and sent Z.A. Bhutto to obtain the approval from Ayub Khan, who was relaxing in Swat, two hundred miles away—strange way to fight a war with the C-in-C unwilling to give decisions and the supreme commander unable to do so. The decision finally arrived on August 29,[37] by which time the Indians had bolstered their defenses in the sector where the operation was to be launched with the induction of three infantry units and an artillery regiment.[38] Still a few more precious hours were wasted by the GHQ, and the operation went to the early morning of September 1, more than a week after the commander in the field had first asked for the go-ahead. By early afternoon of the first day all the objectives were taken, the Indian forces were on the run, and Akhnur lay tantalizingly close and inadequately defended. "At this point, someone's prayers worked" says Indian journalist, M.J. Akbar: "An inexplicable change of command took place."[39]

What happened was that, in a surprising turn of events, General Musa landed in the theater of operations and handed the command of the 12th Division over to General Yahya Khan, whom he had brought along. General Malik was asked to get into the helicopter and was flown away by Musa. For nearly thirty-nine years now the Pakistan Army has been trying to cover up this untimely and fateful change of command by suppression and falsification of history.

Loss of time is inherent in any such change, but for reasons that cannot be explained but by citing the intrusion of ego, Yahya insisted on changing Malik's plan and therefore lost even more time. Whereas Malik had basically planned to invest and bypass the strongly defended localities, subordinating everything to reaching and capturing Akhnur with the least delay, Yahya took a different route—he crossed the river Tawi and went straight into Troti, in which crucial time was lost. And this was enough for the Indians to bolster the defenses of Akhnur and launch their strike against Lahore across the international frontier between the two countries. This came on September 6 while the Pakistani forces were still three miles short of Akhnur. This was the contrived end of an operation, which had been meticulously planned and had promised a lot.

And though Lahore was saved in the nick of time by the heroic efforts of officers like Major Aziz Bhatti, a major Indian attack came on September 8, led by their armored division in the Sialkot sector. Pakistan's 24 Brigade was on the way to its battle positions, after having been called to address an emergency situation in the Jassar area of Sialkot, when a soldier in full flight away from the front lines ran square into a startled Brigadier Abdul Ali Malik, the commander of this brigade. This soldier's company (infantry) was deployed as a screen right on the border. He explained that their position had been overrun by a massive Indian attack led by armor. Brigadier Malik concluded that this would have to be the main Indian thrust spearheaded by their armored division, whose whereabouts had been lost to the Pakistani intelligence a good month earlier. The armor regiment under his command, the 25th Cavalry, led by the brave Lt. Col. Nisar Khan was immediately ordered to advance full speed ahead on a broad front to make contact with and engage the advancing forces. Two infantry battalions were ordered to follow. For the duration of the advance, the brigadier ordered wireless communication with the divisional headquarters to be suspended as he was apprehensive that his superior, if told about the latest situation, was likely to come down with any number of confused orders. This independent initiative to move and meet the Indian advance proved to be one of the most crucial decisions of the war on the Pakistani side. To the misfortune of the Indians, it so happened that 24 Brigade reached the village Chawinda just in time to blunt the full might of the Indian attack. An Indian breakthrough here would have meant a clear run for their forces up to the Grand Trunk Road, the most crucial artery of Pakistan, which would have severed the country in two. Incidentally, Brigadier Abdul Ali Malik was the younger brother of Major General Akhtar Malik.

Meanwhile Pakistan had launched its main strike from Kasur, some twenty miles south of Lahore, in the direction of the Indian city of Amritsar. As this attack went in, the Indians gave a general order for withdrawal of their forces from the area (Beas line). But as they did this, they also opened the floodgates of their irrigation works. The inundation caused by this bogged the Pakistan tanks down. The offensive capability of the Pakistan Army was thus checked, and for both sides the situation crystallized in a stalemate because neither could break through the defenses of the other. For Pakistan it was their artillery that had performed consistently well, and their air force was outstanding, and both combined to save many a day.

On September 6, after the Indian attack across the international border, Ayub and Bhutto tried to invoke the 1959 U.S.-Pakistan bilateral agreement, to ask for American help against Indian aggression, but to no avail. Instead, President Johnson suspended military aid to both India and Pakistan. Pakistan immediately turned to China for help. These efforts brought about a strong Chinese condemnation of India's aggression against Pakistan, and this was followed by a Chinese warning against Indian intrusions into Chinese territory. And then on September 16 they sent a note to India to say that as long as Indian aggression against Pakistan continued, it would not stop supporting Pakistan in its just struggle. On September 19, Ayub and Bhutto flew to Beijing for a top secret meeting with the Chinese leadership. China promised Pakistan all the help, but told Ayub that he should be quite prepared to withdraw his army to the hills and fight a long guerrilla war against India. For this neither the Sandhurst-trained Ayub nor the Berkeley-educated Bhutto was quite prepared. On the international scene there was already considerable concern that any direct Chinese involvement in the conflict may escalate and broaden the war involving other countries. Pakistan was pressed by the Western ambassadors to not encourage the Chinese to step up their engagement any further. Pakistan knew it did not have the wherewithal to break through the stalemate on the battlefront. Thus it knew this was the end. Now Pakistan was prepared to accept a cease-fire. The guns fell silent on the afternoon of September 23. As to the final outcome of the war, Dennis Kux aptly says that India "won simply by not losing."[40]

Immediately after the war, on the Pakistan side the major controversy that occupied the minds of many was the change in command of Operation Grand Slam. The "view both in India and even amongst 'sensible army officers' in Pakistan was that Malik's sudden replacement led to the failure of Grand Slam."[41] But the "sensible" Pakistan Army officers were restrained from discussing this subject. It was taboo to do so in the army messes and officers' gatherings, though in private this was most passionately debated. It was only after General Malik's death in 1969 that GHQ gingerly started putting together a theory to justify this change and to propagate it. It was now claimed that the change was preplanned and that this plan laid down that General Malik would command the first phase of the operation up to the river Tawi, and thereafter the command would be assumed by General Yahya Khan. However, there is not a shred of evidence to support this. The operation itself was a set-piece attack for which the operation orders are a part of the historical record, and there is no such mention in these.[42] And any doubts there might have been on the issue were laid to rest by General Gul Hassan, who was director of military operations during the war and the one person who would have known of such a change. He has specifically denied having any knowledge of the same.[43]

Indeed, not a single army officer except Musa and General Yahya seem to have known about this change, which shifted the initiative from Pakistan to the Indian Army. It now seems fair to speculate that the change in command was preplanned only in the sense that it was a conspiracy between Ayub, Musa, and Yahya; that if the operation got into trouble, Malik could keep the command and also the blame that would accrue as a result, but that if it held promise of success, Yahya would be moved in to harvest it.

Lieutenant General Harbaksh Singh, one of the very respected senior Indian military commanders, was one of the few to have appreciated the full military value of Operation Gibraltar as a part of Grand Slam rather than seeing the two in isolation. According to him, "The plan of infiltration was brilliant in conception," and as for Grand Slam, he thought it was "aptly named Grand Slam for had it succeeded, a trail of dazzling results would have followed in its wake, and the infiltration campaign would have had a fresh lease of life,"[44] and that "it was only the last minute frantic rush of reinforcements into the sector . . . that prevented this debacle from deteriorating into major catastrophe."[45] It seems therefore that but for the change of command at a critical time during Operation Grand Slam, the aim of Gibraltar was well within realization, that is, to "defreeze the Kashmir problem, weaken Indian resolve, and bring India to the conference table without provoking general war."[46] It would be highly educative to read General Akhtar Malik's views on the subject. This unpublished letter[47] from General Malik to his younger brother, Lieutenant General Abdul Ali Malik, is a new source of information on the subject, and for this purpose is quoted here in full:

Pakistan's Permanent Military Deputy
Embassy of Pakistan
Ankara
23-11-67

My Dear brother,
I hope you and the family are very well. Thank you for your letter of 14 Oct. 67. The answers to your questions are as follows:

a. The defacto command changed the very first day of the ops [operations] after the fall of Chamb when Azmat Hayat broke off wireless communications with me. I personally tried to find his HQ [headquarters] by chopper and failed. In late afternoon I sent Gulzar and Vahid, my MP [military police] officers, to try and locate him, but they too failed. The next day I tore into him and he sheepishly and nervously informed me that he was 'Yahya's brigadier'. I had no doubt left that Yahya had reached him the previous day and instructed him not to take further orders from me, while the formal change in command had yet to take place. This was a betrayal of many dimensions.

b. I reasoned and then pleaded with Yahya that if it was credit he was looking for, he should take the overall command but let me go up to Akhnur as his subordinate, but he refused. He went a step further and even changed the plan. He kept banging his head against Troti, letting the Indian fall back to Akhnur. We lost the initiative on the very first day of the war and never recovered it. Eventually it was the desperate stand at Chawinda that prevented the Indians from cutting through.

c. At no time was I assigned any reason for being removed from command by Ayub, Musa or Yahya. They were all sheepish at best. I think the reasons will be given when I am no more.

d. Not informing pro-Pak Kashmiri elements before launching Gibraltar was a command decision and it was mine. The aim of the op was to defreeze the Kashmir issue, raise it from its moribund state, and bring it to the notice of the world. To achieve this aim the first phase of the op was vital, that is, to effect undetected infiltration of thousands across the CFL [cease-fire line]. I was not willing to compromise this in any event. And the whole op could be made stillborn by just one double agent.

e. Haji Pir [Pass] did not cause me much anxiety. Because [the] impending Grand Slam Indian concentration in Haji Pir could only help us after Akhnur, and they would have to pull out troops from there to counter the new threats and surrender their gains, and maybe more, in the process. Actually it was only after the fall of Akhnur that we would have encashed the full value of Gibraltar, but that was not to be!

f. Bhutto kept insisting that his sources had assured him that India would not attack if we did not violate the international border. I however was certain that Gibraltar would lead to war and told GHQ so. I needed no op intelligence to come to this conclusion. It was simple common sense. If I got you by the throat, it would be silly for me to expect that you will kiss me for it. Because I was certain that war would follow, my first choice as objective for Grand Slam was Jammu. From there we could have exploited our success either toward Samba or Kashmir proper as the situation demanded. In any case whether it was Jammu or Akhnur, if we had taken the objective, I do not see how the Indians could have attacked Sialkot before clearing out either of these towns.

g. I have given serious consideration to writing a book, but given up the idea. The book would be the truth. And truth and the popular reaction to it would be good for my ego. But in the long run it would be an unpatriotic act. It will destroy the morale of the army, lower its prestige among the people, be banned in Pakistan, and become a textbook for the Indians. I have little doubt that the Indians will never forgive us the slight of 65 and will avenge it at the first opportunity. I am certain they will hit us in E. Pak [East Pakistan] and we will need all we have to save the situation. The first day of Grand Slam will be fateful in many ways. The worst has still to come and we have to prepare for it. The book is therefore out.

I hope this gives you the gist of what you needed to know. And yes, Ayub was fully involved in the enterprise. As a matter of fact it was his idea. And it was he who ordered me to by-pass Musa while Gibraltar etc. was being planned. I was dealing more with him and Sher Bahadur than with the C-in-C. It is tragic that despite having a good military mind, the FM's [Field Marshal's] heart was prone to give way. The biggest tragedy is that in this instance it gave way before the eruption of a crisis. Or were they already celebrating a final victory!!

In case you need a more exact description of events, I will need war diaries and maps, which you could send me through the diplomatic bag.

Please remember me to all the family.

Yours,
Akhtar Hussain Malik

It is quite obvious what had happened. In the words of Justice Muhammad Saraf: "Had Akhtar been continued in his duty . . . he would have been the only General in Pakistan with a spectacular victory to his credit and it would then have been very difficult for President Ayub to ignore his claim to the office of the Commander-in-Chief, after the retirement of Musa, which was quite near."[48] Zulfiqar Ali Bhutto, one of the main players of this game, also later argued that, "Had General Akhtar Malik not been stopped in the Chamb-Jaurian Sector, the Indian forces in Kashmir would have suffered serious reverses, but Ayub Khan wanted to make his favorite, General Yahya Khan, a hero."[49]

However, the very idea of Operation Gibraltar was controversial in itself. The military initiative robbed Pakistan of its moral high ground vis-à-vis the Kashmir conflict. In retrospect, it would have been better if Pakistan had focused more on continuing its efforts toward the resolution of the dispute through U.N. or third-party mediation. Ayub and his top generals also misread how far Kashmiris in (on the Indian side) were willing to cooperate with Pakistan in this kind of adventure.

The general resentment at the conclusion of the Tashkent Agreement, which formally brought the war to an end, was no less controversial than the change of command in the Chamb sector. In January 1966 both Ayub and Indian prime minister Shastri met in Tashkent, where Soviet prime minister Kosygin played unofficial mediator. Both countries agreed to solve their disputes by peaceful means and to withdraw to the positions they had held before August 5, 1965. And though it recognized the existence of the Kashmir dispute, it said nothing further about it. Within hours after signing the agreement, the Indian prime minister died of a heart attack. The cynical among the Pakistanis let it be known that he had died of joy. There was huge disillusionment among the Pakistanis, who had been led throughout the war to believe that Pakistan was on the verge of a historic victory. In mid-January 1966 there were demonstrations led by students, labor, and other groups, and though they were suppressed by the state apparatus, they signaled the end of the Ayub era. Further, the war had brought home to the East Pakistanis how insecure and practically undefended they were during the entire duration of the war, and the strategy that "the defense of the East lies in the West" was woefully farcical. This feeling was just the wrong palliative for the simmering resentment they had been nursing against West Pakistan ever since independence.

The army also underwent major though subtle changes in personnel. Musa retired soon after the war, to be replaced by General Yahya Khan as C-in-C of the army. This was not a popular choice, but as Yahya settled in, he subtly started to gather power by promoting and placing his own loyalists in critical spots. A sick and disheartened Ayub was too careworn to notice this. And besides, he had implicit faith in Yahya's loyalty. He may also have been quite certain that his new choice of army chief came with the kind of baggage that would foreclose the possibility of his gaining the sort of following that could eventually threaten Ayub's position. Ayub was wrong. He could not see that Yahya could collect any number of equally discredited officers around him. Among the first to be swept off the stage was General Akhtar Malik. He was posted out to CENTO in Ankara, Turkey. Yahya told him that Pakistan needed a sensible and mature officer there, and Malik had replied: "Being a sensible and mature officer, I quite realize why I am needed there."[50] Concurrently with this, all officers considered to be Malik loyalists were sidelined. This was a major step along the road inaugurated by Ayub himself, of promoting the interests of personal loyalty over those of competence and professionalism. Professional pride progressively gave way to servile behavior. Already the army had embarked on a crash program of making up shortages in the ranks of the officer class. To meet the target, standards were consciously and conspicuously lowered, thus making it a self-defeating exercise.

Also, in the aftermath of the war, one would have expected the army to analyze its performance. Not only was such an appraisal not carried out beyond the merest whitewash, the attempt deliberately falsified the record to save reputations, because after the war many of those were promoted whose reputations needed to be saved. But the formality of a war analysis had to be fulfilled, and most ironically the task was entrusted to General Akhtar Malik. He did this in two parts; one dealt with the performance of junior leadership, and the other with that of the higher command. Brigadier Mohammad Afzal Khan, who read the latter in manuscript form, and Major Qayyum, under whose supervision it was typed, both commented upon the scathing criticism to which this document subjected the prosecution of the war at higher levels. After the death of the general, no one has seen the record of this document in the army GHQ.

The result of the 1965 war left Ayub Khan devastated. He was not the same invincible icon of a man he had been before. His confidence was shattered, as was the prestige of Pakistan and its army. Z.A. Bhutto, a supporter of the war, was the first to jump ship. He returned from Tashkent crying betrayal. He promised to tell all about the secret clauses of the treaty whereby Ayub had sold the honor of Pakistan for a pittance. Though the official news agency of the Soviet Union, Tass, came to Ayub's rescue with a clarification that the treaty had no secret clauses, in the prevailing mood this did not seem to matter. The war had brought the halo of his invincibility crashing, and the people were now baying for the head around which that halo stood.

Ayub was on tour to East Pakistan in December 1967 when an attempt was made on his life. This was successfully covered up in the local media. Coming on the heels of this shock, he was further shaken by what came to be known as the Agarthala conspiracy case. In January 1968 the government of Pakistan announced that it had unearthed a conspiracy between India and some East Pakistani intellectuals and politicians that aimed at the secession of East Pakistan from West. The leader of the conspiracy was Sheikh Mujib ur-Rahman, a mid-ranking East Pakistani politician. His agenda was such a loose confederation between the two wings of Pakistan so as to make the East virtually independent. This was exactly the sort of music the disenchanted Bengalis wanted to hear. Mujib's arrest made him an instant martyr and the most popular leader in East Pakistan—enough for him to become the father of an independent nation in the not-too-distant future. Z.A. Bhutto, who was now heading a newly emerged, popular Pakistan People's Party, whipped up the sentiments of the people against the president to the extent he could.

At this moment of mass discontent against Ayub in both wings of the country, Altaf Gauhar, the media czar, most ill-advisedly chose to deflect the anti-Ayub focus of the people by launching a yearlong celebration of Ayub's ten years in power by highlighting what came to be called the Decade of Progress. All this succeeded in conjuring up among the people in the West was that Ayub had already been at the helm too long, and that his rule had been only for the benefit of the chosen few at the cost of the have-nots, who were exactly where they had been ten years earlier. The East Pakistanis knew only too well that whatever progress there had been was confined only to West Pakistan. And this new propaganda blitz had come very quickly on the heels of the earlier one that had worked up the people to expect a dazzling victory in the war. But that had proved not to be the case. Thus there was a tendency to discount anything the government channels had to say.

With all this happening, Ayub's health broke down just when he could least afford it. But as soon as he had partially recovered, he ordered the U.S. base in Peshawar to be wound down. This was the formal notice in a long, pending divorce between two allies—a relationship that had done much to help Pakistan stand on its own feet in its early, very uncertain years—perhaps its very survival was due to this relationship. But it was the U.S. rebuff during the Indo-Pak War that was closer to memory, and most Pakistanis felt that they had been let down by the senior ally just when its help was most needed.

As Ayub sank, so Yahya became more chirpy. Buoyed up by spirits one evening, which was not uncommon for him, he asked a lady seated next to him at dinner if she knew whom she was having the meal with. And before she could answer, he confessed that it was with the future president of Pakistan. How this lady subsequently paid for this gratuitous sharing of confidence is not recorded.

On November 7, 1968, there was a student demonstration against Ayub in Rawalpindi, and police efforts to disperse the crowd resulted in the death of one student. This was enough to provoke dozens of protest marches, creating a serious law-and-order situation. By the end of the year, Air Marshal Asghar Khan, the respected former C-in-C of the Pakistan Air Force, and Justice Murshed, an equally well-respected member of the East Pakistan judiciary, came out against Ayub Khan. Isolated and out of touch with reality, Ayub now wanted to play his ace—the Pakistan Army. His first effort was to get back Generals Akhtar Malik, Bahadur Sher, and Nawazish Malik from Turkey, the U.K., and Jordan respectively. When this was refused by Yahya, Ayub asked him to put the major cities of Pakistan under martial law. Again Yahya refused. He would have the whole country under martial law, or none of it. Ayub knew that power had changed hands. He resigned on March 25, 1969, and handed the country over to Yahya and thus to another martial law. A decade earlier, when he had taken power in Pakistan, he had spoken about the "total administrative, economic, political, and moral chaos in the country." Now a decade later he left a broken man, citing much the same reasons. He was a decent man brought low by the blandishments of power that are best enjoyed by their negation. He had mistaken servility for loyalty, and encouraged it. The corruption of his family, which he had facilitated, and the hypocritical adulation of the courtiers that he so enjoyed, but which had deprived him of his sense of reality, combined to rob him of the greatness that lay within his grasp.

# ——Chapter 4——

# General Yahya and the Dismemberment of Pakistan

General Agha Mohammad Yahya Khan was a graduate of the Indian Military Academy at Dehradun. He was a man of average height, with an affable manner, high intelligence, and considerable wit. And with all this, there was ambition in equal measure. By the time he took over, he was pudgy and oval in shape. He was not an alcoholic, but intemperate imbibing over the years had eroded his defenses against its effects. Although no one saw him keeled over, his behavior frequently touched or went over the bounds of what was considered reputable. Like most men, he liked women. But unlike them, when in his cups he could not resist them, or keep his hands in check. When he was promoted as army chief, his reputation was anything but sterling. And there was a considerable body of opinion that this was precisely why Ayub had promoted him. Yahya's disrepute was Ayub's insurance against a grab for power. But as things turned out, this disrepute did not stand in Yahya's way, and although he did not overthrow Ayub in the conventional sense, he helped him fall.

Among the politicians, the transition from one military regime to another was not welcome, but it was quietly accepted. There was enough administrative anarchy and chaos generated by the four-month agitation that had just toppled Ayub Khan for any politician to be thinking in terms of joining the government at this hour and getting discredited. Within twenty-four hours of taking over, Yahya promised free and fair elections based on adult franchise. The people were exhausted, and the political leaders were wary of the results of further agitation. This made for a simmering down of the agitational ferment and a hesitant acceptance of Yahya's promise that he would hand over power to the elected representatives of the people.

Yahya's martial law had replaced a discredited dictatorship and was accepted with resignation and a half-arrested hope that it would bring about democracy, which would usher in a dispensation of good governance. The immediate challenge confronting Yahya though was the rise of Bengali nationalism made distinct and articulate by Sheikh Mujib ur-Rahman and his popular Awami League party. This was a genie that had taken form and would be difficult to cajole back into the bottle. And if there was any hope of this, it became an instant nonstarter with the realization that it was the Indians that had a hold on the bottle, and that they had sealed its opening so that there was no place for the genie to go and rest.

Unlike Ayub, Yahya was not an absolute dictator. He was the first among equals in a coterie of generals, with whom he ruled by consensus. Given the Pakistan Army's strict hierarchical tradition, this does not seem to have been a situation brought about by any countervailing force exerted by the generals against the authority of Yahya. Had it suited him, he could quite easily have put to pasture a few obtrusive generals, and not a bird would have flapped its wings. Yahya preferred it that way. He was not a very serious administrator, and beyond pursuing a few briefs, had no inclination to get into the detailed grind of governance. He was more for fun and would have made a popular prince had he been born a few centuries earlier.

Unlike Ayub Khan's government, which had started off as a dictatorship of the military and the bureaucracy, Yahya's was an all-military affair run by cronies whom he had preserved, raised, and placed when he took over as army chief. His number two was his friend and batchmate, Lieutenant General Abdul Hamid, who was made chief of staff of the army. In physical shape he resembled Yahya, and shared much with him except his overt indiscretions. Also being a beneficiary of the post–1965 war whitewash, he was close and loyal to Yahya. Major General S.G.M. Peerzada was Yahya's chief of staff in the presidency. He was a conspiratorial figure and the Rasputin of the regime. Though there is no evidence that Yahya had personally encouraged Z.A. Bhutto to destabilize the Ayub regime, Peerzada proudly claimed the credit for this,[1] and Yahya certainly must have known. After some time, Yahya did induct a civilian cabinet of an equal number of members from both wings of the country, but nothing of crucial importance was ever discussed in this body, which seems to have been put together to fulfill the formality of merely having a cabinet. Moreso, the members of this cabinet seemed happy enough with little work to do and a lot of time for socializing.

Surprisingly, Yahya did not seem to have a foreign policy. At any rate, he did not feel the need to have a foreign minister, and felt that between himself and Generals Peerzada and Ghulam Umar (chief of the National Security Cell) the job could be neatly handled. The latter two insisted on their expertise in foreign affairs and often helped Yahya stumble into many blunders. A good example of this was when his magnanimity allowed an Indian delegation to attend the Islamic Summit Conference in Rabat in 1969. Soon he realized that this would allow India, with 60 million Muslims then, a voice in the Muslim world as well, which would inevitably go against Pakistan. He was in a terrible fix when King Hassan of Morocco and the Shah of Iran bailed him out. The Indian delegation, which had already arrived in Morocco, was unceremoniously asked not to attend the conference and it had to leave. This converted an embarrassing mistake into a diplomatic triumph for Yahya.[2] Similarly, in May 1969, when Soviet premier Kosygin visited Pakistan and proposed transit trade through Afghanistan and Pakistan to the rest of South Asia, Yahya readily agreed, but then he was made to realize that this could be the first step around which an anti-Chinese grouping would be built by the USSR, and he was forced to retreat.[3]

The religious parties were also on the lookout for a new opening to pursue their agenda of "Islamizing" the state. Maududi met Yahya early on and declared him a "champion of Islam," expecting that this would sufficiently work on Yahya and the new constitution that he would envisage would be Islamic.[4] Maududi had no clue that Yahya would be the last man on earth to usher in the Islamization of Pakistan.

Still, between the bouts of his favorite indulgence of sampling living flesh and Black Dog whiskey, Yahya was enlightened by a realization unique among a West Pakistani of his influence and position of power. He conceded that the Bengalis (in East Pakistan) had been unfairly treated right from independence onward, and he was determined to take all the necessary steps to remedy this situation.[5] One of his first steps in this direction was to promote six Bengali civil servants to the rank of secretary in the central government—the highest position in the bureaucratic ladder. He also issued instructions that henceforth senior Bengali bureaucrats were to be promoted, irrespective of seniority, till a balance in such positions was achieved between officers of the two wings of Pakistan. And in the allocation of financial resources in the next five-year development plan, he ensured that a lion's share went to East Pakistan. But this was too little too late; especially when it is considered that in this he was attempting to swim against the tide—a tide swollen no less by the opinion of most of his inner circle.

The humiliating attitude of West Pakistan's military, bureaucracy, and political elite toward Bengalis was institutionalized during Ayub's regime, though the early years of Pakistan were not very different. But at the least, Bengali politicians were a part of the mainstream politics of the country before the 1958 martial law. The country leaped forward in economic terms in the Ayub era, but the political rights of the people were buried in the process. Bengalis felt it more because their presence in the civil-military bureaucracy was only symbolic.[6] In the army, the most important institution in the country, there were only 300 Bengali officers out of 6,000.[7]

Moreover, their share in various sectors of the economy such as revenue expenditure, the development budget, and utilization of foreign aid remained most unsatisfactory and unjust.[8] The realization of these facts had resulted in the Six Points agenda of the Awami League, first projected in 1966. The points were:

1. Pakistan should be a federation under the Pakistan or Lahore Resolution of 1940, which implied the existence of two similar entities. Any new constitution according to the Bengalis had to reflect this reality.
2. The federal government should deal solely with defense and foreign affairs.
3. There should be two separate but freely convertible currencies. East Pakistan would have a separate banking reserve as well as separate fiscal and monetary policies.
4. The federated units would have the sole power to tax. The central government should be granted funds to meet its expenditures.
5. Separate accounts from foreign exchange earnings would be maintained. The federating units would be free to establish trade links with foreign countries.
6. East Pakistan would have a separate militia.

The Ayub regime's reaction to these demands can be gauged from the statement of Mr. S.M. Zafar, the federal law minister, on December 15, 1966, in Dhaka. He had categorically declared that demanding "greater provincial autonomy" would be "a treasonous act" and its protagonists "would be identified, hunted, crushed and destroyed."[9] Such tendencies had caused Bengali alienation, and the stage was set for a violent confrontation between West and East Pakistan at some point in the not-too-distant future.

Thus on the political front, the situation was anything but easy. Yahya's main difficulties were the various political demands that were difficult to reconcile, and therefore to meet, to the satisfaction of all the parties. The easiest for him to concede was that One Unit, a scheme under which the four provinces of West Pakistan were grouped into one province in 1955, would be done away with. This was primarily the demand of the smaller provinces of West Pakistan, which believed that in a single province their interests were swamped by the sheer weight and size of Punjab Province. On this issue, Sheikh Mujib ur-Rahman really did not care, though he tacitly supported the breakup of One Unit, as indirectly that would reduce the influence of a combined West wing vis-à-vis the East. The next main demand was that elections be held on the basis of adult franchise, which had already been promised by Yahya immediately after taking over. Another issue was the date of the elections and indeed, whether the Yahya regime was at all serious in the promises it had made in this regard. Soon, Yahya announced that the elections were to be held in October 1970.

The main sticking point still outstanding, and the most contentious, was whether there would be East-West parity at the center, or would the central legislature be filled in proportion to the population ratios of the provinces. The second point was to determine the center-province relationship in the new constitution that would be framed after the elections, and if the constitution would be passed by a simple majority in the legislature. On these issues Mujib was very clear. He would not accept East-West parity nor the center-province relationship envisaged in the 1956 constitution, as these had proved to be tools of the establishment for keeping the power center in the hands of West Pakistanis. In comparison, Z.A. Bhutto was spending all his time organizing his Pakistan People's Party (PPP) and expanding his influence in the ruling junta.

Yahya, to the disregard of the opinions of the rest of the junta, was willing to bend over backward to meet Mujib's demands. But the central difficulty in this was, how to meet his demands and yet guarantee the integrity of Pakistan. Mujib ur-Rahman was entirely committed to his Six Points. Depending on how broadly or narrowly they were to be interpreted would make the difference between a minimal federal Pakistan or one that was a sundered entity. If the government gave way on all of Mujib's demands, it would have nothing to go on but his good faith to keep the country together. Beyond the word he gave, continually and unstintingly, there was nothing to encourage the government to keep faith in him. All the reports of his public meetings, the actions of the toughs and thugs of his party, and the tape recordings of his confidential conversations with his inner group[10] merely went to emphasize his insincerity to the cause of a united Pakistan. Pakistan's intelligence circles believed that Mujib had close links with Indian intelligence, especially in reference to the Agarthala conspiracy case in 1968, in which he was charged with conspiracy to bring about the secession of East Pakistan through armed uprisings in cahoots with India. However, no evidence was ever made public and Ayub had withdrawn the case, though apparently for political reasons.

As a political strategy, Mujib steadfastly refused to define his Six Points in a manner that would allow a minimal federal arrangement guaranteeing the unity of Pakistan, but in autumn 1969, Mujib declared that the Six Points were not the words of the Quran and thereby not immutable. Hence, on November 28, 1969, Yahya conceded all the major demands of Mujib in reference to the coming elections.[11] He announced that there would be no parity between East and West Pakistan, and that the future constitution would be passed by a simple majority vote in a unicameral legislature. As for the center-province relationship, that would be for the new constitution to decide. The *New York Times* hailed the decision by saying that "Yahya Khan has set a prudent example for other military rulers with his move to restore democratic civilian rule."[12] Mujib though was still suspicious of the military regime and its intentions. He increasingly started trusting Yahya but he was not as sure about the other generals, and he was right.

As expected, Yahya came in for strong criticism for making such far-reaching concessions to Mujib. Most of the generals had insisted that a two-thirds majority be required to pass the constitution, or at the very least 60 percent of the members should be required to vote for its passage, but Yahya refused to back out of the commitment he had made to Mujib. This made the future dependent entirely on the good faith of Mujib.

Still to cater to the views of his generals, who were suspicious of Mujib, Yahya promulgated the Legal Framework Order (LFO) on March 31, 1970. It required the future Constituent Assembly to come up with a constitution within 120 days after the elections; the draft constitution would require authentication by the president before being formally presented to the assembly for passage; and it laid down five "fundamental principles" to ensure the integrity of the country. These principles were included because any attempt to limit the provincial autonomy were not acceptable to Mujib. The only alternative was to include at least the minimum provisions that would ensure the unity and integrity of the country.[13] In East Pakistan the LFO came in for a fair degree of criticism, but not enough to withhold Mujib's approval of it. It therefore seemed that all was now in order for the elections to go ahead in October 1970. Yahya had indeed cracked the toughest nut. He was happy with himself, but he did not realize that he was treading on the thin ice of Mujib's faith. In reality, Mujib in public started saying that "Pakistan has come to stay and there is no force that can destroy it," but in private he maintained that "My aim is to establish Bangladesh; I will tear the LFO into pieces as soon as the elections are over."[14] This last remark was reported to Yahya by the intelligence service, but he chose to ignore it, probably thinking that it must have been his political compulsion to say so in front of his associates and that he was not serious about it. Or was it that he had a hangover and could not really decipher the report well?

After a two-month postponement due to massive floods in East Pakistan, elections were finally held on December 7, 1970, as promised. The results were a disaster for the future of a unified Pakistan. Mujib's Awami League virtually swept the Eastern wing, winning 162 seats out of 164, but went without a win in the West. Z.A. Bhutto's PPP, which had no candidate in the East, was the big winner in the Western wing—grabbing 81 seats out of 138. Religious parties also did well by taking 14 percent of the overall electoral vote, but it was Bhutto who had emerged as the most popular choice in the Western wing. Bhutto's slogan of "Roti, Kapra aur Makan" (food, clothes, and shelter) for everyone was the buzzword that worked wonders. The election result was an obvious outcome of regional disparities and class inequalities perpetuated by a decade-long military dictatorship. There is no doubt that the elections were completely free and fair, but there is considerable doubt if the motive behind fair elections was altruistic. There is a reason to believe that the intelligence reports reaching the junta predicted a hung Parliament, which meant that the real power would have been retained by the military, if this were the case. In fact, Yahya had told Henry Kissinger, the visiting U.S. secretary of state, that according to his estimate numerous political parties would win seats, that there would be quarrels between them, and that he would remain the arbiter of his country's politics.[15] As it turned out, there was no national party to emerge. It was a hung Parliament only in this sense. The future was in the hands of two political parties, having a mass support base in two different regions, each of whose leaders wanted to be prime minister. This was the virtual end of Pakistan, but no one in the Western wing could have gathered the wisdom and the courage to accept this. Civil war was thus in the cards.

In principle, Mujib should have been acceptable as a prime minister to both Yahya and Z.A. Bhutto. On the other hand, a strong showing at the polls had turned Mujib's head and he was no longer in a mood for compromise. Yahya invited Mujib and Bhutto to the capital, but Mujib turned down the invitation. Yahya swallowed this and instead traveled to Dhaka himself to meet him on January 12, 1971. The postballot Mujib was a different man. He went back on every point of understanding he had reached with the president during their months of talks, on the basis of which Yahya had sought to accommodate him. The intransigence of Mujib was an invitation to Bhutto to harden his position as well, which was in consonance with the views of the majority in the army junta. Though Mujib had a standing offer to become the prime minister of Pakistan, his terms of acceptance had steadily grown unreasonable, to the extent of being unacceptable. It was becoming clear that he was only for secession.

In February 1971 the Indian intelligence stage-managed the hijacking of an Air India plane to Lahore to justify the banning of all Pakistani flights over Indian territory, cutting a vital link between the two wings of Pakistan. Mujib was quick to blame this as a Pakistani ploy to delay the transfer of power, which he was now demanding. Bhutto was of the view that, being a majority party in West Pakistan, PPP should be sharing power with Mujib's Awami League in the center. Bhutto's reaction to Mujib's demand to be handed over power before the meeting of the National Assembly or the framing of the constitution only provided Mujib with further excuses not to move to a mutually acceptable middle ground where the solution to the problem lay.

On March 14, when Yahya was on his way to make a last-ditch effort to keep Mujib within the bounds of reason, and Pakistan within the bounds of unity, Bhutto declared: "If power is to be transferred to the people before any constitutional settlement as demanded by Sheikh Mujib ur-Rahman, it should be transferred to the majority party in East Pakistan and the majority party here [West Pakistan]."[16]

This was a rapidly deteriorating situation. Mujib's was no simple case of intransigence pegged to a principle. India's part in the faked hijacking and Mujib's reaction to it was interpreted by the military junta as only a further confirmation of their belief that he was not entirely his own master and was following a course that had been charted out for him by New Delhi. Therefore they had little hope of change in his attitude. Second, by banning flights over Indian territory, India had cut off a vital avenue that Pakistan needed to bolster its forces in the East for the civil war. Bhutto's contentious statements in these circumstances could only add to the problem, though it can be argued that conciliatory statements from him would not have changed Mujib's mind. Others argue that "Bhutto's responsibility for the events which ensued is undeniable."[17] By March 15, 1971, Mujib had almost declared the independence of Bangladesh.[18] In the hardening of Mujib's stance, Mr. Archer Blood, the U.S. consul general in Dhaka, also had a role to play. Mujib had understood from Blood that the United States would support his confrontation with the central authorities in Pakistan. And though the U.S. ambassador J. Farland later disabused Mujib of such expectations, some damage was already done.[19]

It was in these circumstances that Yahya reached Dhaka on March 15, 1971, virtually as a foreign guest to placate Mujib and bring him to accept some sort of constitutional arrangement. Between March 16 and 20 the two met daily, and it was rumored that a settlement was in the cards, but the reality was that Mujib was not ready to budge an inch. Reportedly, Yahya was even ready to sign a proclamation of an agreement between the central government and the "state of Bangladesh" in a confederation arrangement, but then Mujib's associates conveyed to Yahya that instead they wanted power to be transferred to East and West Pakistan, that is, a partition of Pakistan. This was the end. The only alternative now remaining was between a peaceful split of the country or a civil war. Mujib had left these alternatives to Yahya by making a choice in favor of secession.

Finally, on March 25, 1971, the Pakistan Army launched Operation Searchlight and cracked down on all dissent in the East. It had the option of doing this by using minimal force and maximum restraint, and the military commander in East Pakistan, Lieutenant General Yaqub Ali Khan, had suggested so, but it fell on deaf ears and Yaqub honorably walked out of the scene. The new commander, Lieutenant General Tikka Khan, in line with the military junta's dictates, inflicted on East Pakistan a reign of horror—of random rape, mindless arson, and gratuitous murder of the innocents. It brought upon Pakistan eternal shame. The orders that led to this carnage could only have been given by half-formed men untouched by any higher value that separates humans from animals. The passions unleashed could have been so only because the Bengalis could not have been considered anything but a subject people—and even among the comparatively refined imperialists of the Western nations, subject peoples were considered only subhuman, to be treated with nothing more than condescension, and that only as long as they behaved themselves. The tragedy of East Pakistan had been implanted right at the inception of the state. It merely lay dormant for a number of years. The unified state of Pakistan, divided by eight hundred miles of hostile territory, was a contradiction in terms. It was unnatural. West Pakistani chauvinism only accentuated the differences between the two wings and nourished a simmering tragedy; Mujib's ambition brought it to final maturity; the Pakistan Army consummated it; and it was the Bengali people who paid the price.

In this unholy drama, Jamaat-i-Islami formed an alliance with the army in East Pakistan and played an active part in the military action against what they believed to be "enemies of Islam."[20] This party along with other rightwing parties had initially launched a propaganda campaign to convince the Bengalis that their loyalties lay first with Islam and Pakistan and not with their ethnic roots, but to no avail.

Pakistan has consistently argued that the reports of the atrocities were greatly exaggerated. Here it misses the moral point, that is, that even minus the exaggeration, the conduct of the army was unconscionable. Bengali regiments and paramilitary units had also killed many West Pakistani men, women, and children who were residing in the nation's eastern wing, and this could only extend the spiral of gratuitous violence. Among the first to react to this was the U.S. consulate in Dhaka. It urged Washington to express "shock" at these events, and the U.S. embassy in Islamabad backed up this demand. When Washington remained silent, the staff at the consulate in Dhaka sent a "dissent channel" telegram to the State Department. But there was a reason for the silence of the U.S. government. After Johnson, President Richard Nixon had moved into the White House, and quite apart from his earlier leaning toward Pakistan when he was Eisenhower's vice president, and Pakistan was a most allied ally, in mid-1969 he had requested Yahya to help open secret U.S.-China diplomatic channels. This was so secret an assignment that even the secretary of state, William Rogers, did not know anything about it. And Yahya was doing a creditable job of it. This initiative was so important for U.S.

foreign policy that Nixon would do nothing to jeopardize it. And though he was pressured into suspending arms aid to Pakistan, he refused to block economic aid and also allowed the export of such weapons for which export licenses had already been issued.

On July 9, 1971, Henry Kissinger arrived in Islamabad for his secret trip to Beijing, which prepared the way for Nixon's unprecedented visit to China and formalization of the Sino-American rapprochement, to the chagrin of the USSR. This was one service rendered by Pakistan to the United States for which the USSR would soon make it pay. During the discussions Kissinger had with Yahya, he concluded that the latter was not expecting India to attack Pakistan, but if such a thing would happen, Yahya and his generals believed that "they could win."[21] More important, while briefing Yahya on his trip to Beijing, Kissinger told him that the Chinese had indicated that they would intervene militarily if India attacked East Pakistan.

Meanwhile, the civil war in East Pakistan was escalating. The Indians were training and equipping the East Pakistanis, the Mukti Bahini (liberation forces), to launch a guerrilla campaign against the Pakistan Army. There were good reasons to believe that Indian military personnel also directly participated in these operations.[22] The unsettled conditions were causing a large number of Bengali civilians to flee the conflict zone and take refuge in India. According to Indian estimates, the number of refugees was close to 10 million and it was officially the refugee problem that India cited as justification for its saber-rattling and preparation of grounds for war against Pakistan.

When Kissinger reached Washington after his trip to South Asia and China, his assessment was that India was "bent on war," while Yahya lacked the imagination to solve the political problems in time to prevent an Indian assault. In July 1971, after having declined it initially, Yahya agreed to permit the U.N. supervision of relief and resettlement efforts of the refugees, but India scuttled the relief plan and refused the presence of U.N. monitors on the border between India and East Pakistan,[23] as that would have exposed and hence hindered Indian war plans.

The implications of the new U.S.-China relationship and Pakistan's role in bringing it about were not lost on India and the USSR. Indira Gandhi, the prime minister of India, could not feel very secure in these circumstances, and thus on August 9, 1971, she played her own trump card by signing a treaty of friendship with the USSR. What was most friendly about it was that it was a euphemism for a war pact between New Delhi and Moscow.

President Nixon meanwhile stressed that he could not allow India to use the refugee problem as a pretext for breaking up Pakistan, and the United States did all it could to bring about some workable understanding between Mujib and the government of Pakistan. The U.S. officials got Yahya to commit that Mujib (who was in custody in West Pakistan) would not be executed. Yahya then encouraged the Americans to open a dialogue with Mujib's colleagues, who had established their base in the Indian city of Calcutta (West Bengal). Lastly, in November 1971, Yahya sent the newly appointed Indian ambassador to Islamabad back to New Delhi with a five-point peace plan, in which he agreed to release Mujib and also to a referendum to determine whether the East Pakistanis wanted independence or a united Pakistan, so that if Bangladesh were to be established, this would be done through a referendum. India turned down the offer.[24]

On November 22, Indian troops became more aggressive and started to move in and physically occupy certain areas of East Pakistan. The U.S. administration was asking India time and again to resolve the problem, but for India, resolution of the problem by any means short of an invasion was the problem. Indian troops were poised to go on the offensive in East Pakistan on December 4, 1971. A day earlier, the Pakistan Air Force in the western wing attacked Indian bases and saved India from the formal onus of starting a war, though not of firing the first shot. With a small portion of its army virtually marooned a thousand miles away and having no means to support it, the defeat of Pakistan was assured. The story of the Pakistan Army in its final months in East Pakistan is replete with many heroic actions against Indian invading forces, though it was sadly diminished by its earlier excesses against the Bengali people.

On the other hand, President Nixon's worry now shifted to the safety of West Pakistan. He was not certain about India's designs and was anxious that such plans possibly included the final destruction of the country, as a CIA report had indicated. American public opinion had forced him into shutting off military and then economic assistance to Pakistan, but unknown to the State Department, he had encouraged other allies to assist Pakistan. Meanwhile, the U.S.-sponsored resolution in the U.N. Security Council calling for a cease-fire was killed by a Soviet veto. In reaction, Nixon warned, "If the Indians continue their military operations [against West Pakistan], we must inevitably look toward a confrontation between the USSR and the U.S. The Soviet Union has a treaty with India; we have one with Pakistan."[25] After failing to receive a satisfactory reply from the Indian ambassador in Washington about Indian intentions in West Pakistan, Nixon ordered the aircraft carrier *Enterprise* to proceed toward the Bay of Bengal, ostensibly to evacuate U.S. citizens from the war zone.

At about the same time, Kissinger met the Chinese ambassador to the U.N. to coordinate the Sino-U.S. action at the U.N. and informed him that, though barred by law, the administration had told Jordan, Iran, Saudi Arabia, and Turkey to extend all assistance to Pakistan, and that though Washington would "protest" this action, it would nonetheless "understand it."[26] He emphasized that the Pakistan Army in the East would run out of steam in a couple of weeks, but that the western wing had to be saved. Nixon then sent his first-ever message to the Soviet leader Brezhnev over the hotline, warning him that time was of the essence "to avoid consequences neither of us want."[27] All through the war, the generals in Pakistan had believed that the United States and China would not allow India a free hand in Bangladesh. They were wrong. The United States knew that East Pakistan had to go and that China was not going to risk a confrontation with the Soviets on the basis of an assurance from the United States. Therefore, having the support of two major powers, Pakistan could not imagine it would be left to fight an unequal war while the rest of the world looked on, and eventually the country's leaders did not know what hit them.

On December 14, 1971, Major General Rao Farman Ali and Lieutenant General A.A.K. Niazi, the military commander in East Pakistan, asked the U.S. consul in Dhaka (capital of East Pakistan) to transmit a surrender proposal to New Delhi. Before forwarding the proposal, the U.S. ambassador in Islamabad was instructed by Washington to get approval from Yahya. The foreign secretary, Sultan Ahmed, speaking on behalf of the president of Pakistan, gave the necessary approval. Yahya Khan did not have time to attend to this matter personally. On the eve of Pakistan's surrender he was giving a party in his newly constructed house in Peshawar.[28] One of the few guests was Mrs. Shamim, known as "Black Pearl," the Bengali beauty who was Yahya's latest sexual affiliate and whom he had recently appointed as Pakistan's ambassador to Austria.[29] As drinks flowed, so did the affair go progressively nude. It was when the whole party was drunk and unattired, except for Major General Ishaque, Yahya's military secretary, that "Black Pearl" wished to go home. The president insisted that he would drive her personally, both of them stark naked. General Ishaque could not save Pakistan, but he did manage to knock enough sense into the sizzled head of a fun-loving president to put him into his pants. Thus coincided the housewarming of the president's house with the surrender in East Pakistan.

General A.A.K. Niazi signed the surrender of his troops to General Jagjit Singh Arora of the Indian Army in Dhaka on December 16, 1971. Niazi had earlier vowed that before the Indian Army took the capital of East Pakistan, Indian tanks would have to roll over his body. Between the promise and the surrender, many a Bengali woman was raped by Pakistani soldiers in the ardency of their "jihad." Niazi condoned this for sheer practical considerations. He is reported to have said, "One cannot fight a war here in East Pakistan and go all the way to the Western wing to have an ejaculation!" This was thought funny at the time. The general was known primarily for his dirty jokes in the army; perhaps the army leadership of Pakistan thought that it was with these that he would blunt the Indian aggression. Niazi was also known as "Tiger" in army circles—to the ultimate mortification of that noble animal. Before he laid down his weapons he was involved in smuggling betel leaves to his son Habibullah in the western wing on official aircraft.[30] How such officers rose to such heights to disgrace themselves is another story.

A day after the war began, Brigadier Afzal Khan "Boss" went to visit his old friend Brigadier Gul Mawaz, a highly respected retired officer and considered to be Yahya's closest friend.[31] He told his guest that the moment he heard that war had formally been declared on December 3, he went to see Yahya. He found him and Hamid, his chief of staff, totally sloshed. Yahya assured him that as commander, his job was to launch his armies, and that henceforth all lay in the hands of his generals. Meanwhile he received a call from Japan. This was from Nur Jahan, a famous Pakistani singer. Excitedly he told the brigadier who the call was from and asked her to sing him a song. A far cry from Churchill when he saw London burn!

After the surrender of Pakistani armed forces at Dhaka on December 16, 1971, ninety-three thousand Pakistani troops and civilians were marched off into prisoner of war camps in India. Zulfikar Ali Bhutto, being in the United States for the U.N. Security Council session deliberating on the India-Pakistan War, called on President Nixon and told him how Pakistan was "completely in the debt of the U.S. for its support during the recent trying days."[32] He also thanked him for at least saving West Pakistan, and Nixon promised that his country would do all within its power to help Pakistan. From there Bhutto flew to Rome to await developments at home.

Back in Pakistan, the defeat and surrender of its army had left the people stunned, though the "elite" did manage to pull itself together in time for the festivities of the new year that lay a fortnight hence. But these festivities were very far from the minds of the otherwise fun-loving junta, whose incompetence and cronyism had ruined the fabric of the Pakistan Army, destroyed its mettle, and led it to ignominy and defeat. The ruling generals desperately wanted to hang on to power, if not for its own sake, certainly then for the preservation of their skins. The junior army officers did not react with any sympathy to this desperation of a clique equally discredited and dishonored, and their rumblings reached mutinous dimensions.

In Gujranwala, about 150 miles from Rawalpindi, the largest contingent of the uncommitted part of the army was stationed. Here Brigadier F.B. Ali and six other officers put three generals in "protective custody" and took command of the troops. Brigadier Ali was well known for his integrity, moral courage, and professionalism. As it became clear to him that the junta was determined to hang on, he sent Colonels Aleem Afridi and Agha Javed Iqbal, both well-reputed officers, with an ultimatum for Yahya and his generals to resign and leave the stage, otherwise they would march on Rawalpindi.[33]

To initiate yet another coverup, on December 19, 1971, Lieutenant General Hamid decided to address all the officers of the army's GHQ. Considering how he managed to squeeze in his talk between the heckling and hissing[34] of the junior officers, it was a "sterling" performance. Undeterred, he went through his script, often having to leave the stage to collect himself, only to return and pick up right where he had left off. Having fulfilled the formality, which was supposed to have motivated the officers into letting the junta continue in office, he left. After that, a couple of his junior officers took over the stage and expounded on the same theme. This attempt ended only when Brigadier Fazle Razik got up from the audience, worked up a fine froth, and tore into a junta general at the podium, listing the army hierarchy's many sins against the people of Pakistan. Razik was not very well reputed within army circles, but that such a man should have got up to expose the doings of a degenerate clique says a lot about the prevailing scenario then.

Meanwhile, Colonels Afridi and Javed Iqbal met Lieutenant General Gul Hassan, the chief of the general staff (CGS), on the afternoon of December 19 and requested him to deliver Brigadier Ali's ultimatum to Yahya. The general immediately called Air Marshal Rahim Khan, C-in-C of the air force, to his office to discuss the seriousness of the situation. They then drove off together to see Yahya. That evening a disgraced and dispirited president of a distraught nation addressed the people of Pakistan and surrendered his office. An aircraft was sent to fly in Bhutto from Rome, and on December 20, 1971, Zulfikar Ali Bhutto became president and the first civilian chief martial law administrator (CMLA) of Pakistan. Yahya was marched off to house arrest.

# Chapter 5

# Zulfikar Ali Bhutto

## The Charismatic

Zulfikar Ali Bhutto was through all negotiations now. He had reached the pinnacle and was master of all he surveyed. He was hugely popular, and especially so with the youth of the country, whose imagination he had fired up, as also with a host of deprived classes, who were quite certain that soon all the goodies that the rich were enjoying would be snatched away and handed over to them. Bhutto had campaigned on the slogan of "Roti, Kapra aur Makan" (food, clothing, and shelter), and the poor of the land believed that he actually meant to give them even more. He went into a whirl of activity, holding party meetings, addressing large crowds, and announcing all manner of reforms. He had the sort of energy, leadership, and charisma that a disheveled and torn Pakistan then most needed. And with all these, he had credibility. He was the focus of all hopes, and among his peers he stood a yard taller, so that none could challenge him. With all this, he had behind him the power of the presidency and all the authority of martial law. That was lot of power in a pair of hands. The danger was whether this power would leave the hands and go to the head.

Bhutto was the youngest child of Sir Shahnawaz Bhutto, a Sindhi feudal lord who also remained the *dewaan* (equivalent to prime minister) of the Indian state of Junagarh. He was a graduate of the University of California at Berkeley and had also studied law at Christ Church College, Oxford, besides being called to the bar from Lincoln's Inn. In 1958 he became a minister in Iskander Mirza's cabinet at the age of thirty. To those around him, he had everything—looks, elegance, wealth, education, family, and office. And those who saw him up close knew him for a sharp mind, an articulate tongue, a sense of humor, and a wit that at times was sardonic. There was also arrogance and a streak of vindictiveness[1] in him that would show itself in times to come.

When Bhutto moved to consolidate his position, his first action was to retire most of the generals closely associated with the Yahya regime. He made Gul Hassan chief of army staff (CAS) with the rank of lieutenant general instead of promoting him to four-star general. The appointment of commander in chief (C-in-C) was done away with since it now inhered in the office of the president, which he was now holding.

Lieutenant General Gul Hassan was not looking forward to taking over command of the army. Perhaps altruism had little to do with his disinclination. It seemed more a matter of realistic judgment of the way things really stood with a defeated army. Besides, he was a general of the Yahya junta, and such generals were not very popular beings in the Pakistan of the day, either within the army or outside. But compared to most of the rest, Gul Hassan still had much of his reputation unimpaired and was more popular than the rest. He was lucky not to have held one of the more disastrous commands in the war. During the war he reported to Lieutenant General Hamid, and the latter was running the war through the coterie of generals, pretty much bypassing and overriding conventional staff channels. This insulated Gul Hassan from much of the direct blame for the disaster. The junior ranks of the army were happy with his choice as the new army chief. Yet Bhutto's considerations for choosing him were rather different. His immediate aim was to stabilize the country and, in this, the stabilization of the army was very important. He knew Gul Hassan personally and felt that for the task immediately at hand, he was better suited than the rest. Besides, he also knew that it was Gul Hassan who had prevailed over Yahya to hand over power to Bhutto. So in some ways he owed it to Gul Hassan.

Having got himself a new chief for the army, and throwing out a clutch of senior generals who had adequately discredited themselves to have earned their unceremonious exits, Bhutto next turned his attention to Brigadier F.B. Ali and the six officers whose ultimatum to Yahya had eventually tipped the scales and convinced him to leave. Indeed, it was possible that without the enforcing actions of this group the junta would have got a little bit of time, and in the Pakistan Army, nourished on the straitjacket values of strict hierarchy, a few days' time might have been enough for Yahya and company to have swept the pieces of blame to various doorsteps and emerged brimming with innocence. Ironically, it was precisely because Brigadier Ali and company had what it took to forestall and evict Yahya and his gang that they needed to be weeded out. Bhutto was in the saddle and wary of all those with a demonstrated ability of unhorsing him. Thus he was determined to deal harshly with the officers who had violated "good order and military discipline." They were collected in Nowshera (in North-West Frontier Province) to face a court of inquiry, which found them guilty and sent them into forced retirement.

This course was followed by Bhutto more to signal his authority than instill discipline in the army, but the decision was not appreciated in the army. To begin with, Bhutto was extremely popular with the army, and even those who suspected that there was more to his role in the East Pakistan crisis than met the eye were wont to suppress their doubts lest their hopes in their savior suffer impairment. But more or less immediately on taking power, he committed a blunder especially in reference to the psyche of the military. The video footage of the army's surrender in Dhaka was played on Pakistan's official television channel. This move backfired. The army saw it as a blatant attempt to humiliate the very institution that had brought him to power. The public response was also not favorable. According to Khalid Hasan, the renowned journalist who was then on Bhutto's team, "PTV phone lines were literally jammed with protesting calls. . . . Not one person said that it was the right thing to do."[2] At one stroke Bhutto lost quite a bit of support within the army.

General Gul Hassan believed that the government's campaign to denigrate the army was affecting its morale. On the other hand, Bhutto apparently was convinced that the army deserved this treatment. Gul Hassan also formally protested to Bhutto for this, which he did not like. Already the general had refused Bhutto's suggestion of screening and surveillance of army officers by the police on the grounds that the army already had an effective enough procedure for this purpose. In addition, Bhutto suggested that he be invited to sit in during the proceedings of the army promotion boards. By virtue of being chief executive, it was within his right and discretion to do so, but this was turned down by the general.

A little later there was a police strike in Peshawar city and Bhutto wanted the army to move in to break it. In fact, without taking the army chief into confidence, ex-general Akbar Khan of the 1951 Rawalpindi conspiracy case fame, who was now Bhutto's national security adviser, directly ordered troops based in the area to tackle the issue. The moment Gul Hassan was informed of this, he countermanded the orders.[3] The political leadership was creating a new precedent of short-circuiting the military's established chain of command, which was unwarranted. Gul Hassan made it clear that he was having none of this. And when the air force chief also refused to have his command drawn in to quell the police strike, change was in the air.

On March 3, 1972, Gul Hassan was called to Bhutto's residence ostensibly for a briefing, along with the chief of the air force. Bhutto used the occasion to list his grievances with the army and the air force over their lack of cooperation with the government. General Gul Hassan said that he was quite on solid ground to have withheld such cooperation, but that he was also prepared to resign. Two folders were then immediately produced with a typed resignation letter for each of the two service chiefs. All they had to do was sign on the dotted lines. They were then escorted to the waiting car of Mr. Ghulam Mustafa Khar, governor of Punjab. The governor, in company with two of Bhutto's ministers, then sped the newly retired chiefs of the two services away to Lahore. Even for Pakistan this was a novelty. Two of its armed forces chiefs were virtually kidnapped on the orders of the president of the country! But interestingly, shortly thereafter both of them accepted posts as Pakistan's ambassadors to their choice of capitals in Europe.

There was no overt reaction to this within the army, but as this waned, tongues began to wag. Among the junior ranks of the army there was an openly expressed demand that the generals responsible for the East Pakistan debacle be held accountable and tried. Toward this end, Bhutto constituted a commission of inquiry headed by Justice Hamood ur-Rahman. The report was finalized and sent to Bhutto in 1972, but he decided that since the report contained sensitive material, it could not be made public. There were mutterings in the army that the report was a whitewash because its terms of reference were specifically designed to keep Bhutto and General Tikka Khan secure from blame for the roles each had played in the 1971 debacle. Tikka had recently taken over as the new army chief in place of Gul Hassan and was widely known as the "Butcher of Bengal" for his role in the massacres in East Pakistan.

General Tikka Khan was an unpopular choice as army chief, not so much because of his role in East Pakistan—the army of the day being too thick-skinned for any such delicate consideration, but because it was felt that he did not have a clue about his new job. He was known for his honesty, for being straightforward, and for bravery under fire. Yet once more an army chief had been promoted not on the basis of his accomplishments but on those of his incapacity, that is, the basic inability to pull off a coup. Time and again the lesson refused to be learned that given the way the military deck was stacked in Pakistan, any person placed at its head would be able to overthrow a government, but not everyone would be able to successfully command an organization that spends a major chunk of the country's resources.

The establishment of a new organization, the Federal Security Force (FSF), was another indicator of the way in which the government was headed. It was fast becoming an official tool for the party's dirty work. By 1973–74, many stories were in the air about the ruling party's henchmen humiliating and harassing political opponents and dissenting party members alike.[4] And it was Bhutto himself who set the tone for this, when he had Mr. J.A. Rahim (the spiritual father and founder of the PPP) abducted and humiliated in a police station, merely because the old man had dared to say what he thought of Bhutto's arbitrary style of governance.

As Bhutto was slowly settling in, disenchantment with him in army circles was rising steadily. The ranks of the pro-Bhutto military officers were thinning out somewhat. His political detractors and critics in the army were increasingly muttering about Bhutto's role in the dismemberment of Pakistan. These elements believed that Bhutto could have averted the surrender of Pakistani armed forces by accepting the Polish resolution in the U.N. Security Council on the eve of the fall of Dhaka, which in their view he artfully avoided. Others argue that this controversy had been created by anti-Bhutto elements for political purposes, which appears to be closer to the truth. Bhutto's performance in other areas was also causing disillusionment among many of his erstwhile supporters in the army. All this, in addition to the anger generated by the army surrender in Dhaka, led to the crystallization of what came to be called the Attock conspiracy case—an attempted military coup against Bhutto and senior army generals orchestrated by a few dozen middle-ranking army and air force officers.

In its final shape, this was a coalescence of three separate groups of army officers, each thrown up spontaneously as a reaction to what has been recounted above.[5] There was a group in the air force, one in the army in the south, and a third in the army in the north. The army group in the north comprised of the junior-most ranks, but it was the most influential. Many of the officers in the group were war heroes and had name recognition disproportionate to their ranks, as most had served as highly respected instructors in the Pakistan Military Academy, Kakul. It is substantiated by the fact that the U.S. embassy in Pakistan, through interviews with many senior serving and retired army officers, in a confidential correspondence to the Department of State on May 16, 1973, maintained that the "officers were considered among the most promising of younger officers."[6]

Informally, Major Farouk Adam Khan, a Sandhurst[7] commissioned officer, was the acknowledged leader of this group. They came in contact with the group in the air force quite by accident. Wing Commander Ghaus of the air force chanced to meet Colonel Aleem Afridi and opened up to him about the anti-Bhutto feelings prevalent among the junior officers in his service. What gave him the confidence to do so was that the colonel was the same officer who had taken the ultimatum of the officers in Gujranwala to General Gul Hassan, which eventually forced Yahya and company out of office and for which he was compulsorily retired of late. He thus had the credentials to be trusted. It was Colonel Afridi who put the air force officers in touch with Farouk Adam Khan. The group in the south was brought in touch with the latter through one Lieutenant Colonel Iftikhar.

The officers involved in the conspiracy wanted the perpetrators of the East Pakistan fiasco to be held accountable, and that all officers holding the ranks of major general and above who could not prove that they had in some way registered their protest at the way in which the war was being run ought to be considered guilty by association. In this group they also included Bhutto.

What also deeply affected them was the moral degeneracy and corruption of the Yahya regime, which for them only seemed to get a greater fillip with Bhutto's emergence in power. They were also strongly of the view that unless the burgeoning cancer of corruption in government was decisively rooted out, one day it would spell the doom of the country. This was indeed the only military conspiracy in Pakistan where the participants were firmly against the military rule, but they strongly believed that the military must have an institutionalized role in safeguarding the vital national interests of the country and wanted corruption at senior levels to be seen as an element that directly threatened such interests.

But they were never under any illusions that they, with their low seniority, could put their plans into effect. They needed at least some generals with them. But in a supremely rank-conscious institution, generals were least likely to exchange views with captains and majors on such a serious issue as overthrowing a government. This could best be done only if the interlocutors were of like rank and seniority. Therefore, Farouk Adam asked Brigadier F.B. Ali and Colonel Aleem Afridi to help him reach the senior ranks of the army.

In the initial days after the surrender the senior ranks were quite vocal, but soon thereafter the instinct of self-preservation overtook them. There was therefore no headway to be made with them. And while these young officers were yet groping their way into the hesitation of the unresponsive senior officers, whom they badly needed for the success of their enterprise, they were overtaken by events. In March 1973 one of the younger officers involved, Major Saeed Akhtar Malik, through his military contacts came to know that their plan was in the knowledge of the army hierarchy. He was stunned at the accuracy of the information that they had. He became certain that their plan was in the knowledge of military intelligence and immediately made for Lahore to meet Farouk Adam to apprise him of this development. Adam heard him out, thought long and deep, and then said: "We are too deep into this to stop now. The way I look at this is, that this is a no-loss situation. If we pull it off, the chances of which are remote, we win. And if we are arrested and are put on trial, the chances of which are bright, we also win, because at the trial we can expose what has happened." That evening the officers held a meeting. Those present were Brigadier Ali, Colonel Afridi, Lieutenant Colonel Tariq Rafi, Majors Asif Shafi, Farouk Adam, Ishtiaq Asif, Iftikhar Adam, and Lieutenant Sarwar Azhar. Saeed A. Malik recounted what he had heard and then suggested that, for the sake of security, they had now to break cover, throw caution to the wind, and openly contact as many officers as possible because their security would henceforth lie in numbers. It was decided that a week from that day they would spread out in given areas of responsibility and spread the word. This was on March 24, 1973, and they were due to meet next in Gujranwala in the second week of April. But fate had something else in reserve for them. On March 30 they were all arrested!

What had happened was that a month earlier, Lieutenant Colonel Tariq Rafi, a member of the group, had gone to recruit Major Naseer Ahmed (later Major General), but the latter got cold feet and suggested that the matter was very serious and needed to be reported to the authorities. On this, Tariq Rafi got scared and lied to him that he had already made the report and that he had come to check him out merely because his name was being discussed by the others in the group. Thus putting Naseer at his ease, he went and reported the matter to General Tikka Khan, who should have hit the roof, but he did not because he was either not too excitable or did not fully comprehend the import of the report. He passed Tariq Rafi on to the Inter Services Intelligence (ISI). The ISI, after thorough questioning of the colonel, decided that he should carry on and introduce two more officers within the group. Thereafter, army authorities took control of the conspiracy. They were guiding it in a manner to establish contact between these young officers and the political leaders in opposition to Bhutto in order to catch them in the same net when all was ready. Apparently the group's decision to openly recruit as many officers as possible aborted the government plan, and it had no option but to affect their arrests before their planned recruitment drive came into effect.

During the interrogation of these officers, they were encouraged to speak without restraint against the generals and say what they thought about the conduct of the 1971 war. But at the same time, they were discouraged to speak their minds about Bhutto. The refrain of each officer in custody was that it would be politic to leave open an escape route and not annoy the entire hierarchy of power. It became obvious to them that Bhutto had further plans to use this conspiracy against the army leadership and would be able to better do so if his own name were left unstained.

Major General Zia ul-Haq was picked as president of the court-martial that was to try these officers at Attock, and the making of history was set into motion. This assignment opened for Zia a direct channel to Bhutto, who was much interested in this trial and therefore would need regular briefings. And these would give Zia the opportunity to deploy about Bhutto just the right amount of servility that would pass for loyalty.

Toward the end of the trial came the time for the officers to make statements in their own defense. Some of the officers were of the opinion that in their statements they must admit the conspiracy and then proceed to outline the reasons that motivated them toward such a course of action. It was their view that this was their one chance to speak out, and if they did not do so, they would regret it for the rest of their lives, not a single good would come from the trial, and all would be lost. Major Malik led this view, and his written statement was especially harsh and was discussed by his counsel for defense, Mr. S.M. Zafar, among other officers who were codefendants with him. But it was the counsel's view that since this was a joint trial, conspiracy should neither be admitted nor should Bhutto be directly attacked by any of the accused officers, as this would adversely affect the defense of even those officers who disagreed with this line.

Farouk Adam Khan's emotional speech brought tears to the eyes of many present in the court that day, and Major Malik's was a damning indictment of the army high command, a sample paragraph of which will suffice to convey its flavor. He said:

> When the war became imminent, I took leave from the PMA [Pakistan Military Academy] and joined my unit. The next day the war started. But instead of glory, I found only disillusionment. The truth was that we were a defeated army even before a shot was fired. This was a very bitter truth. With each corpse that I saw, my revulsion increased for the men who had signed the death warrants of so many very fine men. Yes, fine men but poor soldiers, who were never given the chance to fight back, because they were not trained to fight back. When they should have been training for war, they were performing the role of laborers, farmers or herdsman, anything but the role of soldiers. This was not *shahadat* [martyrdom]. This was cold-blooded murder. Who was responsible for this? I was responsible! But more than me someone else was responsible. People who get paid more than me were responsible. What were some of these men, these callous, inhuman degenerates, doing when their only job was to prepare this army for war? Were these men not grabbing lands and building houses? Did it not appear in foreign magazines that some of them were pimping for their bloated grandmaster? Yes, generals, wearing that uniform (he pointed at the court's president) pimping and whore mongering.[8]

A day after his statement, General Zia ul-Haq called Saeed A. Malik and told him that there had been a technical error in the proceedings. He explained that the court proceedings were duly recorded on tape, but because of an oversight this had not been done when the statements of the accused officers were made. Thus, the general gave him a schedule according to which all the officers were to record their defense statements again. Major Malik and three others were required to do this on the first day. And when this was done, Zia said that there was no need for any of the other officers to record their statements again! This exercise was not conducted without reason. Knowing well the impact of the emotionally spoken word over its written form, Zia had induced the major to have his statement tape-recorded, which he then played for Bhutto to hear. It is conjectured that this went a long way to convince Bhutto that the general level of resentment in the army was such that he could supersede as many senior officers as he wanted to when the time came for the appointment of the next army chief. When the time did come, he superseded a good eight of them and promoted Zia over their heads! Thus these junior officers unknowingly helped promote the man from whose influence the army should have been saved. ·

Bhutto did not seem to have learned any lessons from the conspiracy itself. According to one of the officers interviewed, Bhutto wanted General Tikka Khan to ensure that Brigadier Ali and Colonel Afridi were given death sentences by the court-martial, with many of the others to be given life terms. Tikka Khan had returned the sentences to the court for reconsideration when the court had finalized the proceedings and sent them to him for confirmation. According to procedure, Tikka Khan, in his capacity of being the convening authority of the court-martial, could have unilaterally reduced any sentence that he wished, but to increase the same he was required under law to send the proceedings back to the court for "reconsideration"—a euphemism for enhancement of the same. With Ali and Afridi already having been given life, any increase would have put their heads in the noose. But the court refused any such reconsideration. This was due primarily to the initiative of Major Muzaffar Usmani, who later rose to the rank of lieutenant general and became a part of Musharraf's inner circle for a while. He was then the juniormost member of the court on a bench of seven. A few days before the sentencing he had brought up the matter with the court—in fact, it was a suggestion by him that, in case there was any pressure on the court as regards the sentences to be awarded, the court should disregard the same. This had been unanimously agreed to, and it would not have been easy for the court to make a backflip so soon after taking a unanimous decision.

The government had a real difficult time keeping the junior lot from visiting the convicted officers in jail. Eventually these officers had to be moved to jails in cities that did not have cantonments. This should have told the government that the jailed officers had lost none of their standing in the army, and the many who visited them in jail were indirectly only validating their aborted action. It is also believed that some of the convicted officers kept the names of some of their "recruited" officers to their hearts during the tough interrogations. At least two from among those later rose to the rank of general.

Soon after taking over, Bhutto also focused his attention on the constitution-making process, and his most remarkable achievement was the adoption of the 1973 constitution. It was the first time in the history of Pakistan that a directly elected legislature had framed a constitution. Though Bhutto had the requisite majority in the Parliament to go ahead with the presidential form of government, which he personally was in favor of, he still agreed to some fundamental modifications in his proposals as suggested by the opposition parties. It seemed at the time that he would not find it easy to come to terms with the opposition to push this through the National Assembly, but behind-the-scenes efforts by the U.S. chargé d'affaires also helped bring the opposition and the government to common ground.[9] Adoption of the constitution by 125 votes out of 128 present in the House of 144 in a short time must be considered miraculous by Pakistani standards.

Another accomplishment worth mentioning was defining, in clear terms, the functions of the armed forces. Article 245 of the 1973 constitution says: "The Armed Forces shall, under the direction of the Federal Government, defend Pakistan against external aggression or threat of war, and subject to Law, act in aid of civil power when called upon to do so." It was an indication for military officers to confine themselves to their barracks and simply stay away from politics. Article 6 further discouraged military adventurers by saying that: "Any person who abrogates or attempts or conspires to abrogate; subverts or attempts or conspires to subvert the constitution by use of force or show of force or by other unconstitutional means shall be guilty of high treason." Article 6(3) supplemented this by authorizing the Parliament to provide "for the punishment of persons found guilty of high treason." Without any delay, the Parliament in September 1973 passed a law pronouncing the death sentence or life imprisonment as the punishment for such a crime.[10] The signal was loud and clear—a military coup would be considered high treason.

Also near miraculous were the unlikely results of the summit between Bhutto and Indian prime minister Indira Gandhi at Simla in mid-1972. This summit was called to resolve the outstanding issues relating to the 1971 war. Indira held all the cards and she wanted Bhutto to accept the status quo in Kashmir as a formal solution to this long-festering problem; a no-war pact between the two countries; and for Pakistan to grant immediate recognition to Bangladesh. Bhutto held no cards, and did not want to accede to any of the Indian demands. But he was quite clear about what he did want, that is, the return of Pakistani prisoners of war and the vacating of six thousand square miles of Pakistani territory still under Indian occupation. Having used the Tashkent Declaration to discredit Ayub Khan, he must have been conscious of the ramifications of a misstep in such negotiations. His only bargaining chip was that, after a war that Pakistan had not foisted on India, the latter had no good reason to hold on to Pakistani prisoners and territory, and that sooner or later this was bound to become an embarrassment for India on the international scene. He was therefore quite prepared for no agreement rather than a flawed one that could erode his political position. As a strategy, he avoided mentioning the issue of Pakistani prisoners, knowing that India could not keep them for long.

Eventually he got back the territory, though not the prisoners, whom India decided to hold on to, so that it could use them to gain Pakistan's recognition of Bangladesh. On Kashmir, he agreed that the cease-fire line be redesignated as the Line of Control (LOC). The most important part of the agreement was that henceforth, both countries were to be committed to a peaceful resolution of all disputes through bilateral discussions and consultations. Though Indian prime minister Indira Gandhi told her delegation that Bhutto expressed a willingness to accept the status quo in Kashmir as the final solution to the problem,[11] there is nothing on record to verify this. His acceptance of the bilateral approach for the solution of all problems between the two countries was later to be interpreted by India as one that superseded all earlier United Nations Security Council (UNSC) resolutions on the subject of Kashmir. Benefiting from this situation, his opponents at home castigated him for having sacrificed Pakistan's position on Kashmir as it had stood defined by virtue of the relevant U.N. resolutions. Strictly from the international law perspective, though, the agreement made no difference as to the significance of the UNSC resolutions, which are legally superior and hence more important than any bilateral agreement between two member countries. But from then on, the U.S. position on the subject shifted from one based on the U.N. resolutions of 1948 and 1949 to one where a bilateral solution was considered acceptable.[12]

Meanwhile, trouble was already brewing in Baluchistan between the Marri tribe and the Bugti-Jamote-Zehri tribal coalition. In February 1973 an arms shipment consigned to the Iraqi embassy in Islamabad by the government in Baghdad was discovered through the commendable efforts of an ISI official—Major (later Lieutenant General) Shahid Tirmizi. According to Pakistani intelligence, these weapons were to be delivered to Marri tribe militants who were involved in anti-Pakistan activities and who also had the support of the chief minister of the province. Bhutto therefore had this government dismissed and put the province under governor's rule, which meant his direct control. He was not prepared for what happened next. Large numbers of Marri tribesmen and Baluchi students took to the hills in armed insurrection against the government of Pakistan. An organization by the name of the Baluch People's Liberation Front came up under the leadership of Khair Baksh Marri (chief of the Marri tribe), who took refuge in Afghanistan, drawing support from both Kabul and Baghdad.

Here, Bhutto faced a dilemma. He had decided early on that in order to weaken the army's potential hold on power in Pakistan, he must eschew reliance on it to bolster the fortunes of his government. But already in mid-1972, the army had been called out in Karachi to restore order in wake of the language riots there. Even later, the army was called out to quell labor disturbances in the same city. Trying to benefit from these developments, the Jamaat-i-Islami had already called on General Tikka Khan to refuse the government and take over the reins of government.[13] So, by the time of the Baluchistan insurgency in 1974, Bhutto was becoming cautious, but he had little choice other than to fall back on the men in uniform, eighty thousand of whom were deployed in the province over a four-year period, to bring the situation back to normal. Eventually the situation was restored as much by the exertions of the army (with generous help from the Shah of Iran) as by the recourse to large-scale development projects involving road-building and electrification. It is a singular novelty of Baluch politics that the tribal chiefs, who tax their people heavily and rule them autocratically, are always in the forefront of every "democratic" movement to restore the rights of their people. Yet almost every such leader has a jail to put away his poor tribesmen who dare to transgress against his authority, but none has as yet been known to have built a school or a medical clinic for his people. They are not known to have allowed anyone else to do so either, and frequently those making any such attempt are liable to be kidnapped or at least chased out of the area. They would like to have democracy to the extent that it enhances their own power, but would check any advance by civilization in areas under their control.

During the same years the political situation in the North-West Frontier Province (NWFP) was becoming complicated. In July 1973, King Zahir Shah of Afghanistan was deposed by Sardar Daud, his pro-Moscow and anti-Pakistani cousin. He had never recognized the Durand Line[14] as the border between Afghanistan and Pakistan, and was a strong advocate of Pakhtunistan, that is, the merger of Pakistan's North-West Frontier Province and Afghanistan, whose population south of the Hindu Kush mountain range was ethnically the same as that of NWFP-Pashtuns. It therefore did not take Bhutto long to accuse the NWFP government of planning an anti-Pakistan conspiracy with Sardar Daud's government in Kabul, to have the province break away from Pakistan and join Afghanistan. Bhutto therefore conveniently packed off the government of the province. And then in 1975, when Hayat Khan Sherpao, Bhutto's favorite and one of the founders of the PPP, was murdered in a mysterious bomb blast in Peshawar, Bhutto accused the pro-Moscow National Awami Party of being behind the crime. Hence, he banned this party and locked up its leaders. However, it is another matter that Hayat Sherpao was quite disillusioned by Bhutto and thinking of even leaving the party when he died.[15]

It was about this time that Bhutto decided to use right-wing Islamic dissidents from Afghanistan, who had taken refuge in Pakistan, to destabilize the Daud regime in Kabul, and the names Gulbadin Hikmatyar and Ahmad Shah Masud were first heard. Nothing much came of this attempt, but it was a precursor to a tactic that would be used with great effect against the Soviets when they invaded Afghanistan in the not-too-distant future. And the name Hikmatyar would then become both commonplace and controversial among the Afghan mujahideen while that of Masud would gain renown as a general and as a natural leader of men.

At this stage Bhutto had no ostensible opposition left. With a comfortable majority at the center and the onerous task of constitution-making behind him, he was in complete command of the situation. The opposition governments in Baluchistan and the NWFP had been taken care of. The army had been cut down to size. None in his own party could dare think in terms of mounting a challenge to his authority. Those suspected of having the inclination of doing so had been disciplined through gangsters or by the "gentler" persuasion of the police.

The only potential sources of trouble for Bhutto were the country's rightwing religious parties. Luckily for Bhutto, those of their members who sat in the central and provincial legislatures of the time had been elected during the 1970 general elections, in which their thunder had been drowned out by the nationalist slogan in East Pakistan and by the socialist one in West Pakistan. They were therefore not entirely certain about their strength and therefore of their capability to make mischief. And Bhutto's constitution had declared Islam to be the state religion (Article 2), provided that all existing laws were to be brought into conformity with the injunctions of Islam (Article 227), and said that it would take steps to teach *Islamiyat* and the Quran in schools (Article 31). Besides, the Council of Islamic Ideology was given the job of identifying laws repugnant to Islam and making recommendations to bring these laws into accordance with Islamic injunctions (Articles 228–31).[16] Surely at that stage, no member of the clergy could ask for more. And to add further to his Islamic credentials, Bhutto had hosted the highly successful and well-attended Islamic Summit Conference in Lahore in 1974.

No one could have expected that within two months of this summit, all the religious parties would be out in the streets in great strength. As in 1953, this time again, their demand was that the Ahmedi community be declared non-Muslim. The agitation had erupted from an incident at the small railway station in Rabwah, a small town in the Punjab almost exclusively inhabited by Ahmedis on May 22, 1974. There are two versions of the incident. Ahmedis maintain that some youngsters belonging to Islami Jamiat-i-Tulaba (IJT), the student wing of Jamaat-i-Islami (JI), uttered some rude remarks against an Ahmedi woman and misbehaved when the train in which they were traveling stopped at the Rabwah railway station. To this the Ahmedis reacted, and the culprits were given a sound beating. The IJT version is that Ahmedi clerics were distributing religious pamphlets to the passengers in the train and to this their activists objected, leading to a confrontation. The quarrel became a huge issue as the IJT leadership in a few days delivered a tirade against Ahmedis and revived their demand to declare them non-Muslims.[17] During the times, JI as a strategy was trying to penetrate into the university campuses to uproot the left-wing student groups, which were known to be Bhutto supporters. Within days, many religious parties joined hands to organize a countrywide agitation, which lasted four months. A few Ahmedis lost their lives while many others lost their businesses through arson. Many fled abroad for refuge. Unlike 1953, there was to be no reprieve for them in 1974. They were soon declared to be out of the pale of Islam by the National Assembly, and when Bhutto left the Parliament, he did so in an open car, acknowledging the cheers of the crowd and claiming the plaudits for "solving" a problem that had bothered the Muslims for the previous ninety years. The Ahmedis had supported Bhutto's bid in the 1970 elections with their votes, funds, and organization. When he ditched them and claimed victory, many of his supporters claimed that he had outmaneuvered the mullahs. Saner voices held the opposite view, that is, that he had been challenged and given way. The mullahs had tasted blood and would be back for more. Rafi Raza, who watched the whole episode from up close, maintains that while doing this, Bhutto had "lost sight of what was the fundamental principle of whether the religious issues can or should be settled in a political forum."[18]

For 1974, the thirst of the mullahs seemed to have been sated. The Ahmedi community had to suffer alone as there was hardly a voice raised in its support. No doubt that Muslims belonging to all other sects were seriously troubled by the Ahmedi faith, especially in reference to its views on the finality of the Prophethood in the person of Mohammad (PBUH), but this difference did not give them a right to persecute and harass Ahmedis and deny them a right to practice their beliefs. By virtue of this development, the mullahs had been invested with the broad right to interpret and make of it an unbridgeable chasm. Henceforth they would constantly reassert this right. Once Bhutto gave way on a vital principle, he helped open a Pandora's box for the genie of divisiveness to crawl out and afflict a people whose very fate depended on unity.

On foreign policy issues, Bhutto had done well. He further shored up Pakistan's relationship with China, and with the opening up of the Karakoram

Highway in 1978, a physical link was also established with that country. He had done extremely well in a short space of time to move closer with the Arab countries and with Iran, which funneled in aid that was vital for Pakistan. Extending recognition to Bangladesh, getting back the prisoners of war, and getting Mujib to drop charges against the 195 officers primarily responsible for the massacres in East Pakistan further shored up his prestige in the country. He left the British Commonwealth and Southeast Asian Treaty Organization (SEATO) to signal Pakistan's independence from the West and to bolster Pakistan's claims for membership in the nonaligned bloc, whose leadership he was hoping to take over now that the older generation like Nehru and Nasser had passed away.

However, Pakistan's relations with the United States were the least touched by rancor and the warmest in years, despite the fact that by this time the alliance had more or less unraveled and Pakistan had extended recognition to both North Vietnam and North Korea. Both President Nixon and Secretary of State Henry Kissinger seemed to set great store by Pakistan's erstwhile status as a firm American ally, and especially by its efforts to bring about a Sino-U.S. rapprochement. In addition, Bhutto had little doubt about the U.S. sincerity of effort in trying to bail out his country in its recent war against India. Also, both Nixon and Kissinger had done their best to lift the U.S. arms embargo against Pakistan that had been imposed by President Johnson in 1965, but Pakistan's poor standing with the Congress,[19] due to the memory of the army action in former East Pakistan, stood in the way. Still, economic aid was soon resumed, and when Nixon told Bhutto that the independence and integrity of Pakistan was a cornerstone of American policy, the Pakistani leader knew that the words were sincerely meant.

But good does not last. On May 8, 1974, India exploded the world's first "peaceful" nuclear bomb and further insisted that it was a "device" and not a bomb. The rest of the world sincerely tried but could not tell the difference and went into shock. Consequently, Pakistan went into a whirl of activity. If India had the bomb, no matter how peaceful, Pakistan had to have one, too. India may have exploded a mere "device," as it claimed, but the fact remained that if such a peaceful device were to be dropped on Islamabad, the city would be no more. Bhutto had collected Pakistani scientists in the city of Multan and stressed Pakistan's need for a nuclear deterrent against Indian superiority in conventional weapons as early as 1972,[20] but it was only after 1974 that Pakistan took an irrevocable decision to build the bomb. This was a matter of serious and immediate concern for the United States and was to remain a source of friction between the two countries beyond the turn of the century.

In 1975, President Gerald Ford lifted the arms embargo on Pakistan and tried to dissuade it from taking the nuclear road. Henry Kissinger, who enjoyed considerable respect and credibility in Islamabad, offered to build up its conventional deterrent if Pakistan forswore nuclear development. Despite all the goodwill on both sides, America failed to persuade Pakistan to give up the nuclear option. It probably never fully understood the central dynamic governing the India-Pakistan relationship, that is, that the driving compulsion of India's inferiority complex to build and project its power abroad and the defensive overreaction of Pakistan fueled by its own complex of insecurity were now forging their way to a logical conclusion. Ever since the U.S. arms embargo on Pakistan imposed during its 1965 war against India, Pakistan's feeling of insecurity, and consequent reliance on America as a guarantor of this security, had only grown. So when the Republican president Ford lost out to Jimmy Carter in the next presidential election and Kissinger left office, whatever little confidence Pakistan still had in the U.S. commitment to its security all but vanished.

On the other hand, Bhutto's confidence in himself was constantly on the ascendant. Internally he had no one left to challenge him; internationally he had scored heavily; and in the regional context, with General Zia ur-Rahman's military coup in Bangladesh and Indira Gandhi's declaration of "emergency" having established her as a virtual dictator in India, Pakistan was the only country on the Indian subcontinent projecting itself quite successfully as an effective democracy. All this made for a very buoyant combination, and so in January 1977, Bhutto announced national elections a year ahead of time. But his high spirits suffered an almost immediate deflation when all the main opposition parties, ranging from the JI on the far right to the secular, pro-Moscow Awami National Party[21] on the left, united in an unlikely election alliance under the name of the Pakistan National Alliance (PNA). When public meetings called by the PNA spontaneously attracted huge and enthusiastic crowds, Bhutto and his Pakistan People's Party (PPP) went into a panic. Prior to this, they did not seem to have had the vaguest idea of the disgust that their conduct and policies had generated. The labor unions, first empowered by new reforms, had later to be disciplined by army action. The huge Mohajir[22] populations in Karachi and Hyderabad felt relegated to a lower rung in terms of status and deprived in terms of job opportunities when Sindhi was declared the official language of the province in 1972. The peasants had just felt the fresh breeze of emancipation only to see their landlords being taken into the bosom of the PPP. Thousands of owners of small businesses like ghee mills and cotton ginning factories felt robbed by Bhutto's nationalization policies. The nationalization of private schools and colleges destroyed the few institutions that had maintained a reasonable standard of education.

The much celebrated 1973 constitution also could not maintain its pristine glory of unanimous approval for long, as it was marred by injudicious amendments one after the other. Out of a total of seven amendments in the constitution between 1973 and 1977, three were widely criticized for being controversial. For instance, the Fourth Amendment Act, passed in September 1976, curtailed the jurisdiction of high courts in matters of preventive detention and was rushed through the Parliament despite the outcry of members of the opposition in the Parliament, who were physically thrown out of the National Assembly at the time the amendment act passed.[23]

The PNA groups had no basis of unity except their shared aversion to the arrogance of Bhutto, his ministers, and their minions. Despite media control, use of government agencies, and intimidation, large crowds still flocked to PNA rallies.[24] The PNA promised freedom from this heel by enforcement of the Islamic system of government, the first time since 1947 that a major national movement had used Islam as its slogan. Bhutto drew all the wrong conclusions from this. Unwilling or unable to see that his policies had resulted in support for the PNA, he concluded that the appeal of the PNA lay in its slogan. He bent and gave way. Addressing a public meeting in Lahore, he declared gambling and horse racing illegal, banned the sale and use of alcohol, and declared Friday as the weekly holiday.

It is also interesting to note Stanley Wolpert's disclosure that Bhutto had hired an academic expert on constitutional government, Professor Leslie Wolf Phillips of the London School of Economics and Political Science, to prepare a new presidential constitution for Pakistan.[25] He flew to Rawalpindi in July 1976 to brief Bhutto on his "top-secret labors." According to Khalid Hasan, Bhutto told Professor Phillips that "he needed to acquire more powers for his office."[26] It is alleged that Bhutto rigged the 1977 elections to realize this constitutional plan, as he needed a two-thirds majority in the parliament to be able to make constitutional amendments. Bhutto won the elections by taking 155 seats out of 200. It was widely believed that polls at 35 to 40 seats were rigged. Bhutto's PPP was expected to win the elections comfortably, but a huge victory was out of question. This brought the opposition out on the streets in full force. They boycotted the provincial assembly elections and started a massive agitation without parallel in the country's history. Bhutto had no option left but to fall back on the army and put to the test the loyalty of General Zia ul-Haq.

Bhutto must certainly have hoped that his fortunes had fallen in safe hands, but if he had had any truck with reality whatever, he should have been suffering from considerable anxiety. He had steadily lost support in the army, particularly among the younger officers. Among the seniors, too, he could hope to engender little loyalty. Reportedly, Bhutto on a few occasions introduced

Zia to foreign dignitaries as his "monkey general."[27] Zia could only give a helpless smile on such occasions and hope that the ape in him was not too apparent to his peers and others. But by the time Zia had become Bhutto's recourse of last resort, he had already smiled his embarrassed smile too long. He now started to smile less and twirl his mustache a little more.

To the PPP leadership, Zia had started to resemble a tiger. And quite beyond Zia's transformation, Bhutto had other reasons to worry. PNA's strong showing in the period leading up to the polls had injected a dose of reality into him, and quite early on he had foreseen that he might ultimately have to rely on the army to shore up his political fortunes. As such he had sent Aziz Ahmed, his foreign minister, to various cantonments to address army officers and motivate them to give their loyalties to the government. In the first such talk of his tour he tediously listed the disqualifications of the PNA leadership. He was quite certain that this would prove edifying for the officers, till a young major got up from the audience and asked him if the PNA leadership would also be allowed to address them, and if not, why not.[28] Stunned silence followed this question. After this, he was dogged by similar questions on his next two stops, after which the exercise was terminated.

This was the mullah parties' finest hour. Their disciplined cadres gave the agitation its organization and skeletal structure. Unarmed civilians confronted police batons and bullets head-on. Street agitation had taken on a new dimension in Pakistan. By the time dozens of civilians had been shot dead, martial law was declared in Lahore, Karachi, and Hyderabad by military authorities on the instructions of Bhutto as the chief executive. Almost immediately Bhutto received his worst bit of news yet. In Lahore, Brigadier Niaz Ahmed refused the instructions of his superior to disperse the demonstrators by ordering his troops to open fire on them.[29] The brigadier was a professional officer of high standing, known as much for his moral courage as for his ability and natural leadership qualities. As a result of his refusal, he was removed from command by Zia, pending disciplinary action. The news traveled around the army circles like wildfire, and it was clear that the brigadier's action enjoyed support in the army. He was asked to hand over his command to Brigadier Ashraf, another fine officer, who followed suit and similarly refused to order his troops to fire on unarmed civilians. He too was removed from command and asked to hand over charge to Brigadier Ishtiaq Ali Khan, who completed the hat trick and decided to go home honorably rather than have his troops fire on and kill unarmed civilians. The refusal of the three brigadiers was as honorable for the army as it was devastating for Bhutto and embarrassing for Zia ul-Haq.

On the evening of July 4, 1977, Bhutto told his senior advisers and Zia in a meeting that he would be resuming the dialogue with the PNA leaders the following day and intended to resolve the deadlock. Retired air marshal Asghar Khan, who was part of the PNA movement, while referring to this meeting maintains that "the possibility of an accord being reached between the government and the PNA was not to his [Zia's] liking and Zia ul-Haq decided to act without delay to obviate that risk."[30]

On July 5, 1977, Bhutto and his ministers were arrested and martial law was imposed. The 1973 constitution was immediately suspended, not abrogated—Zia must have believed that it would save his action from being considered high treason, the punishment for which was nothing less than the death penalty or life imprisonment.

One of the mysteries associated with this episode of Pakistan's history is the alleged U.S. role in the removal of Bhutto, though no substantial evidence exists. It is believed by PPP supporters that the United States had developed an intense dislike for Bhutto due to his insistence on making Pakistan a nuclear power. Bhutto, in his death cell memoirs *If I Am Assassinated*, infers that his decision to acquire nuclear weapons led to the death sentence awarded him, and in this context he refers to his discussion with Henry Kissinger.[31] Kissinger is reported to have threatened to make a "horrible example of him" if he did not abandon his plans to reprocess plutonium.[32] However, Rafi Raza, a close associate of Bhutto's, strongly argues that no such threat was ever made to Bhutto.[33] Moreso, if the United States had conspired with Zia to overthrow Bhutto to halt the nuclear program, then Zia would have, after seizing power, abandoned the program, which certainly didn't happen, thus nullifying this line of argument. Still, what cannot be denied is that the then–U.S. administration was very keen to ensure that Pakistan should halt its nuclear program. For instance, it successfully pressured France into rescinding its contract for building a nuclear processing plant in Pakistan.[34]

Another gesture indicating U.S. displeasure with Bhutto was the State Department's ban on export of a large quantity of tear gas to Pakistan in April 1977 on the grounds that such an export would signal American support for a repressive regime that would run counter to the human rights policy of President Carter. And then there was the case of a telephone conversation intercepted by Pakistani intelligence, which further confirmed Bhutto's suspicions. Apparently a journalist had informed the U.S. consul general in Karachi that Bhutto had been forcibly detained at a reception. The consul general promptly passed the message on to the U.S. embassy in Islamabad. A little while later the same journalist called the consul general to say that his earlier information had been incorrect, and the latter called Islamabad to give the correction. In order to disguise this message, since he was talking over an insecure line, he said: "My source tells me the party is over."[35] This was picked up by Pakistani intelligence and relayed to Bhutto, who pounced on it as ready proof of U.S. plotting and dramatically announced it to the National Assembly on April 28, 1977, in an emotionally charged speech. Among many Pakistani intelligence officials, the belief that the United States was indeed involved in Bhutto's ouster continues to be held, as they point out that "the party is over" was a very poor disguise for the message it was intended to convey, and could only have meant that the party was indeed over.[36]

The other allegation in this context relates to U.S. financial support of the PNA, especially Jamaat-i-Islami, during the street protests in 1977. Those who believe in this theory argue that the flow of dollars in the market witnessed a sudden rise in comparison to normal times and, considering the critical law-and-order situation in Pakistan then, this was certainly an unexpected development.

Bhutto certainly had the romantic vision, the mind, and the energy that every great leader must have. He also had the necessary air of authority and the charisma. He had the belief in himself, which propelled him through his whirlwind tours of the country, addressing mammoth public meetings to restore the morale of the people after the 1971 debacle by establishing personal contact with them so that they would know that they were his and that there was no intermediary between them. In this sense he was no armchair politician. He was the first leader to rid the have-not of his fear of the privileged classes. Indeed, this was to be one of his abiding legacies. It is sad, though, that he did not take this process through in an organized manner, and midway he abandoned his promise of emancipation of the masses to fall back into the lap of the feudal lords, as demonstrated by the candidates he chose to represent his party in the 1977 elections. Thus the social justice promised did not see its dawn.

# ——Chapter 6——

# General Zia ul-Haq

## The Redefinition of a Country

General Mohammad Zia ul-Haq was born in a lower-middle-class family of East Punjab (India) in 1924. His father, a devoutly religious man, held a clerical job in a government department and sent his son to attend St. Stephen's College in Delhi. Later, Zia joined an officers training school of the British Indian Army and, on graduating soon after the Second World War, he was commissioned in the armored corps. At the time of the partition of India in 1947, then Captain Zia was an escort officer on the last Pakistani train with refugees and military consignment to leave the Indian city of Babina for Pakistan.[1] In Pakistan, he was posted to the Guides Cavalry Regiment.

Though he came from a solid conservative background, his ambition gave him flexibility enough so that while he worked to shore up his credentials for eventual entry into paradise, he was not among those who would force their interpretation of religion on others while insisting that they had to get there, too. This made him both a tolerant and a tolerable Muslim. He was a hardworking officer, and though no early brilliance shone through him and despite the fact that he resembled a stuffed-out version of the British comic Terry Thomas, he never played the fool, nor was he taken to be one. He may have retired from the army as a lieutenant colonel to no great detriment of the army and the country, but General Gul Hassan rescued him from probable obscurity and catapulted him among the stars—to the initial delight and the ultimate tragedy of Bhutto.

By the time he first met Bhutto, when he was appointed president of the Attock court-martial, he was fairly well regarded in the army, though his reputation as a soldier under fire could not be assessed because he had missed out on both the 1965 and 1971 wars. During the latter he was on assignment to Jordan, where he had helped King Hussein crush the Palestinians with uncommon gusto—his only experience resembling a war, which allowed him free expression of zeal on a stage larger than any he had yet known. He is said to have created a fairly good reputation with the king, and it is believed that before appointing him army chief, Bhutto had checked him out with His Majesty. But there is little doubt that it was the Attock court-martial[2] that allowed him the opportunity to convince Bhutto about his absolute loyalty, and, more important, about his incapacity to be otherwise.

During his conduct of the trial at Attock, he never lost sight of the fact that he was dealing with a group of young officers who were emotionally highly charged and respected in the army. His main aim seemed to be to not allow any untoward incident to erupt and mar the trial and thereby his own reputation as well. Therefore, the trial became an elaborately choreographed exercise in public relationing for Zia. To the officers under trial, he gave as much latitude as the circumstances allowed him.[3] The counsel defending them were given due deference. And to take this show to its logical end, a day before the sentencing, he even had the court invite the accused officers and their counsels to tea, with himself serving the goodies.[4]

And this came very naturally to him, and was one of the strongest weapons in his armory. However, in itself there was no hypocrisy about all this, though dissimulation could hide in such behavior with considerable comfort, which many of his adversaries would later find out to their great embarrassment and disadvantage. He came from a family in which decency and fear of Allah were both strongly stressed, and ingrained. But he was also ambitious, severely practical, and had plenty of native cunning that would easily have passed for brilliance had he also come from Berkeley or Oxford. And as the demands of decency militated against those of ambition and practical good sense, he had no difficulty rolling back the limits of the former to accommodate the latter.

Indeed, hardly any officer tried by him in the Attock court had much to quibble with him on the demerits of the sentences he handed down. They knew well that their court-martial was not about fine points of law, but was a device for maintaining discipline in the ranks. If anything, his handling of the case only enhanced his reputation in the army, which he had handled as well as anyone could have, and better than most. And when the news spread within army circles that he had refused to enhance the sentences of the officers on the implied instructions of General Tikka Khan, this only went to his credit. But in front of Bhutto he took an entirely different line—"Sir, you may have a soft spot for these men, but I must give the maximum punishment to those who were conspiring against my Prime Minister."[5]

His colors started to change slowly after he was promoted to lieutenant general and given command of the strike corps in Multan, and then only to the extent that his ambition gnawed at him. When Bhutto was visiting the station, Zia ordered all the officers, their wives, and their children to line a part of the route to welcome the prime minister. One army officer, a major, refused to employ his family on the grounds that they did not fall under the general's command.[6] And when this officer was sent home on forced retirement, Zia's stock in the army took a nosedive. Zia never gave even a hint of being uncomfortable at this, and he was not unduly self-conscious as he breached one norm of propriety after another in the process. During another of Bhutto's visits to Multan, while the prime minister met with his inner party circle in a conference room of an army mess, a dutiful Zia, duly decked out in full ceremonial, waited outside. When Bhutto came out to ask him what it was that he was doing there, the general had no difficulty keeping a straight face to say that he felt it his duty to personally stand guard for the security of his leader![7]

Bhutto, himself having been a master of purveying such unction to smooth his way to the top, should have been wary of the dramatics of the general, but instead chose to be disarmed by them. He promoted Zia to army chief over the heads of half a dozen senior and more deserving generals. Zia did not rest there—he did not let go a single opportunity to further ingratiate himself with Bhutto. When Major General Tajammal Hussain Malik remarked to his staff officer, Colonel (later Major General) Aslam Zuberi, that Allah enjoins the believers to remove an unjust ruler, the officer lost no time conveying the conversation to Zia, who in turn recommended to Bhutto that the general, being a practicing Muslim, should be considered a threat and immediately retired from the army. Bhutto endorsed the recommendation and the general was put to pasture.[8]

In instances where Zia did not have an opportunity to further insinuate himself under Bhutto's skin, he was not slow to create one. This happened in the case of Brigadier Saadullah Khan during military operations in Baluchistan. The brigadier had an outstanding military career. He passed out of the military academy with the Sword of Honor and was considered among the best officers of his generation. During the civil war in East Pakistan he had a policy of zero tolerance for those under his command charged with any offense having to do with harassing the civilian population. He was one of the few senior Pakistani officers to be genuinely respected by the Bengalis. For courage during a military operation he was recommended for Pakistan's highest gallantry award, but because tradition has reserved this only for the dead, he had to be satisfied with the second-highest. In Baluchistan he was most effective in dealing with the hostiles who had taken to the hills. It was his standard practice to have a vehicle full of rations follow him when traversing the countryside, to be distributed among the families of the men who were fighting the Pakistan Army. He believed this was the only way of winning the civil war. This gained him the respect and the confidence of the hostiles, who surrendered to him in increasing numbers. Unfortunately, this also gained him the envy of his peers, some of whom had good connections with the General Headquarters (GHQ) of the army. One evening the brigadier received a signal terminating his service without assigning any reason. He was asked to hand over his command within twenty-four hours. It was Zia who had recommended this action to Bhutto on the grounds that the Brigadier was a deeply religious officer, and therefore someone to be wary of. Brigadier Saadullah Khan was indeed deeply religious. He was a practicing Sufi. All his time was divided between prayers and the profession, but he sternly disallowed any discussion on any aspect of religion, believing this to be a matter strictly between man and his God. But for Zia, he was a dangerous man due to his religious convictions.

Lieutenant General Faiz Ali Chishti, one of the most senior generals, who closely worked with Zia during the Bhutto days, intriguingly believes that someone was carefully tutoring Zia on how to win over Bhutto, and he further argues: "It is possible that the CIA got hold of him when he was training in the U.S. I wonder why General Zia made friends with Mrs. Herring, an honorary Consul of Pakistan in Houston, Texas. Maybe Zia's stay in Jordan took him closer to the CIA and the fundamentalist Muslims of Saudi Arabia."[9] Linking Chishti's opinion with that of George Crile's information is quite interesting. George Crile in his insightful book *Charlie Wilson's War* maintains that Joanne Herring "is said to have been Zia's most trusted American adviser."[10]

Anyhow, when Zia imposed martial law in July 1977, the army and the anti-Bhutto elements, primarily religious parties, were solidly behind him. However, Zia was not the sort of man who would burn down any bridge if there was half a chance of using it sometime in the future. He personally went to call on the deposed Prime Minister Bhutto, apologized to him, and explained that matters had gotten so far out of hand that he really did not have a choice but do what he had done. He further assured him: "In ninety days I will hold new elections. You will be elected Prime Minister again, of course, Sir, and I will be saluting you."[11] But on the other hand, in his first address to the nation, delivered on July 5, 1977, he had asserted that, "Pakistan, which was created in the name of Islam, will continue to survive only if it sticks to Islam. That is why I consider the introduction of [the] Islamic system as an essential prerequisite for the country."[12]

Thus on the very first day of the coup, Zia opened for himself a window of opportunity, which he was determined to keep open as an option. At this early stage, the casual observer had no real idea what was on the general's mind, but two things seemed to be certain. One, that his assurance to Bhutto that in ninety days he would again be prime minister and that he would again be saluting him was given only because Zia, on the basis of intelligence reports, believed that Bhutto couldn't win the coming elections. And second, that the Islamic passion and sentiment that had pervaded the anti-Bhutto agitation had been taken note of by Zia, and he would be sure to exploit it to his own advantage if such an occasion were to arise. That such an occasion was upon him already would have been amply clear to him when he met Bhutto. Reacting to Zia's humility, Bhutto drew all the wrong conclusions from it and allowed his bruised ego to go on the offensive. He reminded the general that the constitution provided for a death penalty for anyone trying to overthrow the government,[13] and though the latter protested vehemently that he had intervened only reluctantly, having no other choice, Bhutto had already taken the first irrevocable step of talking his way into the noose. Bhutto had forgotten that this was not the same Zia who had kowtowed his slimy way to the top, and that now the roles were reversed. He still believed that he would somehow manage to scare Zia into reinstating his government. He was only partially right. He did indeed scare Zia, but only managed to spook him in the wrong direction. Zia was a sane man—too sane as a matter of fact. He knew his looks came out second-best when compared to Bhutto's, but he was also quite clear that if one of the two heads were to be saved, he would vote for his own.

Two weeks later, Zia released Bhutto. He was free to prepare for the elections that were to be held "90 days" hence. Then all of a sudden the situation seemed to be turned on its head. Bhutto was being received by large enthusiastic crowds wherever he went.[14] These crowds were larger and more spontaneous than those arranged through the party auspices during the recently aborted elections. Among both the urban and rural poor, Bhutto seemed to have retained his immense popularity. But this was to work to his fatal disadvantage. Zia and his generals had plainly miscalculated. Indeed, the enthusiastic reception of Bhutto by large multitudes seemed as much of a revelation to him as it was to the army. The generals were no longer certain that Bhutto would lose the next elections. Indeed, it seemed likely that he would win easily. Something needed to be done, and in a hurry. Soon Bhutto was charged with conspiracy to murder Nawab Ahmed Kasuri, father of Bhutto's estranged friend and former Pakistan People's Party (PPP) leader Ahmed Raza Kasuri. For this he was picked up by police on September 3, 1977.

During the six weeks he had been out campaigning, Bhutto did not quite hide the plans he had for the generals when he would return to power.[15] On October 1, 1977, Zia postponed elections indefinitely. He also let it be known that during the preceding few weeks, the government had unearthed from official files countless instances of corruption and abuse of power by Bhutto and his government,[16] which had finally opened his eyes to reality. Soon the emphasis shifted from the elections to accountability, but lurking behind the promise of accountability was that of the Islamization of Pakistan, and Zia's quest for legitimacy and, perhaps, immortality. To this the public response was mixed. One single man's interpretation of Islam threatened the faith of many, and the minorities were especially apprehensive of being reduced in status to second-class citizens.

On the domestic front, on March 18, 1978, the Lahore High Court found Bhutto and four other Federal Security Force (FSF) men, who had allegedly executed the plan on Bhutto's instructions, guilty of murder and sentenced them to death. In Pakistan's judicial history, there was no precedent for awarding a death sentence in such a case. Ironically, Mahmud Masud, Bhutto's handpicked director general of FSF, turned a "state approver" by confessing that Bhutto had directly instructed him to kill Kasuri. By virtue of this "status," he escaped any punishment and left Pakistan to live an anonymous life in the United States. But Bhutto was still undeterred from threatening Zia. From the death cell he wrote to Zia: "Politics is not the illegal seizure of state machinery . . . politics is the soul of life. It is my eternal romance with the people . . . you and your coterie [have] no right to take away my spiritual and imperishable links with the beloved people of my country. . . . General, please do not overstep the bounds under the intoxication of power. . . . We will meet one day. You pursue me now. Wait till I pursue you."[17]

The only thing that could have saved Bhutto from being hanged after this was a possibility of a violent reaction from the people of the country. Strangely, despite the proven support Bhutto enjoyed among the poor of Pakistan, there was little street protest to save his life.[18] It was generally rumored that many senior leaders of Bhutto's party would rather have a dead Bhutto than a live one—the former would make a convenient martyr while the latter would make a terrible inquisitor and judge.

On February 2, 1979, the Supreme Court of Pakistan rejected Bhutto's appeal by a four-to-three verdict. Technically this divisive decision should have been grounds enough for Zia to have Bhutto's sentence commuted to life. Zia thought otherwise. While talking to a senior bureaucrat, Roedad Khan, Zia exposed his fears by admitting that "it's either his neck or mine."[19] Hence, Zia rejected all appeals for clemency from world leaders, including that of the U.S. president and Congress, and the clock started to tick for the countdown to the hanging.

Earlier, when Bhutto was told that he would be hung on the morrow, at first he did not believe it. Only when his wife and daughter were allowed their farewell visit to him did the gravity and imminence of the situation finally begin to sink in. He then told his wife to file a mercy petition on his behalf with Zia. He would still not beg for clemency himself. But a while later he asked for his shaving kit—he said he wanted to look good when dead. Soon it was time to go. It was suggested to him that, since he was weak, it would be best if he embarked on his last journey on a stretcher. He refused and walked until he could no more. There he addressed the jail warden and said he was sorry that on occasion he had caused him unnecessary problems. His last words were that the handcuffs were uncomfortably tight, and he asked if someone could loosen them. By then Tara Masih, the official hangman, had pulled the lever, and Zulfikar Ali Bhutto had passed into the ages. *The Economist* aptly wrote: "The quality of the evidence was highly questionable. The prosecution witnesses were a shady bunch. But the task set for the justices by the soldiers who have ruled Pakistan since last July's coup was quite clear: Mr. Bhutto must be removed."[20]

A decade and a half later, a disclosure by the former chief justice of Pakistan, Mr. Naseem Hasan Shah, one of the judges who adjudicated Bhutto's case, gives a clear idea of the reasons behind the controversial verdict: "The higher courts faced the threat of complete closure in the event of a decision against the will of the Martial Law regime."[21]

Meanwhile, Pakistan's relations with the United States continued to go downhill. Here Pakistan found itself in double jeopardy. It was not only refusing to toe the U.S. line on the nuclear issue but had once again fallen to a military dictatorship. This was not likely to enamor Pakistan well with President Jimmy Carter. When the new Indian prime minister was warmly welcomed at the White House in July 1977, followed by Carter's return visit to New Delhi the following January without stopping over at Islamabad, the message to Pakistan was clear and bitter: the United States would much rather woo the regional boss of the area, which India was and Pakistan was not. In these circumstances the United States tried to cajole Pakistan into signing the Nuclear Nonproliferation Treaty. Having already removed the offer of the A-7 bomber as an incentive to build up its conventional deterrent, it is little wonder that Pakistan refused. In March 1979, Warren Christopher, the U.S. deputy secretary of state, had stopped by at Islamabad to alert Zia to the possibility of suspension of American economic aid under the Symington Amendment to the Foreign Assistance Act unless Carter received reliable assurances that Pakistan was not pursuing nuclear weapons development. Zia assured Christopher that the Pakistani nuclear program was at least as "peaceful" as India's, and he failed to rule out an equally "peaceful" nuclear test. He also refused to accept international safeguards at Pakistan's nuclear facilities.[22]

In April 1979 the United States decided to cut off economic aid to Pakistan, as warned a month earlier. What really cut deep and wounded Pakistan was that India, which had introduced nuclear weapons in South Asia, instead of being punished, seemed to be having its efforts rewarded by the United States. To the Pakistanis this was an American betrayal, coming as it did coated with insult. A few months later, when it was revealed that a U.S. interagency task force under the direction of the State Department's Gerald C. Smith was considering an attack on Pakistan's nuclear facilities as one of the options to terminate its nuclear program,[23] the surviving vestige of pro-U.S. sentiment among the Pakistanis seemed stamped out. It was difficult for Pakistanis to understand how the United States could dump an ally of long standing and embrace its most rabid adversary without any apparent shame or compunction.

In 1979, when the general was squirming in the uncomfortable slot of an international pariah who had just hanged his prime minister, he was hell-bent on making the nuclear bomb but did not have the money to feed his people. Suddenly and without notice to the CIA, the Shah of Iran was swept away in the tide of the Khomeini revolution. This left an important vacancy for an American ally in the region. But before the Americans had recovered enough to cast anything resembling an amorous glance in its direction, Pakistan's relations with America had to reach their lowest point. On November 21, 1979, Zia decided to take a bicycle ride around town to popularize this form of locomotion. This was the day that news of the takeover of the Ka'aba (the house of Allah) in Mecca had swept Pakistan. And while the entire security apparatus in the capital had dedicated itself to the protection of Zia and his bicycle, he decided to visit a downtown market place in Rawalpindi, where in response to a question on the Ka'aba takeover issue, "intentionally or inadvertently, Zia answered that according to some international radio transmissions, the Americans had inspired the attack."[24] People responded with cries of "Allah O Akbar" (God is great); "Down with America"; "Zia ul-Haq Zindabad" (Long live Zia); and "Embassy Chalo" (Let's go to the U.S. embassy).[25] Soon processions from Rawalpindi moved toward the U.S. embassy in Islamabad while the students at the Quaid-i-Azam University in Islamabad, under the student wing of the JI, had also concluded that America was somehow involved in the events at Mecca. They marched on the U.S. embassy in Islamabad and lay siege to it. Then, climbing over the walls and smashing everything in sight, they set fire to the building. Two Americans and two Pakistani employees of the embassy died in the carnage. None of the U.S. officials could reach anyone in the Pakistan hierarchy capable of making a decision, because the attention of all the decision-makers lay focused on Zia's bicycle. The army barracks were a mere thirty-minute drive from the embassy, but the troops took a good four hours to come to the rescue of the besieged. The United States therefore had good reason to believe that if the entire show had not been organized by someone in the government, it was nonetheless not too averse to seeing the Americans in a bit of a soup. Few were willing to see in this the soaring incompetence of a degenerating army. But luckily for Pakistan, before the ramifications of this incident could reach their natural conclusion, all hell broke loose when in December 1979 the Soviet Army marched into Kabul. All of Zia's rich range of faults and many sins lay immediately forgotten. Almost overnight, his became a Cinderella story. From the ranking object of international disparagement, he was transformed into the most eligible, though hard to get, heiress.

In the domestic context, getting rid of Bhutto was easy for Zia; the difficulty was, what he would do on the day after? He had a well-thought-out plan in mind for that, however. It did not take him long to hijack the Islamic slogan of the anti-Bhutto agitation and make it his very own. He eased snugly into a situation that was tailor-made for him, because he was the one person who could beat the mullahs at their own game. But he was no great "fundamentalist." Throughout his army career he had befriended many a hard-drinking officer and kept up such friendships till his dying day. He was a practicing Muslim more due to force of habit than temperament. He did not have the sort of commitment to religion that compels one to look down on the nonconformist, though if the political situation or his own interests should require it, he was quite prepared to look down on anyone—or up to anyone for that matter. Indeed, he seemèd totally committed to the formal and visual performance of all religious rites while being quite flexible on the deeper issue of morality itself.

The three brigadiers he had removed from command for refusing to fire on unarmed civilians in Lahore during the anti-Bhutto agitation were compulsorily retired and thrown out of the army after he had pulled off the coup and was all-powerful. It did not seem to bother him at all that most of the handpicked officers that he had raised to senior positions were so obviously corrupt. Womanizing was one thing he never indulged in and was most unforgiving of in others, it was widely believed, but yet, even in this core belief he could be very accommodating when it involved his favorites. There is the story, gleefully told by his detractors, about two of his generals being chased from a house of ill repute and barely making it to their staff car. Unlike the three brigadiers retired for refusing to fire on unarmed civilians, these generals suffered no injury to their careers.[26]

Zia knew the army well, and unlike the dictators who preceded him, he was not in any hurry to retire loads of senior officers perceived to be unreliable. The only officer he retired after the coup was Brigadier Imtiaz Ali, Bhutto's military secretary; and he merely sidelined Major General Abdullah Malik, Bhutto's handpicked chief of the general staff, and denied him further promotion, but was confident enough to give him command of an infantry division. Zia managed to keep his generals ultimately in line by the simple device of surrounding them with staff officers of his choice. Thus the general he posted as the head of the military secretary's branch, responsible for all postings and transfers, was one in whom he had complete trust. Similarly, he selected his director generals of Military Intelligence (MI) and the Inter Services Intelligence (ISI) with equal care and deliberation. Zia was therefore never unduly worried about the applecart being upset from within the army and did not ever need to resort to a night of long knives.

But with all the confidence Zia had in himself and the power he exercised over the army, he ended up destroying the established norms of the institution. It was "the first instance in Pakistan's history when the ruling generals openly declared themselves to be conservative-Islamic in their orientations and cultivated close ties with the political groups of the right."[27] Officers tried to outdo each other in an attempt to be seen at congressional prayers in the mosque that Zia was known to frequent. This brought a sea change in the recruitment of the officer corps. Increasingly, the best sons of the traditional military families gave up joining the army; those that were already serving started to leave; and those that wanted to join nevertheless were increasingly rejected by the selection boards. Over a period of time the military selection boards had come to be dominated by inferior officers who culled and threw out candidates whose backgrounds suggested privilege, superior education, and moderation of religious views. In one particular year the principal of Aitchison College, Lahore, one of the premier and elitist educational institutions in Pakistan, was moved to write to the army chief that twenty-six of his boys had applied for the army and that all twenty-six had been rejected. He made it clear, though, that he was not making a case for the selection of all twenty-six of his boys, but merely against the rejection of all of them.

Zia indeed had a limited commitment to excellence. An inside story of promotion of an officer to the rank of general adequately sums up Zia's criteria for the rank and the respect he had for the institution on which he inflicted such generalship.[28] The case is of an armored corps officer who was not believed to reach beyond the rank of a lieutenant colonel, but Zia had helped him crawl through to brigadier. When his name came up at the promotion board for becoming a general, Zia saw his dossier, looked far away, and remarked: "How life passes. It seems only yesterday when this officer's daughter was just a little girl, and only last week I attended her wedding. Next!"[29] With this, the next dossier came up for consideration. The brigadier stood promoted to major general on the solid grounds that life passes so fast.

The closest to Zia, and the most influential in running the Pakistan of the day, were General Khalid Mahmood Arif and Mr. Ghulam Ishaq Khan, the ultimate bureaucrat. The general belonged to what came to be called "the Jalandher

Mafia," that is, those like Zia who were refugees from East Punjab (India) and especially favored by the president. A tall, humorless officer who exercised absolute economy of speech, Arif had pretensions of being a poet and an intellectual as well, and was the quintessential staff officer, who had commanded a brigade for only eight months. From there onward, all rules were bent for him so that he received rapid promotions without commanding anything, till he was promoted to full general, and his next de facto command was that of the whole Pakistan Army. And though no scandal of corruption brought taint to Arif's name, it is difficult to assess how much his silence contributed to the degradation of his country and the army.

Ghulam Ishaq Khan was given the splendiferous title of secretary general-in-chief to the government of Pakistan. He was an austere Pathan who had started his remarkable career from the lowest rung of the bureaucratic ladder and reached the very top through sheer industry. Apart from prayers and work, he had no other employment for his waking hours. He too had a reputation for honesty, though by a queer coincidence two of his sons-in-law managed to do exceedingly well for themselves with relatively sparse effort, while one of these (Irfanullah Marwat) lived well above the law and brought eminence to all that is disgraceful and cheap—the old man had indeed a lot to pray for. Ishaq Khan was also known for reading every file from cover to cover, and his knowledge of rules and regulations was so exhaustive that his detailed notations and observations on these files, and the clarifications he routinely asked for, ensured that if he was part of any decision-making chain, files just kept moving back and forth, with few cases ever getting settled. Of this ruling triumvirate of Zia, Arif, and Ishaq Khan, it was said that the loquacious Zia always said "yes," the reticent Arif said nothing, and the ascetic Ishaq always said "no," so that they managed to achieve a perfect balance on every issue, so that Pakistan stood still while the world moved on.

The last arrival in the blessed circle of ultimate influence was General Akhtar Abdur Rahman, the head of ISI—Pakistan's "silent" soldier who started to speak to his countrymen from beyond the grave through his posthumous biography, when his sons commissioned a retired brigadier to recast him in the mold of a hero, since he had already achieved his first target of becoming a multimillionaire while still alive. General Akhtar, another member of the infamous "Jalandher Mafia," was probably the most disliked senior officer in the army. He had the reputation of bowing low to everyone higher, as if to accentuate his humility through difference in elevation, and of crushing everyone lower in rank to himself. He struggled through the danger zone of supercession (a junior getting promoted over his head) in every rank after that of lieutenant colonel and eventually found himself a full general under the patronage of Zia. When the Afghan war started and funds started to pour in from the United States to the ISI, he was chosen by Zia to head this organization. By the time the war ended, he shone with unrivaled brilliance in the galaxy of those on whom fortune has unexpectedly and unaccountably smiled.

It is not known if General Akhtar had heard of J. Edgar Hoover or his methods, but sometimes he did make it convenient for senior officers to read embarrassing details in their dossiers. These were the fortunate ones. After reading about themselves, they were normally promoted. The unfortunates were those who had nothing to read. They were thrown out—just as it should be in an army that places a high emphasis on education. In reference to corruption, Air Marshal Anwar Shamim, chief of the air force, was another example. It is widely believed in Pakistan that the latter had ascended heights of corruption never before reached by anyone in uniform, and seemed ever committed to improving upon his mark. This compelled Air Commodore M.M. Alam, a fighter ace and a hero of the 1965 war, to arrange a personal interview with Zia and expose the scandal. Alam was sent into forced retirement for not having followed proper channels in registering his complaint against a senior officer! And the air marshal went on to better his mark after being granted an extension of service. After completing the extension, he went into comfortable retirement in the United States.

Still, Zia was not very comfortable. After all, he had mounted a coup against an elected prime minister and then hanged him. Though the courts had given his military coup legitimacy by citing "doctrine of state necessity," he was only too aware that mere necessity would wear thin with time. He therefore needed not just a onetime act, but a process that would give him continued relevance as the initiator of a larger "necessity." Thus, from the anti-Bhutto agitation he picked up the slogan of Islam and initiated the Islamization of Pakistan. Since he knew that none would muster the courage to challenge the legitimacy of religion, he mingled with it his own legitimacy so the two became inseparable.

The religious parties worked hand-in-glove with Zia in this project. On their part they hoped to use Zia for their own purposes, have him do all the dirty work, take responsibility, and then hand everything over to them when all was in order. By July 1977 a martial law regulation had already decreed the imposition of Islamic punishment for crimes like theft, robbery, and dacoity (robbery by a band or a gang).[30] Leaders of Jamaat-i-Islami (JI), a well-organized and disciplined party of the right, were Zia's favorites in this endeavor. JI had a very select membership of less than a few thousand strong—full membership in JI was given only after years of proven service to the party, but it had thousands of adherents, mostly among the student community, many of whom were toughs adept at strong-arm tactics. They were known to break any law for political purposes, but seldom for personal gain. Their transgressions were not those of common criminals, but harassment of political opponents was their favorite pastime. Their senior leadership, however, was generally educated, selfless, and free from the taint of corruption. The problem was that they were without mass support and had already given up any hope of securing power through the ballot. Hence they adopted the position that they would first bring about a revolution in the thinking of Pakistanis and then achieve political power. Their unstated and most logical hope was that they would be carried home to power on the shoulders of an "adherent." Their time seemed to have come. Zia seemed to fit the role perfectly.

In the initial months after the takeover, JI's support of Zia was of critical importance. JI was the only party with a committed cadre of loyalists that stood in readiness to counter and blunt any anti-Zia agitation launched by any political force. It was for this reason that when Zia banned all political activity, JI was the only party allowed to carry on unhindered. Its press was immune from censorship and its penetration of the media, the bureaucracy, and even the army was looked upon with approval by Zia. No less important was the virtual capture of most of the university campuses in Punjab Province by JI's student wing, the Islami Jamiat-i-Tulaba (IJT). To Zia, the advantage that accrued was that these very important centers of potential agitation came to be denied to his opponents.

Apart from the JI, Zia tapped into a host of *Pirs* (saintly men) and ulema, who may or may not have had their own political parties but who collectively had a huge following nevertheless. Not till they started to creep out of every nook and cranny for the numerous conferences Zia arranged for them was it realized that Pakistan was so richly endowed with divines! For the while that such a conference lasted, the protocol and the media coverage accorded to them had the effect of stealing the limelight from organized religious parties. Through such forums he deflected the Islamization debate into the sterile expanse of nonissues. For example, a great deal of time was spent debating whether government servants should be compelled to sprout beards; whether the flag of the country should be altered to give it a more Islamic look; or if Pakistani women ought to be allowed to compete in games with their trousers on, or if it would be more appropriate for them not to step on to the sports field altogether, and so forth.

The army's role was also redefined in the process. They were no longer to be merely the defenders of the borders, but also defenders of Pakistan's "ideological frontiers"[31] as defined by Zia. Lip service to outward religious forms increasingly displaced professionalism as a standard of judging merit. As mentioned earlier, in selection boards for officer candidates, religious knowledge became a determinant for selection in place of secular general knowledge. While considering officers for higher promotion, their social habits (as distinct from morality) came under minute scrutiny. The intelligence agencies, already woefully incompetent, abandoned their prime responsibility to become small-time snoops in a game of pure sleaze. The combined effect of all this signaled a quantum shift in priorities. What suffered was the pride officers and soldiers once took in their profession. Dissimulation, hypocrisy, and deceit flowed in to fill the vacuum.

All this was used by Zia with great adroitness to prune and cull the officer corps of such officers as he and his cronies considered undesirable. For example, among the major generals, Shah Rafi Alam enjoyed the most respect among the rank and file, and so was the case with Khurshid Ali Khan. And long before they were due for promotion, it was common knowledge in the army that both would be ignored for the next rank because they failed to meet the very stringent servility standards of the day and refused to give up their scotch at night. And there was little surprise when both failed to rise any higher. But most instructive of the atmosphere then prevalent in the army is the case of Major General Naseer Ahmed, a soft-spoken officer who was known for integrity and for not allowing nonsense to go unchallenged, irrespective of its source; while a tradition of bootlicking had so established itself that all nonsense issuing from one of higher rank was treated as wisdom. If the parent of the nonsense was Zia, there was an added premium on it and it was elevated to divine wisdom. Naseer had the capacity to revolt in such circumstances, at least verbally. With Zia and Naseer in the same room, therefore, the potential for combustion was always there. During one such conference the horns of the two got inevitably locked, to the mortification of Zia and the great embarrassment of all the others present. When the affair ended and Naseer was the first to leave the conference room in disgust, one of the lackeys attempted to lower the temperature by explaining to Zia that ever since sustaining a head injury in an accident, Naseer had not quite been himself and that therefore he did not always know what he was saying, that is, that he was given to speaking his mind only because he was soft in the head! All present seemed pleased with this explanation, depicting truth as an advanced form of madness, and nodded in grave assent. Naseer, who was also a war hero, could not get a further promotion in the army.

The army had already very nearly become a personal fiefdom. With the relegation of professionalism to an even lower rung in the list of priorities, it had taken a giant step toward degenerating into a militia. Zia had a gift for using power to greater effect than all his predecessors and therefore reduced more comprehensively the standards and stature of every institution he touched. And he touched all of them. But it was for the army that he had reserved the bear hug.

Concurrently with all of the above and as the raison d'être of the regime, the "Islamization" of Pakistan proceeded apace. The major focus of this was "regulative, punitive, and extractive."[32] Very little attempt was made to project other aspects of Islam, that is, social and economic egalitarianism, and accountability of those in power, and thus the socioeconomic structural bases of the existing power arrangements remained unaltered.

As the memory of what Jinnah had stood for gradually faded, Pakistan began increasingly being called an ideological state. But there was no single definition of this, and it meant all things to all people. Zia now proceeded to supply such a definition by giving the country an Islamic character according to his own lights and those of the school of Islamic thought that he subscribed to. This was the Deobandi school,[33] which closely resembles the Wahhabi Islam practiced in Saudi Arabia, whose staunchest supporters in Pakistan were few in number to begin with. Only a small minority in Pakistan adhered to this puritanical school while the great majority followed the Sufi traditions of Barelvi[34] Islam. So when Zia started the process of Islamization, unconsciously he also set into motion a parallel process of converting the already converted—the Barelvis into Deobandis. Ian Talbot, a historian of note, aptly maintains that "the greatest tension of all was between the state's legalistic imposition of Islam and the humanist traditions of Sufism."[35] This was to lead to disastrous results, putting bigotry and intolerance at a premium. Not only did it divide the country along lines of minority and majority sects, it divided the majority into mutually hostile factions of their own.

Zia started with the introduction of certain Islamic laws; then introduced Islamic punishments as prescribed for certain offenses, altered the law of evidence to bring it in consonance with Islamic law as he interpreted it, and set up Islamic (*Qazi*) courts. He forgot that in itself any code of law is a dead letter and is only as good or as bad as its implementation. And if the judges were to be mercenaries, the police corrupt, and witnesses bought, no set of laws could bring order to society nor give it the relief it craved for. Luckily he seemed to have realized this in time, so that no Islamic punishment involving the cutting off of hands for theft or stoning a person to death for adultery was ever carried out, but because these punishments were part of the law, police bribe rates soared in proportion to the harshness of the new punishments because alleged offenders had no way of being certain if these would be invoked or not. Among the new laws, the Zina (sexual offenses) Ordinance was especially outrageous. The way this law was put into force, the very complaint of the poor victim became the equivalent of a confession to be compounded by medical examination, and perhaps a pregnancy. So never mind who did it—as long as it was proved that someone had done so was enough for the raped woman to be convicted for fornication. For the rape victim, therefore, the law provided every disincentive against reporting the crime.

Zia also introduced interest-free banking through a profit-and-loss sharing scheme with the banks. In practice, though, this amounted to interest and all went on as before. The Islamic tax of *ushr* on agricultural produce was also introduced, but since the collection and assessment of it remained with the same corrupt revenue officials, this occasioned no great difficulty that amiable negotiation could not solve. The result was that the only ones to benefit by it were these officials. But Zia had a problem when he introduced the *zakat* (Islamic charity) tax. When Zia made its deduction compulsory through the banks, the Shia minority sect rose up in protest. So the ever-resourceful president settled for a compromise—the Shias could give their *zakat* privately (and voluntarily), but the Sunni majority would have their tax deducted compulsorily through the banks. A safe and practical way was found around this as well. Some Sunnis routinely withdrew their balances from the banks a day before the annual date on which the tax was to be deducted and put them back the very next day, while others handed in declarations to the banks stating that they belonged to the Shia sect, and thus were exempt from compulsory deduction. There was great unity in diversity when it came to hanging onto money.

But laws aimed specifically against minorities could not be so easily circumvented. One such law, notorious for being "open to malicious abuse and arbitrary enforcement"[36] was the Blasphemy Law, which carried a mandatory sentence of death for anyone using derogatory remarks against the sacred person of Prophet Mohammad (PBUH). While drafting this law, it was conveniently forgotten that after the conquest of Mecca, the very same Prophet had decreed a blanket amnesty for all his enemies who had found refuge in the house of his most inveterate blasphemer, Abu Jahl. Such historical precedents were ignored while framing the laws, and in most instances a disputed or controversial incident was taken as the precedent on which to erect an inhuman law. The framers also forgot that in a country with such a tiny non-Muslim minority, as existed in Pakistan, such a law was totally unnecessary for no one would dare heap gratuitous insults on the person of the Prophet, and that any such law would only be used to hound the minorities. Zia introduced it nonetheless as a sop to the insatiable appetite of the intolerant mullahs, who never tired of calling Pakistan "the citadel of Islam," where Islam somehow was considered to be in perpetual "danger." The unfortunate victims of this law were mostly the poor, peaceful, and submissive Christian community of Pakistan. A few of them got charged under this law because of the parry-and-thrust nature of religious debate, which had become and remains the favorite pastime of the chattering classes—and so also, as a matter of fact, of those that do not chatter. A common course these exercises follow is that the Muslim interlocutor tries to prove the other faith wrong by quoting the Scriptures. When a Christian follows the same methodology, despite being careful not to transgress the bounds of the law, he frequently oversteps those of Muslim sensitivity, which in practical terms amounts to the same thing. And this means prison and a long wait for the rope. Most fortunately, the rope has yet not been reached, but this has made the wait of many interminable.

In most cases, however, the object of false accusation was much more mundane, that is, to falsely charge a Christian in order to settle an old score or usurp his property. In all such cases the judges, the police, and the public at large never doubt the innocence of the victim yet cannot gather the courage to protest against the outrage. This has been the bane of Pakistan. Its people have not been able to stand up for the rights of another, so that each has awoken to the danger of the gathering conflagration only when the fire has reached his own dwelling. People like Ms. Asma Jehangir, a leading Pakistani human rights activist, are an honorable exception. She and a few others like her are fighting the battle for the rights of the deprived in the face of threats of every kind, including murder.

The next law against minorities was aimed specifically at the Ahmedi community. In April 1984 Zia inserted sections 298-B and 298-C into the Pakistan Penal Code, which made it a criminal offence for Ahmedis to "pose" as Muslims, to "preach or propagate" their faith, or to use Islamic terminology or Muslim practices of worship. Thus, practicing the Ahmedi faith was practically made a criminal offense. As pointed out in previous chapters, there is no denying the fact that there is a serious theological difference between Ahmedis and all other sects of Islam vis-à-vis the finality of Prophethood in the person of Mohammad (PBUH), and for a great majority of Muslims there can be no compromise on this issue. Still, it does not mean that the Ahmedis' right to practice their version of religion can be taken away by force.

Pakistan's identity crisis finds its most eloquent expression in the case of Pakistan's only Nobel Prize–winner, Dr. Abdus Salam, who was highly respected both as a physicist and as a human being. As he gathered international recognition and honors, and the citizenship of many a Western country was on offer to him, he steadfastly refused to give up his Pakistani passport. In 1956 he came out with his two-component theory of the neutrino, which Wolfgang Pauli discouraged him from publishing and for which he later publicly apologized to him, because in 1958 two American physicists shared a Nobel Prize for the same theory, thus depriving Salam of the prize.[37] But in 1979 he shared the Nobel Prize (which would have been his second) with Steven Weinberg, for his unified electroweak theory.

There should have been jubilation in Pakistan, but there was little, because few came to know about it then. The state media never gave Salam due coverage, as he was an Ahmedi. The government, however, could not ignore him. In recognizing Salam, it had no way out but to officially honor him. Still, the government remained silent, and only when it was learned that India wanted to honor him did Zia finally invite him, pin a civil award on him, and get it over with. But his projected talk at Islamabad's Quaid-i-Azam University had to be canceled under threat of violence by the student wing of Jamaat-i-Islami.[38]

In addition, all references made by Salam to various Quranic verses during interviews were dutifully excised from various texts, because as a non-Muslim he was not supposed to have recourse to them! No monument, street, university, library, or classroom was ever named after him. *Takbeer*, the weekly publication of Jamaat-i-Islami, heaped abuse on Salam. This treatment by Pakistan meted out to one of its greatest sons, who had only bestowed honor upon his country, is an adequate though sad commentary on its confusion of identity. In this context, Pervez Hoodbhoy, a leading Pakistani physicist and writer, aptly remarks: "I have never been able to understand why he [Dr. Salam] was so dedicated to the country of his birth given that he was virtually ostracized there, being an Ahmedi."[39]

The judiciary was another institution severely affected by Zia's policies. Zia had decided to Islamize the courts before bringing any new laws onto the statute books. To begin with, he reconstituted the Council of Islamic Ideology by increasing the representation of the conservatives on this body, which was charged with advising the government on matters concerning Islamization and the review of all existing laws to bring them in conformity with Islamic injunctions. He then set up the *Shariat* (Islamic law) Bench in the High Courts of each of Pakistan's four provinces and also an Appellate Bench at the Supreme Court. Later the provincial *Shariat* Benches were done away with, and a Federal *Shariat* Court (FSC) was set up. And though this court could not hear petitions on constitutional matters and some other subjects, it adjudicated on all other petitions questioning the Islamic character of various laws and administrative matters. Later it was empowered to take *suo moto* notice of such cases as well. And because the president exercised considerable discretion in the appointments, terms of service, and transfers of the judges of this court,[40] he potentially exercised great influence over its judgments as well. It is significant that when the FSC declared that stoning to death for adultery was an un-Islamic sentence because it was not prescribed in the Quran, and it caused the mullahs to start a campaign against this ruling, Zia supported the mullahs. In May 1981 he reconstituted the FSC by making a constitutional amendment conferring upon it, with retrospective effect, the power of "review." Consequently, the government appealed the court's earlier judgment against stoning and had it reversed.

As for the other courts, Zia wasted no time bringing them to heel as well. He started right at the top—the Supreme Court of Pakistan. That was where Mrs. Nusrat Bhutto had filed her petition challenging the military takeover. The presiding chief justice (CJ) was a man whose term of office had been extended beyond superannuation by Bhutto through an amendment to the constitution. It was therefore apprehended that he might have a soft spot for the erstwhile prime minister. Zia promptly rescinded the concerned amendment so that the CJ found himself without a job. Next in line was the man who would have been the CJ, had his predecessor's term not been extended. So it suited all concerned, most of all the affected judge himself, that the latter be the new CJ. And this was done. But danger lights started to flicker when the High Courts started to assert their independence by striking down sentences handed down by military courts. Zia decided to act so that the suspect amiability of the courts was restored. In March 1981 he came out with a Provisional Constitutional Order (PCO) that tore to smithereens the entire fabric of the judicial structure. The Supreme Court and High Courts were rendered totally ineffective. Their judgments delivered against martial law decisions were annulled with retrospective effect. The PCO in an unprecedented fashion required all the judges of the four provincial High Courts and the Supreme Court to take a fresh oath of office, voicing their loyalty to the new constitutional order. Judges suspected of harboring treasonous ideas about the independence of the judiciary were not offered the new oath, while a few others, who had managed to keep parts of their spines intact despite the vicissitudes of Pakistani politics, refused to take it of their own will.[41] By this simple device Zia got himself a judiciary uniformly eager to please.

Concurrently with this, he kept on taking retrogressive strides on the Islamization front. As a shortcut to fulfilling the government's duty to provide affordable primary education to the poor, the regime opened about twelve thousand mosque schools all over the country. As expected, these were neither mosques nor schools, and their products were not aware of which slot in society they were being educated for. A disproportionate largesse from the zakat funds started to be dispensed to the religious seminaries, and their asnad (degrees) received government recognition of equivalence with college degrees, and young men holding these certificates were pronounced fit to preside over Qazi (Sharia) courts. This was the first formal recognition of the Madrasa network by the government. With financial infusion and official encouragement, this was to grow exponentially, and in time it was to become the nursery, and then the assembly line that would churn out tens of thousands of radicalized young men, some of whom would fight at the tail end of the Afghan resistance against the Soviets; others would provide the core element of the Taliban; still others would go on to fight the Indian Army in Kashmir; some would make terrorism a way of life in Pakistan, and eventually they would hold Pakistan hostage. Unknown to Zia, a young Mullah Omar would graduate from one of these seminaries to Islamize a wartorn Afghanistan, which would make Zia's efforts seem facetious by comparison.

Hard on the heels of Islamization came attempts to build up a nationalism that had neither direction nor definition. For instance, instructions were passed prohibiting the use of English as the language of instruction in schools. This created all sorts of confusion and was reversed only when it adversely affected the education of Zia's own children. Censorship against indecent exposure was enforced with vigor in a country where there was no such exposure. In one of the most bizarre but hilarious instances of puritanical zeal gone wild, an oaf in the television hierarchy went so far as to censor the image of the skirted figure of Popeye's girlfriend in the cartoon series. Probably the only reversion to liberalism in the Zia era was when this was discontinued and she was allowed to appear as clad in the cartoon, just the way Popeye liked her. And in a most blatant attempt to distort the truth, even the long-dead Jinnah was made to conform to Zia's jaundiced view of history when, on national media, Jinnah the secularist had now to be depicted as Jinnah the theocrat.[42]

Within a few years of Zia's rise to the top slot, he got so used to the propagation of his sham Islamization that he started to give the impression of a man with a mission, with faint outlines of an aura of a Messiah already dimly visible. A man who loves power, is already riding a tiger, and bears the conviction that Allah wants him to stay there can become a very ruthless man. Those close to him and not overawed enough to lose their powers of observation started to notice the new seriousness with which Zia had now started to take himself.[43]

In the political field meanwhile, the opposition political parties began to chafe under the puritanical burden of the regime, especially as it was being used to bar their rightful way to power. Persecution of PPP political activists had become a norm by then. The political leaders from various liberal and progressive parties repeatedly tried to hammer out sufficient unity to be able to translate their sentiments into an anti-Zia movement, but he frustrated them time and again by using the political wing of the ISI. Despite such efforts the opposition in February 1981 had succeeded in cobbling together the Movement for Restoration of Democracy (MRD) under the leadership of the PPP. In March its campaign had a promising start, but the ill-timed hijacking of a Pakistan International Airlines plane by Al-Zulfikar, an underground organization led by Murtaza Bhutto (son of the executed prime minister), which was supported by elements in Afghanistan, came to discredit the movement in Punjab, the largest province. Still the MRD movement was gaining strength in the country overall in the early 1980s, especially in Sindh Province as the PPP's popularity among the masses was still well entrenched.

Zia could not have maneuvered and managed all of this without the peculiar international political scenario in which he found himself within a couple of years after his military coup in 1977. After the Soviet invasion of Afghanistan in late 1979, Zia was wooed by the United States, which lost little time in giving him a makeover. And out came a different Zia. He was now a knight in shining armor at the forefront of a war in defense of freedom and democracy, which he redefined to suit himself. The Western nations had no quarrel with this as they were infinitely more concerned with stopping the Soviets in Afghanistan and, hopefully, of pushing them back. Zia knew their stakes well, and with this knowledge he resituated himself in the new equation, confidently elevating himself to the position of primacy. Never short of confidence, his new position could only add to his self-assurance. He was therefore not to be satisfied with accepting any crumbs from the West for the task to be assigned to him. So when President Carter upped his initial offer of $150 million to $400 million, Zia rebuffed it as "peanuts." If the pun was intended, he preferred to remain silent on the issue, smugly lapping up the odes to his wit. President Carter was once a peanut farmer from Georgia, but he was not too upset. Because of the altered situation, he had decided to overlook some of the uglier aspects of Zia's government. Zia, however, had realized that Ronald Reagan could very soon be the next president of America, and therefore any agreement with Carter would not really matter with the next administration; but if Carter were to be returned a second time, a minimal position was already on the table and negotiations could always be picked up from there. So when Zia met Carter in the White House in October 1980, he did not bring up the subject of U.S. assistance to Pakistan. This was left for the American president to do. And when Carter brought up the matter and informed Zia that he would be quite happy to include F-16 fighter aircraft in the aid package, Zia sidestepped the issue by saying that, since the president must be quite busy with the elections, discussion on that subject would be best deferred to another time.[44]

By then of course Zia had fully considered the situation in Afghanistan and taken a firm position on it. Knowing that the Soviets could create serious problems in Pakistan's Baluchistan and North-West Frontier Province (NWFP), and would certainly do so the moment they had fully settled in Kabul, he had decided to oppose them to the hilt. He would lead the diplomatic offensive against them, give shelter to the fleeing Afghan refugees, and provide clandestine military assistance to the Afghan resistance (the mujahideen) while publicly denying help. After the Shah of Iran had fled Iran, Zia allowed the CIA to set up an electronic eavesdropping facility in Pakistan operated by Pakistanis trained by U.S. intelligence,[45] and by July 1979 a limited amount of nonmilitary U.S. aid was starting to be funneled to the Afghan resistance through Pakistan. Pakistan was also leading the diplomatic charge against the USSR and had managed a resolution against it (that prevailed by a vote of 104 to 18) in the U.N. General Assembly—India being the only major country outside the Soviet orbit to have voted in favor of their Afghan adventure. Thus, no one had any doubt about where Zia stood on this issue. The only doubt that existed was how far he was committed to go in the direction he had chosen.

Zia himself had no doubt. He would go the whole hog, but for this the United States would have to loosen its purse strings sufficiently to make it worth his while; otherwise, being a practical and flexible man, he was quite capable of coming around to a deal with the Soviets. But it was the United States, Pakistan's traditional ally, that was to have the first right of refusal. Pakistan was clearly unsatisfied with the initial offers of the United States as not being worth the candle. And apart from assistance, Pakistan was also looking for a treaty commitment from the United States to counter the military threat from India, while the United States was not willing to go beyond the 1959 bilateral security agreement with Pakistan, with Warren Christopher insisting that an executive agreement had the same force as a treaty. Already Zia had decided that when and if an expanded American role in Afghanistan came about, he would not allow any direct contacts between U.S. intelligence and the Afghan resistance groups. The conduit of all material assistance would be the ISI in Pakistan, and in case any training was to be imparted to the Afghans, it would be ISI personnel who would receive such training from the Americans and then train the Afghans. This was the decision that led to the ISI becoming a large, clumsy, frequently blundering, hydraheaded monster of great influence in the 1990s.

In 1981, Ronald Reagan took the oath as the president of the United States. As all Republican presidents, he was bound to be popular with the people in Pakistan, and he did nothing to disappoint them. His position on Afghanistan was simple, clear, and total. He wanted the Soviets to suffer and then to get out of there, and he was not going to quibble on the price. This brought joy to Zia, whose position coincided exactly with Reagan's except that, when the Soviets left, he wanted to stay on in Kabul through a proxy of choice. This was to become the driving compulsion of Pakistan's Afghan policy, and it would eventually destroy all the goodwill it had created among the Afghans during their most trying days.

As for himself, he was quite clear that he too was opting to be a tool for the United States in its proxy war in Afghanistan. But in this he saw a coincidence of interest between Pakistan and the United States. This would make them allies, and they would remain such till the time these interests diverged. There was no idealism bringing this relationship about, and he knew what service he would be prepared to render in this partnership, how he would render it, and what he would charge for it. In view of past difficulties and misunderstandings, he was therefore not going to accept any vague promises from the United States. He wanted both sides to understand exactly what the relationship involved and what each side was committed to do for the furtherance of their joint objective. When General K.M. Arif and the foreign minister Agha Shahi were preparing to visit Washington to hammer out an understanding on the basis of which the two countries would cooperate, he instructed them not to get into any details till the issues of concern to Pakistan had first found accommodation with the U.S. administration. What he wanted was that the United States stop badgering Pakistan about its nuclear program or insisting on its return to democracy, and so forth; nor should it ask Pakistan for military bases that would compromise its nonaligned status; and to ensure that in the event of cooperation, the United States would not ask for direct access to the Afghan resistance, which would be controlled by Pakistan; and that the United States should sign a defense treaty with Pakistan to deter Indian aggression.

Arif and Shahi met Alexander Haig in Washington and got nearly all they had come to get. On the nuclear issue Haig gave them the impression that the new administration in Washington could live with Pakistan's nuclear program, but warned them about testing the nuclear device, which would likely take matters out of Reagan's hands and place them in the lap of Congress.[46] On the domestic front in Pakistan, he said that the U.S. government would not presume to advise Pakistan on the type of government it should have.[47] He did not bring up the subject of U.S. military bases in Pakistan and was quite amenable to the suggestion that U.S. military assistance to the Afghans should be channeled through the ISI. The U.S. government was so positive and forthcoming that the Pakistani delegation did not feel the need to press for a treaty against possible Indian aggression and dropped their demand on this matter. Reagan also pushed through a $3.2 billion aid package to be spread over five years and threw the F-16s into the basket as well. This was certainly more than the "peanuts" that Zia had earlier rejected and helped shore up his anticommunist commitment to make Pakistan the most allied ally of the United States all over again.

Way back in mid-1973, when King Zahir Shah of Afghanistan had been overthrown by his cousin Sardar Daud, it was a signal for Pakistan to expect trouble. Daud was a Moscow man, as pro-India as he was anti-Pakistan. He immediately revived the dormant Pakhtunistan issue, started to aid the rebels in Baluchistan, and refused to accept the Pak-Afghan border (the Durand Line) as drawn by the British. Concurrently with all this, he arranged for large quantities of arms to be smuggled from Afghanistan into Pakistan in addition to the bomb blasts that took place in the NWFP. This was Pakistan's first taste of terror on a major scale, and it was to be the beginning of an era of blood and cordite for the region as the two superpowers, vying for supremacy over the globe, chose to make it the battleground for their proxy war. This would eventually result in the final defeat of one of them while raising the other to a position of unrivaled primacy among the nations of the world. The inhabitants of the battlefield, though, would be used, abandoned, and pushed down the road to anarchy, and then perhaps nihilism. A stunned America would then naively ask, "Why do they hate us?"—but would steadfastly refuse to gather the moral courage to look the obvious answer in the face. It would resort to bombing the symptoms of the cancer implanted in part by them without addressing the cancer itself, and in so doing, it would further fortify its claims to supremacy while abandoning those to greatness.

Islamabad's response to Afghan belligerence was to organize an anti-Daud resistance around religious groups opposed to the anticommunist secular government in Kabul. Among these were two students who had escaped the Afghan secret police to flee to Pakistan—Gulbadin Hikmatyar and Ahmed Shah Masud, who were to find notoriety and fame, depending on which side one stood, over the next quarter of a century. Major General Naseerullah Khan Babar, then commanding the Frontier Corps, a paramilitary force, was the real father of this nascent resistance, which was as idealistic at this stage as it was ineffective. When the Soviets took over Kabul in 1979, this group became the responsibility of the ISI. And as military aid began to flow in, the Frontier Corps started to grow in size, organization, and effectiveness. The psy-war experts of ISI coined the slogans "Islam in Danger" and "Holy War" as apt motivation for the Afghan resistance against a godless foe, and the CIA could not have improved on this. Quite early on, Zia had already started to fund the seminaries whose graduates, he expected, would swell the ranks of his supporters. Now many of these foot soldiers of Islam would turn north for a tour of duty in Afghanistan, though most of the fighting was to be done by the indigenous Afghans themselves. And as the United States got Saudi Arabia to match its own contribution to the war effort on a "dollar for dollar" basis, the seminaries mushroomed and their output increased exponentially, as did the radicalization of Sufi Islam when the puritanical strain of Wahhabism from Saudi Arabia found fertile soil for conversion in the Deobandi seminaries. Thus the seeds of almost all such elements that could interact and grow into the radical anti-Western Islam we were to see in the new millennium had already been sowed. The only thing missing was anti-Westernism itself, the vital ingredient of the formula. And this seemed improbable at the time because the prevailing sentiment was pro-Western. Only indifference, selfishness, myopia, and incompetence of flawless pedigree could have reversed this. But Pakistan and the United States would combine to produce this missing ingredient and add it to the volatile mix of elements that was to split the world anew and array it along new battle lines.

The Islamization process and active support of the Afghan jihad also laid the foundation of violent sectarianism in Pakistan. When Zia had decided on the Islamization of Pakistan, the unspoken and unappreciated assumption was that the entire population would conform to an official version of Islam, where many schools of Islamic thought had flourished with tolerable accommodation through the ages. Emphasis on religious conformity was therefore to be a baleful novelty to be enforced by religious zeal, only to be opposed by the same zeal by those whose persuasions were different. This could only accentuate the already existing sectarian differences and widen them into deep chasms of intolerance and mutual exclusivity garnished by bloodshed and brutality.

Thus when Zia had introduced his first set of Islamic laws and made the deduction of the *zakat* compulsory, he opened the first fissure with the Shia minority sect of the country, who believe that although payment of *zakat* is obligatory on all Muslims, nevertheless the state has nothing to do with the enforcement of this obligation, which is a matter strictly between man and his God. They therefore saw the compulsion introduced by the state as something repugnant to Islam and opposed the measure with the same religious conviction by which it had sought to be imposed. Equal and opposite convictions can only be the death of harmony. The Shias feared that the majority would end up ramming their version of Islam down the throats of all the minority sects and force them to comply with laws that, according to their interpretation of Islam, they saw as being violative of Islamic injunctions. In response to these fears, they had already formed the Tehrik-i-Nifaz-i-Fiqh-Jafaria (TNFJ) in 1981, an organization dedicated to guard against infringement of their set of beliefs. So when the government announced the compulsory deduction of *zakat*, the TNFJ led a massive protest demonstration in Islamabad, which forced Zia to back down. But the seed of militant Shia-Sunni conflict had been sown. The Khomeini revolution in Iran had already bolstered the confidence of the Shias, and they were not about to take Sunni dictates in religious matters lying down. Hard-liners among Sunni, for their part, felt that such dictation was their right, and those on the extreme right of the Sunni spectrum simply cut the Gordian knot by taking a position that, correct or not, Pakistan had a Sunni majority and as such it should be declared a Sunni Muslim state in which Shias should be treated as a minority. Since the achievement of this holy goal would likely take some time, some of them decided that the interregnum ought not to be wasted. Thus in 1985 they formed the Anjuman Sipah-i-Sahaba (ASS)—an organization piously dedicated to ridding the country of the nettlesome presence of the Shias by eliminating them physically. Later, when they realized what the organization's acronym meant in English, they changed the name to Sipah-i-Sahaba Pakistan (SSP).

However, Zia was riding the crest. The darling of the free world led by America, he was in hot pursuit of leadership of the Muslim world and buoyed by the exhilarating thought that he was the chosen one of Allah taking one step after another that would make the Pakistan of the future ungovernable but his immediate position impregnable. American support and consequent aid for the prosecution of the Afghan war was mounting. In Bill Casey, the new boss of the CIA who was directing the U.S. part in this war, he found a "soul mate"[48] and an ally who was both powerful and effective. Whenever Zia wanted something from the United States or, as Bob Woodward says, "just needed someone to listen," Casey was his avenue.[49] World leaders were united in their praise for the Pakistani dictator. The ISI was never richer or more powerful. The *Madrasa* assembly lines had started to turn out gun fodder in increasing quantities. According to a retired Pakistani general, Kamal Matinuddin, Zia "established a chain of *deeni madaris* [religious schools] along the Afghan-Pakistan border . . . in order to create a belt of religiously oriented students who would assist the Afghan Mujahideen to evict the Soviets from Afghanistan."[50]

Donated by their parents at a tender age, these soldiers of God were crafted for one function alone—to kill the infidel communists or die trying, and view either outcome as the ultimate victory. It is hard enough to produce such men, and ten times harder to decommission them. But that was something their sponsors would learn in the future, and it was only the present that counted. In that present they were the ill-clad, lean, hungry, weatherbeaten heroes who were bleeding a superpower to a standstill. The number of Afghan resistance groups had been reduced from an unmanageable forty-plus to a more manageable "officially recognized" seven. Each had its headquarters in Peshawar. In theory they were given weapons and monetary aid in proportion to their fighting capability and effectiveness. In practice they got it in accordance with the "recognition" they received from the government of Pakistan. And this depended on religious belief. The greater the coincidence of this with Islamabad's (and Riyadh's) version of Islam, the greater was the recognition accorded. This formula for aid was dictated by what Zia and his principal henchmen chose to see as their "foresight"—the ambition to become the first "power" in four thousand years to rule Afghanistan through proxy by having its own man placed on the throne in Kabul. For this the selected proxy had to have the power and the credibility to keep and hold the power asserted on his behalf by Pakistan. To achieve this he needed an effective band of followers drawing their authority and power from victories won in the war. This aim led to Gulbadin Hikmatyar becoming the most recognized Afghan guerrilla leader (despite the fact that he had no tribal following of his own and drew nearly all his strength from the *Madrasas* through government sponsorship) while alienating Ahmad Shah Masud, the most brilliant Afghan general of the war. And that Hikmatyar was a Pashtun and Masud a Tajik also had a lot to do with this choice.

Despite ISI efforts to hammer out some semblance of unity among the mujahideen groups, or at least bring about some sort of coordination in their war effort, each group operated more or less independently, treating all others more with suspicion than trust. They fought their war organized primarily along tribal lines, pretty much following their traditional tactics of warfare when faced with a superior enemy—of sniping, of a series of hit-and-run operations, of raids and ambushes, and of occupying vacant sites of tactical value and then withdrawing in the face of Soviet advances, thus denying the enemy the opportunity of launching an attack, which suited its organization, training, and equipment. And with all this, the Afghans reserved a singular lack of mercy for those of the enemy unfortunate enough to be caught alive. For the first few years the ebb and flow of operations gave the impression of a fluid stalemate to the uncritical observer. But the Soviets were hurting. Their casualties were mounting and becoming unacceptable, as was the financial cost of the war, while the increasing toll of desertions was destroying morale. The United States, which was taking great pleasure at the discomfiture of the Soviets, soon got bored and wanted the Soviet pain to be consummated in the final humiliation of defeat and surrender. An impatient Casey wanted Zia to have the mujahideen effort redoubled, but a very patient Zia only redoubled the excuses why this was not possible. He was in no hurry, and what he was absolutely not prepared to risk was pushing the Soviets against the wall, even if there was half a chance that this would invite a direct Soviet retaliatory strike against Pakistan. His country was already bleeding and suffering grievously from Afghan and Soviet sponsored acts of terror against all manner of civilian targets, and it could not take any more punishment. He was therefore for keeping "the pot boiling," but not so much that it would boil over onto Pakistan.[51] In mid-1986 the mujahideen supporters in Washington, especially Congressman Charles Wilson, won the most important concession on their behalf when the U.S. government agreed to release shoulder-fired Stinger missiles to them. Thus far the Soviet gunship helicopter Hind was the one weapons system against which the Afghans were helpless and found themselves completely vulnerable. With the introduction of the Stinger in Afghanistan, a major shift in the balance of power occurred in favor of the mujahideen.

Besides handing out Stingers, renowned journalist and analyst Ahmed Rashid recounts two other major secret measures taken by CIA chief William Casey in 1986 that had a profound effect on the Afghan resistance movement:

1. The CIA, Britain's MI6, and the ISI also agreed on a provocative plan to launch guerrilla attacks into the Soviet Socialist Republics of Tajikistan and Uzbekistan, the "soft Muslim underbelly" from where the Soviets received their supplies.
2. Casey also committed CIA support to recruit radical Muslims from around the world to fight the Soviets along with the Afghan mujahideen. It was an ISI idea supported by the CIA. It worked out well as the U.S. "wanted to demonstrate that the entire Muslim world was fighting communism."[52]

As the arms supplies became more massive, large depots were located in Pakistan, but weapons intended to be used by Afghanis often found their way to the arms market. The Americans tolerated this regular siphoning off of aid passed across the border, the proceeds of which paid for a comfortable life for many resistance leaders in Peshawar. These leaders and the ISI are believed to have stolen and sold hundreds, even thousands of weapons from the CIA arsenal. According to Robert G. Wirsing's estimate, around 30 percent of the weapons never reached the destined points.[53]

On the domestic front, leading political parties and a good part of the international media were still raising the clamor for elections and a civilian parliament. Initially, Zia had decided to meet them halfway. He gave them a parliament without giving them elections. In 1981 he had already assembled a handpicked 350-member Majlis-i-Shoora (Assembly for Consultation). Charged with masquerading as an elected parliament, it became the most glorified debating society of the day, with its members elevating the trivial by bringing it to serious debate while being borne down in the process by their own self-importance. If all this made Zia smile under his mustache (he was never caught at it), the rest of the country clearly thought this was a joke in bad taste. So his quest for legitimacy was still on. The MRD movement as discussed earlier was also becoming increasingly problematic for the military regime. The next step he took to secure legitimacy was a presidential referendum in December 1984. It became famous for the wording of its proposition, which so packaged him with Islam that the voters opposing him could not do so without giving the appearance of voting against Islam itself, whereas voting for Islam constituted accepting him as president for the next five years.[54] On polling day, despite the booths being deserted, the official media announced that no less than 62 percent of the population had voted, of whom 97.71 percent had voted "yes" to Zia and Islam. The turnout was approximately 10 percent according to the credible newspaper *The Muslim* in its edition on December 20, 1984. The said issue was withdrawn from public circulation by the military regime.

He had now accumulated the confidence to bend a part of the way to accommodate the public demand for the holding of elections without appearing to be doing so under pressure. He promised elections for February 1985. These were to be free and fair but with a string of provisos. No political party was to be allowed to take part, and all candidates were to fight as independents; no processions of congregations were to be allowed during electioneering; and use of the loudspeaker was prohibited. Sharing the fear of the Caesars, Zia was not going to take the risk of allowing crowds to be formed whose frenzy could lead them anywhere. And if the PPP could not have the crowds, it did not want the elections, which it aptly named "deaf and dumb," and this could only have helped the president sleep all the better, for there was no dearth of eager candidates. And even if there was not going to be the usual din for the elections, there would be interest enough to divert public attention from more pressing matters. Finally, the newly elected National Assembly met on March 23, 1985. It was one keen, leaderless, and confused lot that did not know where to go from there on. As the king's candidate for the slot, the clean and docile Mohammad Khan Junejo from Sindh was given a vote of confidence by the house as prime minister. He was the man destined to play a highly significant role in determining Pakistan's position at the Geneva peace talks to bring the Afghan war to an end.

While Pakistan was at the forefront of doing all it could to assist the efforts of Afghan resistance while issuing equally strident public denials of being in any way involved in this, it was also at the forefront of the diplomatic offensive to bring an end to the Soviet occupation of Afghanistan. Zia already had some experience in diplomacy as a nominee of the Organization of Islamic Countries (OIC) charged with negotiating an end to the Iran-Iraq War. Pakistan had led the ensuing diplomatic offensive at the U.N. by marshaling the Islamic and nonaligned votes to condemn the USSR—and of course if in the same process India was also made to feel wretched, as the only democracy of the world in support of the Soviet occupation, all the better. As an additional prong to this effort, Pakistan urged the U.N. to initiate peace talks between the concerned parties to end the Afghan imbroglio. In 1981 the U.N. had initiated this process under the stewardship of Javier Pérez de Cuellar, who would later become secretary-general of the U.N. and hand over his Afghan assignment to Diego Cordovez. Despite the fact that there was little interest in these talks in Moscow, Kabul, or Washington, and that the Afghan resistance, not being a part of the process, treated them with antipathy, Pakistan still kept the pressure on and Cordovez never lost his optimism. By 1982, Geneva became the venue of these talks, and because Pakistan did not recognize the government in Kabul, the two negotiating teams never met face-to-face, which meant that Cordovez had to shuttle from one team to the other, and so carry these indirect negotiations forward. Because both the negotiating teams were housed in the same building, these came to be called "proximity" talks.

Zia's diplomatic skills and resources were stretched to the limit by India, with whom there was no proximity except in terms of geography. He wanted to be freed of concern with his eastern border to concentrate on Afghanistan, but Indian cooperation was wanting. Not only did India support the USSR's action verbally, it was actively involved in distracting Pakistan from its war effort in Afghanistan to the extent that circumstances would safely allow. There was also a suspicion in Pakistan that its elevation to the position of a frontline state, where it was hogging all the limelight, was not sitting well at all with Mrs. Indira Gandhi's ego, so that she was behaving like the proverbial toddler stretching for an out-of-reach candy bar. Zia did everything to normalize relations, but was rebuffed on every occasion. His offers of a no-war pact with India received a cool response, and his proposal to make South Asia a nuclear-free zone did no better. And when the traditional Indo-Pak animus found an outlet in the world's highest battlefield at Siachen, relations became so strained that in 1984 it was apprehended that India was preparing to launch an attack on Pakistan. In December 1985, Zia made a brief visit to India and met Indian prime minister Rajiv Gandhi, thereby initiating a dialogue process, but he failed to convince Rajiv to visit Pakistan as Rajiv wanted a step-by-step approach,[55] which meant a polite no or "wait and see" policy at best under the circumstances.

The Reagan administration, however, required no encouragement from him to start talks on Pakistan's nuclear program, and all comers down the well-worn path from Washington to Islamabad had plenty of good advice to give, to bring home to the Pakistani president the extent of apprehension with which lawmakers on Capitol Hill viewed his nuclear program. Notwithstanding Reagan's wink of convenience toward Pakistan in this matter, it was with great difficulty that on May 13, 1981, the Senate Foreign Relations Committee passed a six-year waiver on sanctions barring aid to Pakistan. But to emphasize the U.S. concern on the issue, Stephen Solarz got an amendment accepted that prohibited U.S. aid to any country detonating a nuclear device. At this time many in the United States had good grounds to believe that Pakistan was pursuing a nuclear weapons program with total dedication, but not many believed this dedication would lead to much, and perhaps there were a few who would rather have liked to believe this in view of Pakistan being indispensable to the war effort in Afghanistan. The unspoken American position seemed to be that as long as Pakistan went about its business quietly and resisted the temptation of doing something that would embarrass the United States, the administration could live with it.

Zia's nuclear policy was to pursue his weapons program full tilt while emphasizing its "peaceful" intent, and this policy was interspersed with outright denials of certain details of the program, as exemplified by General Vernon Walters' experience when he met Zia to discuss the issue. When the general showed Zia a satellite photograph of the Kahutta facility as proof that the United States knew more about Pakistan's nuclear effort than it suspected, Pakistan's president simply dismissed the photograph as being that of a "goat shed."[56] But it was the minder of this goat shed who created a major stir that was eventually to expose Pakistan's nuclear capabilities a couple of years later. Dr. Abdul Qadeer Khan, the father of Pakistan's nuclear program, who was known to be chasing after money and publicity as well, opened his mouth to a leading Pakistani newspaper, and when the story appeared in newspapers in early 1987, it sent a shudder all across. In it there was Qadeer's claim that Pakistan had already succeeded in enriching uranium to weapons grade level. To Pakistan's bad luck, within three months of this, three Pakistanis in America and two in Canada were arrested for illegally trying to export materials and equipment that could help advance Pakistan's nuclear program. Much as Pakistan ducked and denied any involvement in these activities, the performance was not good enough to impress the Americans.

Prior to this development, Senator John Glenn had argued with the U.S. administration that the waiver of sanctions in 1981 had removed all restraints on Pakistan, and as long as it abstained from exploding a nuclear device, it was left free to pursue the nuclear course without let or hindrance. He had therefore proposed an amendment to the foreign assistance act that would require the U.S. president to annually certify that Pakistan neither had the bomb nor was developing one for the aid to continue. The White House reacted to this by exerting strong pressure to make this amendment milder, so that the president would only have to certify that Pakistan did not possess a nuclear device and that U.S. assistance was advancing the goals of nonproliferation. Senator Larry Pressler, who was in no way involved in the issue of Pakistan's nuclear program, was asked to move this reworded amendment, which did not allow for a presidential waiver. Because Pakistan understood that this amendment was the result of the U.S. government's efforts to relax the stringency of the original proposal by Glenn, it heaved a sigh of relief. It overlooked the fact that once the Afghan problem was settled and Pakistan lost its frontline status, and the sympathy and support that came with it, this amendment would immediately be allowed to come into effect. Being Pakistan-specific, it would discriminate specifically against it, which would once again be tantamount to rewarding India for having brought about the nuclearization of South Asia while punishing Pakistan. And if this were to haunt Pakistan for years to come and give a major impetus to an anti-Americanism that had largely eroded due to U.S. assistance in the Afghan war, the pro-Indian senator Solarz pushed through an amendment in March 1985 that required the barring of U.S. aid to any country whose government (or any of its departments) illegally imported nuclear technology from the United States.[57]

At home, Zia's chief concern in 1985 was to negotiate an agreement with his newly chosen prime minister, so that in return for lifting martial law, the latter was to arrange to have the National Assembly pass such amendments to the constitution as would give Zia and his generals blanket immunity from any manner of prosecution for all acts of commission or omission after the July 1977 coup; mention him by name as the president of the country for the next five years while concurrently holding the appointment of the chief of army staff; and give him powers to dismiss the prime minister and the National Assembly. He got what he wanted through bribery, blackmail, and in some cases threats, and at long last lifted martial law in December 1985.

Mohammad Khan Junejo was a gentleman among the politicians of Pakistan who carried himself in a manner that behooved his high office. Being above corruption and nepotism made him a truly rare bird among those whose company would now be forced upon him in his capacity as prime minister. Tall, lean, and sober, he resembled an emaciated cat, hiding a diffident smile under his mustache. But it was his supposed docility that came to confound both friend and foe, and eventually this gave Zia apoplectic fits. He was his own man, and an honorable one at that, and since his firmness lay bound up in politeness instead of finding expression in loud bravado, he was expected to be weak. He first disappointed such expectations by becoming the first prime minister of the country to dismiss three of his ministers on grounds of corruption. But having no party support in a house of individuals, all elected independently, he had to compromise in order to build any semblance of a parliamentary group in support of the government. This came in the form of distribution of pelf, privilege, and patronage, a precedence that was to have most unfortunate consequences when it went into embrace with the unfettered avarice of future political leaders of Pakistan.

With Zia, Junejo's first clash came over the issue of promotions in the army when Zia promoted one general while he sat on the papers of another with remarkably similar credentials. Major General Pirdad Khan was promoted to lieutenant general by Zia, but he deferred a decision in the case of Major General Shamim Alam Khan. Both were equally qualified: both had served in the elite Special Services Group; and both had the same decoration for gallantry. Junejo made clear that it would have to be promotion for both or neither, and the president had to back down and both officers were promoted.

But the real locking of horns came over the terms on which each wanted to see an end to the Afghan war. At the start of the war, Zia would have considered himself blessed if the Soviets could be held on the Afghan side of the Pak-Afghan border. But as the war progressed and Soviet defeat, or at least withdrawal from Afghanistan, began to loom as a distinct possibility, so Zia's ambitions started to soar. He was now thinking in terms of placing a firmly pro-Pakistan government in charge of affairs in Kabul and thus have a friend cover his back so that he could enjoy the rare luxury of being able to look India squarely in the face without having to look over his shoulder. Toward this end his government had strived mightily, unfairly, and injudiciously to build up Gulbadin Hikmatyar as the next ruler of Kabul.

As the Geneva talks moved forward, by about the autumn of 1987 there were indications that the impossible was fast becoming a possibility, and in a repeat of Vienna, for the second time in their recent history, the Soviets might actually be leaving a country under their occupation—though this time they needed a fair bit of thrashing to help them make up their minds. Then in December of the same year, Mikhail Gorbachev, the Soviet leader then on a visit to the United States, declared that his forces would withdraw from Afghanistan during the coming twelve months. At this point a divergence of Pak-U.S. interests manifested itself in the different expectations of each ally. The United States just wanted to see the USSR out of Afghanistan and did not much care what happened to the country after that, as is evident from the statement of the U.S. State Department's Michael Armacost: "Our main interest was getting the Russians out. Afghanistan, as such, was remote from U.S. concerns. The United States was not much interested in the internal Afghan setup and did not have much capacity to understand this."[58] This attitude was to lay the groundwork of a tragedy, the full ramifications of which cannot be measured or predicted at this stage. Pakistan also wanted the Soviets out, but first it wanted a provisional government in Kabul made up of the resistance groups. Zia could not agree to a pro-USSR ex-head of the notorious Afghan secret service KHAD, in the person of Najibullah, staying on as Afghan president.

Pakistan and Zia cared deeply about what would happen to Afghanistan after the departure of the Soviets. After having put itself in the firing line for eight years and accepting all the risks inherent in giving all-out support to the Afghan resistance against a superpower, housing 3 million refugees with all its many consequences, and inviting retaliatory terror strikes from the Afghan secret service, it felt justified in looking forward to a friendly regime in Kabul. By 1987, of 777 terrorist incidents recorded worldwide, 90 percent had taken place in Pakistan.[59] Zia did not agree with the assessment that, after the Soviet withdrawal, the Najib regime would quickly fold. Najib may have been pro-Soviet and a communist, but he was also an Afghan. With the withdrawal of the Soviets, the situation in Afghanistan would become an all-Afghan affair, and alliances would likely be redrawn, and none could safely predict the shape of the power equation that would emerge. Any equation that did not have a distinctly pro-Pakistan bias would not be acceptable to him.

Zia knew that if the issue of Soviet withdrawal from Afghanistan was tied up with that of a prior formation of an Afghan provisional government around the resistance groups, both the superpowers would have a stake in pushing for the formation of such a government and would make the achievement of his goal that much easier; but if this matter were left to be settled after the Soviet pullout, Afghanistan would likely become a matter of indifference in Washington, and Pakistan would be left waging an unequal struggle against a Kabul regime enjoying full support from Moscow. There is also good reason to suspect that he could not have been averse to a limited prolongation of this war. This would give Pakistan's nuclear program time to reach a stage in development where it would hopefully find security in a fait accompli. He therefore made it clear that unless the Soviet withdrawal was made contingent upon the prior installation of a provisional government in Kabul, he would sabotage the emerging Geneva Accords. Previous to this stage, Pakistan's position did not go beyond stipulating the exit of the Soviet forces from Afghanistan. This new condition made Moscow furious, and it let Zia know in no uncertain terms that by trying to enforce such a condition on the USSR, he was laying Pakistan open to measures, the consequences of which could only be serious. The United States was equally unhappy with the wrench he was threatening to throw into the works, though the expression of their misgivings was more civil.

Thus the only option left to Zia was to explore if somehow the resistance groups could reach an accommodation with the pro-Soviet regime in Kabul, but this proved to be a nonstarter. The Afghans who had fought the communists for eight long years, sacrificing home and hearth, body and limb, and freedom and life, found any such suggestion deeply offensive. Before Zia had the time to juggle the situation in his favor, in which he had become so adept, Junejo made the move that was to knock him completely off balance. Over Zia's head, he arranged an all-parties conference to consider the issue. The consensus of this meeting was to pledge full support to the mujahideen but without accepting any delay in the Soviet program of withdrawal from Afghanistan. This was the first time since his climb to a position of absolute power that Zia had been checkmated on any important issue. It was now his turn to be furious, but he could do little except relent. There was more than a feeling of mere suspicion among the ISI bosses that the United States had extended a helping hand for Junejo to find his claws just when Washington needed them most. Zia could not have helped but feel betrayed by the United States at the finish line. It was not in his reconstructed nature to take such things lying down.

But on April 10, 1988, four days before the Accords were to be signed, there was a massive explosion in the Ojhri Camp midway between Islamabad and Rawalpindi. This was the depot where all ordnance coming in as aid for the Afghan resistance was stored. Rockets, missiles, and shells rained on the twin cities for a good few hours, bringing death, destruction, and panic in their wake. Sabotage was strongly suspected as the cause of the explosion, but no proof of this was forthcoming. While Zia was more interested in getting the destroyed ammunition stores replaced by the United States,[60] his prime minister wanted to focus on identifying those responsible for having sited the huge ammunition dump in the middle of a densely inhabited area and holding them accountable. Before long, all fingers started to point toward General Akhtar Abdur Rahman, the ex-chief of the ISI who had since been promoted to full general and elevated as joint chief of the staff committee. Junejo wanted him dismissed. Zia had earlier been forced to tolerate what he considered disloyalty from the prime minister, but gunning for Rahman's head was lèse-majesté, or at any rate as near to it as anyone could possibly be allowed to get. Zia and Rahman were not only brothers in arms but, as widely suspected, brothers in the ample ISI till as well.

Besides signing the Geneva Accords, another crime of Junejo in the eyes of Zia was his initiative in trying to slash the defense budget for the first time in the history of the country. In May 1988 the finance minister in Junejo's cabinet announced that a special review committee of the government had even decided to reduce the defense expenditure. He added that the said committee, composed of members of Parliament and officials from the economic ministries, had also forwarded proposals for raising a small professional army, comprehensive training for all citizens, and the setting up of a National Defence Council functioning under the Parliament to scrutinize defense spending.[61] In a rejoinder, on May 22, 1988, General Zia said, "Pakistan cannot afford any cut or freeze in defence expenditure, since you cannot freeze threats to Pakistan's security."[62]

The cup of Zia's patience had finally boiled over. On May 29, 1988, in a televised address to the nation, he dismissed Junejo and the National Assembly on grounds of "corruption," besides its inability to enforce Islamic law in the country. During his speech he blinked back a spurious tear or two and choked on fake emotion. It was an unconvincing performance from a master who had lost his touch and was soon to lose his life. Unaware of such a fate, he secretly instructed his constitutional advisers to frame a *Sharia* bill, as if there were room for that, to be enforced soon.

On August 17, Zia flew to the Bahawalpur desert in the C-130B Hercules transport plane designated as Pak One to witness the trials of the U.S.-made M-1 Abrams tank, which was then under consideration for induction into the Pakistan Army. General Akhtar Abdur Rahman, a host of senior Pakistani generals, the U.S. ambassador to Pakistan, Arnold Lewis Raphel, and Brigadier General Herbert Wasson, the U.S. defense representative, were present to witness the demonstration. On the way back, Zia and General Rahman along with eight other senior Pakistani generals were on board the C-130, besides the two Americans. About four minutes after takeoff, the plane crashed, killing all thirty-one persons on board. The event is deeply shrouded in mystery, and the cause of the crash is still unresolved. An effort is made here to recast the episode in light of an ISI inquiry report, the conclusions of the Pakistan Air Force Board of Enquiry, and that of the USAF team. Various interviews conducted with Pakistani and U.S. sources also helped in this evaluation.

General Zia had gone to Bahawalpur reluctantly. It was his former military secretary and Pakistan's former defense attaché in Washington, D.C., Major General Mahmood Durrani, then commanding the armored division in Bahawalpur, who was "extraordinarily insistent in his phone calls"[63] to Zia to convince him to attend the event, as he considered it "diplomatically desirable."[64] Three months before the incident, Lieutenant General Hamid Gul, the director general of the ISI, on the recommendation of Brigadier Saghir Hussain, a director in ISI, had personally informed Zia that as per ISI's assessment and information, an assassination attempt on Zia was a strong possibility and that he should take extraordinary precautions.[65] A Western intelligence agency had also given a lead to the ISI in this context, saying that a person with the nickname Gogi, who was the son of an army officer, was involved in a conspiracy to kill Zia. Aslam Khattak, a senior minister in Zia's cabinet, also warned him not to travel by air only forty-eight hours before this fateful Bahawalpur flight. Intriguingly, General Akhtar Abdur Rahman was reportedly "convinced" by Brigadier Imtiaz, a former ISI director, to seek an urgent appointment with Zia hardly a day before the Bahawalpur visit, which he asked for, and Zia told him to accompany him to Bahawalpur as that would be the earliest meeting possibility.[66] The probability that this was a coincidence is quite remote. Someone was orchestrating these moves from inside.

After the demonstration, Zia was ready to return to Islamabad. He invited the two American officials at the last minute to accompany him, which they accepted. Soon, they all boarded the plane that was fitted with a special capsule—a 21-foot-long by 8-foot-wide plywood-and-metal structure with an independent air conditioning and lighting system, to give some comfort to an otherwise uncomfortable aircraft. Zia, all the Pakistani generals, and the American guests fit into the capsule. General Aslam Beg, the vice chief of army staff, was the only top general in the chain of command not aboard the plane, as he would fly back in another plane. He also politely but firmly refused to accompany Zia on the flight despite an invitation, as he maintained that he had to go somewhere else before returning to Islamabad.

A military guard was on duty around the aircraft during the intervening time, but there had been a problem with a cargo door, so seven Pakistan Air Force technicians worked on it. It is also reported that shortly before departure, two crates of mangoes arrived, which were loaded in the rear without any check, together with a model of the M-1 Abrams tank, but this is more of a myth than reality. According to an ISI insider who was also a member of the ISI team that investigated the crash, an elaborate three-pronged sabotage plan was well into the implementation stage by then. These findings became a part of the ISI inquiry report, but some parts of it were scrapped by the ISI chief, General Hamid Gul, when he was instructed by the military hierarchy to call off his investigations.

According to the ISI insider's story, an army captain named Majid Raza Gillani, during his service tenure in the 111th Brigade at Islamabad during 1988, was cultivated by two army officers belonging to two foreign countries. The two officers, one from Iraq and the other from a European country, were assigned with the brigade for a short time as per the practice, after they had participated in the National Defense College course in Rawalpindi. They somehow convinced Gillani to murder the Shia leader Arif Hussain al-Hussaini because of his "anti-Islam" activities. Arif al-Hussaini, the head of TNFJ, was murdered in Peshawar on August 5, 1988, and Majid Gillani was allegedly involved as later officially charged. He was on a one-day leave from his duty.

At this stage, the planners of Zia's murder convinced Flight Lieutenant Sajid, a Shia who was copilot of the ill-fated C-130, that Zia was anti-Shia and had ordered the killing of Arif. So Sajid, according to the ISI report, was motivated to take revenge and crash Zia's plane.[67] Sajid was told that for accomplishing this task, besides "earning a place in heaven," his family would be taken care of and be paid Rupees 30 lakhs (around $150,000 at that time) as compensation, besides a pension and more. The second option was to use nerve gas in the cockpit to kill the pilots instantaneously soon after takeoff, ensuring a crash. The nerve gas container would burst by remote control, operated from another plane in the area. The third option, to be availed in case of failure of the first two options, was to shoot all the passengers of the plane after it landed at the Chaklala Air Base in Rawalpindi/Islamabad. For this last plan an armed contingent was in place. In ISI's view, both or either of the first two plans worked. The report does not openly say who was responsible, but clearly indicates the involvement of officers from the Pakistan Army and Air Chief Marshal Hakeemullah in operational matters and hint at U.S. involvement in the planning phase, though neither Pakistani nor U.S. authorities were directly blamed. Still, the concluding part of the report was scrapped later.

The facts, as ascertained through interviews and conclusions of other enquiry reports, do not fully support this theory. The ISI version indicates that the two Shia pilots (of Zia's plane and the alternate/cover plane) were directly involved in the act, which is not substantiated by any other source. However, the predominant view in the Pakistan Army is that U.S. involvement in the episode was certain, besides that of the then military leadership that survived the crash, but no evidence is quoted in support of this assertion in such conversations.

The best investigation and analysis of the mysterious crash has been done by renowned American journalist Edward Jay Epstein in his *Vanity Fair* article published in September 1989.[68] Epstein establishes two major facts: that there was an official cover-up of the crash within the Pakistan Army, and that the U.S. State Department intentionally gave the impression that the crash resulted due to a malfunction, whereas the seven-member USAF team under Colonel Daniel E. Sowada and the Pakistan Air Force's Board of Enquiry had proved that sabotage was the only possibility behind the crash. For this purpose, the Pakistani military authorities at the helm of affairs ensured that no autopsies were done so that there was no proof of the use of nerve gas, and the U.S. administration kept the FBI away from the crime scene despite the fact that two senior American officials had died in the "accident." Amazingly, no black box or cockpit recorder was ever found, according to Epstein. More so, a record of telephone calls made to Generals Zia and Rahman were destroyed within hours after the incident. Epstein argues that without a doubt both the USSR and India had the capability to orchestrate this kind of sabotage, but of course they never had the capability to ensure that the Pakistan Army and ISI would not pursue the investigations as per the standard procedures.

The then *Washington Post* correspondent Steve Coll in his book *On The Grand Trunk Road* also covers the episode based on his independent investigations in Pakistan and the United States, speculating on the linkage between Zia's death and the suspicious activities of one Mark Alphonzo Artis, an American citizen who was in Pakistan just before the crash and then vanished from the scene when Steve pursued him.[69] Brigadier Mohammad Yousaf's narration of the episode in his book *The Bear Trap* is also an interesting read, but the work is clearly influenced by Epstein's information and interpretation of events.

The way the *New York Times* reported the crash and investigations is also enlightening. On August 18, 1988, it carried a news report on its front page entitled "Zia of Pakistan Killed As Blast Downs Plane," which maintained that a midair explosion was the cause and quoted an American official as saying that the United States offered "to send forensic and aviation experts and agents from the FBI to help with the inquiry."[70] But the very next day it carried another report quoting a senior Pentagon official involved in the investigation whose "instincts" told him that the "crash might well have been accidental and caused by mechanical problems."[71] The eight-member U.S. Air Force team designated to help Pakistani authorities determine the cause of the crash was still on its way to Pakistan. The source of the Pentagon official's "instinct" is still an unanswered question.

On September 11, 1988, Elaine Sciolino, the same reporter who wrote the first story in the newspaper (August 18), wrote that Pakistani and U.S. authorities were "increasingly suspect[ing] that a mechanical failure brought down the C-130 transport plane" and that "the plane did not blow up in midair, as was previously reported." She also mentioned that the FBI was not being allowed to participate in the investigations. Giving a new tilt, she concluded the story by quoting Soviet foreign minister Eduard Shevardnadze, who in a conversation with Pakistani foreign minister Sahibzada Yaqub Ali Khan a few weeks before the incident had warned him that Pakistani support for the Afghan mujahideen would not "go unpunished."[72]

The next news story carried by the esteemed paper on the subject was a government leak to the paper, according to Edward Epstein.[73] This news item, on October 14, 1988, categorically maintained that U.S. experts "have concluded that the crash was caused by a malfunction in the aircraft and not by a bomb or a missile."[74] It further said that the absence of a flight recorder/ black box in the plane was hampering the investigation, in addition to the lack of information about radio transmissions from the aircraft in its final moments. In fact, three other planes in the area were tuned to the same frequency that Pak One was using for communications: (1) General Aslam Beg's turbojet; (2) Pak 379, the backup for Pak One; and finally (3) a Cessna security plane that took off before Pak One to scout for any terrorist attempt. Epstein interviewed the pilots of all three planes, and they all maintained that, except for the word "standby," uttered by Chief Pilot/Wing Commander Mashood Hasan, there was silence throughout. The only other voice overheard by the three pilots and the control tower was a faint voice saying, "Mashood, Mashood." This was Brigadier Najib Ahmed, Zia's military secretary who had come to the cockpit to see why the plane was tumbling in its final moments. Mashood was not responding. This also means that the radio was switched on and picking up background sounds. The million-dollar question is why nobody from the cockpit sent a "Mayday" signal to the control tower. Even if there was a scuffle or some other crisis, why didn't the pilots converse with each other? More so, there were no screams even seconds before the plane hit the ground. The obvious inference is that everyone, at least in the cockpit, was already dead. The USAF team couldn't get any transmission records because there were none. But it is interesting that the *New York Times* report maintains that "most C-130s do not carry flight recorders," as in this case, whereas Elaine Sciolino's piece published on September 11, 1988, which contained much inside information from Pentagon sources, had already said that "there is no indication from conversations on the plane recorded by the control tower or retrieved from the flight recorder that the pilot knew anything was wrong before the crash." The same article informed that some of the debris of the ill-fated C-130 had been transferred to the Pentagon and to the Lockheed corporation earlier. The fact as ascertained through many sources in the Pakistan Air Force is that Pak One (C-130 B, registration number 23494; cn/In no. 3708) was indeed fitted with a flight data recorder. Who collected the equipment from the scene is another question that remains unanswered.

By early October 1988 the Pakistan Air Force's Board of Enquiry, with the aid of U.S. experts, completed its investigative deliberations and finalized a 350-page report. The report (complete version still classified) concluded that "most probably sabotage" was what downed the plane. The report ruled out weather, inflight fire, a missile, a high-intensity blast, an attack from the ground, fuel contamination, propeller, structural, or engine failure, and pilot error as possible causes, leading to the deduction that "a criminal act or sabotage" was the cause. The report also strongly hinted that an odorless, colorless, undetectable chemical agent might have been used to incapacitate the crew, besides mentioning the contamination of the main hydraulic system. The board concluded that "the use of ultra-sophisticated techniques would necessitate the involvement of a specialist organization well versed with carrying out such covert operations and possessing all the means and abilities for its execution."[75] The board was so definite about the sabotage theory that it recommended constitution of a broad-based committee to investigate who was behind the sabotage.[76] Such a committee was established under the leadership of a senior Pakistani civil servant, meaning thereby to dump further investigations. In Pakistan's political context, no civilian bureaucrat can dare enter the precincts of internal military-related affairs, which this case was all about.

Meanwhile, the FBI was completely kept out of the investigations. According to John H. Cushman of the *New York Times*, an FBI official disclosed to him that the Bureau had wanted to join the investigations right from the beginning, but "State and Defense Departments" excluded them.[77] The article also reported the conflicting interpretations of various congressmen who, being members of the House Foreign Affairs Committee, had listened to Colonel Daniel Sowada, the head of the USAF team that had helped the Pakistani team in its investigations, in a closed hearing. But clearly the predominant view was that Colonel Sowada was not ruling out anything, including sabotage. The FBI was finally heard ten months after the event, and it landed in Pakistan in mid-June 1989 to pursue its independent investigation in the matter. Congressional hearings had made all the difference. Representative William J. Hughes from New Jersey, who presided over two hearings on the subject, aptly remarked that "something was terribly wrong with the manner in which our government pursued its role in the investigation."[78] Robert Oakley, the new American ambassador to Pakistan, being on the staff of the National Security Council supervising Near East and South Asian affairs in August 1988, had played an important role in deciding the U.S. policy options vis-à-vis Pakistan in the aftermath of the crash. He accepted his "mistake" of keeping the FBI out of the investigations, but gave an unconvincing justification for this. He said that when senior officials had met at the White House on the day of the crash to analyze the situation, "it didn't occur to anyone to send criminal investigators to the site."[79] It is indeed surprising that it "didn't occur" to anyone, because a senior American diplomat and a brigadier general had perished in a plane crash that, at the time, was widely believed to have resulted from a midair explosion. Mr. Oakley, in an interview with Ambassador Dennis Kux, even said that he wanted to keep the FBI on the sidelines because he was worried that the FBI would leak the information, and he further disclosed that the opportunity came when FBI missed the flight bringing the U.S. experts to Pakistan.[80]

The FBI inquiry report was never made public, though according to Ambassador Dennis Kux, it also reached "inconclusive findings."[81] One wonders if, in such a case, it would have been advisable for the U.S. administration to declassify it, as it was supportive of its general stance on the issue. It would have also helped in the context of Pakistani public opinion. However, the topic is no longer of any significance in the U.S. context, hence it is a dead issue there; but for Pakistan it is still relevant and routinely referred to, and there are no two views on the subject that there was a big cover-up. As to the perpetrators of the crime, the near consensus among the Pakistani public is that the "CIA did it," as is the case with everything that goes wrong in Pakistan, but the ones who understand the dynamics of such conspiracies better argue that such an operation had a very limited chance of success without support from within the Pakistan Army. Lieutenant General Faiz Ali Chishti for one clearly maintains that the "Pakistani armed forces could not be above suspicion" in this drama.[82] Ijaz ul-Haq, son of General Zia, also earnestly believes that the "cover-up of the crash started immediately after it happened" and that "the Americans, the army [Pakistan's] and the president of Pakistan [Ghulam Ishaq Khan] are all involved," though he suspected the involvement of Al-Zulfikar guerrillas (associated with the late brother of Benazir Bhutto) as well.[83] Contrary to these assertions and beliefs, Mrs. Arnold Raphel is more convinced by the USAF report, which, according to her, pointed out a mechanical fault in the plane's hydraulic system as causing the crash.[84]

One insightful conclusion seldom referred to in Pakistan is that of the judicial commission, called the Justice Shafiqur Rahman Commission (1992), which, after conducting a detailed enquiry of the Bahawalpur crash, exonerated the Americans—in fact, the report praised the Americans for holding a Senate inquiry.[85] The commission accused the Pakistan Army of preventing it from proceeding further and in fact pointed a finger at the army as being the culprits behind the whole show. The commission was shocked to discover that witnesses were accompanied by military "minders," and that some crucial evidence had been made to simply disappear. The commission had also exonerated the Ahmedis and the Shia as possible killers of General Zia.[86]

It is also pertinent to mention here that when CIA headquarters at Langley suggested to its CIA chief in Islamabad, Milton Bearden, that he dispatch a U.S. Air Force team (already in Pakistan for examining a downed Soviet SU-25 aircraft) to the C-130 crash site, he sent a reply cable that said:

> It would be a mistake to use the visiting technicians. Whatever good they might be able to do would be outweighed by the fact that the CIA had people poking around in the rubble of Zia's plane a day after it went down. Questions would linger as to what we were doing at the crash site and what we'd added or removed to cover up our hand in the crash.[87]

Hours after the crash, the U.S. administration also sent cable warnings all over the world, saying, in Robert Oakley's paraphrase, "Don't mess with the Paks, or the United States is going to be on your ass."[88] This was reportedly in response to the Pakistani fear conveyed to the Americans that the Zia assassination might be a first attack in a series of strikes aimed at the country's very existence. Richard Clarke's comments on Zia's plane crash and the Ojhri's arms depot disaster in Pakistan, in his recent book *Against All Enemies,* is also insightful: "I could never find the evidence to prove that the Soviet KGB had ordered these two acts as payback for their bitter defeat, but in my bones I knew they had."[89]

Based on the available information, various possible scenarios can be deduced. One, that General Aslam Beg, the new army chief after Zia, and Robert Oakley, the newly appointed American ambassador to Pakistan, during the very first days in their respective new offices came to know that Soviets or for that matter the Indians were behind the sabotage, and then they both decided that it was against the United States' and Pakistani interests in the region to expose the actual culprits. Hence, the coordinated cover-up and lack of interest on the part of both the U.S. and Pakistani authorities to probe the matter further. By inference, the other possibility could be that elements from within the Pakistan Army planned and implemented the assassination of General Zia because Zia's policies were increasingly at loggerheads with the institutional interests of the army, and they did it after taking the relevant American authorities into their confidence. The United States, for whom Zia was also becoming a liability because of his views on the postwar setup in Afghanistan and his secret friendly overtures toward Iran, could also have orchestrated the act on its own.

It is quite convenient for Pakistanis to blame the Americans for this incident because it is fashionable to do so in Pakistani power corridors and in the military establishment, but there are also counterarguments to such a conclusion. No American intelligence agency has had the constitutional or legal authority to kill foreign leaders since 1976, when President Gerald Ford signed Executive Order 11905 that categorically prohibits the killing of foreign leaders by U.S. government agencies: "No employee of the United States Government shall engage in, or conspire to engage in, political assassination."[90] President Jimmy Carter in Executive Order 12036[91] on January 24, 1978, retained this provision, and President Reagan in Executive order 12333 on December 4, 1981, extended the provision to include hired assassins by specifically providing that "no agency of the Intelligence Community shall participate in or request any person to undertake activities forbidden by this Order."[92] Presumably no American agency would attempt to violate such a clear-cut executive order and, after all, Zia was no Saddam Hussein or Osama bin Laden.

However, in the absence of any substantial evidence, nothing can be concluded with certainty. The individuals who have a lot of inside information on the subject are still alive and may someday spill the beans. Intriguingly, Majid Raza Gillani, who according to an ISI insider was a tool used in this sabotage, was in fact charged with the murder of Arif al-Hussaini but was acquitted in 1993 by the district court in Peshawar. He also remained in ISI custody for some time after the August 17 crash but was later freed and thrown out of the Pakistan Army. The state appealed this verdict and the case is still pending. Interestingly, in April 2003 the Peshawar High Court took up the hearing of the case against the 1993 acquittal.[93] Another suspect, the pilot of the backup plane, Pak 379, was later promoted to a very senior level in the Pakistan Air Force after he survived the tough interrogation of the ISI for few weeks.

Zia's funeral was massively attended by people from all walks of life, a very large number of whom were Afghans, among whom he was probably the most popular man in the world. Among his own people, though, his stock had fallen steadily as his bag ran out of tricks. In popular esteem he was reduced to the ranks of ordinary mortals before his coffin reached its place of final rest. A rumor had gone around that all that had survived of him was his jawbone. By the next morning, the bus stop nearest to his grave had already entered the jargon of the bus drivers as "*jubbra* [jaw] crossing."

When he came upon the scene, Zia seemed an unlikely ruler. By the time he was lowered into his grave he had proved himself to be the most remarkable man ever to have held the reigns of power in Pakistan. He disarmed every man behind the hand he shook and never allowed the surge of arrogance to belittle even the humblest. He seemed to know exactly where he wanted to go and how he would get there. He hoodwinked so many adversaries so often that it became the favorite speculation of Pakistanis to try and guess who his advisers were, as few were willing to credit him with much wisdom—a misplaced assessment that worked greatly to his advantage. He was a master of the restrained response when it came to keeping his opponents in line, but was cold and ruthless enough and could calibrate it to any extent required. Even his detractors would have to tip their hats to him for the mastery with which he managed to carry on Pakistan's nuclear program, for which he deserves credit and acknowledgment from all Pakistanis. The way he kept his balance while dealing simultaneously with the United States, the USSR, and of course India was also no ordinary achievement.

Still, the way he handled domestic issues did great long-term damage to the interests of his country by sowing the seeds of a tragedy that is likely to keep sprouting for decades.

Islamabad. Activists of Millat-i-Islamia coming toward the parade avenue near the Presidential Palace to participate in the funeral prayer of their leader Mullana Azam Tariq.

*(ONLINE Photo)*

Peshawar. Police official talking with prisoner at Peshawar airbase.

*(ONLINE Photo by Ghafar Baig)*

Mohammad Ali Jinnah, founder
of Pakistan.   *(Courtesy of ONLINE)*

Rawalpindi. Qazi Hussain Ahmed, Vice President Mutahida Majilas-e-Amal
(MMA), a coalition of six religious parties, waving in response to supporters during
a "Million March" in Rawalpindi near the Pakistan Capital of Islamabad.
*(ONLINE Photo by Anjum Naveed)*

Governor General Mountbatten, Mohammad Ali Jinnah, and Indian Prime Minister Nehru, 1947. *(Courtesy of ONLINE)*

Peshawar. Taliban supporters donating money to show sympathy for Afghan people. *(ONLINE Photo)*

Mohamand Agency. Gold and money contributed to support the Taliban in their struggle against the U.S. at Ghalanai, Mohamand Agency. *(ONLINE Photo)*

Lt. General Akhtar Hussain Malik

Zulfikar Ali Bhutto.
*(Photograph courtesy of Barry Hoffman)*

Islamabad. Late Lt. General Ghulam Ahmad, Chief of staff to the President/Chief Executive of Pakistan.
*(ONLINE Photo)*

Washington, D.C. George W. Bush, president of the United States and Pakistan's president General Pervez Musharraf addressing a joint press conference.

*(ONLINE Photo)*

Karachi. Ahmed Omar Saeed Sheikh, alleged mastermind behind Wall Street Journal reporter Daniel Pearl's abduction, arrives at court under tight security.

*(ONLINE Photo by Mehmood Qureshi)*

General Mohammad Ayub Khan.

*(Photograph courtesy of Barry Hoffman)*

Islamabad. President General Pervez Musharraf with Chairman Joint Chiefs of Staff Committee Gen. Aziz Khan (left) and Commandant NDC Lt. Gen. Javed Hasan (right). *(ONLINE Photo)*

Islamabad. Army personnel stands on guard in a makeshift bunker near Parliament House. *(ONLINE Photo)*

Islamabad. Sipah-e-Sahaba activists collecting donations.
*(ONLINE Photo)*

Peshawar. Mullana Masood Azhar leader of Kuddam-ul-Islam coming to add a prayer gathering in a mosque.

*(ONLINE Photo)*

George H.W. Bush with Benazir Bhutto at White House Meeting.

*(Photograph courtesy of Barry Hoffman)*

President Ronald Reagan
with President General
Mohammad Zia-ul-Haq.
*(Photograph courtesy
of Barry Hoffman)*

Prime Minister Nawaz Sharif in his office with "missile souvenir" in the background.
*(Press Information Department, Government of Pakistan)*

# ——Chapter 7——

# A Return to Democracy

## Benazir Bhutto and Nawaz Sharif

With Zia's death, the firm hand that had ruled Pakistan for more than a decade was gone in a puff of smoke. General Mirza Aslam Beg, vice chief of the army staff (VCOAS), emerged as the de facto army chief and therefore became the most powerful man in the country. When Zia dismissed the Junejo government on May 29, 1988, he had announced that national elections would take place on November 16, 1988, but now Beg was the chief interpreter of the last major pronouncement of his dead boss. He had to quickly decide if he wanted to become president or be satisfied with being the principal power behind the throne and go ahead with the promised elections. Many of Zia's former colleagues made it clear that they would be prepared to pay homage to him should he decide to move into the presidency.[1] Under the constitution though, this office should have devolved on the chairman of the Senate, Mr. Ghulam Ishaq Khan.

There was perhaps just enough hesitation among the army high command to suggest that it might be a good idea for the military to get off the nation's back for a while. But given the army's strong tradition of playing "follow the leader," it is more probable that any such suggestion must have come from Beg himself, with the rest nodding their heads in vigorous assent. Thus, Ishaq Khan became the president, and it was declared that Pakistan would have general elections as scheduled.[2]

The favorite to win the coming ballot was Benazir Bhutto and her Pakistan People's Party (PPP). After her father was hanged, many party activists had left the country in order to save themselves from state persecution while many senior politicians of the party had either changed their loyalties or were in political oblivion. It was primarily Benazir and her mother alone, among those close to Bhutto, who held aloft the party standard in the harshest days of the Zia repression and preferred incarceration to submission.[3] Murtaza, the elder son of Z.A. Bhutto, with serious charges pending against him in Pakistani courts, decided not to return. Benazir had gone into exile in 1984 after spending four years in jail or under house arrest under very harsh circumstances, but when she returned in 1986 it was to a tumultuous reception. This was in equal part an expression of public feeling against Zia and his policies as it was an expression of hope in the Bhutto family, now being represented by Benazir. The massive scale of this welcome was not lost on the army or the ISI, and despite the latter's inordinate capacity for the analytical blunder, even they could not but conclude that, left to itself, the PPP would sweep the next elections.

Among the middle and lower ranks of the army, fed up with the miasma of cant and hypocrisy spread over the land by the decadelong rule of Zia, the feeling was that if Benazir won in a fair fight, she ought to be given a fair chance to prove herself in government. At the upper reaches of the army, however, the possibility of Benazir in power was treated with a mixture of suspicion and apprehension, and a clean sweep by her party was considered entirely unacceptable. The mullahs also just could not square with the idea of having a Muslim country being ruled by a woman! They hollered and howled at the mere thought of it, and tore their beards in anguish at the prospect that things may indeed come to such a sorry pass! And President Ishaq Khan, having no beard of his own to pull, tugged in panic at those of others and scratched his own head for ideas.

Another man doing a lot of scratching was Lieutenant General Hamid Gul, director general of the ISI, a loudly religious man without a beard. According to the U.S. Defense Intelligence Agency's (DIA) biographical sketch (declassified), he used to "drink in moderation" and "his religious practice does not appear to affect his political views."[4] The DIA's source was certainly ill informed. Gul had a versatile mind whose agility was severely constrained by a predisposition to viewing everything through an ideological prism. But there certainly was a quality of inspiration and commitment about his leadership. Although he was better educated than most of his colleagues and a keen student of history, his religious ideals robbed him of objectivity in historical analysis. His analysis of Pakistani politics, however, was considerably more accurate, that is, if a credible political alliance was not put together in opposition to the PPP, the latter would run away with the elections by a landslide. Such a prospect was deeply disturbing not only to him but to the president and General Beg also, who all doubted if she would be a big enough person to surmount the vengeance she nursed against Zia and army. More so, they were not sure if Benazir would accept how the army's leadership wanted to play its game in Afghanistan. Her outbursts in private, routinely conveyed to the authorities,[5] did nothing to calm their fears. It was thus that Hamid Gul cobbled together the Islamic Democratic Alliance (IJI), an electoral coalition of the two main factions of the Pakistan Muslim League and most of the important right-wing religious parties.[6] This was the first time the army supported and used religious parties in electoral politics.

The leader that Hamid Gul picked to lead this pack was forty-one-year-old Mian Nawaz Sharif. He was a truly amazing choice. His family had immigrated to Lahore from East Punjab in 1947. Mian Mohammad Sharif, the family patriarch, soon to become known as Abbaji (Daddy) in Pakistani politics, built up the family steel business quite literally from scratch with little more than his own industry and effort. The family was typically conservative, religious, and middle-class, with a loving mother minding the household, obedient children, and a hard-driving but gentle father whose word was law. By the time the family business had grown into a chain of steel factories, Z.A. Bhutto had appeared on the scene and nationalized it in the early 1970s. The Sharifs joined the ranks of many families who had a personal grudge against the PPP and Z.A. Bhutto. When Zia took over in 1977 and the family business was restored to them, they became strong champions of the general's cause. At about this time General Ghulam Jillani Khan became the governor of Punjab and decided to build his private house. Not having the time to oversee construction, the chore was taken over by Major Niazi, a retired friend and colleague who was then employed as secretary of the Defence Club Lahore. Niazi sublet the responsibility to an overeager Mian Mohammad Sharif. It was thus that the governor bumped into Mian Sharif and gave birth to a new twist to the history of Pakistan.

During his visits to the house as it was being constructed, the governor often ran into Mian Shabaz Sharif, Mian Sharif's second son. The youngster was exceptionally sharp and did not fail to impress the governor. So, when Zia decided to humanize his martial law by having civilian cabinets in the provinces, Mian Mohammad Sharif, having won his spurs in the personal service of the governor, did not lose the opportunity to put in a request that his son be considered for suitable employment. A few days later, when the elder Sharif was informed that Shabaz had been earmarked as the finance minister in the Punjab cabinet, he had a fit. It was obvious to all that the old man had not been able to contain his joy, till it was discovered that it was a fit of genuine consternation. Shabaz was holding up the family business and was vital for its continued success. If he were to be plucked out of it, the enterprise could suffer irremediable harm. Mian Sharif reverted to the governor and begged his indulgence for the terrible misunderstanding, and explained that while making the request he had had the other son in mind—the elder one who was only good enough for public relations for the business. Jillani was big enough to accept Mian Sharif's correction in good grace, and Mian Nawaz Sharif was transformed from a PR man of a steel mill into the finance minister of the largest province of Pakistan. Later he became chief minister of the province. A polite, well-mannered young man who smiled easily and was difficult to dislike, Nawaz Sharif was a graduate of the famed

Government College of Lahore, even though education did not sit well with him. Sumptuous repasts exerted the greatest pull on him, and even those very partial to him could not help but comment on the amazing brevity of his attention span.

### Benazir Bhutto in Power (November 1988–August 1990)

Despite all that the ISI could manage, Benazir came out ahead in the elections.[7] It was her right to form the government, but Ishaq Khan dithered and procrastinated. It was a nudge by U.S. ambassador Robert Oakley that eventually got him to do the right thing.[8] But before he did this, Benazir had to give an assurance that she would not interfere in Pakistan's nuclear program, its Afghan policy, or the promotions/transfers and budget of the armed forces.[9] She went a step further and promised also to retain Sahibzada Yakub Ali Khan as Pakistan's foreign minister. It would be safe to conjecture that this last was as much a concession to the army as it was to the United States, whose longtime favorite Sahibzada undoubtedly was.[10]

At the mere age of thirty-five, Benazir thus had the truly stupendous distinction of becoming the first woman to become a prime minister of a Muslim state, despite the state machinery having done all it could to prevent the "catastrophe." Despite the aversion of Ishaq Khan and the doubts of the army brass, when she took office most Pakistanis looked to her with hope. There was also sympathy for her. She was obviously beautiful and had a well-rounded education both at Harvard and Oxford, and she was articulate. Her education in the hard school of life had given her more grit than almost all the politicians around. She held a lot of charm and appeal for the West, mainly for the novelty she represented—the novelty of being an urbane, eloquent, and liberal woman, grown in the unlikely soil of the "decadent" East and polished in the West, who had become prime minister of a large Muslim state. Among her own people, though, the considerations were different. What mattered to them most was that she was Bhutto's daughter. They remembered the promise Bhutto once represented. This promise they now transferred to his daughter. How much of this promise was real and how much of it was foisted upon her by their disillusionment with the preceding years, they did not know.

Benazir was to be one of the power players in a troika, of which the other two were Ishaq Khan, who was a very-well-known entity, and General Mirza Aslam Beg, who was not. Beg was an infantry officer who had also served in the elite Special Services Group. Of average height and medium build, he was soft-spoken, had an easygoing air about him, and was well liked by both his subordinates and superiors. His baby face hid an acute mind and an ambition to match. He was also not averse to the odd scotch. When Zia chose him to be his VCOAS to deal with the routine functioning of the army, Lieutenant General Shams ur-Rahman Kallue, a close friend of Zia's, was expected to fill the slot. Kallue would also have been the more popular choice. It was then rumored by the uninitiated that Beg had been preferred because he was a Mohajir officer and therefore did not have a "constituency" in the army, constituting less of a potential threat to Zia.[11] This is the standard nonsense generally bandied about as an explanation for the unexpected. With all its deterioration, the Pakistan Army is the one institution in the country where a good officer, irrespective of his sectarian or ethnic affiliation, can still create a "constituency" through the agency of personal merit. Kallue was not given the coveted slot because he had refused to hold any appointment having anything to do with martial law, and in this preference there was a message Zia could not have been comfortable with. Beg's appointment in preference to Kallue, however, put the former on the defensive and created a rift between the two men that was to have its consequences for the country and the army.

More consequential for Pakistan and the future of democracy in it was the fact that instead of sitting as the leader of the opposition in the National Assembly, Nawaz Sharif, in line with ISI instructions, became the chief minister of Punjab Province. In this capacity Nawaz Sharif would not only be in a position to exercise direct power, but he would largely be beyond the power to be exercised by Benazir Bhutto as prime minister. The election campaign had set the tone for the postelection relationship between the two sides. It was to be one of mutual suspicion, lack of cooperation, and outright defiance. Sharif was obviously the heir to the Zia legacy as Benazir was that of her father's, and there was no shortage of contempt each had for the other. The dawn of the democratic era in Pakistan was therefore announced by the sounding of war drums promising action right from where Zia and Bhutto had left off. And the ISI under the able command of Hamid Gul had a lot to do with it. He is on record as having said that "although we could not take Jalalabad, we managed to save the Punjab."[12] Hamid Gul and Major General Asad Durrani (director general military intelligence then) often remarked with delight that Nawaz Sharif was a product of their agency, their pride and symbol.[13]

If there were to be any realistic chance of Benazir muddling through the troubled waters of Pakistan, this was spoiled by her inexperience in governance and ISI's interference in politics. When Benazir started off as prime minister, she did so hobbled by many external obstacles that obstructed her. To these she was generous in adding self-inflicted ones. Most of the old party stalwarts were ignored, and upstarts and opportunists who would take instructions from her without question were encouraged. As a matter of party policy, Benazir started to distribute patronage and largesse to the party faithful who had suffered under Zia's whip. Allegations of corruption on Benazir's husband Asif Ali Zardari and some federal cabinet ministers also had an impact on the government's credibility. Partly this was the result of a coordinated effort by the intelligence services to tarnish Asif Zardari's name to bring Benazir into disrepute. Asif Zardari belonged to a Sindhi landlord family. He was known for having a sharp mind and a heart that was uncommonly large and warm.

At first she had few problems in her relationship with the army. That changed when she decided that, like her father, she must attend the army's corps commander conferences and promotion boards. Beg did not like this suggestion but could do little about it. He let her know, though, that she could attend only as an observer but not as a participant. And each time he received her in the army headquarters, he did so bareheaded so that he could avoid saluting her formally. During these visits she was treated as a nuisance to be tolerated. Her next clash with the army came when she wanted to rehabilitate the few pro-Bhutto army officers who had deserted the service after Zia's July 1977 coup to take asylum abroad.[14] As per army regulations they were to be penalized, but she wanted to rehabilitate them. This was something the army did not take kindly to and rather viewed it as direct meddling in army discipline. Army leadership was not ready to accept her as a powerful civilian chief executive.

But much more serious was the conduct of Lieutenant General Hamid Gul. As head of the ISI, he continued a liaison with the IJI, which was not only entirely unethical but could only inspire fears of conspiracy in the prime minister's mind—fears that were justified. So she did not take long to see him out of the ISI and in his place appointed Lieutenant General S.R. Kallue, who had by now retired. Appointing a retired officer as an ISI chief was a new precedent. He became Benazir's choice mainly because of his reputation of being an upright and nonpolitical professional officer whose opposition to martial law was well known. Beg, who had been preferred as VCAS over him by Zia, was also defensive where Kallue was concerned because of their rivalry. Now that Benazir was appointing Kallue director general of the ISI, Beg turned suspicious of the prime minister's motives and worked up a new hostility toward Kallue. He isolated the ISI and hamstrung it the best he could by instructing the Military Intelligence (MI) directorate under Major General Asad Durrani to move in and fill in the functions of the former. He thus partially moved another army institution away from its prime function, degrading it in the process, and set yet another watchdog over the politicians. With this change in the ISI, the battle lines between her and the army were drawn.

Politically, Benazir was in a mess almost as soon as the bell rang. The fact that the Mohajir Qaumi Movement (MQM)[15] under the leadership of Altaf Hussain had by now become a highly monolithic and violence-friendly organization masquerading as a political party was not her fault. However, dealing with it was her responsibility, but apparently she was not ready for that. From having held no significant office of any responsibility, she was catapulted to that of a prime minister of a country not easy to govern. She needed to understand the power of the MQM in urban Sindh, and also that she could not hope to govern the province without its active cooperation. The first step toward gaining this cooperation had to be equitable power-sharing, but the PPP leadership in Sindh was not ready to permit that. Thus, the MQM was pushed from the position of an ally to that of an inveterate adversary. With the active hostility of this party, the governance of Karachi and Hyderabad virtually came to a halt.

As the MQM leadership's terror tactics made Karachi ungovernable, the PPP asked the army to restore order. General Beg wanted to control law and order in Sindh only if the army were granted powers under Article 245 of the constitution, which meant immunity from judicial monitoring, whereas Benazir wanted its deployment under Article 147, which allows the civilian authority to keep an eye on army performance. This rift created a further estrangement between the two.

If any form of compromise could bring about harmony on the political stage, Nawaz Sharif in Punjab Province was demonstrating exactly how this should not be done. He was leading his own charge and letting no chance go by that could embarrass the prime minister. And in the spirit of give and take, she was responding likewise. This was to prove fatal for democracy in Pakistan. The logic of mutual animus spread the war to Islamabad, with the opposition preparing to file a motion of no confidence against Benazir in the National Assembly. Hectic activity started, with each side attempting to buy the loyalties of the legislators of the other. The combination of the types of amounts being offered, and the defenselessness of most of the legislators against an assault by serious money, made the political situation extremely fluid. To keep their loyalties and virtue intact, eventually each side was driven to the extreme measure of holding these champions of democracy in virtual house arrest so that none from the other side could reach them. ISI was not behind in this game by any means—they launched Operation Midnight Jackals[16] to sway some members from the government to the opposition, but eventually Benazir survived. Happiest of all was a subinspector of police who got 10 million rupees (approximately $400,000 then) from one party to buy a legislator of the other. He decided to buy an air ticket instead and left the country.

U.S.-Pakistan relations meanwhile turned out to be better than could have been expected. Before leaving the White House at the end of his second term, President Reagan had issued his third certification required under the Pressler Amendment for U.S. military and economic aid to Pakistan to continue, but he left behind a warning that a similar certification for the following year would need looking into rather closely. At the beginning of 1989, when General Beg visited the United States, he was warned that, with the Cold War over and the Soviets preparing to leave Afghanistan, the U.S. Congress would likely be more assertive and sensitive to Pakistan's nuclear program, which would make it that much more difficult for President Bush to give the certification if Pakistan were to be found in the danger zone.[17] General Beg understood the message and acted accordingly, as U.S. intelligence reports soon indicated that Pakistan had halted production of weapons grade uranium.[18] But what the Americans did not know was that Pakistan had already developed a nuclear explosive capability.

As per the initial agreement among the troika, nuclear-program-related issues lay entirely in the domain of the army, though, courtesy of a CIA briefing[19] in December 1988, Benazir had acquired enough information to become relevant to the other members of the troika on this subject. On the Afghanistan front the Americans wanted to be out, though they retained sufficient loyalties with the mujahideen to back them in their bid for power in Kabul; Pakistan could not countenance any but a friendly regime in Afghanistan, and Najibullah continued as president of the country. In February 1989 the Soviet foreign minister visited Islamabad and urged Pakistan to opt for a political compromise in Kabul, to which Benazir agreed but the army and the mujahideen, who were expecting the Najib regime to fold anytime, did not find this suggestion acceptable. Soon afterward the United States decided to wash its hands of the whole affair.

On February 15, 1989, the Soviet occupation army marched out of Afghanistan, and Lieutenant General Hamid Gul started to lobby for recognition of the Afghan Interim Government (AIG), but Sahibzada Yaqub Ali Khan (the foreign minister) and U.S. ambassador Robert Oakley were insistent that such recognition would have no meaning with the AIG sitting around in Peshawar without being in control over a chunk of Afghan territory. Hence, Hamid Gul was tasked to ensure that the mujahideen should capture at least one major city across the border. Jalalabad was selected as the target city. The decision was taken in the meeting of the Afghan Cell on March 6, 1989, which was attended among others by Benazir and U.S. ambassador Oakley. Surprisingly, no Afghan commander was present at this meeting. In the event, the operation turned out to be a costly failure because the attacking troops had no clue of conventional operations, while Najibullah's forces put up a great resistance.

In June 1989, Benazir visited the United States, where she did a commendable job of presenting Pakistan as a moderate and progressive Islamic state. Pakistan's freeze on its nuclear program helped put President George H.W. Bush at ease, and he was therefore in a position to promise the release of sixty additional F-16s that Pakistan had asked for as well as the additional $400 million in U.S. aid due for that year. On her return, she felt sufficiently emboldened by the plaudits received in Washington to cross swords with the two other members of the troika. To test the waters, the path she took was an indirect one by signing the retirement orders of the chairman of the Joint Chiefs of Staff Committee, Admiral Iftikhar Ahmed Sirohey. Though Ishaq Khan took little time to reverse the order, there was little doubt in the minds of the army hierarchy that Benazir was becoming assertive. They were also critical of the way she was tackling Pakistan-India relations.

Meanwhile, another crisis was brewing in South Asia. Kashmiris had always chafed under Indian rule, which had come as an act of usurpation to deny them their right of freedom, but Kashmir did not have a history of seething and simmering, much less that of boiling over. The heroism of the Afghan mujahideen not only had beaten back the Soviets, but in doing so it had also successfully broadcast the message that the courage and will of a people could destroy the powerful machinery of an oppressing state. This idea was at work in Indian Punjab among the Sikhs, to whom it was not new, but it also took hold of the Kashmiris, to whom it was sort of a novelty. The Indians had learned nothing from the Soviet humiliation in Afghanistan, and had so blatantly manipulated the state elections in Kashmir in 1987 that the lid flew off the proverbial docility of the Kashmiri people, which erupted in popular rebellion against the Indian occupation. For Pakistan it was the opportunity of a lifetime. It had supported and financed the Sikh movement for independence and now started to aid the Kashmiris as well. Relations with India, never good, could only deteriorate at an alarming rate. In the two summits between Benazir and Rajiv Gandhi, the prime minister of India, in December 1988 and July 1989, Pakistan attempted to cool the tensions the best it could. One result of these efforts was an agreement between the two not to attack the nuclear facilities of the other. But it was also suspected by the military intelligence that in trying to assuage Rajiv Gandhi, Benazir had given him the lists of Sikh activists who were working in league with Pakistani intelligence. PPP sources continue to deny this allegation as vehemently as sources of Pakistani intelligence support that and hold up as proof the fact that soon after the Indian leader's visit, almost the entire crop of ISI contacts in the Sikh movement was liquidated. To a neutral observer it is inconceivable that Pakistani intelligence services gave the names and locations of their "assets" in India to Benazir or to the interior minister, Aitizaz Ahsan, who was specifically named as the one who leaked the information to the Indians. In any event, matters became so serious that toward the end of 1990, it was feared that the two countries might go to war. Both being suspected nuclear states, the situation was serious enough to call for U.S. intercession through the good offices of Robert Gates, the deputy national security adviser who succeeded in lowering the temperature and deescalating the standoff.

The temperature in Sindh too needed lowering, for which Mr. Gates was not available, and left to its own devices the government fumbled. In May 1990 the Sindh police went into the largely Mohajir locality of Pucca Qila in Hyderabad in search of illegal weapons. By the time it withdrew, forty people, almost all Mohajirs, had been shot to death by the police. The police claimed that they had come under sniper fire and had only fired back in self defense. Whatever the facts, to the army it was also proof that governance was not PPP's forte. And if any doubt remained, it was dissipated when random firing on a bus in Karachi a little later claimed another twenty-four lives.

Thus, on August 6, 1990, with General's Beg's full support, Ishaq Khan, benefiting from the arbitrary powers bestowed on his office courtesy of Zia's constitutional amendments in 1985, dismissed Benazir and her government on multifarious charges of corruption and malfeasance in governance. "The Military Intelligence (MI) was conspiring against my government from the first day,"[20] said Benazir to local and foreign correspondents a day after her dismissal, but she was only partially correct. Economic mismanagement and lack of experience in governance had also played a crucial role in this episode. A little later Dr. Abdul Qadeer Khan, the father of Pakistan's nuclear program, in a lecture at the National University of Science and Technology in Rawalpindi, a military-run institution, disclosed to a selected audience that he had repeatedly asked General Beg to get rid of Benazir, as she was creating hindrances to the further development of Pakistan's nuclear program.[21]

### The First Nawaz Sharif Government (November 1990–July 1993)

Ishaq Khan announced fresh elections for November 1990 and put in place interim governments at the center and in the provinces that were uniformly anti-PPP. Politically, the stage was now set for the IJI, as the ISI had no qualms about trying to stack the deck in their favor in pre-poll rigging. The ISI "persuaded" Younis Habib, a corrupt banker, to stuff 140 million rupees (approximately $6 million then) in the coffers of the IJI political campaign through ISI and MI accounts.[22] Consequently, as Paula R. Newberg accurately contends, "an overwhelming victory for the IJI coalition was managed by the caretaker government 'with remarkable deftness.'"[23]

After a "convincing" electoral victory, Nawaz Sharif took the oath as prime minister of the country. Soon thereafter he had a reason to quail, and that reason was General Beg. On Zia's death, Beg had gone into the background as the politic thing to do, but in his own mind he had merely lent the presidency to Ishaq Khan. In the two years since then he had done all in his power to project himself. He had used the Inter Services Public Relations (ISPR) directorate as a private firm to build up and project his image round the country. His much-publicized military exercise, the Zarb-i-Momin, was an extravaganza designed to achieve similar ends. His courtship with many journalists had them paint him as a stabilizing presence behind the disruptive gimmicks and policies of the politicians. To begin with, he had endorsed the government's pro-U.S. position on the impending war in the Gulf (after Saddam's attack on Kuwait in 1991), in direct opposition to public sentiment. As time passed and this sentiment only solidified and expanded further, he reassessed his position. After a briefing by Major General Agha Masud, chief of Pakistan's antiaircraft command, he made a 180–degree turn. He was informed that, irrespective of U.S. airpower, the last battle would have to be fought on land, resulting in unacceptably high American casualties that could well stalemate the U.S. effort. It would seem that his chief adviser was not reading his science newsletter[24] and, considering that Beg agreed with his assessment, neither was he. In any case, it would seem that he was counting on a popular uprising in Pakistan the moment U.S. operations hit a snag. That would be the time they would accept him as the leader whose views on the war coincided with theirs. It was in this context that he coined the term "strategic defiance" as the prescribed posture for Pakistan in the Gulf War.[25] What this really meant only he could tell, though of course there was a great deal of support when this brilliant, hitherto unknown concept was mentioned among senior army officers due for promotion. This was the time by which professionalism in the army was increasingly being measured by high-falutin' terminology like the "strategic depth" of Hamid Gul, the "ideological frontiers" of Zia, and the "postural difficulties" of the rest of the army. But with his theory of strategic defiance, Beg also warned that the real purpose of the U.S. war against Iraq was to make Israel feel more secure, and that toward the same end the next target would be Iran, and then a day might come when Pakistan might face such wrath.[26] In private, he was laughed at then. To counter such a possibility, Beg also proposed an alliance among Pakistan, Iran, and Afghanistan.

When the U.S.-led coalition launched its air strikes, the Iraqi army was destroyed before it could even see the attacking forces. The crowds that Beg had expected to rise in Pakistan and carry him to his appointed destiny turned around and simply went home. Now his fate lay entirely in the hands of the same Ishaq Khan who had been quite willing to offer him the presidency just a few short years ago. He now prayed that Ishaq would remember the favor done to him and grant him an extension in service as army chief at the least. The president, however, was that much more advanced in age and also in selective amnesia, though he did remember all the right things. To abort any fancy scheme that his army chief might have been hatching, he broke precedence and announced the name of Beg's successor ahead of the customary three weeks before the retirement of the incumbent. This effectively made Beg the first lame duck army chief in Pakistan's history. With all avenues closed to him, strong rumors started to go the rounds that Beg was preparing to launch a coup. It was a good thing for the general that if he did have any such thoughts, he did not attempt to translate them into action because plausible rumors of his corruption had severely eroded his prestige and credibility in the army.

Allegedly, General Beg was also involved in the transfer of nuclear technology to Iran. As is evident from recent reports on the nuclear proliferation issue in the Pakistani as well as international media, Dr. Qadeer and some other Pakistani scientists cooperated with Iranian scientists in their nuclear pursuits during the times when General Beg was custodian of Pakistan's nuclear assets.[27] Such an undertaking, though lately being projected as a work of scientists in their private capacity, was impossible without the approval and support of the general, and this also makes sense as that was indeed in line with his security perspective and worldview, as discussed earlier. According to a *New York Times* story, General Beg told U.S. ambassador Oakley in 1991 that he was consulting with the Iranian Revolutionary Guards about nuclear and conventional military cooperation.[28]

However, on August 18, 1991, General Asif Nawaz Janjua took over as the new chief of army staff. He was cast in a mold entirely dissimilar to that of any of his predecessors. A tall, handsome Sandhurst-trained officer, he was straight enough to be brusque, and though he could smile, he was given to scowling with greater ease. He was easily slighted and would go into a paroxysm of nervous energy at the mere hint of being challenged. With all of this, he had no time for fools and had an enormously long memory. In short, he was not someone that a Pakistani politician would like to see as army chief.

The most serious situation that the new government had to face was the Pressler axe, which fell on Pakistan on October 1, 1990, when President George H.W. Bush refused to provide the requisite certification to Congress. The U.S. president and many in his administration were genuinely sad about this and the consequent aid cutoff to Pakistan. These regrets must have had to do with the conscious abandonment of an ally, a poor country that had volunteered to stand in the front line against Soviet expansionism and had helped fight a proxy war on behalf of the United States, which eventually led to the dismantling of the Soviet empire, making the United States the sole superpower on the globe. And if Bush was sad, the Pakistani leadership was absolutely outraged. To them this was a simple case of a U.S.-Pakistan contract, which bound each to separate and well-defined obligations. It was Pakistan's duty under the terms of this contract to give all assistance to the Afghan mujahideen to turn the Soviets out of Afghanistan, accepting all the attendant risks including that of the threat of declaration of war by the Soviet Union against Pakistan. In return the United States was obliged to give Pakistan military and economic support commensurate to the threat it was inviting. The way the people of Pakistan saw it, when their country had fulfilled its part of the contract and the United States had no further need of Pakistan, it simply struck camp and left, leaving the balance of the bills unpaid while still trumpeting American values, an American sense of fair play, and an American support of freedom. To the Pakistanis this freedom also included the freedom to abandon a friend who is of no further use. The injustice inflicted on Pakistan was so patent and so brazen that the only American friends left in the country were presumably the CIA's faithful moles.

The U.S. position was that since the last certification, its intelligence reports indicated that Pakistan had produced more weapons grade uranium and machined it to form uranium cores for weapons manufacturing. It asked Pakistan to melt the cores and take the level back to that existing before the previous certification. Pakistan absolutely denied any further enrichment beyond the level at which it had frozen its weapons program and insisted that any reports by U.S. intelligence were based more on conjecture and speculation than on verifiable facts, and that the United States had simply shifted the goalposts from "stay where you are" to "roll back."[29] But this was not all. Pakistan suffered even further when, after the suspension of U.S. aid, the Pentagon advised it not to stop payments to the manufacturer, General Dynamics, even if delivery of the F-16 fighter aircraft had been frozen.[30] The reason given was that any stoppage of payment would constitute a breach of contract and make it difficult to gain congressional support for easing the Pressler sanctions, though it may be suspected that an equal reason for the said suggestion was that the manufacturer was strapped for cash. In any event, the ridiculous situation that Pakistan walked into was that of an abandoned ally, paying for equipment it was not to receive, benefiting a Pentagon contractor who would get to keep the money and also the goods!

By September 1991 the United States had formally washed its hands of

Afghanistan, and Pakistan was left to reap the whirlwind the best it could. The scramble for the spoils of power among the Afghan mujahideen was as unruly as the war that had thrown the Soviets out. Professor Rabbani (a Tajik) was named Afghanistan's president, Gulbadin Hikmatyar became prime minister, and Ahmad Shah Masud, the lion of Panjshir and another Tajik, the defense minister in the new cabinet. But Hikmatyar developed some misgivings and refused to join the government, and in a novel expression of dissent started to shell Kabul, killing thousands of its residents.

All this was happening while the Kashmir insurgency heated up. Demobilized Afghan veterans, mostly of Arab origin, and Pakistanis who had received their battle inoculation in Afghanistan had found another arena for the employment of their talents and started to drift into Kashmir. Pakistani intelligence was only too happy to facilitate this shift, both to rid itself of elements it had little control over and to put one past India for its role in East Pakistan in 1971.

At the home front, Nawaz Sharif was increasingly being associated with shady deals. In 1991 a number of cooperative banks in Punjab collapsed, rendering destitute thousands of widows, orphans, and retired personnel who had kept their meager savings in these. Many owners of such banks belonged to Nawaz Sharif's party, and not a single one of them went to jail or returned the misappropriated funds. More so, the personal business of the Sharifs prospered. Tariff and customs duty manipulation benefited Ittefaq foundries, owned by the Sharifs. In a mere decade the earnings of their family business increased from a modest $10 million to $400 million.[31] Side by side, however, Nawaz also introduced a number of measures to address poverty and underdevelopment issues that brought his party considerable popularity.

In the domestic political context, though his pro-U.S. policy during the Gulf War was unpopular among the people, especially so among his mullah allies, they were also unhappy over the excuse of a *Shariat* Bill he had introduced in the Parliament, but there was nothing about these problems he could not quite easily handle. Sindh would have given him the greatest cause for worry, but he had abandoned the province to the tender mercies of Jam Sadiq Ali, a clever and ruthless politician. Jam Sadiq had convinced President Ishaq Khan and Prime Minister Sharif that if things were left entirely to him, he would be able to break the back of the PPP in Sindh. Ishaq not only gave him an unrestricted mandate to do this in his capacity as chief minister of the province, but went further to loan him his thoroughly disreputable son-in-law, Mr. Irfanullah Marwat, to help out in the noble task. Between Jam, Marwat, and Altaf Hussain of the MQM, Karachi was in for an unending night of unbridled loot, rape, and murder.

Both Nawaz Sharif and Jam were a bit worried though by the dacoit (band of armed robbers) menace in rural Sindh, where about two thousand of them had taken refuge, murdering, plundering, and kidnapping without much hindrance by the police. The army was requisitioned, which started Operation Cleanup in rural Sindh in May 1992, and soon the dacoits were on the run. But interestingly, the army commanders on their own decided to extend their operation to major cities in Sindh that had become strongholds of the MQM.[32] This resulted in a direct confrontation between the army and MQM in urban Sindh, furthering the political problems faced by the Nawaz government, as the MQM was a coalition partner with Nawaz in Sindh.

Meanwhile, in December 1991, the MQM, which had reigned supreme and functioned above and beyond the law, was about to be cut down to size by an internal split—about the only way its power could be contained. The perpetrators of the attempt were Afaq Ahmad, Aamir Khan, and Badar Iqbal, who were thoroughly repelled by Altaf's despotic style and corruption. They gave ideological reasons as the cause of the split, but the ISI was behind this split. Lieutenant Colonel Obaidullah of the ISI was the man in charge of this operation.[33] A short, stocky man, he was an officer of unusual ability, intelligence, and dedication, so that he had developed an unerring instinct for his job. He met Lieutenant General Asad Durrani, the new director general of the ISI, and recommended to him that these young men be taken under protection by the ISI and helped to organize their forces, as they were the only ones with the courage and capacity to break the terror of the MQM. In his view the MQM could be brought to heel only by terrorizing the terrorists. Durrani was not verbose. He was decisive and a notch or two above the best of his colleagues in the province of the mind. He did not take long to give his assent to Obaid's proposals, and the three dissidents were shifted to an ISI safe house in Rawalpindi. Soon the two MQM groups were at loggerheads. Jam Sadiq Ali's death in March 1992 created further problems for the MQM, and consequently Altaf Hussain had to go into exile. The ISI recipe worked for the time being.

Jamaat-i-Islami (JI), a member of the ruling IJI coalition, was also increasingly distancing itself from the government. It was also apprehensive of MQM's close ties with the Nawaz government, as MQM was the party that had broken its hold in major urban centers in Sindh. Qazi Hussain Ahmed, the leader of JI, had joined the IJI due to the ISI pressure[34] and had justified this decision to JI cadres by projecting this as an opportunity to continue its policy in Afghanistan and support Islamization measures in which JI had a major stake. But sitting on government benches in the Parliament was not something to which JI was accustomed. They were champions of street agitation with a proven record. Their problems with Nawaz had erupted when JI had taken an anti-American stance during the first

Gulf War. Its members had organized fifty-seven "jihad rallies" and two dozen "coffin-clad" protest marches to express their readiness to participate in the jihad against the West.[35] Nawaz Sharif, in response, was forced to mend fences with JI for political reasons, though he did not abandon his pro-American foreign policy, especially in reference to the Iraq issue. As a token, Nawaz had removed Sahibzada Yaqub Ali Khan from the cabinet when Qazi Hussain publicly criticized Yaqub for "pursuing American interests."[36] The mullah forces were making their presence felt. Realizing that Nawaz was not coming up to their expectations vis-à-vis enforcing Islamic laws and supporting JI interests in Afghanistan, they parted ways with him in late 1992, declaring that the government was infected with the "American virus"!

Another crucial development on the national scene that had international ramifications was the selection of Lieutenant General Javed Nasir as the head of ISI. A born-again Muslim with a flowing beard and flowery speech, he was as religious as he was patriotic, but his concept of patriotism was overextended. His vision of Pakistan was that of an Islamic state that was obliged to help out Muslims in distress wherever they were. By inference, he believed that he had a worldwide jurisdiction for ISI's activities! COAS General Janjua was not amused by this selection, but he could not do much about it as this appointment was solely within the prime minister's discretion. Nawaz had little idea that he was launching an unguided missile that would ultimately land Pakistan in trouble. Javed Nasir confesses that "despite the U.N. ban on supplying arms to the besieged Bosnians, he successfully airlifted sophisticated antitank guided missiles which turned the tide in favor of Bosnian Muslims and forced the Serbs to lift the siege."[37] Under his leadership the ISI also got involved in supporting Chinese Muslims in Xinjiang Province, rebel Muslim groups in the Philippines, and some religious groups in Central Asia.[38] The Chinese leadership was very angry when such Pakistani activities were exposed to them. This was surely a blunder committed by Pakistani intelligence services, creating a dent in Pakistan-China relations. ISI stretched itself far and wide during these times, though things were not much different even before Javed Nasir's arrival in the ISI. Nawaz Sharif's disclosure that General Aslam Beg and ISI director general Lieutenant General Asad Durrani had approached him earlier in 1991 with a proposal to generate finances for ISI's ongoing covert operations through the drug trade is a case in point.[39] Nawaz claims that he categorically refused to approve the plan. However, Generals Beg and Durrani vehemently deny that such a conversation ever took place. However, it is a known fact in army circles that in 1983, all of the staff at ISI headquarters in Quetta city had been removed for involvement in the drug business. It is quite unlikely that the Pakistan Army as an institution was generating revenues in this manner, though such allegations are widespread in the Western capitals.

So when Pakistan was put on the State Department's watch list for terrorist states, its people were stunned. When the U.S. administration warned Pakistan to remove Javed Nasir from his position in April 1993,[40] Nawaz readily agreed. Pakistan's continued support of Kashmiri militants was also troubling for the United States, but on this issue the Pakistani military establishment was not ready to give in. In the end Pakistan escaped honorable mention on the terror list by the skin of its teeth due to Israeli intercession. The Israelis were not too keen to see a nuclear-capable state driven to desperation.

In reference to the nuclear capability issue, Pakistan was trying its best to match India's missile capability, but its infrastructure for technological development in this field was not able to deliver. Hence Pakistan looked elsewhere and finally its old friend China obliged. An ISI station was established in Urumqi, the capital of Chinese Xinjiang Province, for the technology transfer, probably around 1990. Pakistan soon acquired medium-range mobile M-11 missiles as well as the requisite launchers. This development was picked up by U.S. intelligence, and the U.S. administration immediately warned China that such a project violates the Missile Technology Control Regime[41] (MTCR), but it was already too late. The scientists and officials managing Pakistan's nuclear project were smart people who consistently proved that they were two steps ahead of the Western intelligence agencies, especially the CIA, which was regularly trying to monitor and stop Pakistan's endeavor in this sphere.

According to a senior army intelligence official who has the distinct credential of having served in all the leading intelligence agencies of Pakistan, namely MI, ISI, and IB (Intelligence Bureau) during the 1980s and early 1990s, the CIA cultivated a Pakistani nuclear scientist, R.M., in the early 1980s. This agent along with a few CIA officials successfully penetrated into the system (locations: Nilour, Kundian, and Kahutta) and were planning a "technical sabotage" of the project, but military intelligence got wind of it and was able to arrest the group in 1982. Reportedly the CIA agents were soon handed over to U.S. authorities.[42]

Nawaz Sharif's real troubles began when General Asif Janjua died of a heart attack on January 8, 1993.[43] Janjua was all set to impose martial law in the country[44] when the unexpected happened. According to the coup d'état plan, Yusuf Haroon, a senior politician,[45] widely believed to be in the good books of the United States, was to be appointed as prime minister after the takeover. Mr. Yusuf Haroon contends that the secret was leaked when General Janjua disclosed this plan at a gathering in the residence of the corps commander at Lahore a few days before his death.[46] Many in the family of Janjua, including his wife, believed and publicly declared that Janjua had been assassinated, though nothing was proved in the postmortem report.

Nawaz Sharif now started maneuvering for his own man (Lieutenant General Ashraf: corps commander, Lahore) to become the new army chief. It is also known that Nawaz Sharif was trying to buy off some senior army generals,[47] but President Ishaq Khan was smart enough to gauge what was being cooked. He knew well that in the case of a pro-Nawaz general occupying the army's chief post, his own days in power would be numbered. As president, he had the discretion to appoint the new chief anyway. Besides Lieutenant General Ashraf, Lieutenant General Farrukh Khan was also in the running for the job. Farrukh Khan was an intelligent and genial officer known for his quick wit and for never taking a stand on any issue. He would have suited Nawaz Sharif, but was rejected because a brother of his had affiliations with the PPP. Hence, luck smiled on Lieutenant General Abdul Waheed Kakar, a short man with a shorter fuse and bull terrier canines who, once he bit on something, would never let go. He soon took charge as the new army chief. This led Nawaz Sharif to make the fatal decision to take on Ishaq Khan, his long-time benefactor and protector.

Nawaz did not realize that his sponsors in the army and the ISI were already out and the president was too powerful under the constitution. He openly started talking about restricting the powers of the president through a constitutional amendment.[48] Benazir fully benefited from this scenario and started an effective campaign against the government. Within a span of two months (March–April 1993) the political elite realigned itself with either the president or the prime minister, calculating who would win the battle. Consequently, the functioning of government came to a standstill, leading to an open confrontation between the president and the prime minister. Different conspiracy theories were in the air as to what caused the final rift between the two power-holders. The most interesting of these was propounded by Maulana Kausar Niazi, a religious scholar of sorts associated with the PPP. He alleged that Nawaz Sharif was trying to curb Ishaq's powers through repeal of the Eighth Amendment at the behest of the United States, as he had refused to accept the American line on Pakistan's nuclear program. Referring to a statement by Dr. Qadeer Khan that the president was guarding the nuclear program as a rock, Maulana further deliberated that, as per his sources, the United States had asked Nawaz to cut the president down to size![49]

Finally, Nawaz Sharif blasted the president in a televised address to the nation on April 17, 1993. Keeping in line with the political traditions of Pakistan, Ishaq dismissed the government two days later on the charges of maladministration and corruption. Yet it was not all over for Nawaz. In an unprecedented move, the Supreme Court of Pakistan reinstated the Nawaz government within a month of its removal, maintaining that the president had not enough grounds to take such a drastic step. This was humiliating for Ishaq Khan, but he decided not to give up. He was a seasoned bureaucrat who had witnessed political intrigues in the country for many decades and knew the art of dismantling governments quite well. The political opponents of Nawaz were at his beck and call, as Nawaz's ouster meant their chance to enter the power corridors. Soon another choreographed crisis erupted. The people of Pakistan were watching their elected leaders in utter disgust but were helpless. The political mess forced General Waheed Kakar to move in. He could have imposed martial law but, being a professional soldier committed to his job, he did not. He instead "convinced" both the president and prime minister to resign. Before leaving office, Ishaq Khan, with the approval of both Nawaz Sharif and Benazir Bhutto, installed a neutral caretaker government under Moeen Qureshi, a retired World Bank vice president, for three months until fresh elections could be held in the country.

### Benazir Back in the Saddle (October 1993–November 1996)

Moeen Qureshi, the caretaker prime minister, was an outsider in the sense that he was resident in the United States, and many believed that he was imposed on Pakistan by the Americans. Irrespective of this controversy, it was only after a long time that Pakistanis had the experience of seeing someone carrying this office with the grace that it required. His three months in office will be remembered for the lists he made public of all the loan defaulters, and those that had got such loans written off through their political influence. A good part of the country's elite received mention in these lists, and for the first time the people got to know how so many of the "honorable" of their country had managed to keep up their respectability over so many years. Most important, he ensured free and fair elections within the stipulated time and did not attempt to "earn" a place in the next political setup.

The electoral coalition between the PPP and the Muslim League (the Junejo group, consisting of politicians who had left Nawaz in support of the president), JI's decision to contest the elections independently, and the MQM's boycott of National Assembly elections[50] made it possible for Benazir Bhutto to return to power on October 6, 1993. This was Pakistan's third election in five years. On the other hand, the PPP's performance in the provincial elections ensured that Benazir could manage to have a PPP leader elected as president. Within a month, Sardar Farooq Khan Leghari, a PPP stalwart known for his honesty, became president of Pakistan, declaring that, "I won't be a President who encourages intrigues or subverts the democratic process."[51] In addition, with an army that was neutral, an experienced Benazir now had a real chance to deliver. But her personalized style of management and stories of rampant corruption by her ministers and bureaucracy tarnished her government's image. Widespread allegations against Asif Ali Zardari for taking kickbacks in government contracts were increasingly believed by all and sundry, though in many cases corrupt bureaucrats and politicians used Asif's name to cover their own shady practices. The times also witnessed an upsurge in ethnic and sectarian terrorism, making the country increasingly ungovernable.

General Waheed Kakar, the COAS, who was quite supportive of Benazir, was a clean man and had a reasonably good reputation in the army. Unfortunately, he rapidly lost his standing in the army first because he sidelined many senior and middle-ranking officers who were known to be close to his predecessor, the late General Janjua, and second for being perceived as pro-Benazir. The deleterious effects of Zia's army recruitment policies were increasingly emerging. Where religion was once a taboo topic for discussion, apart from politics it became the most discussed subject. This was done at the cost of professional discussions and led to group formations around not only the sectarian divisions, but also around various schools of thought within the same sect.

In 1993, Sufi Iqbal, a self-proclaimed divine who claimed to be a resident of Medina (Saudi Arabia), came and settled in Taxila, a city about twenty miles from Rawalpindi city that houses the military headquarters. Soon he had disciples among the seniormost ranks of the army. He went further and created his own loose organization, bestowing status and seniority to his disciples, which was frequently in conflict with their military ranks. This led to the ridiculous spectacle of Major General Saeed uz-Zaffar, commandant of the Staff College, standing up in deference whenever Colonel Azad Minhas entered his office! Concurrently, Lieutenant General Ghulam Mohammad Malik (known as GM), corps commander of Rawalpindi, was running a character-building course for the benefit of officers under his command. GM was known to be a very religious man.

Intriguingly, the graduates of Lieutenant General GM's character-building courses and Sufi Iqbal's disciples overlapped. In September 1994 the MI stumbled upon a conspiracy by Major General Zaheer ul-Islam Abbassi, Brigadier Mustansar Billa, Colonel Azad Minhas, and a few others to take over the reins of government and declare Pakistan a Sunni religious state. Most of the officers belonged to the Sufi Iqbal circle and were also the pets of Lieutenant General GM. Their plan was simple. They would kill all the generals in the army's General Headquarters (GHQ) on September 30, 1994, when they were scheduled to meet for the promotion board, and then announce their act on national television. They were then counting on the rest of the army to follow their direction. There was one snag, though, and that was that General Abbassi was functioning as director general of the National Guards, and neither he nor any other of his collaborators had any troops under their command. Further, they were not entities with any personal following in the army, and Abbassi was certainly disliked by many. Yet Abbassi was not so bereft of gray matter to have seriously thought that he could take over the country alone. Somebody much more powerful had to be backing him. The conjecture in the army was that that somebody was General GM, who was due for retirement three weeks hence. Everyone knew that GM was very close to Abbassi. As second in seniority to Waheed and being commander of the Rawalpindi corps, he was ideally placed to take over after the only general senior to him was killed. Pakistan was therefore within an inch of becoming a radical Muslim state. Ironically, GM was never charged. As corps commander of Rawalpindi, he knew too much and was privy to most of Pakistan's nuclear secrets. His court-martial would have been both embarrassing and a possible security disaster. When confronted by the general belief in the army that General GM was the man behind the Abbassi conspiracy, Waheed always denied it. But his denials were always tepid and seemed to carry little conviction.[52]

Waheed was assertive, however, on another front. He sent two former chiefs of the ISI, Lieutenant General Asad Durrani and Lieutenant General Javed Nasir, home for violating the channels of command and mandated the new director general of the ISI, Lieutenant General Javed Ashraf Qazi, to not only cleanse the ISI of "Islamists" but to rein in the jihadis in Kashmir as well. Qazi mercilessly cleansed the ISI—many officers involved in the Afghan war were posted back to regular army units, and quite a few of them were soon retired. Many ISI officials who were shunted out soon became consultants for various religious extremist groups. The handler-agent relationship continued in this sense.

Benazir's return to power also marked an improvement in U.S.-Pakistan relations, and in large part this was due to William Perry, then U.S. defense secretary, and the Pentagon, which had traditionally nurtured a soft spot for Pakistan. Robin Lynn Raphel, another person favorably inclined toward Pakistan, also became the first head of the newly created Bureau of South Asian Affairs at the State Department during these days. In October 1993 she made a statement that created quite a stir in Indian circles: "We view Kashmir as a disputed territory and that means that we do not recognize that Instrument of Accession as meaning that Kashmir is forever more an integral part of India."[53] Pakistan read this as a friendly overture encouraging normalization of relations. This effort received a boost when Senator Hank Brown, a Republican from Colorado, after a visit to South Asia, contended that the "draconian sanctions against Pakistan were damaging U.S. interests."[54] As chairman of the Senate Foreign Relations Committee's South Asia Subcommittee, Brown was an influential lawmaker. He soon initiated a proposal for easing sanctions by lifting the ban on economic assistance and releasing frozen U.S. military equipment. Pakistan's government was delighted at this development. In a matter of months, Pakistan reciprocated when its law enforcement agencies helped the U.S. Federal Bureau of Investigation (FBI) in nabbing Ramzi Yousaf from Islamabad. Ramzi was the mastermind behind the February 26, 1993, terrorist bombing of World Trade Center in New York that killed six people.

Benazir's visit to Washington in April 1995 gave further impetus to the warming up of bilateral relations. A successful media blitz highlighted Pakistan's role in U.N. peacekeeping missions in Somalia, Bosnia, and Haiti, and projected Pakistan as a force of moderation and stability in a troubled region. Soon thereafter, Senator Brown, despite strong opposition from Senator Pressler and Indian-American lobbyists, had his amendment passed in Congress, which partially relaxed the pressure of the Pressler sanctions on Pakistan. It was also a diplomatic victory of Pakistan's very able ambassador to the United States, Maleeha Lodhi, over her Indian counterpart. And though President Clinton chose not to resume economic aid to Pakistan in full, it nevertheless constituted a psychological relief for an embattled country.

Meanwhile, a monumental development had taken place in Afghanistan. In 1994, Afghanistan saw the outbreak of the Taliban phenomenon that caught the CIA, the ISI, and anyone who cared napping. The Taliban was composed of the younger generation of Pakistani-Afghans, those Afghan children who had grown up in Pakistani refugee camps and were blooded in the last years of the Afghan war. They were the product of the *Madrasas*, whose growth had been facilitated by Zia, funded by the Saudis, and encouraged by the United States for the cannon fodder they promised to produce for a ragtag army fighting in defense of the free world. To start with, theirs was a local revolt against the corruption and tyranny of the warlord around Kandahar, whom they overpowered and executed in a spontaneous movement of pure rage and determined action. Maulana Fazl ur-Rahman, leader of the right-wing Jamiat-i-Ulema-i-Islam-F (JUI-F), which was running a vast network of *Madrasas* in Pakistan, was an ardent supporter of the Taliban campaign. Being a political ally of Benazir, he played a crucial role in opening up communication channels between the Pakistan government and the Taliban leadership. Retired major general Naseerullah Babar, Pakistan's interior minister, immediately realized the Taliban's potential, sent them more recruits from Pakistani *Madrasas* to beef up their strength, and encouraged them to take over Gulbadin Hikmatyar's massive arms dump at Spin Boldak. After clearing the environs, the Taliban never looked back. Thousands of Pakistani students from hundreds of *Madrasas* spread all over the country joined them as they extended their power from one Afghan province to another. Fighting, cajoling, and bribing, they brought almost the whole country under their control in less than five years. Only Ahmad Shah Masud held out, in the Panjshir Valley.

The devastated people of Afghanistan, ravaged by unending years of war, welcomed the Taliban peace, which was later to enforce a draconian uniformity on them. Pakistan welcomed the change in Kabul because at long last it had a friendly government in power there. The initial American reaction was also favorable because in the Taliban they saw a power that was anti-Iran. They also hoped that unification of the country under a strong central government would increase the chances of a U.S. company, Unocal, laying a gas pipeline through Afghanistan. The U.S. administration, however, was quick to see through the reality of the Taliban and later withdrew whatever support it had extended to them. Pakistan simply closed its eyes to them. In May 1994, when Salamat and Rehmat Masih, two poor Christians charged under the Blasphemy Law, were having their case heard in court, thousands of mullahs were parading outside the court. They were calling for the Taliban to come and protect Islam in Pakistan. They were chanting the slogan: "Kabul Ke baad Islamabad . . . Taliban, Taliban" (After Kabul, Islamabad . . . Taliban, Taliban).[55] The Benazir government could not muster the courage to see what was going on.

While the Taliban were on the ascendance in Afghanistan, Pakistan also experienced its first brush with its indigenous Taliban-style movement in November 1994. This was the black-turbaned Tehrik-i-Nifaz-i-Shariat-i-Mohammadi (Movement for the Enforcement of Mohammad's Law; TNSM) led by Sufi Mohammad. This movement spread in the Malakand area of the North-West Frontier Province (NWFP) of Pakistan bordering Afghanistan, with many of its members boasting about their participation in the jihad in Afghanistan. They occupied the local airport (Saidu Sharif), forced government offices to close down, and blocked traffic on all major roads in the area, demanding enforcement of the Islamic law in Malakand. The government used the Frontier Corps (a federal paramilitary agency) to arrest Sufi Mohammad and restore order, but also succumbed to the TNSM demand of introducing Islamic law in the area.

The government had hardly recovered from the Malakand crisis when, in November 1995, an Arab-Afghan veteran of the Afghan jihad blew up a sizable portion of the Egyptian embassy in Islamabad in the first case of a suicide bombing in Pakistan. With it came a warning that, unless the government eased pressure on Arab volunteers of the Afghan war, it could expect more of the same. For Pakistan, the payback time for its role as a frontline ally of the United States had arrived in earnest.

Sectarian confrontations between Sunni and Shia communities were also on the rise. Sipah-i-Sahaba, an extremist Deobandi organization and its militant wing Lashkar-e-Jhangvi (details in chapter 9), were implementing their agenda of murdering Shias with impunity. The worst incident took place in Kurram Agency, where Shia and Sunni tribes went to war in 1996, using rockets and heavy machine guns. After a week, two hundred people were lying dead on the streets.[56]

But the Taliban were in Afghanistan while Malakand and Kurram Agency were on the fringes of Pakistan, and though events there were an augury for the days to come, they posed no immediate threat to the government. Anything that was not immediate was just not there. A more urgent problem for Benazir was Karachi, where intra-MQM violence had claimed more than a thousand lives in 1994 alone. Altaf Hussain's organization was progressively degenerating into a number of gangs loosely hanging together under the label of MQM, operating like the mafia, sustaining themselves by extortion and affording protection to those in need of it, and spending a considerable part of their energies in revenge killings and keeping themselves from getting killed. The man they had most to fear from was Naseerullah Babar, Benazir's minister of the interior. Decorated for gallantry in both the 1965 and 1971 wars, he was courageous and constituted a small island of cleanliness in a political sea filled with thugs. He took upon himself direct charge of antiterrorist operations in Karachi, and his methods proved highly effective in bringing peace back to the city. This operation was conducted almost entirely by the police force under the operative command of deputy inspector general of police Dr. Shoaib Suddle, establishing that, given sufficient resources, the police could deliver the goods.

However, Benazir plunged herself into another crisis. She appointed twenty new judges to the Punjab High Court, some of whom were known to be her party sympathizers and had a "dubious professional reputation."[57] As soon as these appointments were made, appeals were filed against them in the Supreme Court, and she brought pressure on the chief justice (CJ), Mr. Sajjad Ali Shah, not to accept such appeals. Benazir had appointed him as the CJ thinking that he was her supporter, and because most such supporters acted like poodles, she thought he would toe her policy line. But CJ Shah was a very honest man, as stubborn as he was honest and as proud as he was inflexible. Thus the Supreme Court gave a judgment on March 20, 1996, disallowing Benazir's appointments in Judiciary and laying out principles for the appointment, promotion, and transfer of judges. In a state of shock, she refused to implement the court's decision. The CJ approached the president to help the prime minister see the light and abstain from unnecessarily locking horns with the Judiciary.

The president did manage to prevail over Benazir, but only just, and the strain of doing so ruptured the relationship between the two. In Benazir's vocabulary, Leghari's job description did not include holding opinions of his own. According to Benazir, the turning point in the relationship came when the opposition parties leveled allegations of corruption against the president, in which he was alleged to have made a fictitious land deal. Leghari came to believe that the specific material and evidence of his wrongdoing was let out deliberately by Asif Zardari.[58] Benazir maintains that though she assured him several times that neither she nor her husband had anything to do with it, he became bitter and hostile.[59] The opposition, led by Nawaz Sharif, was also looking for an opportunity to discredit the government, and rumors of a power tussle between the president and prime minister came as music to their ears. Nawaz was furious that Benazir had locked up his aged father on charges of fraud, which was certainly a hit below the belt.

Meanwhile, the issue of selection of a new army chief came up at the time of General Waheed's retirement. Waheed retired in January 1996 after refusing an extension of tenure, which was highly commended in the army for the principle it held. Lieutenant General Nasir Akhtar and Lieutenant General Javed Ashraf Qazi lobbied extensively for promotion, but to no avail. The only one of the front-runners who sat back and did not lend himself to ridicule was Lieutenant General Jahangir Karamat, the seniormost and best of the lot. Before leaving office, the favor that Waheed did for the army was to recommend Karamat to succeed him, and President Leghari endorsed the recommendation.

Activities of the Intelligence Bureau (IB) under its director general, retired major Masood Sharif, also created problems for Benazir. Reportedly, the IB secretly listened to the telephone conversations of the president's family members,[60] and when Leghari came to know of these activities, he was not amused at all. IB was also filing reports to the prime minister on the movement and activities of various corps commanders, ISI and MI field officials, and their bosses.[61] This could not remain a secret, as these agencies were monitoring IB, leading to confrontation between the civilian government and the military establishment. It would have been much more fruitful for the health of the country if all the intelligence agencies would have focused on tracking the activities of extremist outfits who were creating havoc in the country rather than spying on each other.

Interestingly, IB was also specifically tasked by the government to monitor the activities and conversations of Sahibzada Yaqub Ali Khan, as it was believed that being close to the Americans, his conversation with the U.S. ambassador and frequency of meetings with him would give the government enough idea about how the United States was perceiving the developing political scenario. It is a belief in power corridors of Pakistan that the United States has something to do with every political change in Pakistan. The following extracts from the IB report in this regard, covering Yaqub Khan's activities and conversations of March 1996, gives a fair idea about what attracts the attention of a Pakistani intelligence agent and how they link issues:

1. American Ambassador invited Sahibzada Yaqub for dinner on 6th March, which was accepted by him. . . .
2. Col Ayyaz wanted to meet Sahibzada Yaqub on 25 March 1996 but was told that he was sitting with American Ambassador. . . .
3. A very close and confident source confided that Begum Abida Hussain hosted dinner twice for Sahibzada at her residence in second week of March, 1996. It appears that she is active in forming a pressure group against PPP government. It has been noticed that Sahibzada Yaqub Ali Khan has become active and is keenly watching political situation in the country. He is making contacts with various political leaders frequently.[62]

Meanwhile the breach between the president and the prime minister had been steadily widening. In the midst of all this, Murtaza Bhutto, Benazir's estranged brother who had set up his own faction of the PPP, died in a hail of police bullets in Karachi on September 20, 1996. The tragedy was devastating for Benazir. A couple of days later, twenty-one Shia Muslims were killed in a terrorist act in Multan city. Benazir saw these developments as part of a conspiracy to dislodge her government and publicly hinted that Leghari and Military Intelligence were behind the murder.[63] The time for a showdown between the two had finally arrived. The president got in touch with General Karamat and, after ascertaining his views,[64] dismissed Benazir and her government on November 5, 1996. A fourth consecutive civilian government was sent home before completing its stipulated five years in office.

Many Pakistanis were of the view that before the next elections were held, an accountability process of politicians be initiated. President Leghari felt swayed by this opinion but then wriggled out of it, as such an agenda could have hampered his personal political plans. According to Kamran Khan, the leading Pakistani investigative journalist, the top leadership of the Muslim League, including the Sharif family, Saif ur-Rahman, and the Chaudhry family of Gujarat, were very close to being barred from contesting these elections, being loan defaulters, but Leghari rescued them at the last moment.[65] This was probably done due to the fear that the PPP might stage a comeback in the absence of the leading members of the only other major contesting party.

President Farooq Leghari also issued a presidential decree at this time to set up the Council for Defense and National Security (CDNS), with chiefs of the armed forces as members along with elected officeholders. The purpose of this body was to aid and advise the government on key matters, including the proclamation of emergencies. Legal experts doubted its constitutional position,[66] and others believed that at last the army was being given a direct say in governmental affairs. But Qazi Hussain Ahmed of JI interpreted it in an entirely different light—he believed that the CDNS was a tool to strengthen the "Washington plan" of imposing the hegemony of the World Bank and IMF and cutting the Islamic movement down to size.[67]

## Nawaz Sharif Returns to Power (February 1997–October 1999)

Elections on February 3, 1997, were won by Nawaz Sharif in a landslide, a vote that was as much due to his popularity as it was a wholesale indictment of Benazir's economic and political mismanagement. A jubilant and glowing Nawaz Sharif took on the mantle of prime minister amid a shower of promises to a tired and beaten people. But his governance pattern proved that it was old wine in an old bottle with just a new label.

Nawaz Sharif's Muslim League was in power in all the provinces except Baluchistan, while in the center he had a majority with which he could just walk over the opposition. But President Leghari, who had made all this possible, wanted to play a dominant role in running the government.[68] Nawaz simply considered this as interference. Hence he acted swiftly, and on April 1, 1997, the parliament unanimously decided to take the sting out of presidential powers, including the discretionary authority that allowed the president to dismiss the government and dissolve the National Assembly. Courtesy of Zia's Eighth Amendment to the constitution, the division of powers between the president and the prime minister was crafted in such a way that it welcomed intrigues and power tussles.[69] The Thirteenth Amendment finally eliminated the ominous shadows that had stretched across the parliamentary form of government since 1985. Besides making the president toothless, the office of the prime minister had also acquired the power to dismiss and appoint the chiefs of all the three armed services.

Nawaz Sharif had thus become the most powerful man in the country, but he was not entirely satisfied with this. To take the opposition parties to task, he formed the Ehtesab (Accountability) Bureau and placed Saif ur-Rahman over it. Saif was a businessman of humble origins whose services to the cause of Nawaz Sharif had opened up avenues for his substantial enrichment. So by the time he took over the bureau, there was nothing humble about him. Saif lacked the capability to distinguish right from wrong as long as he was doing his master's bidding. Hence the bureau soon became both an instrument of extortion, and one that kept political opponents hostage.

Next, Nawaz decided to test the efficacy of his new power by dismissing the corrupt chief of the navy, Mansur ul-Haq, for the unconscionable crime of helping load his coffers in the French submarine deal. The chief justice (CJ) of the Supreme Court, Sajjad Ali Shah, was another person with whom Nawaz was not comfortable, though for different reasons. The CJ had sent him names of five senior judges serving in provincial High Courts, with the recommendation that they be elevated to fill the vacant slots in the Supreme Court. The list included the name of a judge who had previously adjudicated against him and another who was considered to be unfriendly toward his government, and though they were both known to be men of integrity and ability, Nawaz declared that they could not be promoted. Though he eventually gave way under the advice and persuasion of the army and the president,[70] the beginning of his second tenure was not the most auspicious.

His next step toward the further enhancement of personal power came via another amendment in the constitution, which took the right of parliamentary dissent away from the legislators so that they could not henceforth vote against the position of the party (read prime minister). Any such dissent would automatically lead to the offending legislator being disqualified as a member of parliament, and no court was to have the power to give relief in such cases. This was a naked attempt by Nawaz Sharif to foreclose the possibility of any opposition arising within the ranks of his own party. Soon, members of the opposition filed a writ petition in the Supreme Court against this amendment (the 14th) as being violative of the spirit of parliamentary democracy itself. When the Supreme Court held this amendment to be illegal and scrapped it, Nawaz Sharif was furious and chose to criticize the decision in the National Assembly.

A crisis was in the making. General Karamat was forced to play the role of mediator between Nawaz and the CJ, the latter being fully supported by President Leghari as well. Nawaz finally asked the CJ discreetly to give him one week to settle the issue for good, and the CJ agreed, believing it to be a sincere offer,[71] but Nawaz had something else in mind. He utilized this time to encourage a revolt against the CJ among the judges of the highest court of the land. On November 26, 1997, a day before the contempt case hearing against the prime minister was due to resume, two retired judges of the Supreme Court, the chief minister of Punjab and Sharifuddin Pirzada, the archvillain of every legal drama to be enacted in Pakistan, flew to Quetta.[72] A petition was then presented in the Quetta bench of the Supreme Court challenging the appointment of the CJ himself as being violative of the seniority principle, which lay enshrined in his own judgment of March 1996. The court restrained the chief justice from performing his functions till the petition could be disposed of. The CJ reacted by suspending the decision of the Quetta bench through an administrative order, but in the meanwhile the government had the Peshawar bench of the Supreme Court issue a similar order, with Justice Saeed uz-Zaman of that bench going a step further and taking upon himself the administrative powers of the CJ. When CJ Shah refused to be browbeaten, the ruling party on November 27, 1997, arranged for a demonstration against CJ Shah outside the Court, calling on him to leave the Court. The next day, when he resumed hearing the petition against Nawaz, a mob of ruling party supporters, led by sitting ministers, stormed the courthouse itself. It was as unruly a performance as it was disgraceful. When the show was over, the assailants were feted in a government guest house, and their performance in defense of democracy received fulsome praise from Mr. Shabaz Sharif, chief minister of Punjab and younger brother of the prime minister. The CJ thereon requested the president to provide him army protection so he could discharge his duties secure from the threats of the mob, but nothing transpired.

Meanwhile, the prime minister was pressing President Leghari to appoint a new chief justice, with Leghari refusing to do so. The CJ on the other hand struck down the 13th Amendment to the constitution, thus rehabilitating the full powers of the president. But the army stayed clear of the fracas and, without army intervention, the position of the president had become untenable. He was certain of being impeached. To avoid this he tendered his resignation. The first thing the acting president did was to appoint a new CJ, and Mr. Sajjad Ali Shah walked into the sunset—a stubborn man, but the only one with the guts to stand for the independence of the judiciary and the courage to stand against all the pressure that any government could bring on him. He was also entirely free of the taint of corruption and the bias arising from caste color or creed. He was everything therefore that a country like Pakistan could ill afford to lose.

During these times, politics in South Asia took a very interesting turn. In March 1998 the Bharatiya Janata Party (BJP) won the elections in India, with Mr. Atal Behari Vajpayee becoming prime minister. It was Pakistan that had been declared an ideological state, and though its surrender to the forces of fundamentalism was expected sometime in the future, it was India that fell to a Hindu fundamentalist party that counted among its leading lights (by extension) the murderers of Mohandas Gandhi. The BJP was as committed

to antisecularism as the Pakistani parties on the right were, but the vital difference was that the Pakistani mullah was still waiting to get into power
while his Hindu counterpart across the border was already there. And this
change was not without repercussions. On May 11, 1998, India shook the
world by detonating three atomic devices, followed by an additional two
tests on May 13. President Clinton was appalled and announced a cutoff of
all aid to the country, including a pledge to vote against Indian efforts to
obtain loans from international lending agencies. Concurrent with the moves
to penalize India, U.S. attention was focused on Pakistan, whose reaction
was considered absolutely predictable, and this had to be contained. President Clinton personally called Nawaz Sharif no less than four times to urge
restraint,[73] promising that should Pakistan respect international opinion on
this issue, the United States would write off its bilateral loans to Pakistan,
prevail over Japan to do the same, have its repayments to international lending agencies rescheduled, and try to get through Congress a conventional
military aid package that would add considerable credibility to the country's
conventional deterrence.

Nawaz was under tremendous conflicting pressures from all sides. There
was the United States and the rest of the Western world counseling restraint,
and supported in this by a fairly influential body of opinion within Pakistan,
but all the right-wing parties and the overwhelming majority in the country
demanded that he go ahead with similar tests and disregard all other opinion.
The religious parties openly warned the prime minister that unless he put
Pakistan on the nuclear map, now that India had formally entered the nuclear
club without any fear or regard for international opinion, he would for all
times be considered a traitor to his country. The temper of the prevailing
sentiment was not helped by the gloating and taunting attitude of Indian
leadership immediately following the tests, with the Indian minister for the
interior L.K. Advani condescendingly advising Pakistan to accept the new
power realities in South Asia. Meanwhile, there was a meeting of the G-8
countries in Europe, which condemned the Indian tests but left Pakistan with
the impression that there was more bluster behind their condemnation than
any serious commitment. The Pakistan Army, though conservative and expected to be strongly hawkish on the issue, handled the matter with clinical
detachment. General Karamat called a meeting of his senior generals, got
their opinions, discussed the issue at length, and forwarded to the government a paper detailing the pros and cons of either course open to it, but
refrained from giving a final recommendation one way or the other, leaving
the final decision with the cabinet.[74] Two factors that weighed strongly in
favor of the decision to go ahead with the tests were lack of faith in the
American promises and the encouragement of the Saudi government to go

ahead. The very fact that Nawaz had taken the Saudis in confidence and thought them important enough to be asked their opinion on such an important issue did a lot for the Saudi ego and made for a very special relationship between Nawaz and Prince Abdullah. An additional factor that cannot be discounted was Nawaz's belief that Pakistan's nuclear status would attract more funding from Muslim countries around the world than anything promised by the Americans. On May 28, 1998, Pakistan detonated five nuclear devices in the remote hills of Baluchistan to become the newest, the poorest, and the proudest member of the nuclear club.

It may have been part of an Indian plot to egg Pakistan on into a trap so that when the inevitable international opprobrium followed, Pakistan would be there to share it and thus divide the unwelcome attention that India would otherwise have attracted. Perhaps India was also secretly hoping that the Pakistani nuclear program was a hoax. But the whole of Pakistan exploded in spontaneous joy upon hearing the news of the detonations. Nothing more cogently demonstrated how important it was to understand Pakistan in the context of its relationship with India, and to what extent so many of the policies of the one were determined by those of the other. For the first time, though, it seemed that, if the United States showed no sympathetic understanding of the Pakistani position underlying its reaction to Pakistan's tests, there was at least a veneer of empathy. Reflecting President Clinton's views, his press secretary declared: "Prime Minister Nawaz Sharif was honest and straightforward in the description of his decision, and India was manifestly not."[75] And though all types of international sanctions were slapped on Pakistan, the U.S. Congress voted to give the president the authority to waive all sanctions because the United States did not think it was good policy to let a nuclear Pakistan be pushed to the economic brink. Pakistan was in bad need of economic assistance because, even before the new sanctions, financially it was in a perilous state. In the aftermath of the tests, the government announced the freezing of all private foreign currency accounts that the people had opened consequent to its repeated enticements and guarantees. It was enough to shatter government credibility and consequently scare foreign investors. So, though the people had applauded their bomb and gone delirious over it, the time had come for them to eat the promised grass.[76]

On the Afghanistan front, the Taliban took the northern Afghan town of Mazar-i-Sharif in August 1998, and this brought the whole of the country under their control save the Panjshir Valley, which Ahmad Shah Masud still continued to hold by a combination of courage and uncommon skill. And though he was the ablest general to be thrown up by the Afghan war, and in a reversal of roles Russia and the Taliban-fearing neighbors of Afghanistan were supporting him, there was little chance that he would be able to beat his adversaries in an offensive war and reclaim any territory from Mullah Omar's men. In this scenario the United States was getting increasingly worried that a Taliban-type movement might also spread into and destabilize volatile and nuclear Pakistan.

After the bombings of the U.S. embassies in Nairobi and Dar es Salaam in early August 1998, which America blamed on Osama bin Laden, a cruise missile attack was launched against Osama's bases in Afghanistan on August 21, 1998. Though there were minor protests in the country for the violation of Pakistan's airspace by the United States, and a little damage was done to Osama's infrastructure, eleven Pakistanis were killed in this attack. They were members of the Harkat-ul-Ansar Party, a militant organization active in Indian-controlled Kashmir. The other result of the cruise missile attack was that, for the first time, people all across Pakistan heard about Osama bin Laden. Though he was a known figure to religious militants and many in the provinces bordering Afghanistan had heard his name, the majority of Pakistanis did not know who Osama was before this attack.

On December 2, 1998, Nawaz Sharif was Clinton's guest at the White House. His first order of business, as had been the case with all his predecessors, was to solicit the U.S. president's intercession in resolving the Kashmir dispute. Though the president expressed his inability to do much on this issue, he nevertheless indicated that Pakistan could expect the repatriation of the monies it had paid for the stranded F-16s, which it had not received yet. This assurance by the U.S. president was not motivated so much by a sense of justice or altruism, but instead because Pakistan had finally decided to resort to the U.S. courts to get its money back, and it was the opinion of the U.S. Justice Department that Pakistan was likely to win the legal battle.[77]

On the home front, Nawaz's appetite for accumulating more power had not abated. So in a completely unexpected move in August 1998, he moved a bill in the National Assembly for the 15th Amendment to the constitution to enforce rule by Islamic law in Pakistan, for the interpretation of which the Nawaz Sharif government would have the ultimate authority. The bill appeared to seek government authority to enforce Islam, but in effect it represented a bid to acquire unfettered power.[78] The amendment also proposed that the directives of the government in this sphere would be beyond the jurisdiction of courts and judicial review. One of the clauses offered some guarantees to non-Muslims, but constitutional lawyers declared it to be eyewash, as minorities would be subject to the public law that would be interpreted by the courts and government in light of what they considered to be Islam.[79] In violation of all the norms of federalism, the constitutional amendment procedure was made so "simple" for the purposes of removal of impediments in the enforcement of *Sharia* as to make a mockery of democracy. Abdul Hamid Jatoi, a veteran Sindhi parliamentarian and a member of the ruling party, reacted sharply and, giving voice to his concerns on the floor of the House, said: "Mr. Speaker, I feel like crying. . . . Ours is a beautiful country. For God's sake don't break it up."[80]

The bill, with minor changes, was passed in the lower house on October 9, 1998, and this sent a shudder through the religious minorities, who instinctively knew how Islamic laws would be implemented, while the moderates who had any imagination at all shouted, protested, warned, or simply fell into a state of shock. But Nawaz was just a little short of the numbers required to get his passport to the caliphate through the Senate. In a shameless replay of the recent hooliganism that had accompanied the besieging of the Supreme Court, he encouraged the mullahs of the land to come out of their lairs and lay siege to the Senate, demanding the passage of the bill.[81] Despite all the threats and promises of violence, miraculously the Senate held out by the skin of its teeth. Pakistan was teetering on the brink and was within an inch of its fall to the caliphate of Mian Nawaz Sharif. In this scenario all Nawaz had to do was wait until March 2000, when new elections for the seats of retiring senators were certain to give him the majority he needed. But luckily for Pakistan, events were to take place that would save Islam from its exploitation by yet another unscrupulous Muslim ruler. It is pertinent to refer here to an open letter addressed to the senators by some prominent citizens, urging them to demonstrate courage by defeating the bill. The following extract from the letter insightfully indicates what would have been the situation if the bill had been approved: "In reality, it will be a nightmare where every '*Imam*' of every mosque across the country will issue '*Fatwas*' [binding religious injunctions issued by religious scholars]. . . . Indeed, fundamental and human rights will be redefined on the grounds of these *Fatwas* and ordinary citizens, specially women, non-Muslims and minority Islamic sects will be facing threats to their right to life and liberty."[82]

As the situation progressively deteriorated and government high-handedness continued to grow with impunity, the man who came in for increasing criticism was General Jahangir Karamat. He was being taken to task for not having come to the assistance of the chief justice when he had asked for army protection, which he was obliged to provide him. The implication of the criticism was that, had Karamat acted then, things would never have come to such a sorry pass. The most immediate danger being felt within both the army and among those who had come to see the army as the opposition party of the last resort was that Nawaz would next destroy the army and make it a partisan body, like he and former leaders had done to the judiciary, the police, and the bureaucracy. Indeed, over the years the latter three institutions had been so infiltrated by political influence and patronage that officers could be clearly identified as extensions of one party or the other.

General Karamat was an educated man, and by conviction noninterventionist. He was very much aware of the current rage of opinion both within his command and among the general public. He was also convinced that there was enough justification for such fears. He conveyed his views to the prime minister on few occasions, which was reported in print.[83] It was a measure of the level of popular frustration, discontent, and general apprehension that a man as imperturbable and as free of political ambition as General Karamat should have felt constrained to speak out against the manner in which the government was running the shop. While addressing faculty and students at the Navy Staff College in early October 1998, he vented his frustration by publicly suggesting the need to create a National Security Council backed by "a team of credible advisers and a think tank of experts" for devising effective policies for resolving the ongoing problems. He also recommended a "neutral competent and secure bureaucracy and administration at the federal and provincial levels" and warned that "Pakistan could not afford the destabilizing effects of polarization, vendettas, and insecurity-expedient policies."[84] This was a very strong indictment of the government. Instead of convincing Nawaz Sharif of the general's sincerity and the seriousness of the situation, all it succeeded in accomplishing was pricking his highly inflated ego. Ill-advised, the prime minister called on General Karamat to resign, and he put in his papers and left the colors. Nawaz was now running around like a small boy with a hammer in his hand, viewing all subjects requiring a solution as nails to be hit on the head.

Next in line for promotion was Lieutenant General Ali Kuli Khan. A tall Pathan officer and a graduate of the Sandhurst Military Academy U.K., he had an impeccable lineage that showed in his manners and never failed to disarm. His conduct was also known to be aboveboard, but the great obstacle that stood in his way was that, being the favorite of General Waheed, who had given Nawaz his marching orders during his first stint in office, he was never going to be very popular with him. In the army, what detracted from an otherwise blameless career was the way Waheed had manipulated his seniority to ensure that when the time came, he would be most senior for promotion to the highest rank. This smacked strongly of favoritism, and the Pakistan Army is too conservative an institution to let such things go unnoticed. However, before General Karamat had handed over his resignation, Ali tried to prevail on him to first hand the command of the army over to him and he would deal with the prime minister howsoever he thought fit. But when he failed to get his way, he had it conveyed to the government through an intermediary that Karamat's remarks at the Navy Staff College were in no way reflective of his own views. This rearguard action did not produce the desired results and he was ignored for promotion. Next in line was Lieutenant

General Khalid Nawaz Malik, an officer too hard and unforgiving to have had a large following in the army, and he too was passed over. The news reached him when he was on an official tour to Peshawar. His first act was to write down his resignation, change into civilian clothes, and return home by public transport. In the manner he departed from the army, he rekindled distant memories of an honorable tradition.

The man whom Sharif chose as his next army chief was Lieutenant General Pervez Musharraf, third in line for the job. He was a good, straight soldier, but not quite straight enough to have rigorously avoided the opportunity of infiltrating himself in the affections of the prime minister, and it seems that the foot he put forward as his best, for Nawaz to inspect, found prime ministerial favor. Though his demeanor at the first meeting he had with Nawaz Sharif is not recorded, it would be reasonable to presume that he would have bent himself just sufficiently to blend in with the temper of the times, though this was much against his nature and his instincts. In selecting Musharraf for the job, he had selected the only senior officer of the army who had any support base at all, and also the only one who had it in him to wring his neck, and all he had to do now was place it in the right spot and have it wrung.

Meanwhile, sectarian killings all across the country were on the rise. Sipah-i-Sahaba and its splinter group Lashkar-e-Jhangvi were openly targeting Shia doctors, businessmen, and intellectuals. In the history of Pakistan, 1997 and 1998 are years that witnessed the highest number of such brutal murders and assassinations.[85] The Shia extremist group Sipah-i-Mohammad retaliated on few occasions, but its forces were outnumbered by the Wahhabi strength that supported this heinous crime. The Wahhabi-sponsored groups were serving the Pakistani intelligence agencies well in their pursuits in Afghanistan and Kashmir, and in the garb of this jihad, these militant outfits were successfully following their agendas inside Pakistan.

Contrary to Nawaz's political style at home, his foreign policy made some sense. In the aftermath of the nuclear tests in 1998, both India and Pakistan were showing signs of opening up to each other, and prospects of bilateral talks improved. A meeting between Indian prime minister Atal Bihari Vajpayee and Nawaz Sharif during a U.N. General Assembly session in New York on September 23, 1998, led to a warming of relations, and Nawaz invited Vajpayee to visit Pakistan, which he accepted. In an unprecedented move, Vajpayee decided to travel to Lahore on the inaugural run of the bus service between the two countries. On hearing this, the Pakistani rightist parties led by JI started protesting and declared that they would disrupt this visit. Shabaz Sharif, the chief minister of Punjab and a very able administrator, had to deal with this menace at the very last moment or the visit would become a great embarrassment. He simply had the leading activists of the religious parties picked up without warning and thrown into jail. Thus a landmark meeting between the two leaders took place on February 20, 1999. In what came to be termed the Lahore Declaration, both nations expressed their agreement to "intensify their efforts to resolve all issues, including the issue of Jammu and Kashmir."[86] Vajpayee also paid a visit to the Minar-i-Pakistan, a national monument marking the site where in 1940 the Muslim League had resolved to work toward the goal of a separate national homeland. This visit was widely interpreted as a profound gesture reflecting India's acceptance of the 1947 partition and an indication that India wanted to bury the hatchet and move forward. The greatest achievement of the summit was that it had taken place at all, because all dialogue between officials and leaders of the two countries had stood suspended for years, and this meeting promised to bring many more in its wake.

In this one-to-one session, both leaders also reached a private understanding.[87] They agreed that they should try to find a viable solution of the Kashmir problem by the end of the year (1999). They knew that it would be difficult for both parties to publicly delink the issue from the standard rigid positions both states had adopted for decades. Hence they decided to opt for a back-channel diplomatic route, which was a creative initiative indeed. Both decided to nominate one person each to carry on the process by discussing fresh conflict resolution approaches. Niaz A. Naik, a talented and reputable retired diplomat, represented Pakistan, while R.K. Mishra, a media tycoon with considerable political influence, was selected as the Indian emissary. Robert Wirsing, a leading and highly respected South Asian scholar from the United States, has covered the details of this effort in his latest book, *Kashmir in the Shadows of War.*[88] Nine secret rounds of discussions between Naik and Mishra took place from March 3 to June 27, 1999, in which they agreed that a viable and final resolution of the Kashmir conflict was possible only by moving beyond their publicly stated positions and by ensuring that the interests of all three parties—Indians, Pakistanis, and Kashmiris—are given due weightage. The negotiations certainly maintained the spirit of this initial understanding and considered many scenarios, ranging from converting the Line of Control (LOC) into an international border to awarding independence to Kashmir. From Wirsing's narration, it is obvious that both individuals respected each other's views and concerns and were willing to think outside of the box. In the Indian-Pakistani negotiating history, this was nothing short of a miracle. Naik and Mishra were keeping their bosses updated on the status of discussions.

Finally, after weighing the pros and cons of various options, Naik and Mishra were considering the proposal of bifurcating Kashmir between India and Pakistan along the Chenab River, which implied that the Valley of Kashmir in Indian-controlled Jammu and Kashmir could become a part of Pakistan. At this juncture, Niaz was given the opportunity to meet Vajpayee. When Niaz broached the issue of the Chenab option, Vajpayee, without discarding it, asked him about Pakistan's views on the Kashmir Study Group proposal known as the Livingston Plan.[89]

The plan is named after the Kashmir Study Group's founder and chairman, Farooq Kathwari, and his farmhouse at Livingston, New York, in the United States, where the sketch of this idea was framed. The plan suggests that the Muslim majority areas of Jammu and Kashmir State should be separated from the rest of the region and provided sovereignty (without giving an international personality) and popular rule, and this arrangement would be guaranteed to the people of this entity by India, Pakistan, and the appropriate international bodies. India and Pakistan would then jointly work out the financial arrangements for such a unit and should allow the unit to develop its own internal security force while the external affairs and defense would be looked after by both India and Pakistan. The new unit would have its own secular and democratic constitution, a flag, citizenship, a legislature, and currency. The LOC would remain in place till both countries removed it in their mutual interest. The Livingston Plan also emphasizes the need for demilitarization of the unit and a mutual pledge not to deploy their forces across the existing LOC. In other words, the plan is based on the idea of joint suzerainty over Kashmir.

Naik was not sure about Pakistan's position on this option, so he was expected to get back to the negotiating table after ascertaining the views of Nawaz Sharif. On Naik's return to Pakistan this issue was discussed in detail, and for the first time the ISI and General Pervez Musharraf were involved in the process. Musharraf called it a good starting point and commented that a combination of the Livingston Plan and the Chenab option "could open the door to a solution." From the Pakistani as well as the Indian perspective, this was a big step forward. Durable peace was in sight.

But that was not to be. In May 1999, just three months after the frozen road to Indo-Pak dialogue had thawed enough to get a promise for more going, Pakistan launched its operation against the Kargil Heights in the far north of Indian-held Kashmir, just across the LOC.[90] These heights dominated the main Indian supply route to Leh, where India had a small cantonment to house one brigade. It was the Indian routine at Kargil to descend the heights at the start of the winter snows and reoccupy them the following spring. With these heights in Pakistani hands, it meant that supplies to Leh could not be maintained. And though India did have an alternate route, it was not an all-weather, all-season road. India would therefore have no option but to recover the heights and open the road to Leh or allow its garrison to perish. Though, of course, even if India had any number of alternative roads, its pride alone would have sufficed for it to mount an operation for the relief of Kargil.

This operation had been discussed at least twice before in earlier years and turned down both times. Zia was the first army chief invited by the Military Operations (MO) directorate to see a presentation on this operation. After sitting through it, he retorted in his most chaste Urdu, which he would normally do only when he wanted to take someone to task. His ensuing conversation with the director general of military operations (DGMO), as narrated by a senior army officer, went somewhat like follows:

> *Zia*: When we take Kargil, what do you expect the Indians to do? . . . I mean, don't you think they will try and recapture it?
>
> *DGMO*: Yes sir, but we think that the position is impregnable and we can hold it against far superior forces.
>
> *Zia*: Now that's very good, but in that case, don't you think the Indians will go for a limited offensive elsewhere along the line of control, take some of our territory, and use it as a bargaining chip?
>
> *DGMO*: Yes sir, this is possible, but . . .
>
> *Zia*: And if they are beaten back there also, don't you think they will attack across the international frontier, which may lead to a full-scale war?
>
> *DGMO*: That's possible, sir.
>
> *Zia*: So in other words, you have prepared a plan to lead us into a full-scale war with India!

This sardonic observation by Zia ul-Haq caused the demise of the first Kargil proposal. The second time the plan was mooted, it was shot down on the same grounds, that is, it was an easy tactical operation that was untenable in the long run unless Pakistan were prepared to go into a full-scale war with India, in which Kargil would be a secondary objective.

The third and final operational plan for Kargil was put forward by its inspirational father, Lieutenant General Mohammad Aziz Khan, chief of the general staff (CGS). Himself a Kashmiri, he was fully committed to the cause of Kashmiri freedom, and not the sort of man who held any commitment lightly. He was very religious and not known to be a hypocrite.

The tactical parents of the Kargil plan were two. The first was Lieutenant General Mahmood Ahmad, the commander of 10th Corps, in whose area of operations the objective lay. He was a comparatively weaker personality than Aziz, with a romance about history. It is believed that he was convinced by the conviction of Aziz, which, combined with his own historical dream, made him a hostage to the Kargil idea. The second parent of the plan was Major

General Javed Hassan, commander of the Pakistani troops in the Northern Areas (Force Command Northern Areas, FCNA) who would actually have to carry out the operation. He had one of the best minds in the army and even more ambition. He gave his unstinting support to the operation, less through any sense of conviction and more because of the promise that such a position held of bringing him into Musharraf's charmed inner circle. Musharraf was taken in by the enthusiasm of two of his closest generals, and, being eternally levitated by an irrepressible streak of unreal optimism, he became the strongest advocate of the operation. The absolute secrecy that was one of the preconditions of the success of the operation, to secure it against any possibility of leaks, also made it proof against any possibility of a second opinion, and thus against any collusion with a sense of reality. According to Maleeha Lodhi, "Even corps commanders and other service chiefs were excluded" from the decision-making process.[91] So much so that even the very able DGMO, Lieutenant General Tauqir Zia, was initiated into the secret after the gang of four had already taken the irrevocable decision of going ahead with the operation.

The next task was to bring the prime minister on board. For this, a presentation was organized. The exact date of this presentation is a million-dollar question, as this may consequently decide how history will judge both Musharraf and Nawaz. According to Naik's narration of the events to Robert Wirsing, Nawaz Sharif was given a briefing by the army on the Kashmir issue on March 27 or 28, 1999,[92] which probably was the one where the Kargil plan was discussed. Similarly, according to Owen Bennett Jones, the army contends that a specific briefing on the Kargil plan was given in the second week of March 1999, where Nawaz granted formal approval of the plan.[93] Most probably, both Naik and Jones are referring to the same meeting, and it certifies that at the time of Nawaz's meeting with Vajpayee on February 20, 1999, he was not aware of the Kargil operation.

Anyhow, Nawaz came to hear the Kargil presentation accompanied by the recently retired CGS of the army, Lieutenant General Iftikhar Ali Khan, who was Nawaz's secretary of defense. Iftikhar knew Musharraf, Mahmood, and Aziz well and should have used his rank and influence to abort the operation, but he did not, though he certainly showed his reservations. Nawaz's other adviser was Majid Malik, a minister in the cabinet and a retired lieutenant general who had served as DGMO and CGS during his military career a generation earlier. He had a sharp mind and asked all the right questions of the assembled generals, and pointed out all the weaknesses in their overall plan, and its immediate and larger implications. This should have educated Nawaz Sharif adequately to put the operation on hold pending a detailed reexamination of the project, but it did not. Sharif agreed with the plan, though the operation was already in its final stages and Nawaz was not aware of that. Probably in his reverie, he was looking to the glory that would come his way when the fruits promised by the operation were harvested.[94] However, close associates of Nawaz contend that the said briefing never mentioned that regular troops would be involved in the operation, and the discussion was framed entirely in terms of "increasing the heat in Kashmir." Interestingly, in the latest book on the Kargil issue, Shireen Mazari, a Pakistani academic known for her pro-military stance, asserts that the Kargil operation was in fact planned to counter similar moves expected by the Indians in the area, and this military move was in reality a defensive action finalized after credible intelligence reports confirmed Indian designs for incursions across the LOC![95] This theory is not corroborated by any other source.

In reality, the Kargil plan was for Pakistan to send in a mixture of Kashmiri fighters and regular/paramilitary troops (the Northern Light Infantry Regiment) to occupy the heights above Kargil before the Indian Army moved in to reoccupy them at the end of the snow season and cut off the supply route to Leh. The operation was to be projected as a solely Kashmiri mujahideen operation, denying absolutely any Pakistani involvement in it or that Pakistan had any control or influence over these elements. It is worth noting that until the occupation of the heights became an accomplished fact, neither any of the other service chiefs nor the rest of the corps commanders or Musharraf's personal staff officers knew anything about the operation. The result was that, when the Indian Air Force joined the action, the Pakistan Air Force was in no position to respond while the army's quartermaster general and master general of ordnance, both of whose support was vital for any army operation, were also left totally in the dark. Thus if Kargil had led to general war, the army would have learned that its newest fleet of tanks, of which it was so proud, had no APDSFS[96] antitank ammunition! The other effect of the secrecy surrounding Kargil was that no one in the Pakistani diplomatic corps was equipped to deal with the questions arising in the wake of the operation, while it also split the generals into two groups, that is, those who were "in" and those who were left "out."

The masterminds of the operation were driven by the belief that their nuclear capability provided a protective shield to Pakistan, and that India would acquiesce to this capture just like Pakistan was compelled to swallow India's seizure of the Siachen peaks in 1984.[97] All the four generals involved in the Kargil project had remained instructors in different military training institutions during their careers, teaching young officers how vital it is to weigh the pros and cons of a military offensive in terms of understanding the possible ramifications and enemy reactions. It is strange that these generals forgot such a basic military lesson and seriously miscalculated Indian capabilities both in terms of military strength and political influence in the international arena.

The Indians reacted in an outburst of justifiable rage, citing Pakistan's bad faith for having welcomed their prime minister to Lahore while concurrent preparations for the Kargil operation were already under way. In Pakistan there was no widespread feeling of regret, though few knew what had really happened. Within the army the general feeling about India was that it conducted nuclear tests in the belief that this would force Pakistan to show its hand, and that if this came short, Pakistan would be pushed into the status of an Indian satellite; but when this did not happen, Vajpayee came to Lahore to restart a long suspended dialogue merely to lull a nuclear Pakistan to sleep while cooking up some other perfidious scheme against it, and any measure against such an enemy was entirely justified. Pakistan's explanation of the events at Kargil, though, had a skeptical reception in international circles to begin with, and later their version was entirely discredited.

For India, the exposure of their neighbor's duplicity must have been satisfying, but surely not enough. After India's first abortive attacks to reclaim the heights, it started a large military buildup by moving all its 130mm artillery regiments to the target area and picking up a substantial amount of smart munitions around the world. It is an amazing commentary on the coordination between the "mujahideen" occupying Kargil heights and those fighting inside held Kashmir that when the Indian reinforcements were snaking up the winding roads in endless convoys, there was no reported attempt at an ambush by the latter to disrupt this operation. When the buildup was complete, India subjected the objective to air strikes and massive artillery barrages day after day, followed by determined and courageous infantry attacks in very difficult conditions. The Pakistan Army top brass had confided to various friends who had their trust that their men on the heights were adequately provisioned and well dug in to withstand the rigors of a long campaign. The truth, as it later transpired, was that the digging in was minimal because the rocky soil just did not allow this. The result was not only that the troops were exposed to harsh weather and the shrapnel of exploding shells, but also to the splinters of rocks that followed the explosions. For most, their only safety was to scramble to the comparative security of the reverse slopes during the bombardment, and then get back to the other side of the hill to meet the infantry attacks that normally followed the artillery barrages. Pakistani reserves of supplies and ammunition were woefully inadequate to begin with, and became alarmingly low as the operation progressed, with many having to survive by eating the pitiful vegetation that braved the rocky slopes. Under these circumstances, the resistance they put up was both heroic and magnificent, and the quality of junior leadership again proved admirable.

But Pakistani generals again failed miserably—as the plan and preparations were defective.

Kargil left an already friendless Pakistan in almost total diplomatic isolation. Even China, whose president had counseled Pakistan as recently as late 1996 to go slow on Kashmir and concentrate instead on the economic viability of the country, felt constrained to distance itself from Islamabad's latest adventure. Major General Javed Hassan, the commander on the spot, was being threatened by words and gestures of subordinates that could only be described as mutinous. Lieutenant General Mahmood, on whom reality started to dawn fatefully late in the day, saw his adequate jaw falling at an alarming rate. And though the conviction and inner reserves of Lieutenant General Aziz, helped by blissful ignorance, kept him as gung-ho as ever and also helped keep Musharraf's optimism afloat, the prime minister had become a case stricken by fright. Under these circumstance, Nawaz was left to plead desperately for a meeting with President Clinton, who found that his schedule allowed him a few free hours on July 4, 1999. It is widely believed that at this meeting Nawaz swore complete ignorance about the Kargil operation till everything terrible hit the fan. Blaming everything on his generals, he just begged to be bailed out. Clinton told him quite unequivocally that whether the "mujahideen" occupying the Kargil heights listened to Pakistan or not, the immediate step it would have to take was to evacuate Kargil. As a sop he promised the Pakistani prime minister that following this evacuation, he would treat the issue of Kashmir with active interest.[98]

In the midst of this crisis in June 1999, General Zinni, then commander in chief of the U.S. Centcom (Central Command), had visited Pakistan accompanied by G. Lanpher, deputy assistant secretary of state for South Asia, to impress upon Pakistan's military commanders the need for deescalation. This team also visited India during the tour. However, according to Shireen Mazari, some senior Pakistani army officers are of the view that the United States prevented India from coming to the negotiating table with Pakistan, and in this context she also mentions the visit of Henry Kissinger to India in early June, who was "apparently carrying a message from the U.S. government not to negotiate with Pakistan."[99] It is a moot point whether such was the case, but it was obvious that U.S. sympathies were with India in this conflict. To any neutral observer of the international political scene, this was a predictable outcome as U.S. interests were increasingly being linked with those of India in the region, but Pakistan's military hierarchy was apparently oblivious of what was so clearly written on the wall.

The evacuation of Kargil was followed by a hum of resentment all over Pakistan. The loved ones of those who had given their lives on the desolate and remote slopes there wanted to know that if unilateral withdrawal was to be the end of the whole exercise, what was the point of sacrificing the lives of their sons and brothers? The people of Pakistan had been subjected to the largest whispering campaign in history to expect a great victory. When the operation fizzled out like a wet firecracker, they were a nation left speechless in anger and disbelief. Musharraf and the planners could not give any excuses in public, but privately they let it be known that the blame for the scuttling of a brilliant operation lay on a panic-prone prime minister, who could not stand up to the U.S. president. Nawaz Sharif too could not say anything in his defense publicly, but privately he let it be known that his generals had taken him for a ride, and that he had to bend over backward to get the U.S. president to help Pakistan out of a very sticky situation. This inevitably brought the army and the government to an irrevocable collision course, which had been in the cards ever since the dismissal of General Karamat. From this point on, every action and word of Musharraf and Nawaz was under the scrutiny of the other, fueling a spiraling of mutual suspicion and distrust.

The army was wary and strongly suspicious that Nawaz would maneuver to sack Musharraf at the first opportunity. It is believed that this possibility was discussed by the corps commanders in a meeting at the end of August 1999. It was the overwhelming opinion among them that this would not be allowed to pass—not after Karamat had allowed the prime minister to push him out of office so recently. This was not entirely a reflection of personal loyalty to Musharraf or to the army as an institution, as it was also an affirmation of the discredit into which the government had fallen, and an expression of genuine fear that Musharraf's ouster would be the first step toward destroying the army by making it a partisan institution. Reportedly, the gist of the discussion at this conference was conveyed to Nawaz Sharif by Lieutenant General Tariq Pervez, commander of the army corps in Quetta, whose cousin Nadir Pervez was a minister in the Nawaz cabinet. Musharraf at this stage instructed MI to monitor the activities and telephone conversations of Nawaz and his close aides and asked for daily reports in this regard.

Around this time, Nawaz Sharif decided to invoke his father's counsel in support of his political fortunes. The old man advised reconciliation with Musharraf. As a result, Musharraf was also made the chairman of the Joint Chiefs of Staff Committee, a position previously kept vacant so that in time of need Musharraf could be adjusted against it while appointing a new army chief. It was then decided that Shabaz Sharif and Chaudhry Nisar Ali (a federal minister) should be sent to charm Musharraf. When the two of them entered his office, the Musharraf they encountered was a cold and unsmiling one. Shabaz told the general that there were too many parties interested in souring the relationship between the army and the government, and therefore serious misunderstandings were being created. But Musharraf's intelligence reports were telling him that these two persons were among the ones trying to convince Nawaz that he must get rid of Musharraf. Musharraf thanked them for clarifying their position but at the same time sacked Lieutenant General Tariq Pervez, corps commander in Quetta. Musharraf was of the view that Lieutenant General Tariq had a streak of insubordination in him, and sources close to Tariq maintain that he was among the few generals who criticized the way the Kargil operation was planned.[100] Also suspecting the corps commander at Mangla of having leanings in favor of the party in power, Musharraf moved him to a staff appointment and also moved a company of the Special Services Group (commandos) to Rawalpindi.

All this made for an ominous combination, which sent alarm bells ringing for the Sharifs, and there was general panic in their party corridors, with the opposition gloating at their discomfiture and hoping that their panic was well founded. For Nawaz, things were now serious enough to invoke the ploy of last resort to shore up the defense of his tottering empire. He sent Shabaz Sharif to the United States, who arrived in Washington on September 17, 1999. Shabaz's case in Washington was that democracy in Pakistan was once again under threat from the generals, and that his brother was paying the price for having followed President Clinton's advice to evacuate Kargil against strong opposition from the army.[101] On September 20 an American government official sent a message to the Pakistan military that read, "We hope there will be no return to days of interrupted democracy in Pakistan."[102] This statement emboldened Nawaz to believe that he had American support in case of a showdown.

Nawaz Sharif had played his last card. The question now was if this would be good enough to trump Musharraf's intentions and prevent him from playing his last ace. Already for some time it seemed that the army had been keeping its eggs distributed, ensuring that they did not find their way into the same basket. Musharraf was due to attend the Sri Lankan Army's fiftieth anniversary celebrations in Colombo in October. It was strongly felt in the army that he ought to turn down this invitation because the situation at home was extremely fluid just under the surface, and the last act of the power play was just about to be played out. Musharraf insisted on going, leaving his fate in the trusted hands of Aziz and Mahmood. The moment Musharraf left, Nawaz got into action. His plan was to sack Musharraf and appoint Lieutenant General Khawaja Zia-ud-din, director general of the ISI and a fellow Kashmiri immigrant, as the new army chief. Zia-ud-din was to be the immediate beneficiary of the conspiracy as well as its most central cog.

While flying somewhere over the Bay of Bengal, Musharraf lost his job at approximately 4:30 P.M. on October 12, 1999. At 5 P.M. the same afternoon,

Pakistan Television announced this extremely significant change in a routine manner and showed the new COAS, General Zia-ud-din, in his new badges of rank. The manner in which it was accomplished cut the rank and file of the army to the quick. Among the very first orders of the new chief was to appoint the quarter master general, Lieutenant General Akram, as the new chief of general staff. His second call was to the master general of ordnance, Lieutenant General Salim Haider, the recently removed corps commander at Mangla, appointing him the new corps commander of the Rawalpindi Corps. Meanwhile, far away in Quetta, Lieutenant General Tariq Pervez, the sacked commander of the Quetta Corps, gave orders to cancel his formal dining out of the army. Among the officers of any consequence who did not have a clue about what was afoot in Pakistan and ought to have known everything were Mahmood and Aziz. They were busy with a game of tennis when they received a call from Lieutenant General Saeed uz-Zafar, the corps commander in Peshawar and acting COAS in the absence of Musharraf. He asked them what the situation was in the capital, and they said all was fine and that they were enjoying a perfectly exhilarating game of tennis. When they heard what had happened, Aziz had absolutely no doubt where duty lay, and it was he who decided to move to GHQ immediately. With this, the most important decision seems already to have been made, that is, Nawaz Sharif had set a precedent that made him absolutely unacceptable to the army, and he would therefore have to go.

Meanwhile, Nawaz Sharif had instructed aviation authorities to not allow the plane carrying Musharraf to land at Karachi airport and divert it elsewhere, though the plane was dangerously low on fuel as the pilot, due to confusing messages from Karachi control tower, was circling the city. Soon the army took over the control tower and the plane landed at Karachi airport. The Musharraf that came out of the plane was the man in charge of Pakistan.

As the Musharraf-Sharif thriller unfolded throughout the evening of October 12, 1999, through the early hours of the next day, the people of Pakistan awaited the final outcome with bated breath. When finally it transpired that Musharraf had landed safely and triumphed, and Nawaz and his government had finally been overthrown, people were relieved. Indeed, every change of government in the country since the very beginning had been accompanied by applause by a majority of the population, which was both an expression of disenchantment with the outgoing administration as it was that of hope for what the future may bring. Sadly, this hope was never positive. More often than not, it lay in negative security, that is, that surely things could never be any worse than the days just left behind.

# ——Chapter 8——
# General Pervez Musharraf

## A Season of Hope

Yet another "new era" began in Pakistan on October 12, 1999. Many in the street danced with joy, and many were those who went into a swoon as the anxiety of the hours preceding Musharraf's safe landing abated. He was not the most popular man in the country, but he had ousted a coterie that had lost credibility with the people. Interestingly, the militant Islamic groups were also jubilant but for different reasons. Abdullah Muntazir, spokesperson for Lashkar-i-Taiba (Army of the Pure), a religious-cum-militant group primarily operating in Indian Kashmir, declared that now Pakistan should have an Islamic system on the pattern of Afghanistan's Taliban.[1] Such elements perhaps were waiting for another General Zia ul-Haq, who had fathered them, not knowing that Musharraf was reputed to be cut from a very different cloth.

Musharraf was born in New Delhi (British India) in August 1943 to a middle-class and well-educated family. Musharraf's father, Syed Musharrafuddin, a graduate of Aligarh University, worked in the Directorate General of Civil Supplies in Delhi, and his mother, Zarrin, was a graduate from Delhi's Indraprastha College with a master's degree in English literature. The family migrated to Pakistan during the turbulent partition of the Indian subcontinent in 1947. They were terrified by the mayhem all around and, in the midst of the communal carnage, the family was lucky to get onto the last train out of Dehli for Karachi.[2] The Muslims who lived in Hindu majority areas of British India were more affected by the Hindu domination in society and hence were more appreciative of the value of Pakistan—certainly more than those already living in Muslim majority areas, which constituted the present-day Pakistan. Also, they had to suffer the pain of leaving their ancestral homes for good. These imprints and psychological influences in the initial and formative years of his childhood must have had a deep impact on Musharraf's mind in terms of his views about India.

Soon, Musharraf along with his parents traveled to Turkey (1949–56) owing to his father's deputation in Ankara, where he quickly learned to speak fluent Turkish. Childhood associations with people and places are often long-lasting. A decade and a half later he opted for Turkey to do his midcareer training course, though the alternate option was the United States. There was something in Turkey that fascinated him. This attachment was reflected in the choice of a Turkish newspaper for his first foreign interview after taking over the reins of government in October 1999. He told the interviewer that Mustafa Kamal Ataturk was his role model, indicating his secular and modernist orientation. More so, he even lists Ataturk as the "most admired person" on his official profile.[3] But he astonished everyone when, during a visit to the Turkish military academy in Istanbul a year later, he revealed that he wanted to fight as a volunteer during Turkey's 1974 invasion of Cyprus. He told the audience what he had said to one of his Turkish class-fellows then: "I have such motivation that I am ready to fight with Turkish forces if Turkey requires volunteers."[4]

He joined the Pakistan Army as a young cadet in 1961 and was commissioned as an officer in 1964 during the reign of General Ayub Khan, who was then flirting with the idea of establishing a "reformed" local government system called Basic Democracies, something very similar to what Musharraf would introduce once he was at the helm of affairs. As a junior officer, he participated in the two wars Pakistan had with India in 1965 and 1971. Later he opted to join the elite Special Services Group (SSG-commandos), where he served for a total of seven years at different times. Few officers serve for this long in this branch owing to the hectic lifestyle one has to endure and the dangerous missions to be undertaken routinely. But Musharraf always took pride in being a commando. SSG personnel are generally very tough and task-oriented people who are known to be aloof from politics. Musharraf also went to the United Kingdom twice for military studies and remained director general of military operations (DGMO) in the early 1990s before becoming a lieutenant general in 1995, when he was given command of a strike corps of the army—an impressive army track record by all counts.

Within a year of his promotion a very close friend of his, Major General Saeed Zaidi, convinced Prime Minister Benazir Bhutto and her husband, Asif Zardari, through a common friend who is a leading lawyer from Lahore, to seriously consider elevating Musharraf to be the new chief of the army staff. The argument was that Musharraf was a "liberal" who would go along well with the Bhutto government.[5] General Zaidi further contended that Musharraf was a professional who would be the last man to consider a military takeover. It is not clear if Benazir was unconvinced or whether the proposal was shot down by the president, Farooq Khan Leghari, who had the constitutional power to appoint the new chief but was not enjoying the best of terms with the prime minister.

After General Jahangir Karamat's resignation due to differences over the military's role in governance with the Nawaz government, Musharraf was appointed the new army chief in October 1998. As discussed in the previous chapter, Musharraf was lucky, as two generals senior to him were passed over primarily for political reasons. Prime Minister Nawaz Sharif thought that Musharraf would be a pliable army chief, being a Mohajir and therefore one with no constituency in the army—an entirely baseless myth. The crisis that led to his clash with Musharraf was largely of Nawaz's own making. In a perfect democracy, Nawaz Sharif, being the prime minister, had all the powers to dismiss any army chief, but in view of the political realities of Pakistan, it was a foolish decision to try and dislodge an army chief, especially in the manner in which he attempted to do it, and most especially when his own credibility had sunk so low.

However, Nawaz Sharif and his party maintains that Musharraf along with Generals Aziz and Mahmood had already decided to get rid of him due to his handling of the Kargil crisis a few months earlier. There is no evidence so far to support this claim, but it is certain that Musharraf was closely following what was being cooked up for him in the corridors of power. Military Intelligence (MI) bugged the prime minister's house and office, and the visitors' list was closely scrutinized in the army's General Headquarters (GHQ), and Nawaz knew this well.[6] On one occasion Musharraf personally told Shabaz Sharif, the chief minister of Punjab, and Chaudhry Nisar Ali Khan, an influential cabinet member, that a few politicians, including Khawaja Asif, chairman of the Privatization Commission, were conspiring against him by advising Nawaz Sharif to remove him. Khawaja Asif was stunned when he heard this as, according to him, nothing of the sort had happened. To clear things up he immediately contacted a close friend of Musharraf to clarify his position.[7] A conciliatory meeting was planned for October 13, 1999, but it turned out to be too late, and Khawaja Asif had to pay heavily for this planted misperception.

The October coup was certainly not to the liking of the Clinton administration. A few weeks before this episode, the U.S. State Department had even gone to the extent of signaling a warning by saying that the United States would "strongly oppose" any attempt by "political and military actors" in Pakistan to take power unconstitutionally.[8] Senior State Department officials confirmed these remarks, originally quoted by Reuters on September 20, 1999.[9] State Department spokesman Jamie Rubin in a briefing on October 12, 1999, further confirmed this stance by saying that "we were concerned about the extraconstitutional measures" and that "Pakistan's constitution must be respected not only in its letter but in its spirit."[10] It is also interesting to note that in testimony by U.S. Assistant Secretary of State Karl F. Inderfurth to the Senate Foreign Relations Committee on October 14, 1999, Inderfurth made a special mention of General Zia-ud-din along with the Prime Minister

Nawaz Sharif and his brother Shabaz Sharif in reference to their being under house arrest and asserted that "we call upon the current Pakistani authorities to assure their safety and well-being."[11]

Some Pakistani political analysts believe that Nawaz Sharif tried to dislodge Musharraf with U.S. support and that Musharraf's takeover was "the first time the army seized power without the approval of Washington."[12] It is a matter of conjecture whether the U.S. authorities had given an okay to Nawaz Sharif to appoint Zia-ud-din as the army chief, but at least Nawaz Sharif believed this to be the case.[13] Two days before the October 12 episode, Nawaz Sharif had taken General Zia-ud-din to Abu Dhabi for a meeting with Sheikh Zayed Bin Sultan Nahyan[14] for the final approval, perhaps. Rightly or wrongly, it is a common perception in the Pakistani power corridors that the sultan of the United Arab Emirates (UAE) is very close to the United States, and that "guidance" on crucial matters, when solicited, often comes by this route. It is intriguing, however, that Zia-ud-din had "coincided" his visit to the United States with that of Shabaz Sharif just a few weeks earlier.

General Zia-ud-din also updated CIA officials on the work of CIA-paid Pakistan's secret team that was on the lookout for Osama bin Laden. During Prime Minister Nawaz Sharif's visit to Washington in early December 1998, he had proposed to President Clinton the involvement of the CIA and ISI in training a secret commando team for the purpose of capturing (or killing) bin Laden. According to the plan, the team could be based in a secret location along the Pakistan-Afghanistan border and could quickly move into Afghanistan whenever a credible sighting of bin Laden was reported to them. Such a team was supposed to comprise retired ISI and SSG officials. According to renowned journalist Steve Coll, despite being "deeply cynical" about the proposal the Americans agreed to it.[15] Quickly, the team was assembled, the members of which already had the requisite training as former soldiers. The CIA paid their salaries and also provided the latest weapons and communication equipment. Intriguingly, Zia-ud-din had some other plans in his mind as well—he believed that the elite force would also act as bodyguards for Nawaz Sharif if the Pakistan Army ever moved against him![16] This indicates, first, that American skepticism about the project was well founded and, second, Zia-ud-din became Nawaz's top choice to become the next army chief most probably for coming up with this brilliant strategy! It is another matter that the strategy failed on all counts.

However, Musharraf dissociated himself and the army from this project soon after taking over by maintaining that the "project was designed by the former Prime Minister and the ex-director general of the ISI and I had no knowledge till I took over," and as to the justification of closing this chapter, he argued that "this project could not have met with success so we shelved it."[17] He made it known loud and clear that he was the man in command and that he had some idea about who supported whom on October 12, 1999.

Channels of communication between Musharraf and the United States soon opened up. Maleeha Lodhi, the able Pakistani journalist cum diplomat, who enjoys excellent relations both with the Pakistan Army and power centers in the United States, connected the two sides. One of Musharraf's old friends, a former military officer, played a crucial role in this linkup, for which Maleeha was rewarded with the ambassadorial slot in Washington later. Marine Corps general Anthony C. Zinni, commander in chief of U.S. Central Command and a good friend of Musharraf, also had an important role to play in bringing the new government of Pakistan and Washington together. He suggested to the U.S. administration that Musharraf should be engaged. This is substantiated by his statement before the U.S. Senate Armed Services Committee a few months later, where he contended:

> Because of the historic importance of the military as a source of stability within the country, I believe that isolating Pakistan's influential military establishment is and will continue to be counterproductive to our long-term interests in the region. When the U.S. isolates the professional Pakistan military, we deny ourselves access to the most powerful institution in Pakistani society. . . . I know Chief Executive General Pervez Musharraf well and have spoken to him on several occasions since his assumption of power. I believe that our strategic interests in South Asia and beyond will best be served by a policy of patient military to military engagement.[18]

The time lag between Musharraf's taking over and his first broadcast to the nation seemed interminable, and from this one can deduce that there was no prior preparation for this coup. After foiling the "conspiracy" and taking Nawaz to task, the army could have returned to its barracks satisfied that it had repelled an attack against its institutional interests, and Musharraf and his team did consider this option but decided against it. It would have been a miracle if the decision was different. The military establishment, as always, thought that they could set the system right, and like all the previous military rulers of Pakistan, Musharraf did not waste time before making a categorical statement about his future plans—"I am not going to perpetuate myself."[19]

After the dust had settled, Musharraf presented his agenda to the nation more or less in the form of a military briefing, committing himself to rebuilding national confidence and morale; removing interprovincial disharmony; reviving the economy and restoring investors' confidence; ensuring law, order, and speedy justice; strengthening and depoliticizing state institutions; devolving more power to the grassroots level; and, most important, conducting across-the-board accountability.[20] None of this was new. All Pakistani leaders had made such promises in the past, but the majority of the citizens were ready to give Musharraf a chance to prove himself. Had there been a referendum to gauge public sentiment, Musharraf would have won it hands down. As it turned out, however, there was to be a referendum later, by which time Musharraf had lost his credibility, and the incompetence of his advisers ensured that history would see the attempt as an impious fraud by a man who eventually had nothing to go on save his timorous claim to "good intentions."

To look different from the previous military regimes, Musharraf declared himself "chief executive" and not chief martial law administrator while suspending only parts of the constitution and artfully avoiding imposition of martial law, though for all practical purposes his word was law. The announcement of the new cabinet after two weeks of introspection was not attended by rave reviews, adorned as it was by many discredited faces. The discerning saw in this a hint of the familiar patterns of the past, but most were willing to live by their hopes and invest these on the new man on horseback.

The new regime had to act differently to shelter itself from the curse of historical precedents associated with the previous military interventions in Pakistan. The pattern so far had been to follow a certain genetic code. Initially they exude a sense of vitality and vigor. Hopes are high and there is talk of reform in every pronouncement. Politicians as a class are despised and stories of their incompetence and corruption are laid bare. Then as time passes, army rule mutates into a hybrid democracy, with a few turncoats and some new political faces becoming willing tools of the new setup. The Ayub and Zia regimes were identical in this way. Yahya was an exception as he was too busy presiding over the disintegration of Pakistan. Musharraf had seen all this during his military career, and people were expecting that he would not commit the same blunders. Behind this very assumption were hidden the hopes and expectations of 140 million Pakistanis.

Even before the new regime could settle in, the offices of the United Nations and the United States Information Center in the heart of Islamabad were targeted with missiles fired from a remote control rocket launcher operated from a parked vehicle on November 12, 1999. No extensive damage was done, but this was a very serious message and a matter of dispute about who had sent the message. The attack had taken place just two days before the U.N. deadline of November 14 to the Taliban to turn over Osama bin Laden. Lieutenant General Mahmood Ahmed, director general of the ISI, had a few sleepless nights trying to find out about the culprits. In the meantime he was approached by two well-known Pakistanis from Karachi, one of them widely known for his close relations with the United States, who offered him inside information from U.S. sources about their take on this terrorist activity under certain conditions. Mahmood agreed to keep the source classified, and the next day he was handed over a confidential intelligence document that explained how Afghanistan's Northern Alliance with the support of the Iranian government had orchestrated this attack. ISI, however, was skeptical about the veracity of this information, and some senior ISI officials interpreted the leak as a possible American effort to discourage Musharraf from continuing with his plans to visit Iran shortly.[21] The visit went ahead as per schedule, where Musharraf took up this issue with the Iranian leadership, who vociferously denied such a role, and instead gave him a lecture on how Pakistan's pro-Taliban policy was destabilizing the whole region. Musharraf promised the Iranians to reevaluate the Pakistan-Taliban relationship.

Meantime, the first decisive step that Musharraf took was on the domestic front—accountability of the corrupt. With every change of government since the revival of democracy in 1985, the cry for accountability had become louder and louder, but as the problem was so widespread and the ramparts of vested interest so invincible, no government dared go beyond a judicious mixture of flimsy steps and lip service toward meeting this demand. By the time Musharraf found himself catapulted to the helm, he had no option but to bow to the overwhelming sentiment of the people. Thus before the month of October 1999 was exhausted, he announced the formation of the National Accountability Bureau (NAB), with Lieutenant General Syed Mohammad Amjad as its first chairman. And by a strange irony, it was fated that the "Attock conspiracy" officers who had paid a heavy price for attempting to conduct accountability twenty-five years before would have a fair representation on the Bureau. Within two days of the formation of the NAB, the services of Saeed Akhtar Malik and Farouk Adam Khan (whom the reader last met at the Attock court martial—chapter 5) were requisitioned.

General Amjad was the ideal and unanimous choice of the senior ranks of the army to be NAB chairman. He was an officer of extraordinary diligence and exemplary character, his name was a byword for integrity. Ayaz Amir, a leading Pakistani journalist, while treating Musharraf's choice of certain cabinet members to scathing criticism, had this to say about Amjad: "Chief [Musharraf] has redeemed himself by picking Lieutenant General Amjad—and if anyone can make NAB work, it is Amjad, and if he falters or fails, or even if the pace of his offensive slackens, General Musharraf can say goodbye to the public goodwill."[22] In the event, Musharraf's credibility and commitment were to be defined by the performance of the NAB, and the words of the journalist were to be prophetic.

From the survey of the NAB team, one could only draw optimism. Farouk Adam had a courtly manner, an impressive personality, and a unique ability to smile through the tedium of a sixteen-hour workday. Saeed A. Malik had much idealism and passion and also a flair for winning the esteem of those working under him. He had written a freelance column for a decade in a leading English-language newspaper of the times (*The Muslim*), invariably exposing the corrupt practices of the ruling elite.

The initial labors of the NAB were dedicated to drawing up the NAB Ordinance to provide a legal framework for this new organization. The central principle that dictated the ordinance was the shifting of the onus of proof to the accused, that is, that if the accused person could not reconcile his wealth, earnings, expenses, and taxes that he had paid, he must be deemed guilty of corruption. The framers of this ordinance were very conscious that this draconic law[23] would be applied to a maximum of only four hundred of the most corrupt in the land, and the principle that would determine the qualification of these "selected few" would be that of either an association with a great crime or having a big name adorned perhaps by a theft not that big. Without such a law, the NAB would essentially have been a nonstarter because of the virtual nonexistence of investigative and prosecutorial resources. Had this ordinance been judiciously used to attain the purpose it was designed for, things would be much different today.

To implement this agenda, Amjad was given full authority to select the "targets," though he regularly consulted the ISI and a few legal experts while making vital decisions in this regard. Amjad had a free hand to hold across-the-board and evenhanded accountability from which no one was exempt, except the judiciary and serving armed forces officials.[24]

On November 17, 1999, the NAB moved in for its first crop of arrests. Many of those arrested were big names.[25] There was great euphoria among the people because many individuals who had always considered themselves beyond the reach of law were now behind bars. Yet most of the arrests were made on the charges of loan default, perhaps the easiest charge to prove, but one that the NAB could be horrendously wrong about because it was very difficult to tell an honest from a willful default. With the first blood having been drawn, the public appetite was whetted and they bayed for more. Their clamor could have been ignored, but not that of the government, whose credibility and performance had nothing but the achievements of the NAB to show for itself.

The ordinary public was under the impression that the ISI and other intelligence agencies had collected enough data on corrupt elements when they were "monitoring" the civilian governments during the 1990s, but when a few ISI files were handed over to NAB officials, these were mostly speculative and devoid of any sound material necessary to prove a case in a court of law. To quicken up things, General Amjad hurriedly developed a core team to run the organization comprising bankers, economists, lawyers, and a few from the intelligence and police backgrounds.[26] It was a combination never tried before, the only handicap being a shortage of time to organize and deliver.

Around that time, a letter from Musharraf's office to the NAB (dated December 11, 1999) adequately reflects the anxiety of the government and its dependence on the NAB to shore up its credibility: "It has been reported with a great concern that corrupt politicians are becoming bold and the press is gradually becoming sympathetic to them. This trend must be stopped and reversed. Following steps are suggested:

1. Move fast on all issues.
2. Expose the corrupt people very expeditiously.
3. Scoop on corruption on a daily basis."[27]

Consequently, more people were arrested based on their filthy reputations, but proof of their corruption was lacking. The NAB could have gained a lot of credibility in its initial days by prosecuting the ones who were already in custody, but the special accountability courts were not in place yet as selection of judges and establishing a new chain of courts and developing a whole new infrastructure was taking time. What the military hierarchy did not realize was that there is a huge difference between deploying a military unit to a new location and establishing a law enforcement institution that has to act within the parameters of law. To overcome this shortage, dozens of retired ISI officials were inducted who perhaps knew the art of interrogation well, but had very little legal and investigative experience, which was the core requirement in this case. There was a reason behind the compulsion that the new inductees had to be former ISI officials—the ISI was providing the funds for this NAB expansion and they opted to benefit their comrades in the process.

As if these problems were not enough to hamper the NAB work, all of the arrested persons were kept in different cities under the custody of respective military commands where the local military officials and intelligence operatives started investigating/interrogating the accused on their own. Every single institution was trying to spy on the NAB, making the task further complicated. This was symbolic of the general state of affairs in Pakistan.

Amjad and Farouk Adam, the two public faces of the NAB, were now under immense pressure from the public, the press, and the government. As they addressed the press, it seemed to the military hierarchy[28] that they were hogging the limelight, and they became victims of gratuitous envy. Shaukat Aziz, the finance minister, who had Musharraf's ear, was for blanket protection to businessmen despite the fact that some of the latter, in cahoots with the bankers, were the biggest crooks. Amjad, on the other hand, was heading toward making an example of those industrialists and businessmen who had established their business empires through corrupt practices. This was a risky business as big money was involved.

One of Amjad's problems was the subtle increase of government interference with his functioning. As it was, NAB had an ominous start to begin with. In its first two weeks of operations, it cracked open a multimillion-dollar case of fraud and corruption. Nortel, a Canadian telecommunications company, had unfairly been handed a fat contract to build a mobile telephone network in Pakistan. This was an open-and-shut case as all the evidence was there, but when Amjad wanted to move in and scuttle the contract, he was refrained from doing so. The only man who had the power to do this was Musharraf himself.

As the NAB moved along, two questions were frequently asked of Amjad, that is, whether there were any holy cows, and if the army generals involved in corruption would also be arrested. The government position was that only serving army officers and the judiciary were exempt from the NAB because both institutions had effective in-house correction systems, but technically, retired armed forces officials were not a part of this category. When a journalist publicly asked Amjad about press reports maintaining that corrupt military officials alone had deposited $1 billion in foreign banks from kickbacks from weapons purchases, he shot back by saying: "We have not been sitting on our butts as regards defense deals."[29] Yet it was daily becoming clearer that all the big names among the retired generals were beyond the province of the NAB. The names of generals Aslam Beg, Hamid Gul, Zahid Ali Akbar, Talat Masood, Saeed Qadir, Farrukh Khan, and Air Marshals Anwar Shamim and Abbas Khattak were discussed more than once, but nothing came of these discussions. Amjad was absolutely dedicated to having them probed, but was restrained from doing so. The reputation of Amjad, however, remained unimpaired. By releasing Khawaja Asif and Nawaz Tiwana, a leading politician and a bureaucrat, respectively, from detention and personally apologizing to them for wrongful arrest by the NAB, Amjad had set a new precedent in Pakistan by accepting that the mighty are often fallible. This only enhanced his stature, and the envy of his peers.

In another high-profile case, a leading politician from the North-West Frontier Province (NWFP) known for his corrupt practices threatened NAB officials during his interrogation by saying that he was a CIA agent, and that political instability would be created in the country if he were not released immediately. Amjad responded by making things harsher for him and by appointing more investigators to probe his case. The politician was ultimately convicted.

It was becoming obvious to the NAB that the task before it was gigantic. Realizing this, the NAB hired a couple of foreign investigative and law firms to get the corruption money stashed in foreign banks back to Pakistan. It did not work well in the long run but at least sent a strong warning to many Pakistanis abroad who had stolen the money and were now enjoying life in Europe and America. Foreign governments were also contacted for cooperation in this endeavor, and the first positive reply came from the U.S. government. In August 2000 a U.S. team led by Mr. Harry Marshall, a senior legal adviser in the U.S. Department of Justice, landed in Pakistan to discuss U.S.-Pakistan cooperation in the domain of the extradition treaty between the two states. The NAB presented its cases for extradition of five Pakistanis who were reported to be in the United States. That led to a successful collaboration between the U.S. Federal Bureau of Investigation (FBI) and the NAB in pursuit of the short-listed cases. From Pakistan's list, one of the cases involved former chief of the Pakistan Navy, Admiral Mansurul-Haq, against whom the NAB had a sound case. The admiral had been involved in the famous French submarines kickback case in the mid-1990s. Due to superb efforts of FBI official Michael Dorris, the accused was traced and picked up by the FBI from Austin, Texas, and extradited to Pakistan for the NAB case.

One of the brightest experiences of the NAB was the performance of its Central Investigation Team (CIT). General Amjad had allowed Saeed Malik to handpick a team of officers to give the NAB a limited in-house investigative capability. A former commander of the army's SSG, Brigadier Mohammad Nazir, an officer of unimpeachable integrity, was selected to head the CIT. The performance of the twelve-member CIT team[30] was outstanding on many counts. For instance, in a mere five months a three-man cell of the CIT (Lieutenant Colonel Riazuddin, Nadir Imtiaz Khan, and Major Taimur Shah) recovered or saved for the government of 3 billion Pakistan rupees (around $500 million). But unfortunately, the most outstanding member of the team Lieutenant Colonel Obaidullah, a former ISI official, tragically died of a massive heart attack shortly after being wrongly accused of "mishandling" a case by a very senior NAB official.

The saddest commentary on Musharraf's much-vaunted commitment to the cause of accountability is that each member of this team of rare officers was hounded out of the NAB soon after Amjad's departure from the institution. Their only handicap was that not one of them was prone to entertaining any adverse dictates. And so ended a heroic chapter of the war against crime by a handful of officers in a corrupt environment.

Reportedly, Amjad had asked to be relieved of his duties more than once. He was not one to take government partiality lying down. He left the NAB at the end of September 2000. The NAB's change of command, in the words of Mohammad Malick's commentary in *Dawn,* was "a clear sign of NAB's tailored, if not changed priorities."[31] No one then knew who the real "tailor" might be, but there was an acknowledgment that "Amjad remained a very fair accountability chief."[32] But Tariq Ali in his book *The Clash of Fundamentalisms: Crusades, Jihadis, and Modernity* was much more perceptive when he observed that Amjad was ready to push through, but "Musharraf balked at the scale of the enterprise."[33] The new chairman was Lieutenant General Khalid Maqbool, whose reputation was no match for Amjad's. The NAB was dead for all practical purposes. A noble experiment had ended because those who had initiated it did not have the moral stamina to carry it through. But it would not be they who would pay the price for this failure. This would be paid once more by those who have always paid it, the people of Pakistan.

Musharraf had made a clear choice—he would compromise with those politicians who were ready to side with him. He had given in to the building pressure from various sectors that wanted the regime to behave "normally" and not as a revolutionary one. This was the dilemma Musharraf faced—the masses were looking for a Messiah in him, whereas the political and military elite wanted the status quo to continue. Musharraf was still swinging in between.

Before Musharraf played the secret executioner of his own dearly beloved NAB, however, he readied himself for the most unequal encounter of his life. Earlier, in March 2000, U.S. president Bill Clinton had been scheduled to visit South Asia, but no clear indications were given till the end, whether he would stop over in Pakistan. Finally, a fairly angry Clinton did visit Pakistan on March 25, 2000, but only for a little more than five hours after a visit to India, where he had stayed for five days. Extraordinary security measures were taken for the visit, and the capital city, Islamabad, was practically handed over to the U.S. Secret Service for the day.

Clinton had a blunt message for Musharraf, though conveyed in a friendly and conciliatory manner.[34] The major issues discussed were Pakistan's foreign policy vis-à-vis the Kashmir insurgency and the Taliban policy of allowing Osama bin Laden to use Afghanistan as his base camp. Musharraf listened patiently, but on Kashmir he was not willing to deescalate unilaterally, though he was much more forthcoming on the Osama issue. He indicated to Clinton that he would personally go to Afghanistan to convince the Taliban leadership, but he stressed that it was a very difficult task dealing with "people who believe that God is on their side."[35] Clinton also gave voice to U.S. concerns about Pakistan's return to democracy, and on this Musharraf was noncommittal, knowing that such considerations have historically been of secondary importance to the United States. Ironically, no pictures of the Musharraf-Clinton meeting were shown on television or printed in newspapers as Clinton wanted to avoid being seen shaking hands with a military dictator, as if America had never supported military regimes before.

After the meeting, President Clinton made an unprecedented television and radio address to the people of Pakistan. His references to the historically friendly relations between the two countries were well made, but he clearly warned Pakistan to change its priorities by saying:

> This era does not reward those who struggle in vain; who redraw borders with blood. . . . I ask Pakistan also to be a leader in nonproliferation. In your own self-interest and to help us prevent dangerous technologies from spreading to those who might have no reservations at all about using them . . . I understand your concerns about Kashmir. I share your conviction that the human rights of all its people must be respected. But a stark truth must also be faced—there is no military solution to Kashmir. . . . I hope you will be able to meet the difficult challenges we have discussed today. If you do not, there is a danger that Pakistan may grow even more isolated, draining even more resources away from the needs of the people, moving even closer to a conflict no one can win. But if you do meet these challenges, our full economic and political partnership can be restored for the benefit of the people of Pakistan.[36]

The overall response to the speech was positive among the people of Pakistan. For the first time in Pakistan's history, many Pakistanis found themselves in complete agreement with what an American president had said.[37] *Dawn*, the leading English daily of Pakistan in its editorial the next day aptly said: "His [Clinton's] speech leaves little scope for mounting the high horse of injured Pakistani patriotism because he was guilty of neither of these solecisms and, if anything, came across as a deeply concerned well-wisher of Pakistan."[38] However, other analysts, like retired Lieutenant General Syed Refaqat, called it an "utterly humiliating treatment from Bill Clinton." While commenting on the speech, Ayesha Jalal rightly argued that Clinton's solution of the Kashmir dispute—reduced to the "four Rs" of restraint, respect for the Line of Control, renunciation of violence, and renewal of talks with India—fell well short of the fifth "R," namely, a resolution of this lingering conflict.[39]

Interestingly, the Pakistani team that met Clinton also included Justice Irshad Hasan Khan, chief justice of the Supreme Court of Pakistan, who along with other judges was conducting a hearing to decide whether Musharraf's coup in October 1999 was legitimate and lawful. It was unprecedented that the head of the judiciary was attending such a meeting. It is believed that Clinton briefly conversed with him in private during this short visit, but what was discussed is not known.[40]

Interestingly, a few weeks later, a twelve-member bench of the Supreme Court of Pakistan validated the military takeover of October 12, 1999, on the basis of the doctrine of state necessity and graciously gave Musharraf three years to accomplish his agenda and hold general elections. This was quite expected as there was no shortage of precedents for such a ruling. Indeed, the Pakistani judiciary had by now become somewhat of an expert at reaching an accommodation with most military masters; though it must be admitted that the majority opinion of the public would have supported it in this instance. This time the judiciary also had gone further and had virtually allowed a military ruler to amend the constitution, thus making Musharraf's power only a little less than absolute. With this power he had it within his province to succeed magnificently or fail spectacularly.

The legal validity for the regime gave him the confidence to make the first crucial changes in the military hierarchy. He decided to appoint General Khalid Maqbool as chief of the general staff (CGS), but some of his very close friends all but begged him to spare the army such gratuitous pain.[41] Maqbool's military reputation was a trifle suspect, as he had honed flattery into a fine art and fainting under pressure a minor profession. And so he was sent to take over the NAB, while Lieutenant General Mohammad Yousuf Khan took over as CGS. Of all the generals of the Pakistan Army, Yousuf was the least pretentious, the most laid back, and the least levitated by ambition. Lieutenant General Mohammad Aziz, the outgoing CGS, was sent to command the army corps at Lahore. So far, Aziz, being in the GHQ, had been involved in all the major decisions taken by Musharraf. If he had to be given a command for service reasons, 10th Corps in Rawalpindi was just a stone's throw away. The speculation in Islamabad was that the Americans wanted him to be away from Musharraf because Aziz was seen as a fundamentalist. Mohammad Malick, a well-informed journalist, in an op-ed in the leading paper *Dawn,* called the move a "conciliatory message to Americans."[42] If this was true, then Musharraf played a masterstroke by sending Aziz to Lahore, a very crucial command by virtue of its location at the heart of Punjab, which in political terms is the most important province, also home to the headquarters of an important jihadi outfit.

Another significant development was the Musharraf decision to allow the jailed Nawaz Sharif to go into exile in Saudi Arabia in December 2000. Prior to this, Nawaz was sentenced to life in prison for corruption, kidnapping, and hijacking charges in July 2000. The NAB had worked very hard to investigate corruption charges against Nawaz and his family and had almost finalized a money-laundering case, but Musharraf came under tremendous pressure to release him. Saad Hariri, the son of Lebanon's prime minister Rafiq Hariri, played a major role in this game. Saad permanently resides in Saudi Arabia and has close links with the Saudi royal family. On behalf of the Saudis, Saad conveyed to Musharraf that continuation of better Pakistani-Saudi relations depended on Musharraf's decision vis-à-vis the Saudi request to release Nawaz and his family members. Saudi Arabia had always been very helpful to Pakistan in terms of financial support and Musharraf was indeed in a dilemma. Earlier on, Prince Abdullah had refused to see Musharraf when he was visiting the kingdom.

Finally, Musharraf negotiated a deal with the Saudis—he would allow Nawaz and his family members to go into exile on the condition that Nawaz and his brothers quit politics for a certain time. It is widely believed in Pakistani power corridors that in fact it was President Clinton who was behind this and that Saad Hariri was approached by Saudi ambassador to the United States Prince Bandar to do the "needful" thing. Whatever the reality was, the decision to release Nawaz was a negative mark for Musharraf. Without doubt, the court decision against Nawaz (hijacking case) was excessive and manipulated by the state, but corruption cases against Nawaz should have been probed fully and proceeded with. The episode also explains how unpredictable things are in Pakistan.

Another crucial arena of Musharraf's pre-9/11 policies included a concerted effort to tackle the religious extremists. His speeches and remarks made to the media sufficiently indicate that Musharraf intended to target the religious fanatics from the start, but was unable to do much in the face of their clout and due to the perceived repercussions of such a policy shift on the country's foreign policy agenda vis-à-vis Afghanistan and Kashmir. He had given an early indication of his thinking on the subject in his very first major policy speech on October 17, 1999, in which he had asserted that "Islam teaches tolerance not hatred" and categorically asked the clergy to "curb elements which are exploiting religion for vested interests and bring bad name to our faith."[43] The message was loud and clear, and soon a discreet campaign was initiated by the religious hard-liners to malign the general by spreading rumors about his drinking habits and womanizing. The gossip came and went without leaving much impact.

Having weathered the first storm after consolidating his power and position, Musharraf decided to test the waters further. In April 2000 he proposed to reform the controversial Blasphemy Law, which was a tool in the hands of the administration and religious groups to persecute and settle scores with the religious minorities. According to the law, any person accused by the state or any individual of blaspheming the Prophet (PBUH) or desecrating the Quran was to be detained immediately even before a preliminary investigation. The punishment for such a crime is death or life imprisonment.[44] Minority communities were very critical of this law, but to no avail. Musharraf was not scrapping the law but only planning a procedural change—that a case under this law should be registered only if the civilian functionaries instead of police officials had first investigated the veracity of the accusation. Even at such a minor change the religious hard-liners created an uproar and, surprisingly, Musharraf backed down in a matter of weeks to the great dismay of moderates. He sheepishly maintained that he was doing so in response to the "unanimous demand of the *Ulema, Mashaikh* [elder religious scholars] and the people."[45] The announcement came just three days before a number of religious groups had planned to hold public demonstrations against the reform.[46] The intelligence services caused him to take fright, and he conceded defeat even before the battle was joined—not the most edifying footnote in the annals of generalship. And coming on the heels of this retreat, his much celebrated deweaponization campaign met a similar end.

Meanwhile, Pakistan was facing increasing isolation internationally due to its support of the Kashmir insurgency and its pro-Taliban stance. In the midst of all this, a U.S. State Department report entitled "Patterns of Global Terrorism—1999,"[47] released in April 2000, pinpointed South Asia for the first time as a major center of international terrorism. The report asserted that Pakistan "has tolerated terrorists living and moving freely within its territory" besides supporting "groups that engage in violence in Kashmir."[48] In addition, the United States urged Islamabad to close certain *Madrasas* "that actually serve as conduits for terrorism."[49] Afghanistan was noted for helping and providing safe haven for known terrorists and for refusing to turn over Osama bin Laden, the terrorist mastermind wanted in the deadly bombings of the U.S. embassies in Africa in 1998. However, neither country was included in the list of seven countries sponsoring terrorism.[50] The report asserted that Pakistan was not on the list because "it is a friendly nation that is trying to tackle the problem," whereas Afghanistan was not named because the United States had not recognized the Taliban government. The report concluded that the threat of terrorism now came less from state-sponsored attacks than from "loose networks" of groups and individuals motivated more by religion or ideology than by politics and financed increasingly by drug trafficking, crime, and illegal trade. This was a clear warning to Pakistan, which was taken seriously by Musharraf, though publicly Pakistan's diplomats in the U.S. vehemently denied the charges and asked for evidence.[51]

Pakistan's relations with India during these times were as cold as ever. In February 2000, India had announced a hefty 28.2 percent increase in its military budget[52]—the largest single-year increase in the country's history. India also continued with its efforts to label Pakistan a terrorist state at the international level. For the Musharraf regime, this was increasingly a worrying issue, and he asked his close associates in the military to "think out of the box" in order to counter this Indian strategy.[53] The director general of the ISI, Lieutenant General Mahmood, finally came up with a novel idea—on June 24, 2000, the Hizb ul-Mujahideen, a powerful Kashmiri militant organization with links to Pakistani intelligence, announced a unilateral three-month cease-fire. This was an indirect dialogue offer. But soon serious differences arose between the ISI leadership and Lieutenant General Aziz on the subject, as Aziz was critical of this approach. Aziz was of the view that Hizb's leadership was carrying the initiative too far and Pakistan might be cut out. No wonder the truce collapsed in a matter of weeks!

Around this time, statements from Musharraf's advisers and a few ministers showed a visible change in the government stance on issues related to terrorism. For instance, the country's interior minister, retired Lieutenant General Moinuddin Haider, in a seminar where Lashkar-i-Taiba chief Hafiz Mohammad Saeed was in attendance, boldly asked the audience to "imagine what would happen to Pakistan when militant cadres of Lashkar-i-Taiba would start trekking back home from Indian Kashmir once their objectives were achieved."[54] He was clearly inferring that the militants would create chaos inside Pakistan and, considering the prevailing environment, this was a pretty bold statement. Because of this approach, Haider became a target of religious groups, and he was personally threatened.[55] Later, his brother was brutally murdered in a terrorist act by religious extremists—a stern message to all those who entertained contrary opinions on the subject.

After recovering from the Blasphemy Law fiasco and the failed deweaponization drive, it was time for Musharraf to act again. Besides, harsher messages from the United States and increasing loss of credibility at home convinced him that without a tangible change in policy, things would get out of hand. The Taliban's increasing madness, as evidenced from the destruction of ancient and historical Buddha statutes in early 2001, was one issue, and the continuous sectarian killings within Pakistan was the other crisis he faced. In mid-January 2001, Musharraf had also received a letter from Mullah Omar urging him to "enforce Islamic Law . . . step by step" in order to appease his country's religious parties and avoid "instability."[56] Musharraf was stunned. During an interview with the *Washington Times* in March 2001, he disclosed that he had sent a strongly worded message admonishing the Taliban leadership to desist from attempting to destroy the statues and had sent his interior minister to Kabul with an unequivocal demand to this effect, but that the Taliban had ignored the message. He called the Taliban worldview "an ignorant, primitive interpretation of Islam that is condemned by the entire Islamic world."[57] Still, he defended his pro-Taliban stand by asserting that national interest and security issues dictated Pakistan's policies and the country could not afford a threat from Afghanistan's side in addition to the one in the East (India). It is highly debatable how a better and multiethnic government in Afghanistan would have been threatening for Pakistan, but this is the line the military was toeing consistently, and Musharraf was also a victim of this strategy. It beggars credulity how often and how consistently the Pakistan military evolved policies in the face of certain sets of circumstances, and even when these situations transformed or changed, the policies stayed on to hold the army their prisoner.

But as time passed and as his embarrassments at the hands of the Taliban increased, Musharraf slowly became aware of the futility of Pakistan's Afghan policy. A handful of officers at the ISI were handling Afghan operations, and Lieutenant General Mahmood was personally monitoring the small unit. According to an ISI official, around two dozen Pakistan Army officers were deputed to Afghanistan along with a couple of hundred soldiers to assist in training the Taliban forces fighting the Northern Alliance,[58] but Pakistan had a very limited say in the political decisions taken by the Taliban leadership. According to one such officer, who was a part of the secret Pakistani military contingent in Afghanistan, he was a witness to the massacre of the Shia Hazara community in Bamian in 1999 by the Taliban forces, but could do nothing to halt the outrage, as his protests against the vengeful killings fell on deaf ears.[59] Musharraf was certainly getting such intelligence reports. These reports and world opinion were beginning to take effect.

At an earlier stage, Musharraf had asked his intelligence chief, Lieutenant General Mahmood, to arrange for his visit to Kabul as he wanted to personally convey the U.S. message to the Taliban demanding the surrender of Osama bin Laden. Mahmood disagreed by maintaining that he needed to prepare the ground for such a visit and suggested that initially the interior minister, Moinuddin Haider, should visit Afghanistan.

About this time (June 2001), in a show of exasperation, Musharraf lashed out against the religious extremists in his most vitriolic outburst to date. In a speech to leading religious scholars and clerics, he declared: "Is there any doubt that we have been left behind although we claim Islam will carry us forward in every age, every circumstance and every land. . . . How does the world judge our claim? It looks upon us as terrorists. We have been killing each other. And now we want to spread violence and terror abroad. Naturally, the world regards us as terrorists. Our claim of tolerance is phony."[60]

The religious hard-liners were stunned by the tone and tenor of Musharraf's argument. Still he was cautious, knowing that an open confrontation with the radicals was not advisable at that stage, but this did not stop him from reassessing his policies and strategy.

On the Kashmir front, Indian prime minister Vajpayee in November 2000 had announced that Indian security forces in Kashmir would observe a monthlong cease-fire with the onset of the holy month of Ramadan. Pakistan responded positively by instructing its troops to exercise "maximum restraint in order to strengthen and stabilize the cease-fire" and by withdrawing part of its forces from the Line of Control.[61] In a clear shift of policy, Pakistan also dropped its insistence that it had to be included in any India–Jammu and Kashmir dialogue from the outset. India extended the cease-fire a few times keeping alive hopes that things were changing for the better. Conciliatory gestures from both India and Pakistan amply testified to the fact that there was a realization on both sides, though for different reasons, that peace in Kashmir was necessary for a positive bilateral dialogue to commence. As for the reasons, Pakistan was pressed because it was struggling to come out of its increasing international isolation, and for India, on the other hand, the Kashmir imbroglio was becoming more expensive day by day, and the widely reported human rights violations committed by its forces in Kashmir were doing scant good to its image as the recipient of the Gandhian legacy of peace and nonviolence besides becoming a hurdle for its "rise-to-great-power-status" image. And there was perceptible American pressure as well. Washington had made it known clearly that it was for the early lifting of post-1998 sanctions against India, but this was not to be the case as far as Islamabad was concerned.[62]

Consequently, in a surprising development in late May 2001, Musharraf received an invitation to visit India, which he immediately accepted and had to, as he was consistently offering that he was ready to talk to India anytime and anywhere. In the midst of high expectations and media hype about the upcoming summit, Musharraf, in an expected move, made himself president of the country. That was good timing from his perspective, as the attention of the media and Pakistani public was focused on the prospects of better India-Pakistan relations. Even Pakistan's foreign minister, Abdul Sattar, who was meeting with U.S. officials in Washington at that moment, was unaware of this move and was in fact embarrassed when asked to comment on it by the State Department.

Musharraf's landmark visit to India began on July 14, 2001, in spite of strong reservations expressed by the religious hard-liners. Jamaat-i-Islami chief Qazi Hussain Ahmed warned Musharraf to avoid any "give or take" on the Kashmir issue as he had no mandate to go beyond Pakistan's stated position on Kashmir.[63] It is believed that the United States played a role in influencing Musharraf and Vajpayee to agree to this meeting,[64] but it will be an exaggeration to say that this was "the" factor behind this development. At best, the United States was a facilitator, and this was what its diplomats had also indicated. In fact, one leading American expert on South Asia, Stephen P. Cohen, in a seminar held at the Brookings Institution a few days before the Agra Summit, argued that possibly an Indian invitation to Musharraf was an effort to preempt a more active American role in South Asia and an attempt to control the process.[65] He also dispelled the impression given by Musharraf before the summit that the United States had pressurized India to start a dialogue, but gave him the benefit of the doubt by saying that "if it made it easier [for] Musharraf to go to Delhi because he could say the Americans were urging a summit and the Americans put pressure on them, fine."[66]

Both sides started the summit with optimism, as Musharraf used the phrases "cautious optimism" and "flexibility" to describe his state of mind for the summit. Vajpayee also promised to take "bold and innovative" measures and to discuss the "core issue" between the two countries. The media hype created a lot of expectations among the people of both countries, but a deadlock on the wording of an India-Pakistan joint statement came as a shocking anticlimax to the summit. The point of contention was the phraseology to be used in the statement explaining the nature of the Kashmir crisis. Indian hard-liners, especially L.K. Advani, were insistent that the issue of cross-border terrorism define the problem, whereas Pakistan wanted to emphasize the freedom struggle and mention the Kashmir dispute as the core issue. The heavens would not have fallen if both these aspects had been mentioned as reflective of the two countries' viewpoints along with an expressed desire to solve the bilateral crisis through dialogue and peaceful means. It would have at least helped in establishing a mechanism for peaceful negotiations. But this was not to be. The summit ended abruptly without a joint statement or a joint press conference. In fact, news conferences by both sides during the initial stages of the visit also played a negative role as contradictory statements about whether the Kashmir issue was the focus of discussions or not poisoned the environment and consequently the chances for a process to emerge. Later, the Pakistani media was told by the officials accompanying the delegation that both heads of state had developed a mutually acceptable draft, but that L.K. Advani sabotaged it and the joint statement idea was dropped by the Indian side at the last moment.

In the run-up to the Agra Summit, and while it was taking place in the shadow of the lovely Taj Mahal, there was an upsurge of violence in Indian Jammu and Kashmir, with eighty people killed in a week. The responsibility for escalating this struggle was claimed by the Lashkars fighting in Kashmir.[67] This was not a helpful gesture by any means. It showed that either Musharraf was not in control of the ISI elements handling the jihadi outfits or that these groups were now largely acting independently. It is hard to believe that he could have supported this activity, especially when he was trying to negotiate with India.

Musharraf was certainly disappointed by the outcome of the Agra Summit, but the hard-liners in Pakistan were exultant at its denouement, and ironically Musharraf's stock went up in their esteem. Many conspiracy theories about an American-backed settlement of the Kashmir conflict though were dashed. However, there is one such analysis consistent with the wildest conspiracy theory that deserves to be detailed. Nayyar Zaidi, chief correspondent of the Jang Group, the largest and most influential media setup in Pakistan, maintains that Musharraf and Vajpayee were involved in secret negotiations through Musharraf's brother, Dr. Naveed Musharraf, based in the United States, Vajpayee's foster son-in-law Ranjan Bhattacharya, and India's top industrialist Dherobhai Ambani, who had an interest in a gas pipeline project from Iran to India via Pakistan.[68] According to Zaidi, it was decided between the two leaders that the Kashmir Valley would be given complete autonomy in all areas except foreign affairs and defense within the Indian framework; that there would be "soft" borders between Indian Kashmir and Pakistani Kashmir, and that the Iranian-Indian pipeline through Pakistan would be blessed officially as marking the beginning of a new era of friendship between the two countries. As to the implementation schedule, Pakistan was to act first by constraining "cross-border terrorism" while India would give "autonomy" to the valley at a future date. Zaidi argues that Musharraf went to Agra all set to sign such an accord, but RSS, a Hindu extremist group, disrupted the whole plan through Advani, as Vajpayee never had the hawks on board. This story is not corroborated by any other source, and gauging from Musharraf's profile and political standing during the times, it is difficult to imagine that he would have opted for such a deal then.

In the aftermath of the Agra Summit, Musharraf appeared to have made up his mind that extremist forces creating chaos inside Pakistan had to be tackled effectively, and he renewed his old campaign with a new vigor directed against sectarianism, which had become a millstone around Pakistan's neck. On Pakistan's Independence Day, August 14, 2001, in a nationwide telecasted speech, Musharraf banned two sectarian outfits, Lashkar-e-Jhangvi and Sipah-i-Muhammad[69]—the two were involved in a civil war representing extremists from Sunni/Wahhabi and Shia communities, respectively. He further warned the sectarian political parties Sipah-i-Sahaba and Tehrik-i-Jafaria to mend their ways, and put them on the watch list. This was an overdue move consistently put back by lingering pusillanimity. Sectarian killings had become a matter of routine. Musharraf tried to show balance, however, by condemning and targeting both sides to the conflict, though the Shias were primarily the victims of this Wahhabi-funded killing spree.

Public reaction to this move was positive, but in passing tough laws and giving sweeping statements, Pakistani governments have never been found wanting. It is in translating words into action that their problems arise. Musharraf, who had been good so far on the side of rhetoric, had gingerly taken his first steps toward action. Soon, offices of the banned groups were sealed, their bank accounts were frozen, and a few dozen of their activists were arrested, but Musharraf had little idea about the widely stretched tentacles of these outfits. The upsurge in sectarian killings was halted, but only for the time being.

There is one other event without a reference to which the story of the pre-9/11 Musharraf era cannot be complete. On August 24, 2001, Musharraf's chief of staff, Lieutenant General Ghulam Ahmed Khan, was killed when a truck crashed head-on into his car. GA, as he was affectionately called by his friends, means "May he live long" in the Urdu language. This was about the only thing where he did not quite live up to his name. He was the quintessential officer and a gentleman who did honor to his profession. In the late nineties he was serving as the number two man in the ISI under General Zia-ud-din. Zia was subtly promoting the agenda of Nawaz Sharif within the army, and GA was the rock on which much of his effort was floundering. By mid-1999 his disgust at the machinations of his superior had filled the cup of his patience, and he was seriously contemplating putting in his papers and going off into early retirement when two of his close friends[70] prevailed on him to reconsider the issue. He changed his mind. But on the eve of Musharraf's takeover, he was sure to be a victim, being a subordinate of Zia-ud-din, who was part of the conspiracy to remove Musharraf from his seat. To GA's good luck, Brigadier Niaz Ahmed, one of Musharraf's most respected friends—the same who had disregarded General Zia's orders to fire on unarmed civilians in 1977 and paid for this refusal with his career—came to his rescue when Musharraf took over the reins of government.[71] GA was allowed to continue in his position.

GA was without a doubt the most respected of Musharraf's generals and his greatest asset, who had him posted as his chief of staff in February 2000. Apart from Generals Amjad and Mushtaq, he was the only one who had the moral courage to dissent with the boss. And this is what stood between Pakistan and many a creeping evil while he lived, and his presence was a damper (in a positive sense) to the power of the kingmakers, Generals Mahmood and

Aziz. His death, which many believe was a conspiracy, was ominous for Pakistan. With his demise, Musharraf increasingly lost touch with reality and became a willing prisoner in a web of flattery. It was GA's absolute abhorrence to the suppression of truth that distinguished him from his peers. I cannot help recalling one of the conversations between Saeed A. Malik and General GA—Malik was strongly asserting that everything was "do-able" provided the Musharraf government had the will to do it, and GA stunned the audience when he said: "But, sir, first they [Musharraf, Mahmood, and Aziz] will have to get out of the cage of Kargil, otherwise all their efforts will be reactive." And he was not being disloyal. He was merely delivering an analytical conclusion, and his tone and tenor were entirely reflective of this. No one in Musharraf's government could have mustered the courage to say this. After his death, Musharraf slid rapidly into the mold of his military predecessors who had stepped in to save their country.

# ——Chapter 9——

# Jihadi Outfits

## Pakistan's "Rent-a-Son" Agencies

Before exploring the post–September 11, 2001, scenario and analyzing Pakistan's role in the war on terror, it is imperative to identify the forces and philosophy that drives Pakistan's religious extremists. When Musharraf stepped in as head of state on October 12, 1999, the harvest he was left to glean was significantly more bitter than those of the leaders who had gone before him. Through the active fostering by Zia ul-Haq, the funding of Saudi Arabia, espousal by the United States, and the venal abandon of Benazir Bhutto and Nawaz Sharif, the seed of religious fanaticism sown more than two decades earlier had come to confront him as fully grown trees perversely balanced by the empty coffers of the state.

In 2001–2, Pakistan was home to fifty-eight religious political parties and twenty-four armed religious militias,[1] the latter category also popularly known as jihadi groups. The term jihad deserves a brief introduction as it signifies a sacred Islamic concept that today stands distorted and tarnished. The word literally means "striving" or "struggle" and by no means is an equivalent of the Western concept of "holy war." Second, there are many kinds of jihad, and most have nothing to do with warfare.[2] At its most basic level, jihad is a struggle with one's inner self against sinful inclinations. In a broader sense of the notion, it is meant to be resistance against aggression and oppression. More so, according to the Prophet of Islam, Mohammad (PBUH), "The best jihad is speaking a word of justice to a tyrannical ruler."[3] However, modern-day religious extremists interpret jihad primarily in terms of the use of force to impose their version of Islam on others and to fight "infidels" to conquer the world. They invoke jihad to help Muslims who are in distress around the world, though their agendas are more political than religious. In their view, even killing of innocent civilians for their higher cause is justified, though this is in clear violation of the established laws of Islamic warfare. According to Islam, noncombatants, especially old men, women, and children, are to be protected at all costs during any form of military conflict. Today's jihadi, however, is least concerned about such Islamic traditions. Furthermore, it is not only Hindus, Jews, and Christians who are their perceived enemies, but even Muslims having views different from theirs are considered heretics and hence worth eliminating.

The mushrooming of extreme right-wing militant organizations in Pakistan began with groups such as Harkat-ul-Jihad-i-Islami and Harkat-ul-Mujahideen in the early 1980s, which were focused on the Afghan jihad. In 1993 these groups merged to form Harkat-ul-Ansar (HUA), for directing its resources and energies supporting militancy or freedom fighters in Indian-controlled Kashmir.[4] The lawless Afghanistan of those days proved to be a perfect base camp for their training activities. As these groups were ideologically associated with a Deobandi religious party, Jamiat-Ulema-i-Islam (JUI),[5] its competitor Jamaat-i-Islami also launched its militant wing Hizb-ul-Mujahideen, purely for operating in Kashmir to remain relevant to the times. Many other minor groups involved in the Afghan war also sprang up to establish new outfits with similar sounding names to penetrate in Kashmir, attracting Saudi donors and ISI funds. Realizing that the Kashmir struggle was proving to be a profitable business venture for many outfits, groups hitherto involved only in sectarian battles inside Pakistan also jumped into this arena. Rivalries soon developed among these groups for financial and political reasons, but for Pakistan it was a "healthy" competition that led to increased subversive operations against Indian forces in Kashmir. By the late 1990s these groups had matured into large armies of dedicated men, quite unafraid to give their lives in pursuit of their aims and in honor of their cause. More than anything else, all these groups were united by their unvarying commitment to free Kashmir from its bondage to India.

They were equally anti-Western and specifically anti-American and anti-Israeli, who they see as two sides of the same coin. The nuclei around which they were structured were the veterans, blooded and battle tested in the Afghan war against the Soviets and in the Taliban operations against the warlords. These jihadis belong to all social classes, and the novelty of their composition is that the majority come from the nonweapon-bearing areas of the country, as opposed to the "martial"[6] areas, indicating that the generally peace-loving people of the country had been sufficiently militarized in the aftermath of the Afghan war. In the Kashmir zone, jihadis suffered frightful losses because of their fearlessness, as they would rather confront their adversaries with open chests, spraying bullets, than resort to clandestine sniping and mine warfare, but despite their losses their numbers increased. On the news of the martyrdom of one son, the family of the deceased celebrated the event by distributing sweets and offered another son to the cause. The unemployed youth of Pakistan had found an occupation, an ideology, and a new family in which they found bonding and brotherhood. They had motivation, dedication, and direction. They were unafraid to die and made light of life. One can call them by any name one desires, but they consider themselves the elite in the cause of Allah, and they have developed the infectious pride to inspire thousands of others into following them.

Osama bin Laden's anti-American tirade, meanwhile, was increasingly catching the attention of the Arab-Afghan war veterans and Islamic hardliners in Pakistan. After Osama's return to Afghanistan in May 1996, his interest in Pakistan increased, though most of his edicts and statements remained focused on criticism of the U.S. military presence in Saudi Arabia.[7] He had even secretly met Nawaz Sharif (chief minister of Punjab then) through a former ISI official, K.K., in 1989, and had offered him financial support to dislodge Benazir Bhutto from power. Pakistani intelligence sources believe that activists of Pakistani outfits like HUA came into close contact with Osama's Al-Qaeda around 1994–95, though he had known many of them since the Afghan war days. Osama's renewed recruitment drive in Afghanistan also attracted many Pakistani youth who were training in the HUA camps then. As an incentive, Osama is believed to have provided direct funding to these camps.[8] This strategic move by Osama certainly won the support of the HUA as well as possibly the admiration of some within the Pakistani intelligence network who were providing logistic support to HUA. Arguably, the ISI and Osama were not working together, as Pakistan was too dependent upon Saudi financial grants and subsidized oil to have worked hand-in-glove with someone who was publicly challenging the House of Saud. In fact, Pakistani intelligence in collaboration with the Saudi government wanted to arrest or kill Osama bin Laden in 1997, but the operation failed as the information was leaked,[9] establishing at least that some elements in Pakistani or Saudi intelligence were his supporters.

It was the *Madrasa* network, though, that proved to be the most essential support base for the jihadi groups. In the context of Islamic history, *Madrasas* were the primary source of religious and scientific learning, especially between the seventh and eleventh centuries, producing luminaries such as Al-Biruni, ibn-Sina (Avicenna), Al-Khawarzmi, and Jabir ibn-Hayyan (Geber), but today's jihadis have converted these into a graveyard of knowledge and scholarship. Contrary to the Quran's emphasis on reflection and contemplation, most *Madrasa* students are taught only to memorize the verses of the book. They are not exposed to its meaning because that is perceived as counterproductive.

As discussed in chapter 6, General Zia had played a vital role in the mushrooming of the *Madrasa* phenomenon during the 1980s as nurseries for the Afghan jihad, but the failure of successive Pakistani governments to invest in the public educational system was another potent factor that led to increased student enrollment in these decadent religious seminaries. Free food, housing, and clothing proved to be an effective incentive for the poor to avail these facilities, at times not knowing that their sons would be inculcated with a distorted version of Islam, and instead of learning to read and write they would be taught how to kill people. At the time of Pakistan's birth, it had only 136 *Madrasas,* but today it is home to around thirty thousand.[10] International Crisis Group's report on Pakistani *Madrasas* aptly says, "Education that creates barriers to modern knowledge, stifling creativity and breeding bigotry, has become the madrasas' defining feature."[11]

A combination of all these factors made Pakistani militant groups a force to be reckoned with. To analyze the capabilities of such groups,[12] two leading jihadi conglomerates, namely Sipah-i-Sahaba and its offshoot Lashkar-e-Jhangvi, and Dawat-ul-Irshad and its militant wing Lashkar-i-Taiba, are discussed in some detail here.

### Sipah-i-Sahaba and Lashkar-e-Jhangvi

The Sipah-i-Sahaba (SSP—Soldier's of the Prophet's Companions), a rabidly anti-Shia party, was initially an outcome of the local Shia-Sunni rivalry in the small city of Jhang, later on to be taken into service by the ISI under the Zia ul-Haq regime. It formally came into existence in September 1985. As for its ideological leanings, SSP was an offshoot of the Jamiat-i-Ulema-i-Islam (JUI),[13] a Deobandi party that had played an active role in the electoral and agitational politics of Pakistan since its inception.

SSP founder Haq Nawaz Jhangvi (1952–90), a prayer leader at a mosque in Jhang, was a product of *Madrasa* education and was known for his anti-Shia oratory. He was groomed during the 1974 anti-Ahmedi agitation, like many other leaders of the group,[14] and later rose to become vice chairman of the Punjab JUI. Extremists among the Sunnis, especially those belonging to the Deobandi and Ahle-Hadith groups, had all along been uncomfortable with the Shias because of their theological differences, and some even considered them heretics, but sectarian violence until then was rare.

However, the 1979 Iranian revolution changed the character and magnitude of sectarian politics in Pakistan. It emboldened Pakistani Shias, who in turn became politicized and started asserting their rights. The zealous emissaries of the Iranian revolutionary regime started financing their organization Tehrik-i-Nifaz-i-Fiqh-i-Jafaria (TNFJ—Movement for the Implementation of *Jafaria* Religious Law)[15] and providing scholarships for Pakistani students to study in Iranian religious seminaries. For the Zia regime though, the problematic issue was Shia activism leading to a strong reaction to his attempts to impose Hanafi Islam (a branch of the Sunni sect). For this he winked to the hard-liners among the Sunni religious groups in order to establish a front to squeeze the Shias. It was in this context that Jhangvi was selected by the intelligence community[16] to do the needful. It is also believed that the JUI recommendation played the decisive part in this choice. The adherents of the Deobandi school were worried about the Shia activism for religious reasons anyhow. State patronage came as an additional incentive. Consequently, in a well-designed effort, Shia assertiveness was projected as their disloyalty to Pakistan and its Islamic ideology.

In a few months, Saudi funds started pouring in, making the project feasible. For Saudi Arabia, the Iranian revolution was quite scary, for its ideals conflicted with that of a Wahhabi monarchy. More so, with an approximately 10 percent Shia population,[17] Saudi Arabia was concerned about the expansion of Shia activism in any Muslim country. Hence, it was more than willing to curb such trends in Pakistan by making a financial investment to bolster its Wahhabi agenda. According to Vali Raza Nasr, a leading expert on the sectarian groups of Pakistan, the flow of these funds was primarily routed through the Pakistan military and the ISI.[18] It is not known whether American support for this scheme was readily available, but the Zia regime knew well that the United States would be glad to acquiesce, given the rising U.S.-Iran hostility. However, some analysts believe that CIA funds were involved in the venture.[19]

The campaign started in Jhang, Jhangvi's hometown, in the form of a movement against the Shia feudal lords of the area—an anti-Shia program in this region was politically an attractive slogan to win public support. The SSP's formal goals were well defined: to combat the Shias at all levels, to strive to have them declared a non-Muslim minority, and to make Sunni Islam the official religion of the state. Though undermining Shias was the immediate target, the creation of a theocratic state was the ultimate aim. To begin with, Jhangvi in his public speeches argued that keeping religion and state apart was a conspiracy hatched by the enemies of Islam, with the outcome that the political sphere was in the hands of corrupt and ungodly politicians.[20]

Another critical repercussion of this movement was a gradual rise of the Deobandis to prominence as against other Sunni groups, most notably at the expense of the Barelvis. This was to have long-term consequences for Pakistan because the Deobandi view of jihad is arguably narrow-minded and violence-prone compared to that of any other Sunni group. For the SSP leadership, murdering Shias was pure jihad, but implementation of this agenda was yet some time off.

In the early days (late 1980s), the SSP confined its activities to publicly abusing Shias and producing jihadi literature declaring them *Kafir* (infidels) implicitly issuing their death warrants. They needed some time to motivate, groom, and train jihadis who would physically eliminate Shias, so in the meantime local criminals and thugs were hired to do the "needful." Criminal elements soon realized that this was a mutually beneficial deal—coming under the umbrella of religious outfits provided a perfect cover for their own activities. Over time, the drug traders also developed their ties with sectarian groups, especially the SSP, reproducing in Pakistan relationships between militant groups and drug traffickers that had already evolved in Afghanistan.[21]

While Shia activists were following these developing trends closely and making themselves ready to counter the SSP propaganda effectively, the leader of TNFJ, Arif Hussaini, was assassinated in August 1988, serving a severe blow to the Shias. Hussaini had lived in Iran for a while and had a close working relationship with the Iranian regime. The ISI hand was suspected in the murder, as a serving army officer, Majid Raza Gillani, had participated in this "operation."[22] Soon it was Jhangvi's turn—he was murdered within a year of Hussaini's elimination, though the SSP suspected a Jhang-based Sunni political leader, Shaikh Iqbal. Iqbal was believed to be the main beneficiary of the rise in Shia-Sunni hostility, as the Sunni majority of Jhang was certain to believe that the murder was perpetrated by Shias, thus creating sympathy for Iqbal and increasing his prospects in the coming elections. A few SSP activists who had inside information thus attacked Iqbal's house in Jhang and brutally murdered his brother in broad daylight, though the message conveyed to the SSP cadres and sympathizers was that Shias killed Jhangvi so as to gain maximum benefit by encouraging hatred against Shias.[23]

This was not without consequences. A few incidents of physical attacks on Shias had taken place in 1988–89, but the event that changed the course of Shia-Sunni confrontation for the worse was the murder of Sadiq Ganji, the Iranian consul general in Lahore in 1990. While Ganji was leaving his hotel premises on Lahore's Mall Road, two assailants riding on a motorcycle emerged on the scene and shot him dead. A twenty-three-year-old SSP activist, Riaz Basra, was the man who delivered for the SSP. After accomplishing the task, he conveniently ran away as police were nowhere near the crime scene. This feat ensured a promising career for Basra as a terrorist. He belonged to a poor family and had studied in a *Madrasa*, Darul Uloom-e-Islamia based in Allama Iqbal town (Lahore Memorizing Quran), but as it turned out, Jhangvi's philosophy sounded more attractive to him. He had joined the SSP in 1988 as an ordinary member, but killing Ganji made him a hero among the party sympathizers, who encouraged him to repeat the performance. There was no shortage of targets, but Iran was angry and the political leadership in Pakistan was quite embarrassed, resulting in increased pressure on the police to arrest the culprits. Basra was arrested on June 5, 1992, bringing some respite for the political government, but he had influential "friends" who wanted to see him in action rather than languishing in jail. They were power-ful enough to ensure that they got what they wanted, or perhaps they owed him a favor. In either case, a successful rescue operation helped Basra escape from police custody while he was being taken from the jail to a special court hearing on April 30, 1994.

No credible information has come to light yet as to the exact identity of his "friends," but most probably they were the same on whose behalf he had eliminated the Iranian diplomat. A former Pakistani intelligence operator re-veals that Basra was operating in league with some junior ISI agents.[24] Ac-cording to his information the other person on the motorcycle with Basra conducting the Ganji murder operation was an ISI official named Athar, a low-level official from the Pakistan Air Force serving with the agency. How-ever, it is not known whether the assassination was an act approved by the military and the ISI command, or if some rogue element in the ISI had given a go-ahead on his own, which was possible as some disgruntled elements in the ISI had started operating independently.[25]

These were the times when the financial endowment of the SSP-run *Madrasas* increased manifold, with the repercussion that factional disputes over the control of the purse also surged.[26] Prospects of a financial bonanza attracted many other religious extremists to jump into this theater and vie for rewards. In the ensuing competition among such scoundrels, sectarian kill-ings in Pakistan increased in the 1990s. Meanwhile, Iranian funding to Shia organizations also increased, making Pakistan a battleground for Saudi Arabia and Iran to settle their scores. No effective measures were taken by the Paki-stan government to halt this slide into chaos.

Realizing that sectarian outfits were untouchable entities, professional criminals hastened to join these groups and benefit from this window of op-portunity. For instance, when around five hundred trained gunmen belong-ing to MQM were abandoned by their masters, they tentatively turned to the SSP in search of a job. They found it to be a promising career. All they had to do was grow beards and learn a few anti-Shia lessons. The rest they were already accustomed to—butchering people.

During the 1990s the SSP spawned many splinter groups, Lashkar-e-Jhangvi (Army of Jhangvi, hereafter called Lashkar) being the most deadly and prominent one, whereas other small outfits were mainly "personal mafias of influential feudals, led by local mullahs."[27] Many of the leaders of the SSP, including Israr ul-Haq Qasmi and Zia ur-Rahman Farooqi, were mur-dered by extremists belonging to Sipah-i-Mohammad (Army of Mohammad), a Shia militant outfit formed in 1994. To tackle such attacks on its leader-ship, the SSP in a planned move largely confined its activities to the political arena under a felon, Azam Tariq, while Lashkar, led by the notorious Riaz

Basra, started operating in 1995–96 as a terrorist group. Basra's direct links with Arab financiers and the Taliban helped him establish his base camp in Afghanistan. Before Lashkar's emergence, sectarian killings were mainly restricted to leaders and activists of both the Shia and Sunnis, but Basra expanded the battlefield by targeting Shia government officials, lawyers, doctors, and traders, giving a new twist to the confrontation. Even Shia mosques came under attack, resulting in random killings of innocent people. By virtue of such terrorist operations, Lashkar distinguished itself as the most violent sectarian force in Pakistan. It also openly admitted to its acts of terror, informing newspapers through telephone calls and its publication *Intiqam-i-Haq* (dual meaning—Revenge of Truth, or Revenge of Jhangvi). It also started operating in Indian-controlled Kashmir but, keeping in line with its philosophy, it embarked on this journey by starting to murder Kashmiri Shia leaders before targeting the Indian forces.

By early 1997, Lashkar was ready for even bigger operations—Iranian cultural centers in Lahore and Multan were burned down, and Iranian diplomat Mohammad Ali Rahimi was killed in cold blood. Basra immediately escaped to Afghanistan after orchestrating this operation, where a HUA guesthouse was ready for him,[28] but Ashraf Marth, a senior police official, apprehended the other Lashkar terrorists involved in the crime. Marth had the competence as well as political support[29] to carry out his investigation. In a few months he was able to track the funding sources of Lashkar and, to everyone's amazement, evidence of foreign financing and records of funds transfers through U.S. banks were on the table of the prime minister. One of the men accused of the attacks was found with a credit card issued from New York.[30] This was enough to cause the prime minister to jump in his seat. He immediately passed the information on to the army chief. Before any action could be taken on the information, Ashraf Marth was assassinated right in front of his official residence, and the inquiry came to an abrupt closure. The attack was so well planned that half a dozen armed guards of Marth could not move and the attackers vanished from the scene. Pakistani intelligence agencies were thunderstruck, and police officials were scared to get involved in such investigations. It is ironic why the military intelligence agencies remained a silent witness to such developments. According to Samina Ahmed, the army used the instability caused by sectarian violence to pressure the democratic governments.[31]

The regional political scenario was also relevant. In Afghanistan, the Shia Hazara community was part of the anti-Taliban alliance under Ahmad Shah Masud, providing additional grounds to the pro-Taliban SSP to continue its onslaught against Shias in Pakistan.[32] Iran-Taliban relations reached their lowest ebb when nine Iranian diplomats were killed in August 1998 by Taliban forces in Mazar-i-Sharif. In reaction, Iran's supreme leader Ayatollah Ali Khamenei demanded that Pakistan, which Iran held partly responsible for the murders, drop its support of the Taliban.[33] The Pakistan Army considered such a possibility as counterproductive to its strategic interests in the region.

Basra had now become a legend among the religious hard-liners in the country. Prime Minister Nawaz Sharif finally decided to target some sectarian groups, including Lashkar, through civilian law enforcement agencies, as he was not expecting much support from military intelligence agencies. Tariq Pervez, an accomplished counterterrorism expert in the police service, was tasked to trace out the Lashkar terrorists and bring them to justice. Tariq's hard work and commitment paid off when his special team was able to trace Basra, though there was a problem. Basra was in Kabul, and that was beyond Tariq's jurisdiction. On getting the report, Nawaz Sharif personally requested the ISI chief to get hold of him, knowing that they had close links with the Taliban and HUA. He was told not to worry and that Basra would be taken care of soon.[34] Ironically, instead of Basra being apprehended, Lashkar stepped up its activities and attempted to assassinate the prime minister on January 3, 1999. The plot failed because a remote-control bomb placed under a bridge that the prime minister had to pass over detonated an hour too early.

How the assassination plan was botched is indeed an interesting story. Gul Khan, Lashkar's top bomb-making expert, was hiding near the location with a remote control device, waiting for the prime minister's vehicle to approach the bridge. Due to a lack of access to sophisticated equipment, he was using an ordinary cordless telephone as a gadget to send the signal. This telephone set was on a VHC frequency, and he was not aware that some police vehicles in the city were also using the same frequency for their wireless communications. Meanwhile, the driver of a police patrol vehicle surveying the prime minister's travel route, by pure coincidence, parked very close to the point where the bomb was planted. As soon as the vehicle's wireless set received a call, the bomb detonator caught the signal too and the bomb exploded. Nawaz Sharif was lucky—Gul Khan's planning was perfect but the technology he was using was outmoded. When he was arrested later, the interrogations led police to connect the dots. Prior to this, the police were of the view that one of the terrorist groups had only sent a warning to Nawaz Sharif, telling him that they were capable of eliminating him.[35]

In reaction, Punjab's chief minister, Shabaz Sharif, gave the go-ahead to the Punjab police to eliminate the Lashkar terrorists through all means possible. Around three dozen operators belonging to SSP and Lashkar were gunned down in staged police encounters,[36] but extrajudicial killings, besides being obviously contrary to the due process of law, were not the solution to the simmering problem. With no sign of abating, Lashkar activities witnessed an upsurge in 1999 when close to a hundred innocent people became victims of its horrendous campaign.

Nawaz Sharif's efforts to curb this menace during 1998–99 had failed miserably because Lashkar activists were using Afghanistan as a sanctuary courtesy of the Taliban, who were known to be hospitable to their guests. Another means of support was HUA's logistic backing, but the factor that really turned the scales in favor of Lashkar was that Basra had developed a close working relationship with Al-Qaeda and Osama bin Laden.[37] This was so lethal a combination that only an event like 9/11 could trigger events that would lead to this conglomerate's dismemberment.

### Dawat-ul-Irshad and Lashkar-i-Taiba

Lashkar-i-Taiba (Army of the Righteous), a militant outfit created in 1990, is a subsidiary of Markaz Dawat-ul-Irshad (MDI—Center for Religious Learning and Propagation; also called Jamaat al-Dawa), which was founded in 1987 by Mr. Zafar Iqbal, Hafiz Mohammad Saeed, and Abdullah Azzam (1941–89),[38] the last being more of an intellectual father of this organization. A brief look at the profiles of the three men who came up with the idea of setting up this institution provides an interesting insight into its goals and objectives.

Azzam, a Palestinian with a Wahhabi bent of mind, was an important player during the Afghan war of the 1980s. He had studied Islamic jurisprudence at Egypt's Al-Azhar University, remained a professor at the University of Jordan in Amman, and taught later in Saudi Arabia. He had left the West Bank in 1967, arguing that he first wanted to learn the skills necessary to fight. According to Stephen Schwartz, Azzam was also disgruntled by the secular nature of the Palestinian resistance and wanted to generate a new zeal among the Arabs for the "lost art and science of Jihad."[39] As soon as the Afghan crisis erupted in 1979–80, he rushed to Pakistan, where a teaching position at Islamic University in Islamabad was waiting for him. This assignment, however, proved to be temporary, and he shifted to Peshawar shortly thereafter, where he established an organization named Mekhtab al-Khadamat (Service Bureau) for mujahideen.

With generous Saudi funds, this group managed to afford travel and training for volunteers coming to participate in the Afghan jihad from all across the Arab world. In a short span of time Azzam proved to be a valuable asset for both the ISI and the CIA, though he largely operated independently and was more loyal to his Saudi financiers than anyone else. He traveled widely around the world to generate finances and support for the Afghan cause, and various cities in the United States were also covered during these "lecture tours." His real "long-lasting" contribution, though, was the inspiration that he provided to Osama bin Laden in the mid-1980s through his speeches in Saudi Arabia.[40] Osama bin Laden's Peshawar-based Bayt-ul-Ansar (House of the Helpers), involved in work similar to that of Azzam's group, provided an opportunity to both Azzam and Osama to work together, though Azzam was already a prominent figure then and Osama was not. It was only a matter of time before Osama would rise high in the ranks of Azzam's protégés.

During these times, Azzam came into contact with Hafiz Saeed, and the two discussed the idea of establishing MDI. Zafar Iqbal was then tasked to draw up a plan for raising the center at Muridke, a city near Lahore, but before the center could become functional, Abdullah Azzam was assassinated along with his two sons in a powerful bomb blast in Peshawar on November 24, 1989. The ISI believed it to be the work of the Israeli intelligence agency Mossad[41] as, according to their assessment, Azzam, after the mujahideen victory, was planning to return to the West Bank to join *Intifada*. Others blame Osama and the ISI for the killing. Peter Bergen, a renowned journalist and the world's leading expert on Al-Qaeda, believes that there is a strong possibility that the Soviets and/or Afghan communists killed him.[42] The murder mystery, however, was never resolved.

MDI under the leadership of Hafiz Saeed, the main architect of the organization, was now standing on its own feet. In late 1989, Saeed started preparing grounds to create Lashkar-i-Taiba (LT), the militant wing of the group. He took it upon himself to lead the outfit during its teething days, leaving Zafar Iqbal to administer MDI's educational activities. Zafar, in comparative terms, had a moderate personality. When confronted by a journalist about jihadi-friendly curriculum adopted by the MDI, in turn encouraging the Talibanization of Pakistan, he responded: "Taliban are a group of misguided elements. We have higher ideals."[43] What those higher ideals were, he did not chose to elaborate then, but Hafiz Saeed's background and philosophy provide sufficient indication about the direction that MDI/LT was destined to take.

Saeed had grown up in a very conservative Muslim environment. His family had migrated from India to Pakistan in 1947 while sadly losing thirty-six members of the extended family unit in the Hindu-Muslim riots that accompanied the partition of India. Saeed was brought up as a believer in the Ahle-Hadith sect,[44] and he received early religious education at home. Later he was sent to a *Madrasa* to memorize the Quran thereby becoming a *Hafiz* at an early age. He did his master's in Arabic language and Islamic studies from Punjab University and left for Saudi Arabia, where he taught at a university in Riyadh. On his return he was employed as a research officer in the government-run Islamic Ideology Council during the General Zia era. From there he moved on to the University of Engineering and Technology, Lahore, as a professor of Islamic studies.

Belonging to the Ahle-Hadith group, which is the South Asian version of Wahhabism, Saudi support was forthcoming for his MDI project. In addition, association with Azzam and participation in the Afghan jihad, though for a short duration, readied him for the task of establishing Pakistan's most powerful jihadi outfit. His political orientation can be gauged from his statement asserting that, "We believe in Huntington's clash of civilizations, and our jihad will continue until Islam becomes the dominant religion."[45]

As to the ideology of MDI, it aspires to develop a jihadi culture by imparting Islamic education in a modern setting and at the same time providing military training to its activists. MDI was made responsible for taking care of the educational requirements and goals while the LT platform was meant to equip the adherents for practical experience in waging jihad. Thus, the foundation of the movement was based on the twin fields of education and jihad. Hafiz Saeed also propounded the theory that when Muslims gave up jihad, scientific and technological advancement went into others' hands.[46] He strongly advocated the learning of computer sciences and modern communication tools along with religious education, though the real purpose he had in mind was to utilize this knowledge in pursuit of waging jihad. This was a clever strategy to attract recruits in the name of education and then divert their energies toward military training.

The Kashmir insurgency beginning in 1989 came at an appropriate time to provide an active battleground for the LT soldiers. Contrary to the general assumption, freedom for Kashmir is not the ultimate goal of this conglomerate. Their ideal is to provide an alternate model for governance and development in Pakistan, and for that MDI's Muridke Headquarters (near Lahore), occupying two hundred acres of land, was built up as a model city. It contains a huge mosque, a garments factory, an iron foundry, a furniture factory, playing/sports facilities, markets, and residential blocks for the trainees/students. A new educational complex is also under construction at the site that will cater to around six thousand additional students. Besides, it runs hundreds of schools providing free education. It also runs many hospitals across Pakistan and is involved in charity work (for details see: www.dawakhidmat.org).

As for the military training imparted to the LT militants, it runs separate courses for trainers as well as new recruits. A typical twenty-one-day course for newcomers starts by indoctrinating the activists on the virtues of jihad. Then they are sent out to nearby towns to spread the message of Islam, to promote civic sense, and preach social responsibility. Their performance vis-à-vis their ability to gather and influence people through public speaking skills is closely monitored and evaluated by their mentors. The emphasis is on becoming a good citizen before becoming a good jihadi. Only after qualifying in this stage is one sent for guerrilla warfare training in military camps, located mostly in Pakistani-controlled Kashmir. This phase includes training in handling weapons ranging from a revolver to a rocket-launcher.[47] It also involves carrying heavy loads while marching through mountainous areas to get accustomed to the Kashmir environment, where they would ultimately operate.

In many ways this jihadi conglomerate was developed on the lines of the Hezbollah. It has separate wings that have different operational and functional responsibilities ranging from intelligence-gathering, research work, and media-monitoring to managing hospitals, schools, and charity clubs. In terms of funding, it receives grants from around the world, mostly from well-to-do Ahle-Hadith/Wahhabi sympathizers, though their primary source has been contributions from Saudi Arabia.[48] Regular fund-raising in local mosques as well as in Islamic centers in North America and Europe also takes place in the name of jihad for supporting Muslims who are victims in conflict zones worldwide. Gauging from LT's extensive operations in Kashmir and MDI's increasing charity work in Pakistan during the late 1990s, the group's financial health appears to be quite promising. Financial strength has been a major factor behind its expansion. Handsome monetary rewards to the families of boys who sacrificed their lives in Kashmir and regular monthly income for the families of jihadis fighting in Kashmir made jihad an attractive venture for unemployed youth, especially among the underprivileged.

MDI was also different from other competitive groups by virtue of employing advanced propaganda techniques. Its publications were available widely, and because of its well-conceived projection of emphasis on modern education, it started attracting people from rich as well as educated families, making it a dynamic outfit. The jihad literature became a popular genre in the 1990s—mostly sold outside mosques after Friday prayers and at regular bookstores. Readers of these materials are often younger people who are searching for meaning in their lives and who have little to look forward to in a stagnant economy and disintegrating society.

However, the primary reason behind the considerable growth of the group can be linked to its successful sabotage operations against Indian forces in Kashmir, as these brought them into the limelight while ensuring immunity from the country's intelligence and law enforcement agencies. Running military training camps inside Pakistan would not be possible without such support. This confidence also led LT to orchestrate killings of innocent Hindus in the Kashmir theater, tarnishing its image of a freedom movement. Few among ordinary Pakistanis knew about this unfortunate development because they were led to believe by the state media that these incidents were managed by Indian agencies to blame Pakistani groups in order to damage their credibility among Kashmiris. It is probable that Indian agencies were in fact involved in some cases, like the massacre of Sikhs when President Clinton was visiting South Asia in 2000, but LT's direct involvement in similar acts is also certain.

LT also prides itself on introducing suicide bombings in the Kashmir theater. Such attacks had a discernible impact on the morale of Indian forces, in turn raising the prestige of LT at home and making it distinguished among all groups fighting in the zone. By virtue of these "accomplishments," criticism of LT was increasingly considered antipatriotic in some Pakistani circles. Their sponsors lacked the vision to see where all this might lead. The group, however, fully benefited from this image and, while motivating more young Pakistanis to participate in the Kashmir jihad, it continued to expand its support base and infrastructure inside Pakistan. LT's annual congregation is one indication of its growing popularity in Pakistan. Reportedly, around half a million people attend this gathering annually, which is second only to Tableeghi-Jamaat's (preaching group) assembly, which attracts around a million people every year. LT used these occasions to expand its network by propagating its success stories in Kashmir; by linking up with extremist groups operating in other parts of the world, as representatives from such groups are routinely invited; and, last but not least, by sending a message to the government about its growing size and strength. Consequently, it earned the goodwill of the army leadership for achieving what they could not.

In operational matters, the ISI provided them with sensitive maps and access to arms and ammunition, but LT local commanders mostly chose their targets by themselves and the ISI did not have much say in this, according to an ISI official. Having independent financial sources was perhaps the reason behind the group's comparative sovereign status. Increased recruitment of retired army and intelligence officials also made the LT increasingly self-sufficient in decision-making processes while at the same time providing strength to its organizational and operational capabilities.

Realizing that the movement was gaining momentum and that it was the appropriate time to expand its operations, Hafiz Saeed declared in June 1999 that LT was not working for the liberation of Kashmir alone, but intended to aid the 200 million Muslims in India. He added that jihad would continue until the independence of Himachal Pradesh, Bihar, Hyderabad, Uttar Pradesh, and Junagarh—mostly Hindu majority areas in India with significant Muslim population.[49] The statement was given at a time when LT jihadis were operating at the Kargil Heights along with army troops, and the military leadership of the country had nothing but appreciation for their efforts.

Emboldened by the Kargil episode and Musharraf's takeover in October

1999, Hafiz Saeed's tone and tenor changed further. During LT's annual gathering in November 1999, he advised the Musharraf government to readjust Pakistan's foreign policy by strengthening ties with the Muslim bloc and reducing its dependence on the United States.[50] Taking another leap forward, he vowed to launch jihad to turn Pakistan into a pure Islamic state.[51] This was not a revelation for those who were following the activities of the group, but the timing was of the essence as the military had taken over the country barely a couple of weeks earlier. This was a clear sign of close links between the MDI and the military leadership. This group's philosophical posture vis-à-vis jihad was also witnessing a transformation during this period. It started projecting five new principles through its website and published materials to entrench itself further. These were:[52]

1.  Attack the intellectual elite (westernized Pakistanis) to discredit them before they even speak out against MDI/LT.
2.  Democratic system of government is un-Islamic.
3.  Sufism dampens the jihad spirit.
4.  Jihad is not preaching or personal purity but fighting in the cause of Allah by sword.
5.  Jihad is an offensive defense.

The crux of the move was to effectively undermine any effort that may challenge their version of jihad. One of the articles on the MDI website relating to the subject, written by Ihsan ul-Haq Shabaz, makes interesting reading. It argues that the traditionally accepted notion that the state's permission was mandatory for waging jihad was a "huge mistake" because the political and military leadership of Pakistan was under the influence of Christians and Jews and hence could not be expected to allow jihadis to perform a duty that is obligatory to them under the circumstances. Thus the group was increasingly expanding its objectives and targets with no one in the government daring to challenge these assertions. Ordinary people kept silent because they could see the gun-toting LT activists often roaming around in the cities, knowing what could be the price of having an argument with them. Weak civil society groups and political instability were additional reasons why groups like these carried on with their business unchallenged by society at large, though a majority felt disturbed by these trends.

Being a moderate and a liberal by force of inclination if not by philosophic persuasion, Musharraf would have wanted to crush the exploitative power of these groups and their likes when he emerged on the national scene in October 1999. Indeed, he moved in that direction more than once in 2000–2001, but the problem was that his bold advances were followed by precipitous retreats. This was not only an admission of the jihadis' power, but also of shoddy homework—a manifestation of the Kargil syndrome. But then came the catastrophic shock waves of 9/11 to stun the world. Musharraf was one of the few who immediately woke up to the glimmer of opportunity this opened up to him. The instantaneous outcry that sounded around the globe shifted the balance against the jihadi, and Musharraf lost no time to move in and usurp the advantage. How far he is willing to go in this direction, especially when it starts affecting the Pakistani establishment's Kashmir policy, is yet to be seen.

——Chapter 10——

# 9/11 and the War on Terror

Within hours of the deadly September 11, 2001, terrorist attacks, the U.S. administration concluded that Osama bin Laden and Al-Qaeda operating from Afghanistan were behind the attacks, and that any successful counterstrike would not be possible without the support and assistance of Pakistan. While addressing the American nation after the tragedy, President George W. Bush left no doubt as to the fate of the Taliban regime when he plainly declared that, "We will make no distinction between those who planned these acts and those who harbor them."[1] This led Colin Powell, the U.S. secretary of state, to assert in the National Security Council (NSC) meeting at the White House the same night: "We have to make it clear to Pakistan and Afghanistan, this is show time."[2]

Lieutenant General Mahmood Ahmed, Pakistan's ISI chief, who was on an official visit to the United States as a CIA guest, and Maleeha Lodhi, Pakistan's ambassador to the United States, were asked to attend a meeting with senior American officials on September 12, 2001. To be fully prepared, Mahmood called Musharraf to discuss the emerging scenario and take instructions for the important meeting. On the morning of September 12, the U.S. deputy secretary of state, Richard Armitage, in a "hard-hitting conversation," told Mahmood that Pakistan has to make a choice: "You are either 100 percent with us or 100 percent against us—there is no gray area."[3] In the words of Armitage, Mahmood "was immediately willing to cooperate."[4] In the afternoon, Mahmood was invited to CIA headquarters at Langley, Virginia, where he told George Tenet, the CIA director, that in his view Mullah Omar, the Taliban chief, was a religious man with humanitarian instincts and not a man of violence![5] This was a bit difficult for the CIA officials to digest and rightly so as the Taliban's track record, especially in the realm of human rights, was no secret. General Mahmood was told politely but firmly that Mullah Omar and the Taliban would have to face U.S. military might if Osama bin Laden along with other Al-Qaeda leaders were not handed over without delay. To send the message across clearly, Richard Armitage held a second meeting with Mahmood the same day, informing him that he would soon be handed specific American demands, to which Mahmood reiterated that Pakistan would cooperate.[6]

Meanwhile, as expected, Musharraf had received his first call from Wendy Chamberlain, the U.S. ambassador to Pakistan. After the pleasantries, she expressed the hope that Pakistan would come on board and extend all its cooperation to the United States in bringing the perpetrators of the terrorist act to justice. He gave her the assurances she sought, but could not restrain himself from enumerating Pakistan's past experiences of cooperation with America, and the list of broken promises that was the compensation Pakistan often received from such alliances. But Ms. Chamberlain assured him that this time it would be different. For lack of an alternative, he dutifully played the part of a reassured Third World leader.

As per the credible narrative of Bob Woodward, General Mahmood on September 13, 2001, was handed a formal list of the U.S. demands by Mr. Armitage and was asked to convey these to Musharraf and was also duly informed, for the sake of emphasis, that these were "not negotiable." Colin Powell, Richard Armitage, and the assistant secretary of state, Christina Rocca, had drafted the list in the shape of a "non-paper." It categorically asked Pakistan to:

1. Stop Al-Qaeda operatives coming from Afghanistan to Pakistan, intercept arms shipments through Pakistan, and end ALL logistical support for Osama bin Laden.
2. Give blanket overflight and landing rights to U.S. aircraft.
3. Give the U.S. access to Pakistani naval and air bases and to the border areas between Pakistan and Afghanistan.
4. Turn over all intelligence and immigration information.
5. Condemn the September 11 attacks and curb all domestic expressions of support for terrorism.
6. Cut off all shipments of fuel to the Taliban, and stop Pakistani volunteers from going into Afghanistan to join the Taliban.
7. Note that, should the evidence strongly implicate Osama bin Laden and the Al-Qaeda network in Afghanistan, and should the Taliban continue to harbor him and his accomplices, Pakistan will break diplomatic relations with the Taliban regime, end support for the Taliban, and assist the U.S. in the aforementioned ways to destroy Osama and his network.[7]

Having gone through the list, Mahmood declared that he was quite clear on the subject and that "he knew how the President thought, and the President would accept these points."[8] Mahmood then faxed the document to

Musharraf. While the latter was going through it and in the process of weighing the pros and cons of each demand, his aide de camp informed him that
Colin Powell was on the line. Musharraf liked and respected Powell, and the
conversation was not going to be a problem. He told him that he understood
and appreciated the U.S. position, but that he would respond to the U.S.
demands after having discussed these with his associates.[9] Powell was far
too polite to remind him that he in fact was the government, but did inform
him that his general in Washington had already assured them that these demands would be acceptable to the government of Pakistan. It is not certain if
Musharraf bit his lip when he heard this, but he did grit his teeth, and his
relationship with Mahmood suffered a crack. Musharraf was in no doubt
that, in the circumstances, he would have accepted every American demand,
but only after putting up the right appearances. Mahmood's presumption had
denied him the act and national prestige had suffered a blow, though the
bruise must have shown more clearly on his personal ego, which has as large
a compass as it is tender.

Musharraf's response to Powell was in line with his earlier statement on
the eve of the 9/11 tragedy—he had condemned it as the "most brutal and
horrible act of terror" and in his message to President Bush had said that the
world must unite to fight against terrorism in all its forms and root out this
modern-day evil.[10] Later, discussions with Wendy Chamberlain and a telephone conversation with General Mahmood in the United States on the issue
had helped him gauge the direction in which the wind was blowing. On the
eve of September 12 he had already discussed the issue in Pakistan's National Security Council and made up his mind. But he was not expecting an
"either you are with us or against us" proposition, with a specific seven-point
demand list and a very short deadline to respond. To reply, he intended to
take the army corps commanders in confidence, but courtesy of Mahmood,
he had to immediately give the U.S. administration all the assurances they
needed from Pakistan, though there was to be no public declaration of the
same because Musharraf needed an ex post facto formalization of the same
after meeting with his corps commanders.

Corps commanders, on the other hand, were unaware of this development
when they all met in a nuclear bunker near Islamabad on September 14,
2001, believing that they could talk without the risk of U.S. surveillance in a
highly secured location. Nine corps commanders and a dozen other senior
staff officers at the army's General Headquarters (GHQ) were in attendance,
including the chiefs of the ISI and MI. Musharraf gave out a cogent exposi-
tion of why Pakistan had to stand with America. He told them that Pakistan
faced a stark choice—it could either join the U.S. coalition that was supported by the United Nations Security Council, or expect to be declared a

terrorist state, leading to economic sanctions. Most of his commanders nodded in sage agreement, but General Mahmood sat in sullen silence; Lieutenant General Aziz registered his polite disagreement; General Mushtaq was entirely consistent and honorable in dissent; and the unfortunate Lieutenant General Jamshed Gulzar seemed to have lost his sanity and discovered his nonexistent heroism to join the dissenters. But it was General Khalid Maqbool who really sparkled, giving a glittering performance of unctuous courtiership. In the process he won the heart of Musharraf by pleading his infallibility. And Lieutenant General Muzaffar Usmani, the number two man in the army, a self-confessed "soldier of god," registered his impolite disagreement. Usmani had started out as a moderate and an open-minded officer, but later in his career he found the intolerant fringe of Islam, where he saw his own piety in discovering the imperfections in others. By the time he became deputy chief of army staff, he had become reclusive, shutting himself in his house and walking about in a Saudi *jubba* (gown) topped by a green turban. All this was widely known when Musharraf promoted him.

General Usmani's argument was that ditching the long-standing Pakistan policy of supporting the Taliban without any specific American incentive in return should be avoided.[11] On the contrary, Musharraf was of the view that Pakistan should be supportive of the United States as a matter of principle, and any hint of economic incentives would be inappropriate at a time when the United States was in a "shock and anger" mood.[12] Lieutenant General Aziz, on the other hand, was of the view that there was a possibility of a domestic backlash if Afghanistan were attacked, to which Musharraf agreed, but he insisted that in case of any delay in agreeing to the U.S. terms, India would benefit by currying favor with the United States. This was a sufficient argument for the Pakistani military commanders to agree with Musharraf's opinion, though it took them six hours to reach this "consensus."

The next day, on September 15, Musharraf conveyed General Aziz's concerns about a possible domestic fallout to Wendy Chamberlain without naming him, explaining that in such an eventuality Pakistan would expect the United States to understand such pressures and continue to support him.[13] The message was duly conveyed to senior officials in the U.S. administration.

The point that had helped Musharraf clinch the argument during the corps commanders' meeting a day earlier, in reference to India, was in fact substantial. Of course, Musharraf and his corps commanders were unaware that hardly a few hours before their meeting had commenced, the leading Indian intelligence service, named the Research and Analysis Wing (RAW), had convinced the CIA that "Pakistani jihadists" were planning an "imminent attack on the White House," and as a precautionary measure the U.S. Secret Service had even made arrangements to evacuate President Bush from the

White House.[14] President Bush was understandably exhausted by the hectic schedule and attendant pressures, hence to the surprise of everyone he refused to leave the White House until shown the exact information. U.S. Secret Service director Brian Stafford told him that he was in immediate danger and that the report was credible, as Indian intelligence was well wired into Pakistan, but the president was unmoved. Still, the threat was considered so serious that Vice President Dick Cheney was shifted to a safe location and nonessential staff at the White House were allowed to go home early. This explains the credibility of Indian intelligence in the eyes of the CIA, but most likely its privilege and trust was misused in this case. Arguably, it was an effort on the part of India to push the U.S. administration to include Pakistan on the hit list. Without a doubt, religious extremists are narrow-minded bigots and violence indeed is their bread and butter, but to make a case that any of the domestic Pakistani groups (e.g., Lashkar-i-Taiba and Lashkar-e-Jhangvi) were capable of launching a terrorist attack on the White House was an exaggerated assessment. The report also inferred that Pakistani intelligence possibly was sponsoring this attack, which was not possible. For the sake of argument, even if the Pakistani jihadi groups were capable of orchestrating such a strike, Indian intentions behind providing this "timely" intelligence assessment were less than noble.

On September 16, 2001, Musharraf sent a delegation to the Taliban with the mission to convince them to hand over Osama bin Laden. It included Lieutenant General Mahmood, the ISI chief, and Mufti Nizamuddin Shamzai, head of the famous Deobandi *Madrasa* in Binori town, Karachi. It is the same *Madrasa* where Osama bin Laden first met Mullah Omar, the leader of the Taliban, a few years ago. The mission failed, which was expected, but more worrisome was the revelation that Mufti Shamzai, instead of conveying the official message, encouraged Mullah Omar to start a jihad against the United States if it attacked Afghanistan.[15] After this, Mahmood, whose arrogance and presumption had come to grate on Musharraf's expansive tolerance by now, was offered the ceremonial slot of chairman of the Joint Chiefs of Staff Committee.[16] He refused.

However, Musharraf was under immense pressure, both domestically and from the United States on how to proceed vis-à-vis U.S. demands and expectations. While talking to a selected gathering of retired generals, seasoned diplomats, and politicians, on September 18, Musharraf argued that the decision to extend "unstinting support" to the United States was taken under tremendous pressure and in the face of fears, that in case of refusal, a direct military action by a coalition of the United States, India, and Israel against Pakistan was a real possibility. When confronted by the audience that he still should have consulted a cross-section of society before taking any decision, he mentioned the short deadline he was given for a response.[17] It was easy for Musharraf to have a dialogue with this group, but leaders of Jamaat-i-Islami and Jamiat-i-Ulema-i-Islam (both Sami and Fazl groups) were not ready to listen to Musharraf's justifications. They asked for a review of government policy and insisted that Musharraf demand from the United States a credible evidence of bin Laden's involvement in the 9/11 attacks. This was what the Taliban also asked for a day earlier. On September 18, when a journalist posed this question to the U.S. secretary of defense, Donald Rumsfeld, his reply was that sharing intelligence with other countries posed a dilemma as that could lead to a drying up of sources of information.[18] But Musharraf was finally shown some evidence on October 3, 2001. A day later the Pakistan Foreign Office declared that the "material provides sufficient basis for [bin Laden's] indictment in a court of law."[19] Musharraf should have been allowed to share the information with the people of Pakistan.

Anyhow, Musharraf knew that war was coming to Afghanistan. On October 7, 2001, the U.S. attack on Afghanistan commenced, and what was left of the country was bombed to smithereens. The many dead did not receive the dignity of even a decent count. The sheer magnitude of the effort stunned the people, and the Pakistani clerics were unnerved for the first time since their steady rise in influence and power, which helped Musharraf consolidate his position. Pakistan had taken a historical U-turn in its policy toward the Taliban by fully supporting the U.S. military campaign. On the domestic scene, Musharraf started to announce measures against the hard-line religious groups and limit the license of the mullahs. Most Pakistanis heaved a sigh of relief—for those oppressed by all and sundry, suppression of the mullahs was to be one oppression less.

This change in policy needed a change of faces as well. Gauging the mood, Mahmood, through a close friend of Musharraf, put in a request to be retained as director general of ISI.[20] Musharraf refused and Mahmood had to go home. General Aziz retained the esteem and affection of his boss to fill the office so recently refused by Mahmood, and General Usmani packed his bags and vanished. Shortly thereafter Generals Mushtaq and Gulzar lost their commands and were sidelined, and Khalid Maqbool was made governor of the largest and most populous province in the country. With General Ghulam Ahmed already having passed away, and General Amjad not being a part of Musharraf's inner core, there was no one left in the fighting army with courage enough to register a disagreement with their chief. Ironically, Musharraf mistakenly took this as an omen of his rising popularity in the army.

For a few days after the beginning of the U.S.-led Afghan campaign there were street protests in Pakistan, but a determined Musharraf managed to discourage the trend successfully. Contrary to Western media projections, most of the gatherings were small and controllable from the law enforcement angle, though the popularity of Osama witnessed a rise, especially in the two provinces bordering Afghanistan.[21] A letter ostensibly from Mullah Omar voicing his defiance was widely circulated across thousands of *Madrasas* in the country, and the call for jihad in support of the Taliban resounded from mosques all across Pakistan.[22] Readership of Jaish-e-Mohammad's magazine *Zarb-e-Momin* and that of Harkat-ul-Mujahideen's *Al-Hilal* broke all records. These were filled with emotional appeals for donations in cash for aid to "Afghan victims of the U.S. terrorism" and carried phone numbers and office locations of Al-Rasheed Trust.[23] It is estimated that around ten thousand Pakistani jihadis crossed into Afghanistan to fight along with the Taliban. A policy change at the government level was easy to pronounce but difficult to translate into reality. People who expected that jihadis could be decommissioned at will were living in a fool's paradise.

As the events of 9/11 came to be discussed in Pakistan, a rash of doubts and skepticism rose to afflict the minds of the people in the country. They thought it uncanny that most of the U.S. news channels could so confidently name Osama as the perpetrator of the outrage while the dust of the World Trade Center was still rising. How, they asked, could half-trained pilots maneuver jumbo jets through a maze of skyscrapers to direct them into their chosen targets? Or how could Osama, a man holed up in a remote cave in Afghanistan, bereft of any means of communication save that of a human messenger, coordinate such an intricate operation? A senior Pakistani intelligence officer, while discussing the event with the author, argued that this operation needed a gestation time of at least two years in which the "don'ts" seemed to be of far greater importance than the "dos." He contended that the men preparing for it had to know what all the major American and European intelligence agencies were routinely on the lookout for. "Who in an organization like Al-Qaeda could be expected to have such detailed knowledge?" he questioned.

Also, the conclusion of a sizable number of people in Pakistan was that such an intricate operation was well beyond the capability of Osama and company. Others had hallucinations that Al-Qaeda must have been infiltrated by Mossad agents, one of whom must have assumed leadership of the cell that eventually wrought the havoc at the behest of his masters, while his subordinates joyfully carried out his orders in the belief that they were carrying out Osama's instructions. They thought of Mossad, believing that Israel has gained the most from 9/11 as its enemies have been severely crippled as a consequence of the tragedy. Former ISI chief and now retired Lieutenant General Hamid Gul went to the extent of arguing that, besides Zionist collaborators, elements from within the U.S. government were involved in the terrorist act. Their agenda, according to him, was to subjugate the Muslim world and for this they needed a pretext and a cause célèbre to justify their actions in Afghanistan.[24] Such meanderings of Pakistani minds are likely to continue given their passion for conspiracy theories.

Irrespective of such notions, a majority of Pakistanis supported Musharraf's domestic campaign against religious extremists. According to a poll commissioned by the U.S. State Department, a large majority backed Musharraf in his efforts to curb extremism in Pakistan.[25] Leaders of religious political parties like Fazl ur-Rahman (Jamiat-i-Ulema-i-Islam) and Qazi Hussain Ahmed (Jamaat-i-Islami) were arrested, and many Pakistani and Arab militants who were returning from their sanctuaries in Afghanistan were taken into custody. In an important policy speech addressing the nation on January 12, 2002, Musharraf banned Jaish-i-Mohammad (Army of Mohammad: hereafter Jaish), Lashkar-i-Taiba, Sipah-i-Sahaba, Tehrik-i-Jafaria, and Tanzim Nifaz-i-Shariat-i-Mohammadi.[26] His remarks made on the occasion were indeed courageous and bold:

> The day of reckoning has come. Do we want Pakistan to become a theocratic state? Do we believe that religious education alone is enough for governance or do we want Pakistan to emerge as a progressive and dynamic Islamic welfare state? . . . Look at what this extremist minority is doing. They are indulging in fratricidal killings. . . . Mosques are being misused for propagating and inciting hatred against each other's sect and beliefs. . . . The extremist minority must realize that Pakistan is not responsible for waging armed Jihad in the world.

The forces of religious extremism for once were on the receiving end, which further demoralized and weakened hard-liner religious groups, providing Musharraf a golden opportunity to take effective measures to curb extremism, but like most of Musharraf's measures, his antijihadi campaign too was to be a half measure. As time passed and the miracle of reconstruction that was to be wrought in Afghanistan failed to show itself, the religious groups started to get their confidence back, the U.S. presence in Afghanistan became increasingly unpopular, and Musharraf became a marked man.

Around two hundred religious extremists and militants who were arrested by law enforcement forces in November 2001 were released after a few months as the government declared that there was insufficient evidence to implicate them in plots to harm the country. In reality, the government had instructed police authorities to do so after "negotiating" a deal with these elements. The understanding was that these militants would thereafter lie low and strictly refrain from participation in any violent activities. This was a gross miscal-culation. A few of the extremists from this group were found to be involved in the two assassination attempts on Musharraf in December 2003!

The obstacle in the way of a complete and effective clampdown on jihadi outfits was Pakistan's Kashmir policy. A suicide attack on Indian-controlled Kashmir's legislative assembly on October 1, 2001, and a December 13, 2001, attack on the Indian parliament by jihadis brought the dilemma to light. India, while alleging that Pakistani-sponsored jihadi groups had com-mitted the terrorist acts, amassed its troops on the India-Pakistan border. Pakistan had no option but to reciprocate. There was little doubt as to the involvement of Lashkar-i-Taiba and Jaish-e-Mohammad in these attacks, but the Indian understanding was that the ISI had sanctioned these. An objective analysis would be more in line with the assessment of *The Economist,* ac-cording to which the attack on the Indian parliament was "almost certainly [a] freelance affair."[27] Musharraf condemned these terrorist strikes but at the same time refused to hand over to India the leaders of these groups,[28] as that he could not afford for domestic political reasons. More so, ditching the Taliban was possible and logical under the circumstances, but giving up jihadis who had been groomed and financed to operate in Kashmir was considered a suicidal step for Musharraf and the army. What Musharraf and his advisers in the ISI failed to understand was that extremism inside Pakistan was inher-ently and inextricably linked with the actions and ideology of jihadi groups operating in Kashmir.

True that Lashkar-i-Taiba was among the banned outfits and its chief Hafiz Saeed was under arrest, but this group's parent organization, Dawat ul-Irshad (see chapter 9), was operating without any hindrance or restric-tions. Even in jail Hafiz Saeed had access to an international telephone and reportedly he even remained in touch with his sympathizers and friends in the United States.[29]

However, a crackdown on Lashkar-e-Jhangvi and Jaish was already in the offing, as these were banned outfits though still operating under new names. Jaish had more than suspicious origins. There is considerable speculation whether this was a creation of the ISI, or at least had found adoption by this doubtful parent after having splintered off its parent party Harkat-ul-Ansar. Considering the bloom of his health when its leader, Maulana Masood Azhar, was released by the Indians in exchange for the passengers of the hijacked Air India plane in 1999, there are grounds to suspect that his erstwhile cap-tors did not think too harshly of him, either. The possibility therefore that the Jaish may be running with the hare and hunting with the hounds cannot be entirely discounted. With its credibility suspect, the Jaish should have been the logical target of the Pakistan Army if a stern message were to be sent to terrorist organizations, but it took the brutal murder of the American journalist Daniel Pearl by Jaish terrorists to give the government a wake-up call.

Pearl's elimination is one of the many mysteries that Pakistan might never be able to unravel. Musharraf apparently implied in a public statement that Pearl had overstepped certain limits despite advice to lay off.[30] Omar Saeed Shaikh, the accused, was associated with Harkat-ul-Ansar and had lately been operating under the Jaish platform. He remained in ISI custody before being handed over to the police for production in a court of law, where he initially confessed to the crime but then backed off. Pakistan refused to extradite him to the United States, but ensured that he was awarded the death sentence in the case.

Meanwhile, war clouds were looming over South Asia once again, but the United States played an effective mediation role. According to Stephen P. Cohen, a leading American expert on South Asia, some Indian generals were then advocating a "limited war" to teach Pakistan a lesson, but they could not ensure that such a strike would not go nuclear. Hence the Indian political leadership, realizing the high risks of such a gamble, opted to deescalate.[31] Though in the process, American diplomats extracted from Musharraf a promise to end infiltration by jihadis into Indian Kashmir.[32] In return, India was expected to open a dialogue on Kashmir. The crisis passed, but the problem remains. Musharraf later argued that he delivered what was promised, but the Indians never reciprocated, making it difficult for him to defend his actions in Pakistan. To everyone's surprise, he even warned that, "I am not going to give an assurance that for years nothing will happen" vis-à-vis Pakistan's commitment to end infiltration permanently.[33] This was no political rhetoric—he meant exactly what he had said. The only way the general could sustain his policy of stopping militants from crossing the border was to show that something was moving on Kashmir. Here India's attitude was lamentable. It refused to accept that the Kashmir dispute was a subject fit for international mediation. Pakistan also offered that it was ready to allow a third party to monitor the Line of Control and judge whether cross-border infiltration was taking place. India again refused, making things increasingly difficult for Musharraf.

In May 2002, under enormous pressure from the United States, Musharraf had instructed the ISI to convey to the jihadi outfits in categorical terms that their activities in Kashmir had to be stopped. When a senior ISI officer told this to a roomful of leaders of jihadi groups, they resented it, and, voicing everyone's concern, one of them said: "General Musharraf has now betrayed the Kashmiris after ditching the Taliban."[34] An exact reportage of this supposedly secret meeting was published in a few newspapers in Pakistan, giving rise to the suspicion that it might have been an ISI leak trying to establish that jihadis were increasingly getting out of control. This might have been the case, but it is equally probable that the ISI itself had a limited idea about the growing potential of these groups. Whatever the case, in late 2002, jihadi outfits were allowed by Musharraf to resume small-scale infiltrations into Indian Kashmir.[35] Reacting to this, Nancy Powell, the U.S. ambassador to Pakistan, criticized the Musharraf government on this count publicly in January 2003 and asserted that Pakistan must "ensure that its pledges are implemented to prevent infiltration across the Line of Control and end the use of Pakistan as a platform for terrorism."[36]

There were two major reasons for this "adjustment" in policy. Terrorist attacks inside Pakistan against local Christians, Shia Muslims, and foreigners carried out by the banned jihadi outfits Jaish and Lashkar-e-Jhangvi were enough for the government to determine that, with the closure of access to the Afghan and Kashmir theaters, the jihadis were opening up new avenues inside Pakistan.[37] One can argue that rediversion of this outburst was hence deemed necessary for peace in Pakistan! Second, the Pakistan Army's influence and importance depended upon its Kashmir policy, and it believed that silence on the issue in the face of continued Indian oppression of Kashmiris would be interpreted in Pakistan as acceptance of the status quo. The only argument that potentially nullifies this perspective is that jihadi groups have become Frankenstein monsters and that the ISI is no longer able to control them effectively. Repeated attempts on Musharraf's life establishes that at least some elements among the jihadis have decided to turn the tables on him.[38] Or was it that Musharraf calculated that his support of the U.S. war on terror and handing over of hundreds of terrorists to the United States earned him immunity and he could continue with Pakistan's prior policy of actively supporting militancy in Kashmir? On the other hand, some Pakistani officials assert that U.S. authorities only want cross-border infiltration to be lowered but not completely blocked, as that keeps the United States relevant to Indians as a guarantor to keep Pakistan in check.

In early May 2002, Musharraf imprudently tried to test his popularity by holding a national referendum to seek a term of five years as president of the country. Government money was wasted on plastering the country with posters of Musharraf in a startling variety of dresses and poses. Though Musharraf won the vote comfortably and predictably, the real test of his support was the turnout, barely 15 percent, though highly exaggerated figures of the turnout and results were projected through the state-run media. From thereon, he plodded from one blunder to next, losing credibility with the silent majority that was supportive of him.

The October 2002 national election was another reflection of how Musharraf was mishandling the domestic political scene. With all the prepoll rigging charted out by the masterminds of the intelligence services, the mullah parties under the banner of Muttihada Majlis-e-Amal[39] (United Action Council—MMA) still swept into Parliament in their greatest-ever numbers. The ISI was so busy in ensuring that the Pakistan People's Party (PPP) of Benazir Bhutto and a section of Pakistan Muslim League led by Nawaz Sharif (PML-N) be defeated in elections that they failed to gauge that MMA's popularity was on the ascendance. The pro-Musharraf Pakistan Muslim League (Quiad-e-Azam group), widely known as the King's Party, was created by the ISI, and local military commanders in different constituencies interviewed the potential candidates who aspired to run on this party's platform.[40]

On the other hand, the MMA candidates went to the electorate asking whether they wanted to vote for the Quran or America. The results were predictable. Anti-American feeling in the wake of the Afghanistan situation and the predictable American attack on Iraq translated into an increased vote bank for the MMA. It was also a measure of the foresight and competence of Musharraf's government that both Irfanullah Marwat, a despicable criminal, and Maulana Azam Tariq, a committed and self-advertised terrorist, became members of the houses of the legislature while some of the most corrupt politicians were also inducted in the King's Party. It was obvious that Musharraf had not just forgiven corruption but sanctified it.

Despite all such efforts, the military regime failed to get the requisite number of seats for the King's Party in the National Assembly. They had to charm a few members of the PPP to desert their party by bribing them with the most sought after cabinet posts to be able to form the central government. The MMA, winning 53 seats out of a directly contested 272, managed the highest number of seats for any Islamist group since Pakistan's creation in 1947 (receiving 11.10 percent of the total votes). It became the third-largest force in the National Assembly after the pro-Musharraf ruling coalition and the PPP. The MMA though was able to form a government in the North-West Frontier Province (NWFP), where it had a majority in the provincial assembly (52 out of 99 seats), and it became a part of the ruling coalition in the Baluchistan Province (14 out of 51 seats).[41] There were also allegations that the ISI secretly supported the MMA as a bulwark against the mainstream political elite and also wanted to use the Islamic card in its dealings with the United States, but this was unlikely.

Musharraf also incorporated a Legal Framework Order (LFO) in the constitution just before the 2002 elections through a presidential ordinance, making the position of president much more powerful than the prime minister's. A similar pattern of undemocratic division of power between the two positions was responsible for the failure of the democratic system in the 1990s, but no lessons were learned from that era. For a change, the U.S. administration criticized the move, but to no avail.

The MMA government in the NWFP did not lose much time in launching its Islamization campaign in the province, sending shudders all across Pakistan. They started with a crackdown on cable TV operators (by blocking people's access to international entertainment channels), cinema owners, and musicians. The next attack was on billboards featuring women. Shabab-e-Milli, the youth faction of the Jamaat-i-Islami, smeared such billboards with black paint. The police were helpless, as the provincial administration had sanctioned the attacks.[42] Further, the MMA espoused terminating coeducation, veiling women, and Islamizing education curricula.[43] To cap it off, the NWFP assembly adopted a *Sharia* bill in June 2003 to bring the judicial, educational, and economic systems of the province in consonance with the injunctions of Islam as interpreted by them. The NWFP government had already converted to Urdu and had asked the federal government to banish English as an official medium. MMA members in the Baluchistan assembly were fast catching up with this. One of their members led an attack on a circus, destroying it, killing the animals, and looting the earnings.[44] It was done because the circus was deemed un-Islamic. These signs were significant steps toward the Talibanization of Pakistan.

Musharraf countered this MMA trend by criticizing it,[45] but it was for everyone to see that the cat was out of the bag. The senior minister of the NWFP government appeared on official Pakistan Television and boldly said that the Taliban-like actions of his government, far from arousing fear among the public, were according to the expectations of the electorate.[46] With the passage of time, MMA gained further confidence and started a confrontation with the government on its policies. The military campaign in Iraq created such an anti-American perception in Pakistan that Musharraf's pro-U.S. policies came under increasing attack. For instance, Qazi Hussain Ahmed of the MMA, in a public meeting in March 2003, declared that, "I salute the Iraqi soldier who killed five U.S. marines in a suicide attack" and added that jihad was the only option to halt the U.S. aggression in Iraq.[47] Under these circumstances, the U.S. State Department's "request" to Musharraf to send Pakistani troops to Iraq in 2003, if accepted, would have proved to be a recipe for disaster in Pakistan.

Another major reason behind Musharraf's declining support is the widely held belief among Pakistanis that, despite his strong support for the U.S. war on terror, Pakistan had not been compensated sufficiently in financial terms. The war in Afghanistan had stopped Pakistan's industry in its tracks just as it was heading for recovery, and international aid did little even to cover the cost of its participation in the war on terror. According to the U.S. Central Command (Centcom), Pakistan's economy suffered a loss of over US$10 billion from October 2001 to October 2002 in terms of a decline in tourism and investments and losses caused to civil aviation and due to rises in the rates of insurance. This information and assessment by Centcom was immediately taken off its official website as soon as it was reported in the Pakistani press in May 2003.[48] The report did not help Musharraf, to say the least. He was accused of selling Pakistan short.

Musharraf's crackdown on militant groups had led to the arrest of leading Al-Qaeda members like Abu Zubaida and Khalid Sheikh Mohammad, besides hundreds of suspected Al-Qaeda militants currently being held in Guantanamo by the United States. Such efforts were regularly praised by the U.S. authorities, including President Bush, but on the ground Musharraf faces stiff resistance, especially in the border areas between Afghanistan and Pakistan. For the first time the Pakistan Army is operating in the Waziristan region, which was always considered largely autonomous though lying within Pakistani territorial jurisdiction. As a reward, President Bush in June 2003 pledged a $3 billion aid package to Pakistan to be disbursed over five years, which is also tied to annual reviews of Pakistan's cooperation in the war on terrorism. It surprised many that half of it would be earmarked for armed forces and defense procurements. Ordinary Pakistanis justifiably interpreted it as a revival of the Pakistan Army–Pentagon relationship rather than anything else, though for Musharraf's prestige within army circles it was a boost. Arguably, it was meant to be so. It is questionable whether this is a prudent policy for the United States to pursue from a long-term perspective. Interestingly, according to Richard Clarke's book *Against All Enemies,* Musharraf, during his visit to the United States in 2003, complained to the U.S. administration that they were offering him military assistance fund that he did not need and not providing the economic development help he desperately required.[49]

The U.S.-Pakistan relationship in the aftermath of the 9/11 terror attacks has not always remained smooth, however. In fact, relations became dangerously strained following leaked stories in the American press of a Pakistani hand in the development of North Korea's nuclear program. Musharraf vehemently denied the allegation initially, though he stated that nothing had happened since he was in charge of the country, implying that some cooperation might have taken place before. It is widely known that Pakistan had imported North Korean missile technology, and its nuclear-capable missile "Ghauri" greatly resembles North Korea's Nodong, but this new information on nuclear collaboration was troubling for the United States. U.S. intelligence had tracked a Pakistani military cargo plane landing in North Korea with suspicious containers. It was suspected by the CIA that Pakistan had been sharing sophisticated technology, warhead-design information, and weapons-testing data with the North Koreans.[50] When confronted with the cargo plane issue, Pakistan contested that the said flight was carrying the defective missiles that Pakistan had bought from North Korea and was returning for replacements.[51] The U.S. administration was "tentatively" satisfied with this response and the matter was closed, at least for the time being.

The focus on this issue had hardly subsided when Pakistani nuclear scientists' links with Iranian and Libyan nuclear programs were unearthed in late 2003, putting Pakistan again in the international "limelight." While on a tour of eight Asian countries in the summer of 2002, Colin Powell had asked General Pervez Musharraf to arrest Abdul Qadeer Khan, the mastermind and father of Pakistan's nuclear weapons program.[52] Musharraf asked for time to probe the matter thoroughly. Even in 2000, the National Accountability Bureau (NAB) had briefly and discreetly investigated the matter when a dossier covering the financial activities and assets of Dr. Qadeer Khan was handed over to it. The matter was considered so "top secret" that the file did not leave the NAB office. The NAB decided that the time was not ripe to undertake such an initiative, and that the subject would be tackled a year hence.[53] In March 2001, Qadeer Khan was removed from his position in the Khan Research Laboratories (KRL) and given a ceremonious position as adviser to the president. General Musharraf had a fair idea, at the least, about the financial irregularities of Qadeer Khan, which led him to distance the scientist from the nuclear program, much before the issue became "internationalized."

According to a Pakistani government-sponsored news item in the waning days of 2003, intensive investigations on the subject pinpointed "those who stole and sold the country's nuclear secrets for their personal financial glory," and "several top Pakistani scientists were found involved in nuclear proliferation."[54] If indeed these scientists were rogue elements, then what were the military intelligence agencies and army chiefs (during the era) doing? Qadeer Khan was severely criticized and exposed by the government-leaked stories in the Pakistani press in early 2004, and all the blame for the nuclear technology transfers to Iran, Libya, and North Korea was laid at his door. But the fact remains that to a majority of Pakistanis, Qadeer Khan continues to be viewed as a national hero because very few people in Pakistan are ready to believe that he did all this on his own.

To borrow Ayaz Amir's terminology, in Pakistan's temple of national security, nothing was more holy than its nuclear program. Pakistan managed to acquire its nuclear capability and delivery system the hard way, at an enormous cost, through painstaking effort spread over two decades and in the face of implacable American efforts to halt this acquisition. The man who pulled it off was Qadeer Khan. His achievement for Pakistan cannot be denied. At the same time, nuclear proliferation is a serious crime and calls for a thorough probe and not a whitewash. Pakistan has to realize that Western countries, especially the United States, are seriously concerned about "rogue" scientists peddling nuclear secrets that can possibly land into the hands of freelance terrorists. On the other hand, analysts like Pervez Hoodbhoy, voicing the opinion of many Muslims, argue that doing away with the menace of nuclear proliferation "will require the United States, as the world's only superpower, to take the lead by reducing its own nuclear arsenal, as well as dealing with all proliferators, including its ally Israel, at the same level."[55] Respected Pakistani columnist Ayaz Amir artfully frames the Pakistani dilemma in this context, when he says:

> Across a national landscape littered with failure, the bomb is a reminder of what Pakistan can achieve when sufficiently inspired. So the question arises: now that Pakistan's nuclear program stands demystified, its halo stripped away and its secrecy seriously compromised, will the Americans stop here? . . . There's just so much that a country can take. . . . Pakistan's guardians have "overloaded the circuit" by giving the impression of retreating on too many fronts and executing too many U-turns. While domestic support is too far behind, they, in their eagerness to please, have run too far ahead.[56]

Allegations in the aftermath of the U.S.-led campaign in Afghanistan in 2001 have also surfaced about Pakistan's discreet support to pro-Taliban elements in its tribal borderlands, who are conducting hit-and-run operations against U.S. and NATO forces in Afghanistan. For neutral observers the real issue is whether Pakistan has been doing enough to deter regrouping of the Taliban and curb its activities rather than being directly involved in supporting the Taliban remnants. Second, Pakistan cannot be held responsible for everything that goes wrong in Afghanistan. Many Afghans are uncomfortable with the way Hamid Karzai has involved some notorious warlords in the affairs of state and the manner in which a "secular" constitution was imposed on them.

In the regional reference, the India-Pakistan diplomatic thaw in early 2004 came as a pleasant surprise to many peace-lovers in South Asia. Religious parties did criticize Musharraf, but only in a hushed tone and created no significant problems for him in the aftermath of the Musharraf-Vajpayee meeting. For Musharraf to pronounce in the India-Pakistan joint statement issued on January 6, 2004, that he had "reassured Prime Minister Vajpayee that he will not permit any territory under Pakistan's control to be used to support terrorism in any manner"[57] was a great leap forward. Consequently, both India and Pakistan initiated many confidence-building measures to improve their relations and set the stage for a peace process. Obviously there are still many obstacles, especially in relation to the solution of the Kashmir dispute, but there is a healthy development worth appreciating, which is that a large number of Pakistanis welcomed the initiation of the peace dialogue, clearly indicating that they are tired of the Kashmir crisis.

The grave crisis facing Pakistan in terms of religious extremism, however, remains relevant. Far from being diminished through Musharraf's mantra of a need for "enlightened moderation," narrow-mindedness and isolationist tendencies in a segment of society are still entrenched. The proportion of supporters of such dogmatic tendencies hardly numbers in double digits, but in a country of around 145 million people it is still a very troubling sign. A few instances in the recent past substantiate this assertion. The Council of Islamic Ideology, a state-run institution, declared in October 2003 that it was against Islam to induct women into the legislative assemblies in the country. It explained its view by arguing that some of these women in assemblies belonged to the westernized and modernized class that was a stranger to the Islamic worldview.[58] Hafiz Saeed, leader of the banned Lashkar-i-Taiba, while addressing a public gathering in mid-2003, announced that Musharraf "has become the biggest enemy of jihad and if we can get him out of the picture, we can take care of the infidels."[59] Such a statement coming from Hafiz Saeed was indeed alarming, but not as unexpected as a statement from General Aziz Khan, Musharraf's longtime right-hand man. In a public forum, Aziz said that America was the No. 1 enemy of the Muslim world, as it was conspiring against Islam, considering it a threat. In the same address he hinted that Musharraf should not get involved in politics while in uniform,[60] voicing what was being demanded by the politicians and religious parties then. The statement created quite a stir.

Coupled with this trend, Pakistan is witnessing an increasing dislike for the army among the masses. Since Musharraf's rise to power, hundreds of civilian positions were given to retired military officials, and a gracious allotment of residential plots and farmland to senior army officers has become the norm rather than a reward for gallantry in the battle zone. Abrupt changes in the military hierarchy and command positions at the corps commander level are also unprecedented, indicating Musharraf's possible lack of confidence in his generals.[61] Musharraf's reluctance to stand by his commitment to give up the position of army chief by the end of 2004 has also eroded his credibility to a great degree. According to Ahmed Rashid, Musharraf's growing unpopularity is causing distress in the officer corps as well, as they fear that the army's prestige is being undermined by their chief's bid to secure more power for himself.[62] For the army, any increase in this perception can potentially be the proverbial last straw on the camel's back. Two assassination attempts on Musharraf's life in the last days of 2003 from Pakistani jihadis, aided by armed forces personnel, are an indication of times to come.

Despite the government's renewed efforts to curb religious extremism and violence, especially after Musharraf survived assassination attempts by the skin of his teeth, the pattern of disturbing events continues unabated. Nine schools (mostly girls) in northern areas of Pakistan were burned or bombed by terrorists in February 2004 alone. The reason behind torching these schools was religious extremists' disappointment with decline in enrollment in *Madrasas* and an increase in government schools.[63] In the first week of March 2004, around four dozen Shias were murdered in Quetta during the tenth Muharram procession. According to media reports and law enforcement agencies, banned militant groups Lashkar-e-Jhangvi and Sipah-i-Mohammad are resurfacing in many parts of the country. After these two groups were banned by Musharraf in 2001, they changed their names to Tehrik-e-Islami and Millat-e-Islamia, respectively. When these were banned in 2004, they emerged now under the titles of Sunni Action Committee and Millat-e-Jafaria.[64] A suicide bomber's attempt on the life of prime minister designate Shaukat Aziz in July 2004 and troubling sparks of insurgency in Balochistan adds fuel to the fire. To say the least, these trends can be fatal for Pakistan.

The military operation against Al-Qaeda operators in the Waziristan region in March–April 2004 resulted in heavy casualties for the Pakistan Army, establishing that the adversary is well entrenched, fully equipped, and motivated. The pro-Taliban elements and Al-Qaeda sympathizers in the tribal belt, despite being outnumbered, fiercely fought back and in retaliation also fired rockets at Peshawar, creating a panic in military circles.[65] Even the residence of Peshawar-based Corps Commander Lieutenant General Safdar Hussain was targeted (though the rocket missed the target), which was unprecedented. This "symbolic gesture" has huge significance for those who are well versed in the traditions and history of the tribesmen of the area. In short, it is not a good omen when these tribals revolt.

During 2004, scores of Shias were murdered in the suicide attacks by the jihadis on Shia mosques and unfortunately, little outrage, if any, has been shown by the civil society over these gruesome acts. Further, a professionally conceived assassination attempt on the life of Lieutenant General Ahsen Saleem Hayat, the corps commander in Karachi, on June 9, 2004, indicates that the final clash between the jihadi elements and the Pakistan Army has moved a vital step closer. The benumbing U.S. bombardment of Afghanistan in late 2001 left the jihadis stunned and disoriented. The resultant brief calm was mistaken for final victory. Musharraf's banning of militant outfits and attempt at crippling their funding was seen as a mopping up operation by the naive; the denial to them of exit into the Kashmir theater was thought to be their death by the optimist. But slowly the illusions are giving way to reality. The disorganized and destabilized jihadi outfits revived themselves and as should have been expected, reorganized their organizations according to changed circumstances. Arguably, the loss of the U.S. prestige in Iraq gave them new heart, new sympathy among whom they live, and new recruits.

Here a brief look at Musharraf's personality traits might help us understand the reasons behind Pakistan's shifting fortunes in the last few years.[66] Musharraf is a man of many parts. He is amiable and very easy to like, but if crossed he is quick to roll up his sleeves and grit his teeth. The threshold of his "diplomacy" is therefore low, and what he feels shows clearly in his countenance. His patriotism and sincerity are palpable and so is his unpretentiousness. He would rather avoid pomp and ceremony, but if it is laid out for him, he is not too uncomfortable with it. Throughout his military career he has enjoyed a reputation of being crisp and to the point, and of being far removed from mendacity. He is not one who is amenable to threats and pressure, which immediately bring his truculence to the fore, but friendship is likely to draw out of him all he possesses. He is not a man of striking intelligence or learning, but is sharper than most. He is a polite and cultured man, and even when angry, which is often, he will not leave the bounds of propriety. He is not a religious man though he takes pride in being a Muslim. He also does not mind scotch on the rocks, though he is not known to sacrifice his deportment to the influence of liquor. With all this, like Napoleon's marshals, he also is lucky.

Such an array of qualities should have made for success in a leader in whom they inhere, but such is unfortunately not quite so. Musharraf is an unhappy mix of the conventional and the revolutionary, and plays either the one or the other at quite the wrong places. His manner of dealing with the problems of his friends is revolutionary, where he will cut through the red tape of convention, but when it comes to dealing with the problems of the country, which beg revolutionary solutions, he will supply conventional applications. For instance, a senior army officer in Lahore spent seven million rupees on the renovation of his official residence in a case of obvious misappropriation, but he was rewarded by a prize posting at army headquarters because, like Musharraf, he too was an artillery officer. His pro-Mohajir bias is also increasingly being talked about in army circles, but fortunately for the army, this is not sticking.

His poor judgment of men combined with prejudice against real or imagined adversaries has, in practical terms, served to restrict Pakistan's already narrow human resources base, so that incompetent "friends" have been inflicted on important offices for which many a competent "adversary" was better suited. With this, his increasing intolerance for the person who disagrees with his position has shut him off from the contrary view and closed his window to all but a one-sided perspective of reality.

What has made a bad situation worse for Musharraf is his failure to establish a mechanism to monitor the progress of implementation of his directives, so that all that he decrees, though entirely in consonance with the needs of the times, is bereft of benefits that ought to follow. And this problem is further accentuated because Musharraf does not have the ability to fire the lax and the laggard as long as they continue making the right noises in his presence and in concert with appropriate gestures of due servility.

As such, it is not for nothing that his government is defined by, and stands arraigned for, a level of incompetence that he could only have worked very hard to achieve. He is therefore best defined as a master of half measures and as the poor man's Ataturk. He can, however, still stage a comeback if he chooses to work with political partners who have broad support among the masses and who by their political and ideological orientation are his natural allies. Changing prime ministers is no solution. In this context, Professor Lawrence Ziring's advice to Musharraf is very relevant and cogent:

> If he truly wants to reconstruct Pakistan, then he has no choice but to invite the free and open play of all politicians . . . it is time to accept the failures along with the frailties and to nurture a generation of leaders unencumbered by blind doctrines. A new generation waits off stage in the wings of obscurity. That generation wishes to see the Pakistan of the twenty-first century realize its potential for greatness, not only as a Muslim nation but as a country that represents the better instincts of humanity.[67]

In this overall scenario, many U.S. officials and journalists[68] wonder whether Pakistan is a reliable ally. The dilemma is that Pakistanis see the U.S. administration in the same light. As far as history is concerned, the U.S. track record is worse than that of Pakistan, in this context. The present Pakistani leadership has already burned its bridges and it is in the larger interest of Pakistan to continue on this path. From the American perspective, continued engagement is the only way forward to build a better future.

—————Chapter 11—————

# The Road Ahead

America has often wondered aloud why many Muslims did not strongly condemn the outrageous terrorist attacks on 9/11. While the reasons behind the Muslim masses' seeming lack of condemnation are complex and varied, one of the more direct and honest answers to this is that a large percentage of Muslims all around the world perceive America itself as, if not the perpetrator, then at least as the instigator of similar outrages and injustices.[1] Others wondered aloud: "Why do they hate us?" and this anguish is heard around the world. But for years before this, many in Muslim countries have been asking: "What compels America to be so unjust?" Except for some intellectuals, journalists, and academics, none in the United States had taken this plaintive cry seriously.

For decades, higher national interests have compelled successive American administrations to support highly repressive regimes in many Muslim countries. A clean example is that of Saddam Hussein, who was a close enough ally to be equipped with weapons by Western countries, including the United States, during the eight-year war that he fought against Iran. After the war, he used these weapons against his own Kurdish and Shia populations. The irony is that, in this age of rapid communications, the average American heard about the plight of these Kurds and Shias only a good ten (or, in some cases, fifteen) years after the gruesome event. Neither did this average American hear about what the secret police of the Shah of Iran, or that of the house of Saud or of the Egyptian dictators do to their own people. These people suffered an unbroken tyranny spanning many decades. Helpless and powerless, they could only hate their leaders. By extension, they hated America, the main prop of these regimes that had treated them inhumanely. Further, no single factor has stoked the fires of hate in Muslim countries as have the U.S. policies affecting Israel and the Palestinians. These were always seen as being tilted in favor of Israel.

But this question of "hate," when posed by the average American, who is the least xenophobic among the peoples of the world, remains germane. Because he harbors no resentment against the peoples of distant countries, the extraordinary lengths that the latter will go for the sole purpose of harming him can only bewilder him. He cannot realize that the illiterate Muslim fanatic is least qualified to tell the difference between some of the U.S. government policies and the American people. Therefore, this spiral of hate, built on real or perceived injustice, got further entrenched with the passage of time.

Pakistan, not being an Arab country and being far from the scene of conflict in the Israel-Palestine region, could have been expected not to harbor anti-American feelings of the strain and virulence of those harbored by many Arabs. That indeed was the case in the early days of Pakistan, and the reasons for this were that Pakistan was a very early ally of America, receiving substantial military and economic aid; the focus of Pakistani animus and suspicions was pointed toward India; the religious parties had good working relations with the United States; and last but not least, the Pakistani military regimes supported by the United States were not as harsh and brutal as those in the Middle East. Because of the combined effect of all these factors, far from being anti-American, the general public sentiment was very much pro-U.S., and this continued to be the case until the mid-1960s.

After the 1965 war there was the first, though muted, burst of anti-Americanism experienced in Pakistan because the United States (despite being an ally) did not come to Pakistan's assistance. This mood did not last. It was after the 1967 Arab-Israeli war that anti-Israeli emotion took root in Pakistan, which eventually extended to the United States as well. Profiting from this opportunity, religious parties declared Jews and Israel the root of much of the malevolence afflicting Muslims all over the world and, by extension, Pakistan. But this newfound scapegoat did not take immediate hold.

The next crucial stage in this context was the Palestinian Intifada, which Pakistanis witnessed through the television screen. They repeatedly saw Israeli attacks on the West Bank and Gaza with the U.S.-made helicopters and tanks while Palestinian youth were shown opposing these attacks with slings and stones. The stark inequality of the contest left an imprint on their minds and thus the issue was constantly discussed. Hence, the religious parties on their recruitment drives needed nothing more. Religious leaders were to cash in on these passions to gain personal popularity, and then turn them into anti-American rage in coming years. The American betrayal in Afghanistan in 1989–1990 was to only add fuel to the fire of anti-Americanism in Pakistan.

Resulting from a lack of educational opportunities, an ongoing sense of strategic insecurity, and streams of financial support from Wahhabi sources in the Arab states, the *Madrasa* industry had also caught on in Pakistan in the aftermath of the Afghan war of the 1980s, and the assembly line was producing tens of thousands of deadly earnest future "heroes." Their one unity is their common hatred of the westernized Pakistani elite, India, America, and Israel. Because of India, their focus and attention on America is divided, but their commitment to give their lives for what they believe in, irrespective of who is on the other side, is not expected to diminish. And though Pakistani generals and politicians are still given to making their habitual noises, the very tepidness of their calls to end the power of religious extremist groups is like the fading strains of a distant retreat; the much vaunted power of the army is increasingly a façade that must crack sooner or later, and the power that is on the ascendant is that of the religious parties.

It was hoped that the anti-Osama operation would stabilize and strengthen Pakistan. It was hoped that the United States would start its reconstruction of Afghanistan through Pakistan—to strengthen first its base, and then move into the area of instability and uncertainty. Unfortunately, this did not happen. The little aid that Pakistan received was more than counterbalanced by the expenses involved in keeping its forces deployed on the borders in response to the Indian threat in 2002–3. Thus, no economic activity came to relieve Pakistan's stagnation. The *Madrasa* remains the only haven for the child whose parents can not afford him. Pakistan's alliance with the United States in the aftermath of the U.S. campaign in Afghanistan yet again brought no tangible benefit to the people of Pakistan.

Criminal incompetence in governance and lack of funds for the public education system further strained Pakistan's capacity to change for the better. The real tragedy is that a country that has produced a Nobel Prize–winner in physics and so many top-class physicians, high-tech geniuses, and some of the finest air force pilots in the world has wasted so much due to the inadequacy of its education system for the masses, robbing so many of a chance to succeed in life. Pakistan preferred acquiring F-16s and submarines over establishing schools and hospitals. Billions of dollars spent on defense procurements provided security only to the military, political, and bureaucratic elite of Pakistan. For ordinary people these policies brought hunger, misery, and hopelessness.

Failing to make a real difference lately, Musharraf has fallen in the esteem of the people of Pakistan, and there is many a hope that lies crushed in the rubble of this fall, and yet no popular movement has been able to generate steam against him. That, however, is only a matter of time, and unfortunately the ones who will lead the public opinion in such a crisis will be the religious leaders, because Musharraf has sidelined the liberal forces and moderate political parties. Without doubt, Musharraf has shown ample courage in fighting religious extremism and terrorism, but has failed to institutionalize his policies. A credible democratic set-up could have strengthened Musharraf, but he opted to sponsor the "King's Party," which will be history the day Musharraf leaves the scene.

Barring a miracle, the influence of the rightist parties is bound to grow in Pakistan, or at the very least they will retain a solid following. The U.S. attack on Iraq is viewed in Pakistan as a step in the establishment of a new imperialism. Indeed, this war has pulled the rug out from under the feet of the Pakistani moderates and given the clerics new strength. Even before the Iraq war started in early 2003, the U.S. campaign in Afghanistan, leading to thousands of civilian deaths,[2] and the U.S. ultimatums to Iraq were enough to convince them about what was ahead, and that gave them sufficient support to demonstrate their power in the October 2002 general elections, in which they had their best showing ever in terms of winning seats in the central and provincial legislatures. Yet it is unlikely that they will come to power in the future through the ballot. It is more likely that an errant spark somewhere will ignite massive street protests, and if these protests are joined by the jihadi groups and the army is called out to contain them, it will be a real disaster for Pakistan.

The Pakistan Army dare not confront them, knowing their strength and suspecting that they have many sympathizers, if not supporters, within its own ranks. It was therefore considered more feasible for the army to continue to direct its energies in the battle zone of Kashmir rather than to face the jihadis. It was for the convenience of its repose that the army, routinely given to having study periods on a myriad of subjects, has apparently not done one on the strength and potential of the jihadi organizations. No one has a clear idea about their exact numbers, but their potential capability resides in the subconscious of those in authority, and this stays there because the reality of it is too hard to confront. Their funding will not dry up because thousands of Pakistanis and Arabs believe in them and contribute to them.

To tackle this, Pakistan must devise ways to lessen the power and influence of religious extremists in the country and support genuine Islamic scholarship as a counter. Most of Islam is very simple to understand and therefore needs little interpretation. Mullah scholarship, as it has turned out to be, moves from the broad to the narrow, emphasizing the arcane over the easily intelligible. By its very nature, therefore, it must reside in narrow crevices and attempt to broaden them into irreconcilable differences. It is in finding and defining such differences that mullah scholarship, as distinct from that of the Sufi (mystic) or a true *alim* (scholar), gains approval of the multitude, who gasp with wonder as they are initiated into the intricate world of hairsplitting. The narrow intellectualism of the mullah can only be divisive, exclusive, and intolerant of those whom it excludes, and is antithetical to all that is eclectic and harmonizing.

If Pakistan is to be saved from its likely future, it must invest in its envisioned future, and start doing so now. It must start by coming to a sincere accommodation with India over Kashmir. To make this possible, India too will have to shed its present position on Kashmir and proffer an equally sincere hand of friendship to Pakistan. Perhaps India should initially enlarge the autonomy in Kashmir, to which Pakistan could respond by creating further space and circumstances for India. In a second stage, India and Pakistan could work out the modalities of a jointly controlled Kashmir Valley, turning the bone of contention into a peace bridge between the two countries. And concurrently with this, Pakistan should take every measure to effect an economic upturn conspicuous enough to give its people real hope.

And all this is impossible to achieve in the absence of strong democratic institutions. Democracy is not alien to Pakistan. It had come into being as a democracy, though autocratic tendencies of the Pakistani elite and military dictators changed its direction. Still, the people of Pakistan yearn for true democracy. For this dream to become a reality, Pakistan's military establishment has to take a back seat.

Pakistan will not be able to do this on its own. It will need U.S. assistance and support to provide economic development and strengthen democracy. At a global level it may be worth America's while to invest in peace, a small price to pay compared to the cost of war. Funds and support must be carefully allocated and invested so as to avoid both a repeat cycle of corruption and an unending rentier-state[3] status for Pakistan. The new confidence that unchallenged power has given to the United States has made it prone to unilateralism and to see war as a solution to problems. Sooner or later it must realize that it cannot bomb an idea out of existence. The answer lies in positing another and more powerful idea. If injustice has sparked a fire, it will be justice that will douse it—not more injustice. If there has to be universal peace, it shall be born not out of the "infinite," but out of universal justice. It is certainly within the United States' means and interests to help usher in such an era.

# Notes

## Chapter 1

1. R. Thapur, "Imagined Religious Communities? Ancient History and the Modern Search for a Hindu Identity," *Modern Asian Studies* 23, no. 2 (1989): 216.

2. The four castes are arranged in a hierarchy. The highest caste is Brahman, the priest, meant to be most powerful and influential. After them are the Kshatriya, the warrior caste. After them are the Vaisya, who are business people. And after them are the Sudra, who are the common peasants and workers. Below these four castes are the casteless, the untouchables. The four castes were not allowed to have any physical contact with the untouchables.

3. Mulla Abdul Qadir Badauni, *Muntakhab al-Twarikh,* vol. 1, ed. Maulavi Ahmad Ali (Calcutta, 1868), pp. 5, 7–8.

4. Akbar S. Ahmed, *Jinnah, Pakistan, and Islamic Identity: The Search for Saladin* (London: Routledge, 1997), p. 37.

5. For a detailed analysis, see P.M. Currie, *The Shrine and Cult of Muin al-din Chishti of Ajmer* (Delhi: Oxford University Press, 1989), and Christian W. Troll, ed., *Muslim Shrines in India: Their Character, History, and Significance* (Delhi: Oxford University Press, 1989).

6. Akbar S. Ahmed, *Discovering Islam: Making Sense of Muslim History and Society,* rev. ed. (London: Routledge, 2002), p. 96.

7. The Lucknow Pact conceded separate electorates for Muslims and provided for provincial autonomy. It also provided a safeguard to the effect that no bill or resolution affecting a community should be proceeded with if three-fourths of the representatives of that community were opposed to it. Under the pact, Muslim representation was also fixed at 33.33 percent of the Indian elected members for the central government, which was a larger share than the Muslim population warranted, though it was balanced out in other ways in reference to provincial quotas.

8. The Nehru Report proposed the replacement of separate electorates by a joint electorate in addition to a new formula of reservation of seats for a community in proportion to its population to be applied selectively. This meant a reducing of the Muslim majority in Punjab and Bengal since adult suffrage was as yet far off and on a franchise restricted by property and education qualifications, Muslim voting strength would have been far below the Muslim proportion of the population. The central government with its fixed Hindu majority was to retain powers over the provinces as it was to be vested with the residuary powers.

244 NOTES TO CHAPTERS 1 AND 2

9. Anthony Read and David Fischer, *The Proudest Day: India's Long Road to Independence* (New York: W.W. Norton, 1999), p. 218.

10. In reaction to the Treaty of Sèvres, whose harsh terms made it obvious that the victorious Allies had plans beyond the dismemberment of the Ottoman Empire, the integrity of the Turkish homeland was in jeopardy. To Indian Muslims, the treaty appeared to be a deliberate attempt by the Christian West to exterminate forever the political power of Islam as symbolized by the caliphat in Turkey. Maulana Mohammad Ali, Shaukat Ali, and Abul Kalam Azad led the popular movement, and soon Gandhi espoused the cause in an effort to engage and involve Muslims in his campaign of noncooperation with the British.

11. H.M. Seervai, *Partition of India: Legend and Reality* (Bombay: Emmenem Publications, 1990), p. 13.

12. Ibid, p. 15.

13. Sugata Bose and Ayesha Jalal, *Modern South Asia: History, Culture, Political Economy* (New York: Routledge, 1998), p. 178.

14. Penderel Moon, ed., *Wavell: The Viceroy's Journal* (London: Oxford University Press, 1973), p. 442.

15. Ahmedi faith is associated with Mirza Ghulam Ahmed (1835–1908), who in 1876 claimed that he had received a revelation and that though Prophet Mohammad (PBUH) was the seal of the prophets, he was the promised Messiah and a prophet without a book and law giving authority to continue the mission of the Prophet of Islam. Most Ahmedis observe the routine rituals of Sunni Islam to a large extent, though a minority group among Ahmedis consider Mirza Ghulam Ahmed as a Godsent reformer and not a prophet. According to a great majority of Muslims, Mirza Ghulam Ahmed's declarations were contrary to the basic precepts of Islam.

16. According to Shaukat Hayat Khan, a senior Muslim League leader, Jinnah asked him to go to the spiritual leader and *khalifa* of the Ahmedi community and request him to pray for and support the Pakistan idea. The leader replied that his community had been praying for the mission from the very beginning and ensured that no Ahmedi would stand against a Muslim Leaguer in the elections (1946), and that if someone disobeyed this instruction, the community would not support the person. Shaukat Hayat Khan, *The Nation That Lost Its Soul* (Lahore: Jang, 1995), p. 147.

17. Ayesha Jalal, *Self and Sovereignty: Individual and Communalism in South Asian Islam Since 1850* (New York: Routledge, 2000), p. 375.

18. Ibid.

## Chapter 2

1. Sugata Bose and Ayesha Jalal, *Modern South Asia: History, Culture, Political Economy* (London and New York: Routledge, 1998), p. 190.

2. Quoted in H.M. Seervai, *Partition of India: Legend and Reality* (Bombay: Emmenem Publications, 1990), p. 131. Original source: Viceroy's Personal Report No. 11, July 4, 1947, in *Constitutional Relations Between Britain and India: Transfer of Power, 1942–47*, vol. 11, ed. Nicholas Mansergh et al. (London: Her Majesty's Stationery Office, 1982), pp. 899–900.

3. Seervai, *Partition of India,* pp. 131–32.

4. For a firsthand account, see Chaudhry Mohammad Ali, *Emergence of Pakistan* (New York: Columbia University Press, 1967).

5. Ibid., pp. 332–87.

6. According to Alastair Lamb, in Jammu about 500,000 Muslims were displaced forcibly by Hindus and Sikhs, and as many as 200,000 of them disappeared in August, September, and October of 1947, prior to the tribesmen raid into Kashmir. Alastair Lamb, *Kashmir: A Disputed Legacy, 1846–1990* (Hertfordshire: Roxford Books, 1991), p. 123.

7. K. Sarwar Hasan, ed., *The Kashmir Question: Documents on the Foreign Relations of Pakistan* (Karachi: Pakistan Institute of International Affairs, 1966), p. 212.

8. Constituent Assembly of Pakistan, *Debates*, vol. 1, August 11, 1947, pp. 18–22.

9. Ali, *Emergence of Pakistan*, p. 372.

10. Penderel Moon, ed., *Wavell: The Viceroy's Journal* (London: Oxford University Press, 1997), p. 442.

11. Stanley Wolpert, *Jinnah of Pakistan* (New York: Oxford University Press, 1984), p. 1.

12. Zulfiqar Khalid Maluka, *The Myth of Constitutionalism in Pakistan* (Karachi: Oxford University Press, 1997), p. 77.

13. Ali, *Emergence of Pakistan*, p. 386.

14. Iftikhar H. Malik, *State and Civil Society in Pakistan: Politics of Authority, Ideology and Ethnicity* (London: Macmillan, 1997), p. 35.

15. Constituent Assembly of Pakistan, *Debates*, vol. 5, March 7, 1949, pp. 2–3.

16. Anthony Read and David Fischer, *The Proudest Day: India's Long Road to Independence* (New York: W.W. Norton, 1999), p. 186.

17. Keith Callard, *Pakistan: A Political Study*, 2d ed. (London: Allen and Unwin, 1958), p. 80.

18. West Pakistan comprised Punjab (language, Punjabi), the North-West Frontier Province (language, Pushto), Baluchistan (languages, Baluchi and Brohi), and Sindh (language, Sindhi). East Pakistan on the other hand was populated only by Bengalis (language, Bengali).

19. Shaukat Hayat Khan, *The Nation That Lost Its Soul* (Lahore: Jang, 1995), pp. 147–48.

20. Lawrence Ziring, *Pakistan in the Twentieth Century: A Political History* (Karachi: Oxford University Press, 1997), p. 146.

21. A.K. Brohi, "Thoughts on the Future Constitution of Pakistan," *Dawn*, Karachi, August 24, 1952.

22. Mr. Brohi wrote two more articles in *Dawn* to clarify his position by saying that, "I have never said that I do not want an Islamic constitution in this country." He further maintained that he in fact wanted to say that an Islamic political system has to be deduced from the Quran and Sunnah, as no clear-cut statement on the issue is available. See, *Dawn*, Karachi, September 7 and 21, 1952.

23. Sir Morrice James, *Pakistan Chronicle* (New York: St. Martin's, 1993), p. 14.

24. Humayun Mirza, *From Plassey to Pakistan: The Family History of Iskander Mirza, the First President of Pakistan* (New York: University Press of America, 1999), pp. 355–56.

25. According to police records, Liaquat Ali Khan was assassinated by Said Akbar, an Afghan, who had been a former British intelligence informer.

26. Official document titled: "Report of the Court of Inquiry Constituted Under Punjab Act II of 1954 to Enquire into the Punjab Disturbances of 1953" (Karachi, 1954), p. 218.

27. Minutes of Cabinet meeting, September 9, 1947, 67/CF/47, National Documentation Center, Cabinet Division, Islamabad.

28. Dennis Kux, *The United States and Pakistan, 1947–2000: Disenchanted Allies* (Washington, DC: Woodrow Wilson Center Press, 2001), p. 9.

29. Ibid., pp. 6–15.

30. "A Report to the National Security Council by the Executive Secretary on the Position of the United States with respect to South Asia (Declassified)," January 5, 1951, NSC 93, NND867400, available at Digital National Security Archive.

31. Ian Talbot, *Pakistan: A Modern History* (New York: St. Martin's, 1998), p. 139.

32. Interview with a senior bureaucrat in the Cabinet Division Secretariat, Islamabad, in July 1994.

33. Mohammad Ayub Khan, *Friends, Not Masters: A Political Autobiography* (London: Oxford University Press, 1967), p. 41.

34. Talbot, *Pakistan: A Modern History*, p. 131.

35. Kux, *The United States and Pakistan, 1947–2000*, p. 54.

36. Ibid., p. 57.

37. Major General Sher Ali Khan, *The Story of Soldiering and Politics in India and Pakistan*, 1978, pp. 116, 126.

38. Hasan Askari Rizvi, *Military, State, and Society in Pakistan* (New York: St. Martin's, 2000), p. 80.

39. For a detailed analysis of the coup, see Hassan Zaheer, *The Times and Trials of the Rawalpindi Conspiracy, 1951: The First Coup Attempt in Pakistan* (Karachi: Oxford University Press, 1998).

40. Mushahid Hussain and Akmal Hussain, *Pakistan: Problems of Governance* (Lahore: Vanguard Books, 1986), p. 30.

41. Ibid., p. 90.

42. Ayub Khan, *Friends, Not Masters*, pp. 51–53.

43. *Foreign Relations of the United States, 1955–57*, vol. 3, South Asia (Washington, DC: United States Government Printing Office, 1987), p. 436.

44. *Dawn*, Karachi, October 31, 1954.

45. Ayesha Jalal, *The State of Martial Rule* (Cambridge: Cambridge University Press, 1990), p. 214.

46. Ziring, *Pakistan in the Twentieth Century*, p. 181.

47. Syed Vali Reza Nasr, *The Vanguard of the Islamic Revolution: The Jamaat-i-Islami of Pakistan* (Los Angeles: University of California Press, 1994), p. 144.

48. Kux, *The United States and Pakistan, 1847–2000*, p. 76.

## Chapter 3

1. Stephen P. Cohen, *The Pakistan Army: 1998 Edition with a New Foreword and Epilogue* (Karachi: Oxford University Press, 1998), p. 7.

2. Hasan Askari Rizvi, *Military, State, and Society in Pakistan* (London: Macmillan, 2000), p. 55.

3. Ayub Khan says that the British were backing General Iftikhar, and that he was short-tempered and difficult to get on with. For details, see Mohammad Ayub Khan, *Friends, Not Masters: A Political Autobiography* (London: Oxford University Press, 1967), pp. 34–35.

4. Humayun Mirza, *From Plassey to Pakistan: The Family History of Iskander Mirza, the First President of Pakistan* (New York: University Press of America, 1999), pp. 156, 225.

5. Ayub Khan, *Friends, Not Masters,* pp. 15–17.

6. Correspondence reproduced in Mirza, *From Plassey to Pakistan,* pp. 216–17.

7. Embassy Karachi telegram to State Department, October 4, 1958, *Foreign Relations of the United States, 1958–60,* vol. 15, p. 664.

8. Mirza, *From Plassey to Pakistan,* p. 225.

9. Stanley Wolpert, *Zulfi Bhutto of Pakistan* (New York: Oxford University Press, 1993), p. 60. Also see Ardeshir Cowasjee, "Referendum 2002-II," *Dawn,* Karachi, April 21, 2002.

10. For details, see Dennis Kux, *The United States and Pakistan, 1947–2000: Disenchanted Allies* (Washington, DC: Woodrow Wilson Center, 2001), pp. 134–35.

11. It was restricted in the sense that only eighty thousand elected representatives known as Basic Democrats participated in it.

12. Altaf Gauhar, *Ayub Khan: Pakistan's First Military Ruler* (Lahore: Sang-e-Meel, 1993), p. 160.

13. The Objectives Resolution with some modifications was retained as the preamble of the 1962 constitution. From the first statement of the resolution, saying that "Sovereignty over the entire universe belongs to God and authority exercisable by the people is a sacred trust," the qualifying phrase "within the limits prescribed by Him" was deleted.

14. Rubya Mehdi, *The Islamization of the Law in Pakistan* (Surrey: Curzon, 1994), p. 87.

15. Javaid Saeed, *Islam and Modernization: A Comparative Analysis of Pakistan, Egypt, and Turkey* (London: Praeger, 1994), p. 96.

16. Zulfiqar Ali Bhutto, *If I Am Assassinated . . .* (New Delhi: Vekas, 1979), p. 21.

17. Kux, *The United States and Pakistan, 1947–2000,* p. 92.

18. Ibid.

19. "Pakistani Leader Berates the West: Noon Attacks Sale of Arms to India, Threatens Policy Shift, Hints at Red Ties," *New York Times,* March 9, 1958, p. 27.

20. Kux, *The United States and Pakistan, 1947–2000,* p. 95.

21. Report of Meeting Between Secretary of State Herter and Pakistani Foreign Minister Manzur Qadir, June 2, 1960, *Foreign Relations of the United States, 1958–60,* vol. 15, p. 812.

22. Conversation with an ISI officer who had read the related inquiry report, March 7, 2001.

23. "Transcript of the President's First Report to the Congress on the State of the Union," *New York Times,* January 31, 1961, p. 16.

24. Kux, *The United States and Pakistan, 1947–2000,* p. 123.

25. Ibid., p. 130.

26. For details, see Alastair Lamb, *Birth of a Tragedy: Kashmir 1947* (Hertingfordbury: Roxford Books, 1994).

27. See statements by Jawaharlal Nehru in the Indian parliament on March 31, 1950, February 12, 1951, June 28, 1952, and August 7, 1952.

28. Mushtaqur Rahman, *Divided Kashmir: Old Problems, New Opportunities for India, Pakistan, and the Kashmiri People* (London: Lynne Rienner, 1996), p. 97.

29. *Times of India,* New Delhi, July 20, 1961. For details about Nehru's change of heart see Stanley Wolpert, *Nehru: A Tryst with Destiny* (New York: Oxford University Press, 1996), pp. 408–83.

30. Rahman, *Divided Kashmir,* p. 96.

31. Kux, *The United States and Pakistan, 1947–2000,* p. 148.

32. Sir Morrice James, *Pakistan Chronicle* (New York: St. Martin's, 1993), pp. 129–30.

33. Ibid., p. 128.

34. Details of Operation Gibraltar are collected through interviews with many army officers who were serving there at the time. War diaries and materials of General Akhtar Hussain Malik were also accessed courtesy of some relatives and family friends of the general.

35. Interview with Lieutenant Colonel Aftab Ali, general staff officer-1 with General Malik during the 1965 war, September 2000.

36. Lieutenant General Harbaksh Singh, *War Dispatches: Indo-Pak Conflict, 1965* (New Dehli: Lancer International, 1991), p. 25.

37. Victoria Schofield, *Kashmir in Conflict: India, Pakistan, and the Unfinished War* (London: I.B. Tauris, 2000), p. 109.

38. Lieutenant General Gul Hassan Khan, *Memoirs* (Karachi: Oxford University Press, 1993), p. 184.

39. Schofield, *Kashmir in Conflict*, p. 109.

40. Kux, *The United States and Pakistan, 1947–2000,* p. 164.

41. Schofield, *Kashmir in Conflict,* p. 109.

42. Courtesy of a senior army officer at GHQ, the author read the documents related to the operation, December 2000.

43. Lieutenant General Gul Hassan Khan, *Memoirs*), pp. 186–87.

44. Singh, *War Dispatches,* p. 26.

45. Ibid., p. 57.

46. These were the declared objectives of the operation. See Gauhar, *Ayub Khan,* p. 328.

47. The letter has been acquired from the family of General Akhtar Hussain Malik.

48. Muhammad Saraf, *Kashmiris Fight for Freedom, Vol. 2* (Lahore: Ferozsons, 1977), pp. 1164–65.

49. Col Rafiuddin, *Bhutto Kay Aakhri 323 Din* (Lahore: Jang, 1991), p. 66.

50. Interview with Major General Javed Afzal, October 1999.

## Chapter 4

1. G.W. Choudhury, *The Last Days of United Pakistan* (London: C. Hurst, 1974), p. 31.

2. Ibid., p. 68.

3. Sultan Mohammad Khan, *Memoirs and Reflections of a Pakistani Diplomat* (London: London Center for Pakistan Studies, 1998), p. 233.

4. S.V.R. Nasr, *The Vanguard of the Islamic Revolution: The Jamaat-i-Islami of Pakistan* (Los Angeles: University of California Press, 1994), p. 162.

5. See Yahya's statement in *Dawn,* Karachi, July 29, 1969.

6. For details, see Mehrunnisa Ali, *Politics of Federalism in Pakistan* (Karachi: Royal, 1996), pp. 68–69.

7. Rounaq Jahan, *Pakistan: Failure of National Integration* (New York: Columbia University Press, 1972), p. 193.

8. Choudhury, *The Last Days of United Pakistan,* p. 143.

9. Lawrence Ziring, *The Ayub Khan Era: Politics in Pakistan, 1958–1969* (Syracuse: Syracuse University Press, 1971), p. 184.

10. Choudhury, *The Last Days of United Pakistan,* p. 98.

11. Ibid., pp. 86–87.

12. "Pakistan Sets an Example," *New York Times,* December 2, 1969.

13. The five points were: (1) Pakistan must be based on Islamic ideology; (2) The country was to have a democratic constitution providing for free and fair elections; (3) Pakistan's territorial integrity must be upheld in the constitution; (4) The disparity between the wings, particularly in the sphere of economic development, must be eliminated by statutory provisions to be guaranteed in the constitution; (5) The distribution of power between the center and provinces must be made in such a way that the provinces enjoyed the maximum degree of autonomy consistent with giving the central government adequate power to discharge its federal responsibilities, including the maintenance of the country's territorial integrity. Choudhury, *The Last Days of United Pakistan,* pp. 93–94.

14. Ibid., pp. 97–98.

15. Henry Kissinger, *The White House Years* (Boston: Little Brown, 1979), p. 850.

16. Choudhury, *The Last Days of United Pakistan,* pp. 162–63.

17. France Bhattacharya, "East Bengal: Between Islam and a Regional Identity," in *A History of Pakistan and Its Origins,* ed. Christophe Jaffrelot (London: Anthem, 2002), p. 54.

18. See *Daily Telegraph,* London, March 9, 1971; *The Economist,* March 13, 1971; *Time,* March 15, 1971.

19. Choudhury, *The Last Days of United Pakistan,* pp. 168–69.

20. For details see Nasr, *Vanguard of the Islamic Revolution,* pp. 165–69.

21. Kissinger, *The White House Years,* pp. 861–62.

22. Richard Sisson and Leo E. Rose, *War and Secession: Pakistan, India, and the Creation of Bangladesh* (Los Angeles: University of California Press, 1990), p. 211.

23. Ibid., pp. 188–91.

24. Choudhury, *The Last Days of United Pakistan,* p. 199.

25. Quoted in Dennis Kux, *The United States and Pakistan, 1947–2000: Disenchanted Allies* (Washington, DC: Woodrow Wilson Center, 2001), p. 201.

26. Ibid.

27. Ibid., p. 202.

28. Interview with an army officer to whom General Ishaque had narrated the story, November 2000.

29. For details, see "The Report of the Commission of Inquiry-1971: War as Declassified by the Government of Pakistan," *Dawn,* Karachi, online, last accessed August 12, 2003, at www.dawn.com/report/hrc/hrmp5c1.htm.

30. Ibid., at www.dawn.com/report/hrc.

31. The incident was narrated by Major General Javed Afzal, son of Brigadier Afzal, November 1999.

32. "Memorandum on President Nixon's Meeting with Deputy Prime Minister Z.A. Bhutto, 18 December 1971," in *The White House and Pakistan: Declassified Documents, 1969–1974,* ed. F.S. Aijazuddin (Karachi: Oxford University Press, 2002), p. 484.

33. Brigadier F.B. Ali, "Conduct Un-becoming," *Newsline,* Karachi, September 2000.

34. "The officers were silent at first; then restless; then vociferous and interruptive; finally, abusive." Brian Cloughley, *A History of the Pakistan Army: Wars and Insurrections,* 2d ed. (Karachi: Oxford University Press, 2000), p. 240.

## Chapter 5

1. Brian Cloughley, *A History of the Pakistan Army: Wars and Insurrections,* 2d ed. (Karachi: Oxford University Press, 2000), p. 239.

2. Khalid Hasan, "Zulfikar Ali Bhutto," online, last accessed April 29, 2003, at www.khalidhasan.net/longerpieces.htm.

3. Lieutenant General Gul Hassan Khan, *Memoirs* (Karachi: Oxford University Press, 1993), pp. 362–63.

4. Ian Talbot, *Pakistan: A Modern History* (New York: St. Martin's, 1998), p. 219.

5. Details of the conspiracy are based on interviews, telephone discussions, and e-mail communication with various officers who either participated in this coup attempt or were involved in investigating and interrogating these officers. Most of the interviews for this episode were conducted in 2000. Some documents in the army records were also accessed.

6. Compiled and selected by Roedad Khan, *The American Papers: Secret and Confidential India-Pakistan-Bangladesh Documents, 1965–1973* (Karachi: Oxford University Press, 1999), p. 909.

7. Refers to the Royal Military Academy, Sandhurst, U.K., where the topmost Pakistani cadets from the Pakistan military academy were sent regularly for military training.

8. Quoted in F.B. Ali, "Conduct Un-becoming," *Newsline,* Karachi, September 2000, p. 37.

9. Dennis Kux, *The United States and Pakistan, 1947–2000: Disenchanted Allies* (Washington, DC: Woodrow Wilson Center Press, 2001), p. 209.

10. Hasan Askari Rizvi, *Military and Politics in Pakistan, 1947–86* (Lahore: Progressive, 1987), p. 201.

11. Kux, *The United States, and Pakistan, 1947–2000,* p. 208.

12. Ibid.

13. Hasan Askari Rizvi, *Military, State, and Society in Pakistan* (New York: St. Martin's, 2000), p. 150.

14. In 1893 the British, after some costly defeats, negotiated the boundary demarcation between Afghanistan and British India, which was done arbitrarily by cutting the lands of the eastern Pashtun (pathan) tribes living in the region, and this fifteen-hundred-mile border came to be known as the Durand Line after Sir Mortimer Durand, who was the negotiator.

15. Quoted in Ardeshir Cowasjee, "The Missing Chapter," *Dawn,* June 27, 1997.

16. Though such advice and recommendations were not binding, according to Article 230(3) of the 1973 constitution.

17. S.V.R. Nasr, *The Vanguard of the Islamic Revolution: The Jamaat-i-Islami of Pakistan* (Los Angeles: University of California Press, 1994), pp. 183–84.

18. Rafi Raza, *Zulfikar Ali Bhutto and Pakistan, 1967–77* (Karachi: Oxford University Press, 1997), p. 294.

19. Sultan Mohammad Khan, *Memoirs and Reflections of a Pakistani Diplomat* (London: London Centre for Pakistan Studies, 1998), p. 134.

20. Talbot, *Pakistan: A Modern History,* p. 238.

21. When Bhutto banned the National Awami Party in 1975, it resurrected itself as the Awami National Party.

22. The word "Mohajir" is used for the people who migrated to Pakistan from India in 1947 or afterward.

23. Hamid Khan, "An Outline of the Constitutional History of Pakistan," *Pakistan Today* (Lahore, 1986), p. 48.

24. Marvin Weinbaum, "The March 1977 Elections in Pakistan: Where Everyone Lost," *Asian Survey* no. 17 (July 1977): 599–618.

25. Stanley Wolpert, *Zulfi Bhutto of Pakistan: His Life and Times* (Karachi: Oxford University Press), p. 267.

26. Khalid Hasan, "Zulfikar Ali Bhutto," online, last accessed April 29, 2003, at www.khalidhasan.net/longerpieces.htm.

27. Ibid., pp. 262–63.

28. Interview with retired Lieutenant Colonel Arif, who in 1977 (as a captain) attended the event; August 2000.

29. Interview with Brigadier Niaz, July 2000.

30. Asghar Khan, "The Hanging of Bhutto," *Dawn*, April 4, 2002.

31. Zulfikar Ali Bhutto, *If I Am Assassinated* ( New Delhi: Vikas, 1979), p. 118.

32. Ashok Kapur, *Pakistan's Nuclear Development* (London: Routledge, 1987), p. 145.

33. Raza, *Zulfikar Ali Bhutto and Pakistan, 1967–77*, pp. 243–48.

34. Shahid M. Amin, *Pakistan's Foreign Policy: A Reappraisal* (Karachi: Oxford University Press, 2000), pp. 79–80.

35. Quoted in Kux, *The United States and Pakistan, 1947–2000*, p. 230.

36. Interview with an Intelligence Bureau official who was serving in a midlevel position in Islamabad in 1977: August 2000.

## Chapter 6

1. Mary Anne Weaver, *Pakistan: In the Shadows of Jihad and Afghanistan* (New York: Farrar, Straus & Giroux, 2002), pp. 56–57.

2. For details about the Attock conspiracy, see chapter 5.

3. Interview with Major (Ret.) Ishtiaq Asif, one of the accused in the Attock conspiracy case; November 10, 2000.

4. Ibid.

5. Khalid Hasan, "Zulfikar Ali Bhutto," online, last accessed April 29, 2003, at www.khalidhasan.net/longerpieces.htm.

6. Lieutenant General Faiz Ali Chishti, *Betrayals of Another Kind: Islam, Democracy, and the Army in Pakistan*, rev. and enlarged (Lahore: Jang, 1996), p. 65.

7. Interview with a middle-ranking army officer then posted in Multan in a command position, under General Zia; November 2000.

8. For details see Tajammal Hussain Malik, *The Story of My Struggle* (Lahore: Jang, 1991) pp. 205–12.

9. Faiz Ali Chishti, *Betrayals of Another Kind*, p. 71.

10. George Crile, *Charlie Wilson's War: The Extraordinary Story of the Largest Covert Operation in History* (New York: Atlantic Monthly, 2003), p. 68.

11. Stanley Wolpert, *Zulfi Bhutto of Pakistan: His Life and Times* (New York: Oxford University Press, 1993), p. 302.

12. Quoted in W.L. Ritcher, "The Political Dynamics of Islamic Resurgence in Pakistan," *Asian Survey*, no. 9 (June 1979): 555.

13. Wolpert, *Zulfi Bhutto of Pakistan*, p. 308.

14. Hasan Askari Rizvi, *Military, State, and Society in Pakistan* (New York: St. Martin's, 2000), p. 167.

15. Ibid.

16. General Khalid Mahmood Arif, *Working with Zia: Pakistan's Power Politics, 1977–88* (Karachi: Oxford University Press, 1995), pp. 99–105.

17. Wolpert, *Zulfi Bhutto of Pakistan,* p. 325.

18. Interview with Major General Rahat Latif, March 1998.

19. Wolpert, *Zulfi Bhutto of Pakistan,* p. 327.

20. *The Economist,* London, March 25–31, 1978.

21. *The News,* Lahore, April 23, 1994.

22. Dennis Kux, *The United States and Pakistan, 1947–2000: Disenchanted Allies* (Washington, DC: Woodrow Wilson Center, 2001), p. 239.

23. Richard Burt, "US Will Press Pakistan to Halt A-Arms Project: Series of Steps Considered for a Last Ditch Effort," *New York Times,* August 12, 1979, p. 1.

24. Faiz Ali Chishti, *Betrayals of Another Kind,* p. 207.

25. Ibid., p. 208.

26. One of these was later elevated to governor of Punjab Province by Benazir Bhutto in 1994.

27. Quoted in Rizvi, *Military, State, and Society in Pakistan,* p. 174.

28. Narrated by a senior military officer who served as General Zia's staff officer at GHQ.

29. Interview with a general who was a corps commander at the time; January 2000.

30. Martial Law Order No. 5, issued on July 8, 1977.

31. Hasan Askari Rizvi, *Military and Politics in Pakistan* (Lahore: Progressive, 1986), p. 242.

32. Ibid., p. 170.

33. Deobandi faith is a branch of Sunni Islam associated with the *Madrasa* Dar-ul-Uloom, that was founded in the city of Deoband in India in 1867. Two forces motivated the leaders of the new seminary in Deoband: (1) a zeal to introduce Muslim youth to Islamic values, and (2) an intense hatred toward the British and all foreign (non-Islamic influences). The seminary from its inception made a sharp distinction between "revealed" or sacred knowledge and "human" or secular knowledge. Hence it forbade Western-style education and the study of any subject not directly related to the Quran. The seminary also became extremely critical of the way Islam was being practiced in the modern world, especially in India. This "purification" effort became a movement establishing kind of a new sect, which came to be known as Deobandi. After the creation of Pakistan, numerous satellite Deobandi *Madrasas* sprang up in the country. The official website of the Dar-ul-Uloom is at www.darululoom-deoband.com/english/index.htm. For a detailed analysis of the movement, see Barbara D. Metcalf, "'Traditionalist' Islamic Activism: Deoband, Tablighis, and Talibs," last accessed April 19, 2004, at www.ssrc.org/Sept 11/essays/metcalf.htm.

34. The Barelvi school of thought owes its origin to Ahmed Raza Khan of Bareilly, who established many *Madrasas* in the late nineteenth century in British India. The Barelvi school is heavily influenced by mystical Sufi traditions and is tolerant of diverse local Islamic traditions in the practice of Islam.

35. Ian Talbot, *Pakistan: A Modern History* (New York: St. Martin's, 1998), p. 251.

36. Ibid., p. 282.

37. Pervez Hoodbhoy, "Abdus Salam—Past and Present," *The News,* January 29, 1996.

38. Ibid.

39. Pervez Hoodbhoy, "A Hero Is Gone," *Dawn,* November 22, 1996.

40. Article 203C, Clause 4B of the 1973 Constitution of Pakistan.

41. Chief Justice of Pakistan Justice Anwar ul-Haq along with Justice Durab Patel and Justice Fakhar-uddin Ibrahim of the Supreme Court and Justice Zaki-ud-din Pal, Justice Aftab Farrukh, Justice Amir Raza A. Khan, and Justice Habibullah of the Lahore High Court resigned, refusing to acknowledge the validity of the PCO. In all, sixteen judges of the High Courts refused or were not invited to take oath. For details, see the official website of the Lahore High Court at www.lhc.gov.pk/history/text.htm.

42. Talbot, *Pakistan: A Modern History,* p. 245.

43. Lieutenant General Faiz Ali Chishti, the corps commander who led the 1977 takeover in operational terms, explains this development in his autobiography in detail. Faiz Ali Chishti, *Betrayals of Another Kind.*

44. Quoted in Kux, *The United States and Pakistan, 1947–2000,* p. 254.

45. Interview with an ISI official. Also see Diego Cordovez and Selig Harrison, *Out of Afghanistan* (New York: Oxford University Press, 1995), pp. 33–34.

46. Kux, *The United States and Pakistan, 1947–2000,* pp. 257–58.

47. Ibid.

48. Ibid., p. 262.

49. Bob Woodward, *Veil: The Secret Wars of the CIA, 1981–1987* (New York: Simon and Schuster, 1987), p. 312.

50. Kamal Matinuddin, *The Taliban Phenomenon: Afghanistan, 1994–1997* (Karachi: Oxford University Press, 1999), p. 14.

51. Crile, *Charlie Wilson's War,* p. 128.

52. Ahmed Rashid, *Taliban: Militant Islam, Oil, and Fundamentalism in Central Asia* (New Haven, CT: Yale University Press, 2000), pp. 129–30.

53. Robert G. Wirsing, *Pakistan's Security Under Zia, 1977–1988: The Policy Imperatives of a Peripheral Asian State* (New York: St. Martin's, 1991), p. 56.

54. The question referred to in the referendum was: "Whether the people of Pakistan endorse the process initiated by General Mohammad Zia ul-Haq, the President of Pakistan, for bringing the laws of Pakistan in conformity with the injunctions as laid down in the Holy Quran and *Sunnah* of the Holy Prophet (peace be upon him), and for the preservation of the ideology of Pakistan, for the continuation and consolidation of that process and for the smooth and orderly transfer of power to the elected representatives of the people."

55. Romesh Bhandari, "When Rajiv Met Zia," *Rediff.com,* July 16, 2001, last accessed June 12, 2003, at www.rediff.com/news/2001/jul/16spec.htm.

56. Kux, *The United States and Pakistan, 1947–2000,* p. 279.

57. For details see Robert Pear, "Legislators Move on Atom Exports," *New York Times,* March 1985.

58. Quoted in Kux, *The United States and Pakistan, 1947–2000,* p. 287.

59. Weaver, *Pakistan: In the Shadows of Jihad and Afghanistan,* p. 8.

60. Crile, *Charlie Wilson's War,* pp. 491–92.

61. Mushahid Hussain and Akmal Hussain, *Pakistan: Problems of Governance* (Lahore: Vanguard, 1993), p. 93.

62. Ibid.

63. Edward Jay Epstein, "Who Killed Zia," *Vanity Fair,* September 1989, last accessed May 15, 2003, at http://edwardjayepstein.com/archived/zia_print.htm.

64. Brigadier Mohammad Yousaf, "The Legends Never Die" (excerpts from *The Bear Trap*), last accessed June 2, 2003, at www.afghanbooks.com/editorial/07.htm.

65. Interview with a retired ISI official; August 2000.

66. However, Brigadier Imtiaz, in a detailed interview with the author (December 2003), says that he had indeed met the general a day before the episode, but he was not the one who convinced him to accompany Zia to Bahawalpur. According to Brigadier Imtiaz, General Rahman was feeling left out when he was not invited to witness the presentation at Bahawalpur and he had invited Brigadier Imtiaz to brainstorm how to make this a possibility.

67. The alleged role of Flight Lieutenant Sajid was mentioned by a senior Pakistani air force officer to Mary Ann Weaver. For details see Weaver, *Pakistan: In the Shadows of Jihad and Afghanistan*, p. 52.

68. Edward Jay Epstein, "Who Killed Zia?" *Vanity Fair*, September 1989, last accessed May 15, 2003, at http://edwardjayepstein.com/archived/zia_print.htm.

69. Steve Coll, *On the Grand Trunk Road* (New York: Random House, 1994), pp. 86–112.

70. Elaine Sciolino, "Zia of Pakistan Killed as Blast Downs Plane; U.S. Envoy, 28 Others Die," *New York Times*, August 18, 1988, p. A1.

71. Robert Pear, "U.S. Experts Helping Zia Crash Inquiry," *New York Times*, August 19, 1988, p. A8.

72. Elaine Sciolino, "No Sabotage Clues Seen in Zia Crash," *New York Times*, September 11, 1988, p. 3.

73. Epstein, "Who Killed Zia?"

74. Bernard E. Trainor, "Malfunction Seen as Cause of Zia Crash," *New York Times*, October 14, 1988, p. A3.

75. "Report of the Proceedings of the Board of Enquiry into C-130 BS No. 62–3494, August 17, 1988"—the official thirty-page summary of the 350-page report prepared by the Pakistan Board for Prime Minister Mohammad Khan Junejo and his cabinet. Also, quoted (almost in similar wording) in Robert Kaplan, "How Zia's Death Helped the U.S.," *New York Times*, August 23, 1989, p. A21.

76. Faiz Ali Chishti, *Betrayals of Another Kind*, p. 309.

77. John H. Cushman, Jr., "FBI Is to Begin Inquiry of Crash That Killed Zia," *New York Times*, October 23, 1988, p. 11.

78. Robert Pear, "FBI Allowed to Investigate Crash That Killed Zia," *New York Times*, June 25, 1989, p. 13.

79. Ibid.

80. Kux, *The United States and Pakistan, 1947–2000*, p. 419 (fn. 166).

81. Ibid., p. 292.

82. Faiz Ali Chishti, *Betrayals of Another Kind*, p. 313.

83. Barbara Crossette, "Son of Former Military Ruler Goes into Politics in Pakistan," *New York Times*, August 9, 1990, p. A8.

84. John K. Cooley, *Unholy War: Afghanistan, America, and International Terrorism* (Virginia: Pluto, 2000), p. 230.

85. Khalid Ahmed, "Second Opinion: Who Killed General Zia?" *Daily Times*, Lahore, July 22, 2003.

86. Ibid.

87. Quoted in Steve Coll, *Ghost Wars: The Secret History of the CIA, Afghanistan, and Bin Laden, from the Soviet Invasion to September 10, 2001* (New York: Penguin, 2004), p. 178.

88. Ibid., 179.

89. Richard Clarke, *Against All Enemies: Inside America's War on Terror* (New York: Free Press, 2004), p. 50.

90. President Gerald R. Ford's Executive Order 11905: United States Foreign Intelligence Activities, February 18, 1976, last accessed on June 1, 2003, at www.ford.utexas.edu/library/speeches/760110e.htm.

91. President Jimmy Carter's Executive Order 12036: United States Foreign Intelligence Activities, January 24, 1978, last accessed June 2, 2003, at www.fas.org/irp/offdocs/eo/eo-12036.htm.

92. President Ronald Reagan's Executive Order 12333: United States Intelligence Activities, December 4, 1981, last accessed June 5, 2003, at www.fas.org/irp/offdocs/eo12333.htm.

93. "PHC Seeks Record of Deaths: Allama Hussaini's Murder," *Dawn,* Internet edition, April 5, 2003.

## Chapter 7

1. Interview with a high-ranking army officer who was holding a senior position in the military hierarchy then.

2. Beg also sent a message to the Supreme Court, which was hearing a petition challenging the dismissal of the last government, asking it to not reinstate the Junejo government now that new elections were just round the corner. For details see General Aslam Beg's confession in *Dawn,* Karachi, February 10, 1993.

3. For details see Benazir Bhutto, *Daughter of the East* (London: Hamish Hamilton, 1988).

4. Biographical sketch of Major General Hamid Gul, January 1989, *Digital National Security Archive,* George Washington University, Washington, DC, last accessed October 12, 2003, at www.gwu.edu/~nsarchiv.

5. Her movements were closely monitored by the ISI and her residences and offices were bugged—interview with an ISI official; September 1998.

6. See Hasan Askari Rizvi, "Civil-Military Relations Under General Beg," *Defence Journal* 7, nos. 6 and 7 (August 1991): 17–21.

7. The PPP won 93 seats and the IJI 54 in the 207-member National Assembly. The third-largest group were the independent candidates, who grabbed 27 seats, and the MQM (explained later in chapter 7) bagged 13 seats.

8. Mary Ann Weaver, *Pakistan: In the Shadows of Jihad and Afghanistan* (New York: Farrar, Straus & Giroux, 2002), p. 191.

9. Mushahid Hussain, Akmal Hussain, *Pakistan: Problems of Governance* (Lahore: Vanguard, 1993), p. 39. Also see *The Economist,* December 3, 1988.

10. Lieutenant General Sahibzada Yaqub Ali Khan had refused to use lethal force against Bengalis in the 1971 military operation in East Pakistan, for which he is highly respected in the army. Later, Prime Minister Zulfikar Ali Bhutto had appointed him as Pakistan's ambassador in the United States in the early 1970s. General Zia ul-Haq was also very respectful toward him, as he had served under him, and due to Yaqub Khan's established diplomatic skills, he was chosen by Zia as his foreign minister. He is also believed to have had influential contacts in the United States. In certain circles, however, he is often criticized for being too pro-American in his approach.

11. A very large majority of the rank and file, and even the officer corps of the Pakistan Army, are drawn from among the Pathans of the North-West Frontier Province and the Punjabis of the Salt Range.

12. Mushahid Hussain, "Civil-Military Relations," *Frontier Post,* Lahore, May 5, 1991.

13. Azhar Sohail, *Agencion ki Hakumat* (Lahore: Vanguard, 1993), p. 10.

14. General Beg's statement is in the Urdu-language daily *Pakistan,* April 27, 1995.

15. This political party comprises an Urdu-speaking immigrant community primarily based in the Sindh Province. The party was formed in 1984, allegedly with military support, to lessen the influence of the PPP in Sindh. However, there were other potent reasons behind its creation in terms of the Mohajirs' just aspirations and feelings of alienation in Sindh.

16. For details see Maleeha Lodhi and Zahid Hussain, "The Night of the Jackals," *Newsline,* October 1992, pp. 32–33.

17. Dennis Kux, *The United States and Pakistan, 1947–2000: Disenchanted Allies* (Washington, DC: Woodrow Wilson Center, 2001), p. 299.

18. Ibid., p. 294.

19. Ibid., p. 299.

20. *Dawn,* Karachi, August 9, 1990.

21. Interview with an army officer who attended the lecture in late August 1990.

22. Ardesher Cowasjee, "We Never Learn from History," *Dawn,* Karachi, July 21, 2002.

23. Paula R. Newberg, *Judging the State: Courts and Constitutional Politics in Pakistan* (Cambridge: Cambridge University Press, 1995), p. 216.

24. A brief routinely issued to all officers in the Pakistan Army to keep them abreast of weapons development in the world.

25. *Dawn,* Karachi, December 7, 1990.

26. Hasan Askari Rizvi, *Military, State, and Society in Pakistan* (New York: St. Martin's, 2000), p. 211.

27. For instance, see "Dr. Qadeer Under Microscopic Scrutiny: Official," *The News,* January 29, 2004; Kamran Khan, "Dr. Qadeer's Fate Hangs in Balance," *The News,* January 24, 2004; David Rohde, "Pakistani Scientist Is Focus of Atomic Sale Investigation," *New York Times,* January 29, 2004; David E. Sanger and William J. Broad, "From Rogue Nuclear Programs, Web of Trails Leads to Pakistan," *New York Times,* January 4, 2004.

28. David Rohde, "Nuclear Inquiry Skips Pakistani Army," *New York Times,* January 30, 2004.

29. Kux, *The United States and Pakistan, 1947–2000,* p. 310.

30. Ibid., p. 313.

31. Ian Talbot, *Pakistan: A Modern History* (New York: St. Martin's, 1998), p. 316.

32. Rizvi, *Military, State, and Society in Pakistan,* p. 211.

33. A series of interviews with Lieutenant Colonel Obaidullah, February–May 2000.

34. Vali Raza Nasr, *The Vanguard of the Islamic Revolution: The Jamaat-i-Islami of Pakistan* (Los Angeles: University of California Press, 1994), p. 207.

35. Ibid., p. 215.

36. Mumtaz Ahmed, "The Politics of War: Islamic Fundamentalism in Pakistan," in *Islamic Fundamentalism and the Gulf Crisis,* ed. James Piscatori (Chicago: University of Chicago Press, 1991), p. 176.

37. Statement submitted by Lieutenant General Javed Nasir in Lahore High Court in December 2002. "Ex-ISI Chief Reveals Secret Missile Shipments to Bosnia, Defying UN Embargo," *South Asia Tribune,* Issue No. 22, December 23–29, 2002, last accessed October 1, 2003, at www.satribune.com/archives/dec23_29_02/P1_bosniastory.htm.

38. Interview with a former ISI chief, January 2002.

39. Ardeshir Cowasjee, "We Never Learn from History," *Dawn,* Karachi, July 21, 2002.

40. "Ex-ISI Chief Reveals Secret Missile Shipments," *South Asia Tribune.*

41. Kux, *The United States and Pakistan, 1947–2000,* p. 319.

42. The official who gave this information retired as a brigadier in the early 1990s. The author could not confirm the report from any other source.

43. There were rumors that Janjua was murdered, and Janjua's wife and younger brother Shahid Nawaz even publicly allege that he was poisoned by Nawaz Sharif minions. However, General Janjua was only the second man in a very large family to cross the age of fifty—all the others died of heart failure at considerably younger ages.

44. Statement of retired general Mirza Aslam Beg making the disclosure. *The News,* Lahore, August 10, 1994.

45. Yusuf Haroon, son of a prominent and respected Sindhi politician, Abdullah Haroon, was associated with the Muslim League of the partition days (1947). Both father and son were close to Jinnah. Yusuf also became the first chief minister of Sindh Province in 1947, and also briefly remained governor of West Pakistan in 1969.

46. Interview with Yusuf Haroon.

47. Rizvi, *Military, State, and Society in Pakistan,* p. 212.

48. See editorial of *The Muslim,* Islamabad, March 23, 1993.

49. *The Frontier Post,* Lahore, March 13, 1993. Also see *The Nation,* Lahore, March 12, 1993.

50. MQM leaders maintained that they were forced by the ISI to boycott the National Assembly elections.

51. *The News,* November 14, 1993.

52. Interviews with many army officers then serving in the GHQ.

53. Quoted in Robert Wirsing, *Kashmir in the Shadow of War: Regional Rivalries in a Nuclear Age* (Armonk, NY: M.E. Sharpe, 2003), p. 93.

54. Kux, *The United States and Pakistan, 1947–2000,* p. 329.

55. Zahid Hussain, "Islamic Warriors," *Newsline,* Karachi, February 1995, p. 22.

56. "Kurram Limping Back to Peace," *Dawn,* September 19, 1996.

57. Rizvi, *Military, State, and Society in Pakistan,* p. 223.

58. *Dawn,* Karachi, November 14, 1996.

59. Ibid.

60. Kamran Khan, "Spooks Who Become Benazir's Achilles' Heel," *The News,* November 13, 1996.

61. Ibid.

62. "Top Secret: Contacts Made by Sahibzada Yaqub Ali Khan During the Month of March 1996," Letter from DG IB to prime minister, March 30, 1996. The file was recovered by the ISI when it took charge of the prime minister house on Benazir's dismissal on November 5, 1996.

63. Zahid Hussain, "Benazir Bhutto: Fall from Grace," *Newsline,* Karachi, November 1996.

64. General Jahangir Karamat reassured President Farooq Leghari that the armed forces would at all costs uphold the constitution and stand by the decisions of the president. For details see Kamran Khan, "Clock Ticking for a Major Political Change," *The News,* October 18, 1996.

65. For details see Kamran Khan, "Why Leghari Stopped Short of Sealing PML's Fate?" *The News,* January 31, 1999.

66. See statement of Justice Fakhruddin G. Ibrahim published in *Jang,* Rawalpindi, January 8, 1997.

67. *Dawn* (Internet edition), January 15, 1997.

68. Within two weeks of Nawaz becoming prime minister, President Leghari called upon the parliamentarians to legislate all the fifty ordinances promulgated during the caretaker government in the shortest possible time. He further warned opponents by saying that courts would do the *ehtesab* (accountability) test if the National Assembly failed. For details see *The News,* March 7, 1997. Second, he wanted the Muslim League to give a Senate ticket to his cousin Sardar Mansoor Leghari instead of Sardar Zulfiqar Khosa, who was Leghari's rival and Nawaz's choice, creating political problems for Nawaz. For details see *The News,* March 8, 1997. Leghari also wanted his friend Khawaja Tariq Rahim to continue as governor of Punjab, to which Nawaz reacted. Finally, Shahid Hamid, another close friend of Leghari, was made governor of Punjab. For details see Amjad Warraich, "Sharifs Want KTR Out," *The News,* Lahore, March 8, 1997.

69. For a detailed analysis of the Eighth Amendment, see Hassan Abbas, *Poleaxe or Politics of the Eighth Amendment, 1985–1997* (Lahore: Watandost, 1997).

70. Zahid Hussain, "Behind the Clash," *Newsline,* Karachi, November 1997.

71. Interview with CJ Sajjad Ali Shah and Yusuf Haroon.

72. Hamid Khan, "A Courthouse Divided Against Itself," *The News,* Lahore, March 12, 1998.

73. Kux, *The United States and Pakistan, 1947–2000,* p. 345.

74. Interview with senior staff officers at the Prime Minister's Secretariat.

75. John F. Burns, "Pakistan, Answering India, Carries Out Nuclear Tests; Clinton's Appeal Rejected," *New York Times,* May 29, 1998.

76. After the Indian test of a nuclear device in 1974, Zulfikar Ali Bhutto had sworn that Pakistan too would have the bomb, even if this meant that the people of Pakistan would have to eat grass for a thousand years.

77. Kux, *The United States and Pakistan, 1947–2000,* pp. 350–51.

78. Maleeha Lodhi, "The Politics of Religion," *The News,* September 7, 1998.

79. Asma Jahangir, "Implications of the 15th Amendment," *The News,* September 13, 1998.

80. Quoted in Nusrat Javed, "Dissent Comes into the Open," *The News,* September 18, 1998.

81. For details see *The News,* November 5, 1998. Also see the editorial "Beating Up on the Senate," *The News,* November 20, 1998.

82. The letter was published in *Dawn,* Internet edition, November 3, 1998.

83. For instance, see *Dawn,* May 5, 1998; *Muslim,* July 12, 1998; and *Dawn,* September 23, 1998.

84. Rizvi, *Military, State, and Society in Pakistan,* pp. 231–32.

85. Owen Bennett Jones, *Pakistan: Eye of the Storm* (New Haven, CT: Yale University Press, 2002), p. 24.

86. Lahore Declaration, last accessed October 7, 2003, at www.usip.org/library/pa/ip/ip_lahore19990221.html.

87. Jones, *Pakistan: Eye of the Storm,* p. 95.

88. Robert Wirsing, *Kashmir in the Shadow of War: Regional Rivalries in a Nuclear Age* (Armonk, NY: M.E. Sharpe, 2003), pp. 25–36.

89. For details, see the Kashmir Study Group's website, www.kashmirstudygroup.net.

90. Events related to planning and implementation of the Kargil Plan are based on interviews with serving and retired army officers who wish to remain anonymous.

91. Maleeha Lodhi, "The Kargil Crisis: Anatomy of a Debacle," *Newsline,* Karachi, July 1999.

92. Wirsing, *Kashmir in the Shadow of War,* p. 29.

93. Jones, *Pakistan: Eye of the Storm,* p. 102.

94. Ibid., pp. 102–3.

95. Shireen M. Mazari, *The Kargil Conflict, 1999: Separating Fact from Fiction* (Islamabad: Institute for Strategic Studies, 2003), pp. 42–43.

96. Stands for "armor-piercing discarding sabot fin-stabilized" projectile.

97. Lodhi, "The Kargil Crisis."

98. Kux, *The United States and Pakistan, 1947–2000,* p. 353.

99. Mazari, *The Kargil Conflict, 1999,* p. 61.

100. Interview with Khawaja Asif; December 2003.

101. Jones, *Pakistan: Eye of the Storm,* p. 40.

102. Reuters, September 20, 1999.

## Chapter 8

1. Quoted in Anthony Spaeth, "Under the Gun," *Time,* vol. 154, no. 16, October 25, 1999.

2. Mary Anne Weaver, *Pakistan: In the Shadow of Jihad and Afghanistan* (New York: Farrar, Straus & Giroux, 2002), pp. 20–21.

3. Ilene R. Prusher, "A Turkish Path for Pakistan?" *Christian Science Monitor,* January 24, 2002.

4. "Musharraf Wanted to Fight with Turkey in 1974: Cyprus Astonished," *Cyprus Mail,* October 16, 2002, last accessed April 25, 2003, at www.cyprus-mail.com/October/16/news10.htm.

5. Interview with the lawyer who arranged these meetings and submitted briefs to the prime minister, August 1997.

6. Interview with the chief of security of the prime minister's house, November 1999.

7. Interview with Khawaja Asif, March 2003.

8. K. Ratnayake and P. Symonds, "US Concerns over Political Stability in Pakistan," *World Socialist Website,* 24 September 1999, last accessed April 30, 2003, at www.wsws.org/articles/1999/sep1999/pak-s24.shtml.

9. Ibid.

10. Transcript: State Department Noon Briefing, October 12, 1999.

11. Karl F. Inderfurth, Assistant Secretary of State for South Asian Affairs, Testimony Before the Senate Foreign Relations Committee, Washington, DC, October 14, 1999, last accessed May 2, 2003, at www.fas.org/spp/starwars/congress/1999_h/991014_inderfurth_tst.htm.

12. Tariq Ali, *The Clash of Fundamentalisms: Crusades, Jihadis, and Modernity* (London: Verso, 2002), p. 200.

13. Interview with a senior staff officer of Nawaz Sharif while the official was in custody, in May 2000.

14. Owen Bennett Jones, *Pakistan: Eye of the Storm* (New Haven, CT: Yale University Press, 2002), p. 42.

15. Steve Coll, *Ghost Wars: The Secret History of the CIA, Afghanistan, and bin*

*Laden, from the Soviet Invasion to September 10, 2001* (New York: Penguin, 2004), p. 442.

16. Ibid., p. 444.

17. "Attacks to Be Short, Targeted, Says Musharraf," *The News,* October 9, 2001; Bob Woodward, Bush at War (New York: Simon & Schuster, 2002), p.5.

18. Statement of General Anthony C. Zinni, commander in chief, U.S. Central Command, before the U.S. Senate Armed Services Committee on February 29, 2000, last accessed May 15, 2003, at http://armed-services.senate.gov/statemnt/2000/000229az.pdf.

19. Star TV interview with General Musharraf, January 28, 2000.

20. *The News,* October 18, 1999.

21. Interview with a senior ISI official, December 1999.

22. Ayaz Amir, "Cynicism Takes a Thrashing," *Dawn,* November 19, 1999, last accessed May 12, 2003, at www.dawn.com/weekly/ayaz/991119.htm.

23. People arrested under the Accountability Ordinance were to be detained for up to ninety days without charge, a period that far exceeds the fifteen days permitted under Pakistan's Criminal Procedure Code. In a further break with the code, the ordinance prohibited courts from granting bail and gave the NAB chairman sole power to decide if and when to release detainees. The ordinance also established special accountability courts, providing that trials should be conducted within thirty days of charges being filed, and automatically bars those convicted under the ordinance from holding public office. For further details see "Reform or Oppression? Post Coup Abuses in Pakistan," Human Rights Watch Report 2000, vol. 12, no. 6 (C), last accessed May 1, 2003, at www.hrw.org/reports/2000/pakistan/pakio09-05.htm#P337_70719.

24. "NAB Explains Its Position," *Pakistan & Gulf Economist,* May 1–7, 2000, issue no. 18, last accessed May 3, 2003, at www.pakistaneconomist.com/issue2000/issue18/i&e1.htm.

25. The arrested defaulters included industrialists, parliamentarians, and high-ranking officers of the armed forces. They included former Punjab chief minister Manzoor Wattoo; senator and former minister Islamuddin Shaikh; Air Marshal (Ret.) Waqar Azim; former member of the National Assembly Jafar Leghari; former Sindh ministers Nadir Ali Magsi and Agha Siraj Durrani; former federal minister Anwar Saifullah; industrialists Asif Sehgal and Nasim Sehgal; and businessmen Zakaria Ghani and Abdul Shakoor Kalodi. Besides the twenty-one defaulters arrested, the NAB also issued a list of defaulters who were already under custody. They included deposed prime minister Nawaz Sharif; his brother and former Punjab chief minister Shabaz Sharif; Saifur Rehman; his brother Mujeebur Rehman; Brigadier (Ret.) Imtiaz; Asif Zardari, the husband of former prime minister Benazir Bhutto; and Ramesh Udeshi. The next day, November 18, three more major defaulters were arrested. They were Naveed Qamar, former finance minister and ex-chairman of the Privatization Commission in the Benazir government, Waqir Akhtar Paganwala, and Agha Shahabuddin. Some of the defaulters arrested on November 16 were also released the same day when they repaid their loans.

26. Details on the NAB's internal affairs are based on interviews with senior officials of the NAB who wish to remain anonymous. The author himself also remained a part of the NAB in 1999–2000.

27. Letter No. 1000/Army/10/CES dated 11 December 1999. The letter was addressed to the chairman of the NAB and signed by Brigadier Haroon Sikander Pasha,

chief of staff to the chief executive. The letter also gave a few tips on certain cases against Nawaz Sharif and Benazir Bhutto.

28. It would include corps commanders, the director general of the ISI, and senior staff officers of General Musharraf at GHQ.

29. "Law Firms Hired to Recover Money from Abroad," *Dawn,* September 14, 2000.

30. The team included Lieutenant Colonel Riazuddin, Nadir Imtiaz Khan, Major Taimur Shah, Zia Ansari, Lieutenant Colonel Waheed Ashraf, Lieutenant Colonel Iftikhar Rasul, and Lieutenant Colonel Obaidullah.

31. Mohammad Malick, "'Inside' Story of the Reshuffle," *Dawn,* September 18, 2000.

32. Ibid.

33. Tariq Ali, *The Clash of Fundamentalisms: Crusades, Jihadis, and Modernity* (London: Verso, 2002), p. 258.

34. Dennis Kux, *The United States and Pakistan, 1947–2000: Disenchanted Allies* (Washington, DC: Woodrow Wilson Center Press, 2001), p. 357.

35. Ibid.

36. Text of President Clinton's address to the people of Pakistan on March 25, 2000, last accessed May 1, 2003, at www.dawn.com/events/clinton_visit/speech.htm.

37. Ayaz Amir, "The Fourth Junta," *Dawn,* March 31, 2000.

38. "Food for Thought," *Dawn* editorial, March 26, 2000.

39. Ayesha Jalal, "New American Agenda in the Region," *Dawn,* May 3, 2000.

40. Interview with a senior security officer of the President House in Pakistan, who was on duty when the meeting took place.

41. Interview with a close friend of General Musharraf, December 2000.

42. Malick, "'Inside' Story of the Reshuffle."

43. Address to the nation by General Pervez Musharraf, October 17, 1999. All major speeches and interviews of General Musharraf are available on the Pakistan government's official website: www.Pak.gov.pk; last accessed May 28, 2003, at http://server1.pak.gov.pk/President_Addresses/presidential_addresses_index.htm.

44. Section 295-C of the Pakistan penal code.

45. "Blasphemy Law: Old FIR Procedure Restored," *Dawn,* May 17, 2000.

46. "Pakistan's Blasphemy Law U-turn," *BBC News Online,* May 17, 2000.

47. "Patterns of Global Terrorism 1999," Department of State; last accessed April 12, 2003, at www.state.gov/www/global/terrorism/1999report/1999index.html.

48. Introduction to "Patterns of Global Terrorism 1999," Department of State; last accessed April 12, 2003, at www.state.gov/www/global/terrorism/1999report/intro.html.

49. Ibid.

50. The seven countries included in the list are: Libya, Iran, Iraq, Syria, Cuba, Sudan, and North Korea. Being named on the list means coping with cut-off aid, loans, and credit.

51. "Pakistan Embassy Denies Charges of Terrorism by US State Department," *Dawn,* April 30, 2000.

52. Barry Bearek, "India, a Nuclear Power, Raises Military Spending 28 Percent," *New York Times,* web service, March 1, 2000.

53. Interview with a senior military staff officer of General Musharraf, August 2000.

54. Ashfaq Bokhari, "When Jihadis Return Home," *Dawn,* November 8, 2000.

55. "Targeted Killings," editorial, *Dawn,* December 23, 2001; last accessed May 17, 2003 at www.dawn.com/2001/12/23/ed.htm.

56. Tim Judah. "The Taliban Papers," *Survival* (Spring 2002): 69–80.

57. General Pervez Musharraf's interview with the *Washington Times,* March 21, 2001; last accessed April 17, 2003, at http://server1.pak.gov.pk/CE_Addresses/CE_Washtimes_inter.htm.

58. Interview with a retired ISI colonel, August 2000.

59. Narrated to the author by a serving Pakistan Army major in December 2000.

60. Zaffar Abbas, "Man on a Mission," *Herald,* Karachi, July 2000, p. 34.

61. "Pakistan to Pull Out Part of Its Troops from LOC," *Dawn,* December 21, 2000.

62. Sridhar Krishnaswami, "US for Sustained Indo-Pak Engagement," *The Hindu,* July 17, 2001.

63. "JI Opposes Give and Take on Kashmir," *Dawn,* July 12, 2001.

64. "Kashmir Prays for Summit Peace," *Telegraph,* July 14, 2001.

65. "A Brookings Press Briefing: The India-Pakistan Summit," Brookings Institution, July 11, 2001, last accessed May 12, 2003, at www.brookings.edu/comm/transcripts/20010711.htm.

66. Ibid.

67. "Bang and Whimper at Agra," *Dawn* editorial, July 18, 2001.

68. Nayyar Zaidi, "How Agra Was Conceived and Aborted," *Milli Gazette,* September 1, 2001; last accessed May 1, 2003, at www.milligazette.com/Archives/01092001/22.htm.

69. Faraz Hashmi, "TJP, SSP Warned: Sipah-i-Muhammad and Lashkar-i-Jhangvi Banned," *The News,* August 15, 2001.

70. Saeed A. Malik and Ishtiaq Asif, interview with Ishtiaq Asif, May 2000.

71. In the early hours of October 13, 1999, Saeed A. Malik told the brigadier the story of how GA had almost said his farewell to the service, and how this had been averted. He then made a solemn request of the brigadier: "Sir, if you can get one sentence across to the Chief, let him know about GA, otherwise there is a good chance that one of the best generals in the army may be wasted out." On the morrow at about midday he received a terse call from the brigadier: "Your message has been conveyed."

## Chapter 9

1. Saeed Shafqat, "From Official Islam to Islamism: The Rise of Dawat-ul-Irshad and Lashkar-e-Taiba," in *Pakistan: Nationalism Without a Nation,* ed. Christophe Jaffrelot (London: Zed Books, 2002), p. 133.

2. Reuven Firestone, *Jihad: The Origins of Holy War in Islam* (New York: Oxford University Press, 1999), p. 17.

3. Abu Dawud, *Sunan Abi Dawud* (Cairo: Daral-Misriyya al-Lubnaniyya, 1988), p. 4344.

4. The group reverted to the name Harkat-ul-Mujahideen in 1997, when HUA was designated a terrorist group by the United States.

5. JUI has two faces in the shape of JUI-F, headed by Maulana Fazl ur-Rahman, and JUI-S led by Maulana Sami ul-Haq.

6. The term came into vogue during the British rule in the Indian subcontinent (1857–1947). During these times, emphasis was put on recruiting in areas where disaffection was least and where the British discerned the existence of "martial races"

(ethnic groups) noted for their military tradition and demonstrated loyalty. By these criteria, the most fertile area for recruitment was considered to be the Punjab region of northwestern India. In present-day Pakistan, Punjab and some areas in North-West Frontier Province are considered "martial areas" in this context.

7. See bin Laden statements in "Hunting bin Laden," *Frontline*, PBS, last accessed September 15, 2003, at www.pbs.org/wgbh/pages/frontline/shows/binladen/who/edicts.html.

8. Peter Fritsch, "Information Bank Abstracts," *Wall Street Journal*, October 12, 2001.

9. See "A Biography of Osama bin Laden," *Frontline*, PBS, last accessed October 2003, at www.pbs.org/wgbh/pages/frontline/shows/binladen/who/bio2.html.

10. S.V.R. Nasr, "Islam, the State, and the Rise of Sectarian Militancy in Pakistan," in Christophe Jaffrelot, ed., *Pakistan: Nationalism Without a Nation?* p. 90.

11. "Pakistan, Madrasas, Extremism, and Military," International Crisis Group, July 29, 2002, last accessed November 15, 2003, at www.crisisweb.org//library/documents/report_archive/A400717_29072002.pdf.

12. For brief details about other groups operating in Indian-controlled Kashmir, see Zaffar Abbas, "A Who's Who of Kashmir Militancy," *Herald*, Karachi, August 2000, pp. 29–31.

13. Jamiat-i-Ulema-i-Islam was formed in 1945 when some ulema separated from Hussain Ahmed Madni and other nationalist Muslim leaders of the Jamiat-ul-Ulema-i-Hind. It actively participated in the 1953 and 1974 anti-Ahmedi campaigns; was part of the coalition governments in the North-West Frontier Province and Baluchistan in 1973; and in 1977 was part of the anti-Bhutto Pakistan National Alliance movement that crippled the Bhutto government and led to the imposition of Zia's martial law.

14. Muhammad Qasim Zaman, *The Ulama in Contemporary Islam: Custodians of Change* (Princeton: Princeton University Press, 2002), p. 119.

15. Mushahid Hussain, "Pakistan-Iran Relations in the Changing World Scenario: Challenges and Response," in *Pakistan Foreign Policy Debate: The Years Ahead*, ed. Tariq Jan (Islamabad: Institute of Foreign Policy Studies, 1993), pp. 211–12.

16. Mariam Abou Zahab, "The Regional Dimension of Sectarian Conflicts in Pakistan," in Jaffrelot, *Pakistan: Nationalism Without a Nation?* p. 118.

17. The Shia are concentrated primarily in the Eastern Province in the oases of Qatif and Al Ahsa, where they constitute around 40 percent of the population.

18. Nasr, "Islam, the State, and the Rise of Sectarian Militancy," p. 92.

19. Mariam Abou Zahab, "The Regional Dimension of Sectarian Conflicts in Pakistan," p. 118.

20. Haq Nawaz Jhangvi, *Maulana Nawaz Jhangvi ki pandara tarikhsaz taqrirain* (Lahore: Idara-i-Nashriyyat-i-Islam, 1991), p. 272.

21. Nasr, "Islam, the State, and the Rise of Sectarian Militancy," p. 95.

22. For details, see chapter 6.

23. Interviews with many former SSP activists in Jhang, courtesy of Mr. Sami Ibrahim, a prominent Pakistani journalist who belongs to Jhang.

24. Interview with T.M.

25. The ISI handlers of the Afghan mujahideen were angry over the Geneva Accords that Pakistan's civilian government had signed in 1989 under U.N. auspices, without any guarantees of handing over of power in Kabul to the mujahideen.

26. Nasr, "Islam, the State, and the Rise of Sectarian Militancy in Pakistan," p. 98.

27. *Herald*, Karachi, June 1994, p. 29.

28. Hundreds of SSP/LEJ activists were trained in HUA camps in Afghanistan, and on many occasions HUA operators accompanied Lashkar agents to Pakistan to conduct sectarian killings. For details see Ejaz Haider, "Price of Kashmir-Afghanistan Policies," *Friday Times,* July 3–9, 1998, and Ejaz Haider, "Have Your Cake and Eat It Too," *Friday Times,* July 10–16, 1998.

29. Ashraf Marth was a cousin as well as brother-in-law of sitting interior minister Chaudhry Shujaat Hussain.

30. Details of the investigation were given to the author by a former police colleague.

31. Samina Ahmed, "Centralization, Authoritarianism, and the Mismanagement of Ethnic Relations in Pakistan," in *Government Policies and Ethnic Relations in Asia and the Pacific,* ed. Michael E. Brown and Sumit Ganguly (Cambridge, MA: MIT Press, 1997), pp. 107–27.

32. The Taliban massacred hundreds of Shia Hazaras in 1998, enlarging the sectarian confrontation in the region.

33. "Tensions Mount Between Iran, Afghanistan's Taliban," CNN, September 14, 1998; last accessed December 6, 2003, at www.cnn.com/WORLD/meast/9809/14/iran.afghan.border.

34. Interview with Shabaz Sharif, a Staff officer of Prime Minister Nawaz Sharif, May 2003.

35. Interview with a police officer who investigated the bomb blast; November 2000.

36. Azhar Abbas, "Tentacles of Hatred," *Herald,* September 2001, p, 62.

37. Jessica Stern, *Terror in the Name of God: Why Religious Militants Kill* (New York: HarperCollins, 2003), p. 341.

38. Saeed Shafqat, "From Official Islam to Islamism: The Rise of Dawat-ul-Irshad and Lashkar-e-Taiba," in Jaffrelot, *Pakistan: Nationalism Without a Nation?* p. 141.

39. Stephen Schwartz, *The Two Faces of Islam: The House of Saud from Tradition to Terror* (New York: Doubleday, 2002), pp. 159–60.

40. Peter L. Bergen, *Holy War Inc: Inside the Secret World of Osama bin Laden* (New York: Simon & Schuster, 2001), pp. 50, 54–55.

41. Interview with a former ISI agent.

42. Telephone interview with Peter Bergen, January 2004.

43. Kamal Siddiqi, "In a Sleepy Lahore Village, Lashkar Trains Kashmir Mujahideen," *Indian Express,* April 27, 2000.

44. Ahle-Hadith is an orthodox and puritanical Sunni group, different in orientation than Deobandis and Barelvis. They argue that the Quran and Hadith provide sufficient guidance to the believers, and one ought to base one's conduct on their teachings rather than the various schools of law. Its adherents are around 10 percent within the Sunni populace of Pakistan but are considered the most radicalized one, especially in the aftermath of the Afghan war (1980s).

45. Zahid Hussain, "Inside Jihad," *Newsline,* February 2001, p. 22.

46. Quoted in *Takbeer,* Karachi, August, 1999.

47. Shahzeb Jillani, "Which Way Ahead," *Herald,* Karachi, March 2001, pp. 55–57.

48. Stern, *Terror in the Name of God,* p. 107.

49. Reported in *Dawn,* Karachi, June 15, 1999.

50. "Lashkar-e-Taiba Chief for Readjusting Foreign Policy," *Dawn,* Karachi, November 2, 1999.

51. "Dawat to Fight for Islamic Pakistan," *The News,* November 4, 1999.

52. Evident from a reading of articles that appeared on MDI's old website www.markazdawa.org (current: www.jamatuddawa.org) during 1999–2000.

## Chapter 10

1. Text of President Bush's speech on September 11, 2001; last accessed May 15, 2003, at www.cnn.com/2001/US/09/11/bush.speech.text.

2. Bob Woodward, *Bush at War* (New York: Simon & Schuster, 2002), p. 32.

3. Owen Bennett Jones, *Pakistan: Eye of the Storm* (New Haven, CT: Yale University Press, 2002), p. 2.

4. Interview: Richard Armitage, "Campaign Against Terror," PBS *(Frontline)*, April 19, 2002; last accessed June 2, 2003, at www.pbs.org/wgbh/pages/frontline/shows/campaign/interviews/armitage.html.

5. Woodward, *Bush at War,* p. 47.

6. Jones, *Pakistan: Eye of the Storm,* p. 2.

7. Woodward, *Bush at War,* pp. 58–59.

8. Interview: Richard Armitage, "Campaign Against Terror," PBS *(Frontline)*, April 19, 2002.

9. Interview with a staff officer of General Pervez Musharraf, June 2002.

10. "Musharraf Condemns Attack," *Dawn,* September 12, 2001.

11. Jones, *Pakistan: Eye of the Storm,* p. 3.

12. Interview: President Pervez Musharraf, Campaign Against Terror, PBS *(Frontline)*, May 14, 2002; last accessed June 6, 2003, at www.pbs.org/wgbh/pages/frontline/shows/campaign/interviews/musharraf.html.

13. Ibid.

14. The episode is narrated in Woodward, *Bush at War,* pp. 55–57.

15. S. Hussain, "Clerics Violated Official Brief During Visit to Afghanistan," *Friday Times,* October 7, 2001.

16. Interview with a senior staff officer at GHQ.

17. "Pakistan Backing U.S. Under Pressure: CE Briefs Think Tanks," *Dawn,* September 19, 2001.

18. Department of Defense News Briefing, September 18, 2001. For the transcript, see www.defenselink.mil.

19. Transcript of the press conference addressed by the Foreign Office Spokesman, October 4, 2001, at www.pak.gov.pk.

20. Interview with a senior army official at GHQ.

21. Douglas Frantz, "Support for Bin Laden Is Still High in Pakistan," *New York Times,* October 22, 2001, p. B5.

22. Nazish Syed Ali and Massoud Ansari, "Mission of Faith," *Newsline,* Karachi, November 2001.

23. Ibid.

24. Lawrence Ziring, *Pakistan: At the Crosscurrent of History* (Lahore: Vanguard, 2004), p. 311.

25. "Bridging the Great Divide," *The Economist,* June 1–7, 2002, p. 39.

26. For full text of the speech see, *Dawn,* January 12, 2002, last accessed October 12, 2003, at www.dawn.com/2002/01/12/speech020112.htm.

27. "The Weakest Link: Why the World Needs Pakistan's Dictator to Survive and How to Rescue Him," *The Economist,* June 1–7, 2002, p. 11.

28. Interview with an American official, April 2003.

29. Interview with a friend of Hafiz Saeed who resides in Baltimore, Maryland.

30. Khalid Ahmed, "Second Opinion: Who Killed Daniel Pearl?" *Daily Times,* Lahore, July 11, 2003.

31. "India and Pakistan: Steps Toward Rapprochement," Testimony of Professor

Stephen P. Cohen, Senate Committee on Foreign Relations, January 28, 2004; last accessed January 29, 2004, at http://foreign.senate.gov/testimony/2004/CohenTestimony040128.pdf.

32. Amy Waldman, "U.S. Presses to Keep India-Pakistan Peace," *New York Times,* August 23, 2002, p. A4.

33. "The Absence of War," *The Economist,* June 29–July 5, 2002, p. 39.

34. Zahid Hussain, "Mission Impossible," *Newsline,* June 2002.

35. David Rhodes, "Pakistan Allows Kashmir Raids, Militants Say," *New York Times,* September 20, 2002, p. A3. Also see "Only One Way Out," editorial, *Friday Times,* April 26–May 2, 2003.

36. Sabihuddin Ghausi, "Pakistan Urged to Fulfill Promises on Infiltration," *Dawn,* January 24, 2003.

37. About Lashkar-e-Jhangvi's involvement in terrorist attacks, see Najam Sethi's editorial, "The 'Real' Terrorist Network," *Friday Times,* August 16–23, 2002.

38. There were at least five attempts made on Musharraf. For details see "Musharraf Assassination Plot Foiled," CNN.com, September 18, 2002. Also see "Musharraf Faces Threat to Life, Says Moin," *Dawn,* July 23, 2002; Anwar Iqbal, "Musharraf Tightens Personal Security," *Washington Times,* August 19, 2002; "Musharraf's Convoy Escapes Bomb Blast," *Dawn,* December 15, 2003.

39. MMA comprised JUI-F led by Fazl ur-Rahman, JUI-S led by Sami ul-Haq, Jamaat-i-Islami led by Qazi Hussain Ahmed, Tahrik-e-Islami led by Sajjid Naqvi, JUP led by Shah Ahmed Noorani and Jamiat-e-Ahle Hadith.

40. Interview with Khawaja Asif and Chaudhry Nisar Ali, members of National Assembly of Pakistan, September 2003.

41. The PPP, which won 62 seats in the National Assembly, received the highest number of votes, 25.01 percent of the total. The pro-Musharraf Pakistan Muslim League (PML-Q) received 24.81 percent of the votes and bagged 77 seats, while PML-N won 14 seats, though it received 11.23 percent of the votes.

42. "Peshawar: Police Avoiding Arrest of Suspects: Billboards Ransacking Case," *Dawn,* October 9, 2003.

43. Aqil Shah, "Obscurantism on the Move," *Dawn,* May 31, 2003.

44. "Government Must Stand Up to Civil Violence," editorial, *Daily Times,* December 21, 2002.

45. "Musharraf or Talibanization," editorial, *Daily Times,* June 12, 2003.

46. Ibid.

47. "Jihad Only Option to Halt US: MMA Leaders Want Bush, Blair to Be Tried," *Dawn,* March 31, 2003.

48. Khalid Hasan, "CENTCOM Blackout on Pakistan," *Daily Times,* May 21, 2003. The report, however, was cached by Google.com, later to be reproduced by the *South Asia Tribune,* which is available at www.satribune.com/archives/may18_24_03/Pakistan_Centcom.htm.

49. Richard Clarke, *Against All Enemies: Inside America's War on Terror* (New York: Free Press, 2004), pp. 280–81.

50. For details about the CIA report, see Seymour Hersh, "The Cold Test," *New Yorker,* January 27, 2003.

51. Interviews with Pakistani diplomats in the Pakistan embassy in Washington, April 2003.

52. Ian Traynor, "Pakistan's Nuclear Hero Throws Open Pandora's Box," *Guardian,* U.K., January 31, 2004.

53. Interview with the NAB official who handled the case.

54. Shakil Shaikh, "Individual Violations of N-Control Rules," *The News,* December 21, 2003.

55. Pervez Hoodbhoy, "The Nuclear Noose Around Pakistan's Neck," *Washington Post,* February 1, 2004.

56. Ayaz Amir, "Overloading the National Grid," *Dawn,* January 23, 2004.

57. "Pakistan, India Joint Statement," *Dawn,* January 7, 2004.

58. Khalid Ahmed, "Second Opinion: Why Against Women," *Daily Times,* October 7, 2003.

59. "Musharraf Blocking Jihad Against US: Hafiz Saeed," *Daily Times,* July 18, 2003.

60. Arnaud de Borchgrave, "Heartbeat Away from Jihadi Nukes," *Washington Times,* July 18, 2003. Also see A.R. Siddiqi, "A Bundle of Contradictions," *Dawn,* July 4, 2003.

61. For instance, see "President Appoints New MI Chief," *Dawn,* December 19, 2003; Kamran Khan, "Ahsan, Javed Made Karachi, Gujranwala Corps Commanders," *The News,* December 21, 2003.

62. Ahmed Rashid, "Pakistan on the Edge," *New York Review of Books,* October 10, 2002.

63. Ibrahim Shahid, "Another School Damaged in Diamer," *Daily Times,* Lahore, February 21, 2004.

64. Amir Rana, "Vengeance, Frictions Reviving LJ and Sipah-i-Mohammad," *Daily Times,* Lahore, April 7, 2004.

65. For details, see Rahimullah Yusufzai, "Pakistani Priorities Were Different Than U.S. in Wana Operations," *South Asia Tribune,* no. 88, April 18–24, 2004, at www.satribune.com.

66. Many close friends and former colleagues of Musharraf were interviewed in this context.

67. Lawrence Ziring, *Pakistan: At the Crosscurrent of History* (Lahoe: Vanguard Books, 2004), p. 354; for instance, see Jim Hoagland, "Pakistan: Pretense of an Ally," *Washington Post,* March 28, 2002.

## Chapter 11

1. For instance, see the results of a relevant survey in Kathleen Cahill, "They Don't Like Us. Worse, They Don't Trust Us," *Washington Post,* June 15, 2003, p. B03.

2. For instance, see Professor Marc W. Harold, "A Dossier on Civilian Victims of United States' Aerial Bombing of Afghanistan," *Cursor,* last accessed October 12, 2003, at www.cursor.org/stories/civilian_deaths.htm. Also see articles of renowned British journalist Robert Fisk at www.robert-fisk.com.

3. "Rentier state" is generally defined as a state reliant not on extraction of the domestic population's surplus production but on externally generated revenues, or rents, such as those derived from oil. In the case of Pakistan, these external sources are mostly in the form of foreign aid and loans. Since paying the "rent" dominates a significant amount of the GDP, a rentier state generally lacks a productive outlook.

# Index

**Hassan Abbas** is currently a visiting scholar at the Negotiation Project, Harvard Law School, and a Ph.D. candidate at the Fletcher School of Law and Diplomacy, Tufts University. He served in the government of Pakistan for ten years and worked in the administrations of Prime Minister Benazir Bhutto (1994–96) and President General Pervez Musharraf (2000). He did his LLM in International Law from the University of Nottingham, United Kingdom (1999) as a Britannia Chevenning Scholar and MALD from the Fletcher School, Tufts University (2002). He also regularly contributes to various newspapers in the United States and Pakistan.